Translated Texts for Historians

This series is designed to meet the needs of students of ancient and medieval history and others who wish to broaden their study by reading source material, but whose knowledge of Latin or Greek is not sufficient to allow them to do so in the original languages. Many important Late Imperial and Dark Age texts are currently unavailable in translation and it is hoped that TTH will help to fill this gap and to complement the secondary literature in English which already exists. The series relates principally to the period 300-800 AD and includes Late Imperial, Greek, Byzantine and Syriac texts as well as source books illustrating a particular period or theme. Each volume is a self-contained scholarly translation with an introductory essay on the text and its author and notes on the text indicating major problems of interpretation, including textual difficulties.

Front cover: left, gold solidus from Constantinople mint, under Justinian II (first reign) 685-95; right, silver dirham from Damascus mint, under CAbd al-Malik 685-705 (photographs by courtesy of the Ashmolean Museum, Oxford).

For a full list of published titles in the Translated Texts for Historians series, please see pages at the end of this book.

Translated Texts for Historians
Volume 15

"The Seventh Century in the West-Syrian Chronicles"

introduced, translated and annotated by
ANDREW PALMER

including two seventh-century Syriac apocalyptic texts
introduced, translated and annotated by
SEBASTIAN BROCK
with added annotation and an historical
introduction by ROBERT HOYLAND

Liverpool
University
Press

First published 1993 by
Liverpool University Press
PO Box 147, Liverpool, L69 3BX

British Library Cataloguing-in-Publication Data
A British Library CIP Record is available
ISBN 0 85323 238 5

Printed in the European Community by
Redwood Press Limited, Melksham, England

PREFACE

The principal aim of this book is to make available to students who do not have the necessary languages a number of historically important, but rather inaccessible texts. Original analysis of the individual texts and a fresh evaluation of Syriac historiography make this more than a text-book based on established scholarly wisdom. Some of the ideas it contains have not previously appeared in print. The chronological tables, the maps and the index should help to make the book useful to advanced scholars and undergraduates alike.

The exact period covered is AD 582 to AD 718, the seventh century with eighteen years on either side. The upper date is that of the beginning of the reign of Maurice, with which the greatest Syriac historian, Dionysius of Tel-Mahrē, is said to have begun his Secular History. The lower date, as it happens, coincides with the first centenary of Islam, according to the lunar calendar of the Arabs; but that was not the reason for choosing it. In 718 the Arabs abandoned a prolonged siege of Constantinople. Dionysius appears to have closed the first half of his Secular History with this siege, which he describes at length. In his account there followed an excursus on the foundation of Constantinople, marking a clear caesura which was reflected in the parallel narrative of his Ecclesiastical History: from that time onwards, the Syrian Orthodox 'had neither opportunity nor need to interest themselves' in the 'heretical' Byzantine Church.

The present book is divided into three parts: Part One, devoted to the minor West-Syrian secular chronicles (East-Syrian and ecclesiastical historiography is excluded); Part Two, which attempts to recover what Dionysius of Tel-Mahrē (d. 845) had to say about secular events in our period; and Part Three, by Sebastian Brock, which presents two apocalyptic texts. Whereas chronicles were concerned with the past, apocalypses claimed to reveal the future; such visions were inspired not only by the prophecies of Scripture, but also by a pattern perceived in past and recent events and projected into the future. The Epilogue contains some reflections on the relationship between chronography and apocalyptic and on the problem of the interpretation of what might appear to be purely factual information about the past. There are three appendices which present the evidence for some problems of chronology, the dates of solar eclipses in the seventh century and the topographical source-books consulted in making the maps. The book closes with an index of proper names and five maps on various scales.

I conclude by acknowledging the help I have received in writing this book. It was Sebastian Brock who, in 1983, first interested me in this venture, bequeathing to me his own project to translate the minor chronicles, and subsequently, in 1988, providing a translation of and introduction to the two apocalypses (not since then revised). Other commitments delayed a final revision until the Spring of 1992 when Robert Hoyland, by his learning, enthusiasm, and tactful criticisms, restored momentum to this languishing project, suggested many improvements and furnished an up-to-date introduction to the historical context.[1] Geert Jan van Gelder, Tom Sinclair and Peter Khoroche

---

[1] Robert Hoyland's initials appear beside a number of notes, in particular adding information from the Arabic sources where they shed light on problems of dates and names. He is not responsible for the main text, except for his section of the Introduction and participation in the Introduction to Text No. 13, although his advice as an Islamicist and a pupil of Patricia Crone has been of great value, all the more so in view of the insights into Byzantine history which he has gained from a close association with such scholars as James Howard-Johnston, Averil Cameron and Peter Brown. His thesis, involving source-criticism of Syriac and other external sources for early Islamic

have advised on the Arabic, Armenian and Persian names respectively and helped to weed out errors. My guidelines were that Greek names should be latinized and that, for all famous names, the form most familiar to non-Orientalist English readers should be used. Gerrit Reinink used his collation of the Mardīn manuscripts to furnish the extract from the *Apocalypse* of Pseudo-Methodius with selected variants and provided me with copies of forthcoming articles. Harvey Butcher and John North supplied information for the Appendix on solar eclipses. Liuwe Westra supplemented my efforts on the index. Sebastian Brock, Larry Conrad, Bernard Flusin, John Haldon, Walter Kaegi, [**] Hubert Kaufhold, Fred Leemhuis, Rob Lente and Michael Whitby also helped me to improve the book (the first and the last with many detailed and valuable suggestions) and saved me from many of my errors. It would be too much to expect that these friends and acquaintances, however wise, should save me from them all. My wife Anne-Marie has remained constant as a rock, while I, like the mining tide, kept ebbing into the seventh century, only to steal back for meals and lap around her with my babble about the past. This book is for my late father, a wonderful man, who, as one who formed me while respecting my freedom, should have all the credit for its merits and none of the blame for its defects.

Andrew Palmer, 5 Argyll Street, Brechin, DD9 6JL

January, 1993

---

history, will be, when it appears in print, a great help to anyone using the texts in the present book. I am particularly grateful to him for his suggestion, worked out in Appendix I, that a simple error on the part of Dionysius of Tel-Mahrē accounts for most of the discrepancies in the chronology of text No. 13.

[**] Unfortunately, Walter Kaegi's *Byzantium and the Early Islamic Conquests* (Cambridge, 1992) was published too recently for me to use it in the preparation of this book. Kaegi provided valuable help at an earlier stage in the preparation of the present book, when it was entitled *In the Shadow of the Moon*, and references in Kaegi to 'Palmer, Shadow' are to this book.

CONTENTS

INTRODUCTION

(i)   The confessional background   xi
(ii) The historical context (by R. H.)   xiv
(iii) The texts   xxviii
(iv) Chronology and Chronological tables   xxxiii
Select bibliography of West-Syrian chronicles   lix
Abbreviations, brackets, signs   lxiv

PART ONE

Minor West-Syrian Chronography   1
1.   A record of the Arab conquest of Syria, AD 637   1
2.   Extract from a chronicle composed about AD 640   5
3.   Extract from the *Melkite Chronicle* (AD 642+)   25
4.   Extract from the *Maronite Chronicle* (AD 664+)   29
5.   Fragment of James of Edessa, AD 691/2   36
6.   A list of caliphs, composed after AD 705   43
7.   A chronicle of disasters dated AD 716 (tr. S. P. B.)   45
8.   A list of caliphs from the Arabic (AD 724+)   49
9.   Extract from an 'Account', written in AD 775   51
10. Extract from the *Chronicle of Zuqnīn*, AD 775   53
11. Inscriptions of Ehnesh, late eighth century   71
12. Extracts from two chronicles up to AD 819/846   75

PART TWO

Dionysius of Tel-Maḥrē, Secular History, introduction   85
Concordance of the contents   105
13. Extract from the *Chronicle of AD 1234*   111

PART THREE

Two Apocalyptic Texts of AD 691+ (by S. P. B.)   222
14. Extract from the *Apocalypse of Ps.-Methodius*   222
15. *The Edessene Apocalyptic Fragment*   243

EPILOGUE   251

APPENDICES, INDEX and MAPS

INTRODUCTION

(i) *The Confessional Background*

In the seventh century of the Christian era the old conformations of the Mediterranean area and of the Middle East were disrupted completely. The opposition between Greece and Rome on the one hand and Persia on the other had characterized the way the history of the Near East was portrayed ever since Herodotus. For many centuries the frontier between East and West had run from the upper Tigris to the middle Euphrates and Rome's enemies had had no access to what the Romans fondly called their sea. All this was changed by the Arab conquest. Persia was incorporated, together with all but the northern Mediterranean sea-board, in the world of the most successful people of the seventh century. Life in those countries has been indelibly printed with the stamp of the seventh-century revolution of the Arabs.

A large part of the area directly affected by the Arab conquest was inhabited by Syriac-speaking Christians. The Syrians had a strong native tradition of literature and they had learned much from the Greeks, many of whose books they translated. They had become part of the Roman world, yet they felt themselves to be distinct from the Romans of Constantinople. This distinctiveness was expressed in the majority's stubborn refusal to be brow-beaten into accepting the Constantinopolitan line in the definition of Christian orthodoxy.

The Christian commonwealth had existed before the Christian emperor Constantine gave it a status parallel to that of the Roman state. In those days it had already consisted of a great variety of people, poor and rich, women and men, Gentiles and Jews, speakers of Greek and speakers of Syriac or another language, natives of Europe, of Asia and of Africa. The only thing all these people had in common was their belief in Christ. The authoritarianism natural to a patriarchal society, which could find justification in the need to defend Christianity against its enemies, required the law to be laid down about what entitled a person to call herself or himself a Christian. In the absence of other criteria the Christians were forced to use that of belief, in spite of the fact that neither the object of that belief, God, nor the mind of the believer was susceptible of analysis in concrete terms.   Humanly speaking, judgment was arbitrary.   The Christians maintained stoutly in the face of all the evidence that decisions were reached on this subject under the unifying guidance of the Holy Spirit of God. Nevertheless, as soon as they were able, they identified this guidance with the judgment of a reigning Christian emperor, a judgment backed by the sanction of legitimized force.

But human beings are obstinate.   Not everyone accepted that orthodoxy was what the emperor decided it would be.   With the christianization of the Roman empire, orthodoxy, which had been seen as the *sine qua non* of the Church's survival, came to be seen as the guarantee of the protection of the empire itself against its enemies.   The Cross may have won a battle for Constantine in 312, but it lost one for Valens in 378.   The failure of the talisman itself was unthinkable, so the supposed 'Arianism' of Valens (the manner in which he professed his Christian convictions) had to have been to blame.   The consequence of this syllogism was that the enemies of orthodoxy, however that might be defined by the Church (working together with the emperor), were also perceived as enemies of the State.   This helped to alienate numerous Christians in Syria from Constantinople and gave them a very different perspective on the Arab conquest.   They found fault with the Ecumenical (General Church) Council of Chalcedon (AD 451) on several points, especially on the definition of Christ as one person in two natures, as opposed to one person *out of* two natures, human and divine, neither of which was changed in the process.   For their resistance to Chalcedon they were sometimes persecuted and frequently put under pressure.   Their status as victims of the Christian emperor was perceived as that of the famous faithful remnant in Israel who did not obey the King's ungodly commands.

The concessions offered by the emperor Justinian AD 532 showed clearly that it was not merely the theological scruples of the opponents of Chalcedon which formed an obstacle to unity in the Church, for he was prepared to tolerate these.   But Justinian refused to give the dissidents a structural role in the running of the empire as bishops. This discrimination led to open schism when a certain Jacob, nicknamed Būrd^{c}ōnō,[2] was consecrated bishop of Edessa AD 543 in opposition to the official incumbent. The 'Jacob-ites' thus formed an autocephalous Church, a development which made it easier for them to cope with the transition to Arab rule than for those Christians in Syria who had taken the Chalcedonian line, the majority of whom lived west of the Euphrates. Nevertheless both Chalcedonians and anti-Chalcedonians continued for a while to believe that the Arab conquest was a temporary chastisement. Even when the Muslim empire proved to be a durable entity, the belief that the Cross would be victorious in the end was present among the Christians, like a seed waiting to germinate. One proof of this may be seen in the eagerness with which the Jacobites were to espouse the ideology of the Crusades.

The Arabs renounced all responsibility for the internal affairs of non-Muslim communities under their rule. But the subject status of the Church under Islam involved the abandonment of grandiose political ambitions and accentuated the tendency to pragmatism. The Jacobite (or Syrian Orthodox) Church was concerned with belief insofar as its conception of orthodoxy was its formal reason for existing, but those responsible for its internal discipline gradually became more concerned with behaviour and less with the imponderables of faith. Where doctrine was concerned, their most certain knowledge was that they were opposed to the Byzantine Church. This would be strikingly revealed by the readiness of one of their patriarchs to submit to the authority of the Roman Church in the thirteenth century. The cement of this short-lived rapprochement was a common distrust of Byzantium.

The prime need, both under Islam and under Crusader rule, was to protect the infrastructure of the Church. This included the legal status and the financial basis of the ecclesiastical institution and the social solidarity and self-esteem of the community; it also included the

---

[2] This is latinized as Baradaeus and occasionally re-orientalized as Bar ⊃Addai, which is wrong.

resourcefulness of community leaders and the readiness of the lay sector to contribute both in human and in financial terms to the clerical sector. The result was a change in mentality which the Greek church would not undergo until much later, under Turkish rule.

(ii) *The Historical Context.*[3]

'There was a time', narrates an eye-witness of the Avar assault upon Constantinople in AD 623, 'when things were going well for us and there was no warfare to terrify us; but the summit of prosperity, as they say, was changed through our carelessness and tripped us up, for we were not able to maintain our prosperity unsullied'.[4] Little more than a decade later, a Jewish merchant, a native of Palestine on business in Carthage, was to confirm this view: 'Indeed the territory of the Romans used to extend until our times from the Ocean, that is from Scotia, Britain, Spain, Frankia, Italy, Greece and Thrace, as far as Antioch, Syria, Persia and all the East, Egypt, Africa and the interior of Africa ... but now we see Rome humbled'.[5] This perception of shrinkage and decline given by contemporaries is shared by modern

---

[3] The following is intended as an introduction to, not an analysis of the period. Since this book is for non-specialist use, I have minimised the number of Arabic works cited; abbreviations used are: Tabarī = Taʾrīkh al-rusul wa 'l-mulūk, ed. M. J. de Goeje (Leiden, 1879-1901); Balādhurī = Futūh al-buldān, ed. M. J. de Goeje (Leiden, 1866); Ibn ʿAsākir = Taʾrīkh madīnat al-Dimashq I, ed. Salah al-dīn al-Munajjid (Damascus, 1951); Azdī = Taʾrīkh futūh al-Shām, ed. ʿAbd al-Munʿim ʿAbd Allāh ʿAmir (Cairo, 1970); Pseudo-Wāqidī = *The Conquest of Syria: commonly ascribed to Aboo ʿAbd Allah Mohammad b. ʿOmar al-Wāqidī*, ed. W. Nassau Lees (Calcutta, 1854). [Robert Hoyland]

[4] Averil Cameron, 'The Virgin's Robe: an episode in the history of early seventh-century Constantinople', *Byzantion*, 49 (1979), p. 49. For the date of the Avar attack see Michael and Mary Whitby, *Chronicon Paschale 284-628 AD* (Liverpool, 1989), appendix 4.

[5] V. Déroche, 'Doctrina Iacobi nuper baptizati', *TM*, 11 (1991), p. 169.

scholars, who frequently portray the seventh century as a 'dark age'.[6] But there is light, too; in the words of a colleague of the aforementioned Jew: 'though it (the Byzantine empire) may be somewhat diminished, we expect that it will rise again.'[7] And when it does emerge from the long dark tunnel of the late sixth, seventh and early eighth centuries, it is a renewed and transformed society, able to repulse the Arabs and set itself on a new footing. This brings us to the second characterization of our period, as a turning-point, a watershed, 'a crucial bridge in the transition from a definable Late Antique world to a medieval one.'[8]

Trying to discern and document the various elements and episodes in this reorganization is an all but impossible task. A figure or phenomenon that one had thought to belong wholly to one era turns out, on closer inspection, to bear traces of a subsequent age.[9] John Lydus, a civil servant of the emperor Justinian (527-65), had noted that 'the emperor's excellence is so great that institutions that have come to

---

[6] J. Herrin, *The Formation of Christendom* (Princeton, 1987), p. 133, citing other literature. On the seventh century see Ostrogorsky, part II; and, for more detailed studies: *DOP*, 13 (1959) - a special volume; F. Winkelmann *et al.*, *Byzanz im 7. Jahrhundert* (Berliner byzantinische Arbeiten, xlviii, Berlin, 1978); M. Hendy, *Studies in the Byzantine Monetary Economy, c. 300-1450* (Cambridge, 1985), pp. 619-61; A. N. Stratos, *Byzantium in the Seventh Century*. An easy introduction to the Muslim view of the period is given by G. R. Hawting, *The First Dynasty of Islam: the Umayyad Caliphate AD 661-750* (London and Sydney, 1986).

[7] Déroche, 'Doctrina', p. 167.

[8] Herrin, *Formation*, p. 133; J. F. Haldon, *Byzantium in the Seventh Century: the Transformation of a Culture* (Cambridge, 1990) examines many aspects of this transition; the general notion is discussed by A. Kazhdan and A. Cutler, 'Continuity and Discontinuity in Byzantine History', *Byzantion*, 52 (1982), pp. 429-78.

[9] cf. Averil Cameron, *Procopius and the Sixth Century* (London, 1985), ch. 2; S. C. MacCormack, 'Christ and Empire: Time and Ceremonial in Sixth-Century Byzantium and Beyond', *Byzantion*, 52 (1982), pp. 287-309 (on Cosmas Indicopleustes as a medieval Byzantine figure).

ruin in the past are eagerly awaiting a rebirth by his intervention'.[10]
From Justinian's failure to achieve a lasting union of the western
Mediterranean under imperial control, his closure of the Academy at
Athens and of the theatre at Rome[11] and his termination of the
consulship,[12] one may infer that the 'rebirth' never really came and
that many of the decaying institutions met their final demise. Certainly
one senses a different rhythm in late sixth- and early seventh-century
life. A number of trends that had begun much earlier reached their
completion at this time. Greek now totally supplants Latin as the
official language of the empire.[13] The town-councils and their
toga-clad members which John Lydus (b. 490) can vaguely recollect
from his childhood[14] have gone, their right to levy the taxes on their
locality usurped by an increasingly centralized bureaucracy, and care
for the welfare of a city's inhabitants now firmly in the hands of its
bishops.[15] Christianity has so permeated the Byzantine world that
it has begun to redefine it. Bath- and theatre-centred life wanes as
public worship rather than public entertainment comes increasingly to

---

[10] John Lydus, *de magistratibus populi romani*, ed. R. Wuensch
(Leipzig, 1903), II.5.

[11] R. C. Beacham, *The Roman Theatre and its Audience* (London,
1991), p. 198.

[12] Alan Cameron and D. Schauer, 'The Last Consul: Basilius and his
Diptych', *JRS*, 72 (1982), pp. 126-45. Justin II revived the consulship
in 566, but only as an adjunct of the imperial office; it was finally
abolished in 642.

[13] In a letter of 597, Pope Gregory laments: 'hodie in
Constantinopolitana civitate, qui de latino in graeco dictata bene
transferunt, non sunt' (*epistolae*, ed. P. Ewald and L. M. Hartmann,
MGH, Berlin, 1891, I, p. 474 = 7.27).

[14] John Lydus, *de magistratibus*, I.28.

[15] Governors sent from Constantinople and wealthy landowners also
participated in administration and policy-making, but clergy and holy
men most represented people's interests. See A. H. M. Jones, *The
Later Roman Empire 284-602* (Oxford, 1964), II, pp. 726ff.; G.
Dagron, 'Le Christianisme dans la ville byzantine', *DOP*, 31 (1977),
esp. pp. 19-25.

be stressed;[16] by contrast, a plethora of churches fills the lands, more than 250 being built in Palestine alone during the fifth and sixth centuries.[17] Classical texts are still being copied in the seventh century, but hagiographies and miracle-stories are what attract readers, while production of new secular literature has all but ceased.[18] The rapprochement between Church and State that began in the time of Constantine I has now become an inextricable bond, and emperors begin to proclaim to all the world their allegiance to Christ.[19]

Fresh developments were also afoot in our period. The prime agents of change were recurring bouts of bubonic plague, commencing in 542, by which 'nearly the whole world was annihilated',[20] and a surge of wars and invasions which culminated in the annexation of most Byzantine provinces, temporarily by the Persians (c.610-28), then, even as the Byzantines were celebrating their victory, permanently by the Arabs. Already in 580, an historian could say: 'nations have been wiped out, cities enslaved, populations uprooted and displaced, so that

---

[16] C. Mango, 'Daily Life in Byzantium', *JÖB*, 31 (1981), pp. 337-53 (repr. in *idem, Byzantium and its Image*, IV).

[17] A. Ovadiah, *Corpus of Byzantine Christian Churches* (Bonn, 1970); *idem* and C. G. De Silva, *Supplementum* (Jerusalem, 1981-84). M. Piccirillo, *Chiese e Mosaici di Giordania I* (Jerusalem, 1981) shows that Jordan, too, was intensively inhabited and endowed with churches in this period.

[18] Averil Cameron, 'New themes and styles in Greek literature, seventh-eighth centuries' in *eadem*, etc., *Byzantine and Early Islamic Near East I*, pp. 81-105. See also *eadem*, 'The Eastern Provinces in the Seventh Century AD. Hellenism and the emergence of Islam' in S. Said, ed., *Ellēnismos. Quelques jalons pour une histoire de l'identité grecque* (Strasbourg, 1991), pp. 289-313.

[19] I. Shahid, 'On the Titulature of the Emperor Heraclius', *BZ*, 51 (1981), pp. 28-96: on the assumption by Heraclius in 629 of the title {Gr. pistós en Christōi basileús}. See also Averil Cameron, 'The early religious policies of Justin II' in *eadem, Continuity and Change in Sixth-Century Byzantium* (London, 1981), X, who discerns in Justin's reign 'a new sort of piety creeping over Byzantine life, the emperor setting the tone'.

[20] Procopius, *Werke*, ed. Otto Veh (Munich, 1970), III, p. 355 (= *de bello persico*, 2.22).

all mankind has been involved in the upheaval'.[21] Furthermore, there was almost no respite, for Arab expeditions, with the capture of Constantinople as their goal, continued with undiminished vigour for a century.[22] Byzantium had to use all its ingenuity just to survive. To facilitate rapid, on-the-spot decision-making, the old Diocletian separation of civil and military offices was now discarded in favour of a concentration of both powers in the military governor of a province {Gr. stratēgós}. Deficiency in agricultural and military manpower was eased by the creation of an army of farmer-soldiers {Gr. stratiōtai}.[23] Cities were abandoned or reduced in size and there was a shift from a city-based towards a more rural society, comprised of villages and small market-towns protected by castles.[24]

The calamities of this era brought about conceptual as well as physical changes. For it seemed as though these were 'the beginning of the sorrows, when nation shall rise against nation and kingdom against kingdom, and there shall be famines and pestilences and

---

[21] Agathias, *History*, ed. R. Keydell (Berlin, 1967), p. 5 (preface); tr. J. D. C. Frendo (Berlin and New York, 1975), p. 5.

[22] R.-J. Lilie, *Die byzantinische Reaktion auf die Ausbreitung der Araber* (Munich, 1976), ch. 4.

[23] The military reorganization of this period is a much debated subject; for an overview and further references see Haldon, *Byzantium in the Seventh Century*, ch. 6.

[24] This applies chiefly to Asia Minor; the first Arab dynasty, the Umayyads, reversed the decline of certain classical cities (see H. Kennedy, 'Recent French archaeological work in Syria and Jordan', *Byzantine and Modern Greek Studies*, 11 [1987], 245-352). There is much discussion as to whether the changes were the result of a decline in prosperity occasioned by numerous plagues and wars - thus H. Kennedy, 'The Last Century of Byzantine Syria: a Reinterpretation', *Byzantinische Forschungen*, 10 (1985), pp. 141-83; or whether they were due to 'internal cultural readjustments' - thus M. Whittow, 'Ruling the late Roman and early Byzantine city: a continuous history', *Past and Present*, 129 (1990), pp. 3-29. A good résumé of the latest scholarship is given by S. Barnish, 'The transformation of classical cities and the Pirenne debate', *Journal of Roman Archaeology*, 2 (1989), pp. 385-400.

earthquakes ... and you shall be hated of all nations for my sake'.[25] Indeed, as Huns, Avars, Persians and Arabs bayed at the very walls of Constantinople, 'the Byzantines regarded themselves no longer as citizens of a world-empire, but as a Chosen People ringed by hostile pagan nations'.[26] Public spaces disappeared, as buildings as well as their inhabitants huddled together for protection.[27] Dissenters were less and less tolerated, and Jews in particular, were suspected of siding with the enemy, and so liable to be persecuted.[28] The enslavement by the Persians and Arabs of large segments of the population occasioned much physical suffering and soul-searching: how could one obtain salvation and remission of one's sins if, having been reduced to slavery or captured in war, one could no longer attend church, fast or observe a vigil freely or at will? What was to be one's attitude towards Christian women who, as slaves and captives, committed certain transgressions?[29] For comfort and aid, the Byzantines turned heavenwards; icons, relics, saints living and dead were called upon to

---

[25] *Matthew* 24:7-9, a frequently cited chapter; *Matthew* 24:15, 'When you see the abomination of desolation ... stand in the holy place ...', was quoted in connection with the arrival of the Arabs in Jerusalem (e.g. Theophanes, p. 339).

[26] Peter Brown, *The World of Late Antiquity AD 150-750* (London, 1971; repr. 1989), p. 174.

[27] B. de Vries, 'Jordan's Churches: their urban context in Late Antiquity', *Biblical Archaeologist*, 51 (1988), pp. 222-6.

[28] G. Dagron, 'Juifs et Chrétiens dans l'Orient du VIIe siècle', *TM*, 11 (1991), pp. 17-46. There was also a proliferation of anti-Jewish disputation-literature: V. Déroche, 'La polémique anti-Judaïque au VIe et au VIIe siècle', *ibid.*, pp. 275-311.

[29] Anastasius the Sinaite (d. *c.*701), 'Quaestiones', *PG* 89, 784C, 773AC; note Anastasius's observation (*PG* 89, 785B) that 'the present generation' faces a period of spiritual crisis like that endured by the Children of Israel during the Babylonian Captivity. See also B. Flusin, 'Démons et Sarrasins. L'auteur et le propos des *Diēgēmata Stēriktiká* d'Anastase le Sinaïte', *TM*, 11 (1991), pp. 400-4.

act as divine intermediaries and intercessors.[30] Thus the citizens of Constantinople could rest easy: 'No one shall capture it - far from it, for it has been entrusted to the Mother of God and no one shall wrest it from her hands'.[31]

But it was not only the enemy at the walls that was to assail the Byzantines in the seventh century; internal religious strife was also to plague them. Wishing to impart a measure of agreement and uniformity of belief to his war-shattered realm, the emperor Heraclius and his patriarch Sergius attempted to impose common ground under the banner of one energy (monoenergism) and one will (monotheletism) in Christ. Deeply-held religious beliefs mingled with issues such as soured East-West relations, resentment of imperial meddling in doctrinal matters and shifting provincial allegiances to produce a storm of furious debate that raged for over half a century (especially from 630 to 680) and resulted in a flurry of synods, embassies and correspondence.[32] The dispute reached a crescendo with the arrests and trials of the monk and mystic, Maximus the Confessor (d. 662) and of Pope Martin (d. 655) and only abated with the convening of the Sixth Ecumenical Council, held at Constantinople in 680/1, which

---

[30] Averil Cameron, 'Images of Authority: élites and icons in late sixth-century Byzantium', *Past and Present*, 84 (1979), pp. 3-35; Peter Brown, 'The rise and function of the holy man in Late Antiquity', *JRS*, 61 (1971), pp. 80-101, repr. in *idem, Society and the Holy in Late Antiquity* (California, 1982), pp. 103-52. On ideological reorientation generally in this period see J. F. Haldon, 'Ideology and social change in the seventh century: military discontent as a barometer', *Klio*, 68 (1986), pp. 139-90.

[31] *PG* 111, 853B; L. Rydèn, ed./tr., 'The Andreas Salos Apocalypse', *DOP*, 28 (1974), pp. 201-2/215. The text is ascribed to the late seventh century by C. Mango, 'The Life of St. Andrew the Fool Reconsidered', *Rivista di Studi Bizantini e Slavi* II, (Bologna, 1982), pp. 297-313, repr. in *idem, Byzantium and its Image*, VIII.

[32] Compare the list of sources compiled by F. Winkelmann, 'Die Quellen zur Erforschung des monoenergetisch-monothelitischen Streites', *Klio*, 69 (1987), pp. 515-59.

secured a degree of accord at least in the imperial camp.[33] The Arabs' occupation of the provinces did nothing to dampen the controversy, but rather fuelled it, since it was manifest to all concerned that it was due to the error of the other party that the Christian community was thus afflicted.[34]

Yet, like Dickens's late eighteenth-century France and England, the seventh-century Near East witnessed not only 'the worst of times' but also 'the best of times'. For the inhabitants of the Arabian peninsular this was certainly the case. After a series of lightning campaigns lasting but a decade (633-42), they established a foothold in the Byzantine provinces which they were never to relinquish. Possessing their own culture and faith, they felt no pressure to become assimilated after the fashion of the sackers of Rome, and their successes only made it clearer to them that they were on the right path: 'It is a sign of God's love for us and pleasure with our faith that he has given us dominion over all regions and all peoples'.[35] The Umayyads, the first Muslim dynasty (660-750), set about laying the foundations of a new empire; they built administrative complexes, palaces and mosques;[36] they

---

[33] The latest résumé of the affair is J. Meyendorff, *Imperial Unity and Christian Divisions. The Church 450-680 AD* (New York, 1989, ch. 10). The relevant texts are translated by F. X. Murphy and P. Sherwood, *Constantinople II et III* (Paris, 1974).

[34] Examples of this view are given in W. E. Kaegi, 'Initial Byzantine Reactions to the Arab Conquest' *Church History*, 38 (1969), pp. 139-49; S. P. Brock, 'Syriac Views of Emergent Islam'.

[35] Dispute between an Arab and a monk of Beth Hālē, Codex Diyarbakir 95, f. 2a (edition and translation being prepared by H. J. W. Drijvers, Groningen). Note the words of Leo III to ᶜUmar II: 'You attribute to your religion the success with which heaven favours you' (A. Jeffery, 'Ghevond's Text of the Correspondence between ᶜUmar II and Leo III', *Harvard Theological Review*, 37 (1944), p. 330).

[36] So much was thus spent that it became an 'election promise' to reduce such expenditure; cf. Yazīd III's accession speech in 744: 'O people, I promise you not to put stone upon stone nor brick upon brick, not to dig canals ...' (Tabarī, II, p. 1834). For the idea that the machinery of the Islamic state was in place at an early date see F. M. Donner, 'The Formation of the Islamic State', *Journal of the American*

reclaimed lands and undertook irrigation projects.[37] For such tasks, competent managers were required and, since the Umayyads paid no heed to the birth, creed or rank of non-Arabs, there were great opportunities for advancement open to the able and willing. Baššār b. Burd's grandfather, a native of Tukhāristān, was captured and taken to Basra where he worked as a bricklayer; Baššār himself (715-85) was in a position to satirize caliphs and to ask: 'Is there a messenger who will carry my message to all the Arabs ... to say that I am a man of ancestry, superior to any other man of ancestry'?[38] Conversion was not essential - thus Athanasius bar Gūmōyē made his fortune as right-hand man to ^CAbd al-^CAzīz b. Marwān, governor of Egypt, while remaining a devout Christian.[39] But among prisoners-of-war and émigrés to Muslim cities, who would be spending all their time among Muslims, conversion was the norm, as was noted with much grief by their erstwhile co-religionaries: 'Many people who were members of the Church will deny the true Faith ... without being subjected to any compulsion, lashings or blows.'[40] The entry into the Islamic fold of such a diffuse mixture of people, from so many different races and of so many different religious and philosophical persuasions, lent a tremendous variety and vitality to the nascent

---

Oriental Society, 106 (1986), pp. 283-96.

[37] A. M. Watson, *Agricultural Innovation in the Early Islamic World* (Cambridge, 1983) makes an interesting, if exaggerated, case for a green revolution, a result of the removal by the Arabs of the old East-West divide; see the review by P. Crone, *JSS*, 80 (1985), pp. 347-50.

[38] A. F. L. Beeston, ed./tr., *Selections from the poetry of Baššār* (Cambridge, 1977), p. 11/50.

[39] See text No. 13, § 132-4.

[40] Text No. 14, XII.3. Apostasy was evidently an issue as early as 690; cf. the ruling of James of Edessa (d. 708) that 'we should not rebaptize a Christian who becomes a Muslim or a pagan, then returns': C. Kayser, ed./tr., *Die Canones Jacobs von Edessa* (Leipzig, 1886), p. 8/37; A. Vööbus, ed./tr., *The Synodicon in the West Syrian Tradition I*, *CSCO* 367/8 (Louvain, 1975), p. 253/231. The phenomenon of Umayyad clientage is discussed by P. Crone, *Slaves on Horses. The Evolution of the Islamic Polity* (Cambridge, 1980), ch. 8.

Muslim world and meant that Byzantium was brought face-to-face with a new and vigorous civilization taking shape within her own provinces and in the heartlands of her old arch-enemy, Persia.

The story of the seventh-century Near East is very much a story of this confrontation and, as it turned out, of the survival of both parties. Though at the cost of their provinces, the Byzantines managed, thanks to the reforms they carried out and the measures they took, as well as to the determination they displayed, to halt the Arab advance at the borders of their heartlands. The divided provincial Church, though it dwindled in the long term,[41] withstood the immediate shock of being severed from its centre: the Jacobites and Copts, because they had already established a degree of autonomy during the sixth century;[42] the Chalcedonians, because they had the advantage of holding many of the positions of power when the Arabs arrived.[43] At the time, surrounded by a hostile majority, the Arabs were not so sure of their survival either and there were many who shared the opinion of the Muslim scholar, ^cUrwa b. al-Zubayr who, ascending Mount Sal^c, warned his comrades: 'the Byzantines shall drive you out of your Syria

---

[41] R. Schick, *Christian Communities of Palestine from Byzantine to Islamic Rule. An historical and archaeological study* (Studies in Late Antiquity and Early Islam, Princeton, 1992); argument summarized in *idem*, 'Christian Life in Palestine during the early Islamic Period', *Biblical Archaeologist*, 51 (1988), pp. 218-21, 239-40.

[42] W. A. Wigram, *The Separation of the Monophysites* (London, 1923); S. Ashbrook-Harvey, 'Remembering Pain: Syriac Historiography and the Separation of the Churches', *Byzantion*, 58 (1988), pp. 295-308.

[43] The Chalcedonian leader Theodore was able to obtain from Yazīd b. Mu^cāwiya (680-3) a diploma giving him authority over the people of Alexandria and Maryūt (*History of the Patriarchs*, ed./tr. B. Evetts, *PO*, 5 (1910), p. 5). See H. Kennedy, 'The Melkite Church from the Islamic Conquest to the Crusades: continuity and adaptation in the Byzantine Legacy', *Seventeenth International Byzantine Congress, Major Papers* (New York, 1986), pp. 325-39.

and their horsemen shall stand on this mountain'.[44] However, [c]Abd al-Malik's building of the Dome of the Rock on the Temple Mount in Jerusalem, his minting of aniconic coins bearing the Muslim profession of faith and his moves to institute Arabic as the official language of the new empire made it clear to all that the Muslim realm was to be no mere temporary phenomenon. Equally, their failure to take Constantinople in 717-18 demonstrated to the Arabs that the Byzantines were not so easily to be dislodged. Strife and conflict there still was and distrust was ingrained, but accommodation and co-existence were now the order of the day. It is thus from this date that we see the beginnings and efflorescence of Christian-Muslim disputation literature,[45] and witness the first steps in the long and stormy course of Muslim-Christian relations.[46]

Turning now from the historical to the historiographical context, we find a similar picture of decline and transformation. The Eusebian tradition of chronography in Greek faltered after the efforts of Panodorus and Annianus in the fifth century and Greek historical writing as a whole went into the doldrums with the onset of Arab rule,[47] only re-emerging in the late eighth and early ninth century under the influence of Syriac and Arabic models.[48] West-Syrian

---

[44] S. Bashear, 'Apocalyptic and other materials on early Muslim-Byzantine wars: a review of Arabic sources', *Journal of the Royal Asiatic Society*, ser. iii, 1 (1991), p. 185.

[45] A.-T. Khoury, *Polémique byzantine contre l'Islam (VIIIe-XIIIe s.)* (Leiden, 1972); A. Ducellier, *Le Miroir de l'Islam* (Paris, 1971); Reinink, 'Syriac Apologetic Literature'.

[46] H. A. R. Gibb, 'Arab-Byzantine relations under the Umayyad caliphate', *DOP*, 12 (1958), pp. 219-33; R. Hoyland, 'Jacob of Edessa on Islam', *Middle Eastern Christian Studies*, 2 (1991; forthcoming); P. Crone, 'Islam, Judaeo-Christianity and Byzantine Iconoclasm', *Jerusalem Studies in Arabic and Islam*, 2 (1980), pp. 59-95.

[47] Michael Whitby, 'Greek historical writing after Procopius: variety and vitality,' in Cameron etc., *Byzantine and Early Islamic Near East I*, pp. 25-80.

[48] C. Mango, 'The Tradition of Byzantine Chronography', pp. 363-369; L. I. Conrad, 'Theophanes and the Arabic Historical Tradition'.

historiography suffered less disruption. The royal annals kept by the Abgarid kings of Edessa had inspired a subsequent episcopal tradition of annalistic record-keeping, of which we find extracts in a mid-sixth-century anonymous Edessene compilation and in the early seventh-century work of Thomas the Presbyter.[49] At monasteries such as Qēnneshrē and Qartmīn in northern Mesopotamia, the tradition appears to have continued throughout the seventh century. After the fashion of Eusebius, 'other men charted the succession of years, namely James of Edessa and John the Stylite of Litarba',[50] both active in the late seventh and early eighth centuries and James, at least, having been educated at Qēnneshrē. The work of earlier authors is clearly discernible in the *Chronicle of 846* and its immediate source, the Qartmīnite *Chronicle of 819*.[51] The same is true for the narrative of the Zuqnīn monk, whose source for the Arab siege of Constantinople (717-18) was evidently a contemporary of the emperor Leo III.[52]

But although it did not cease, history-writing in Syriac did become rather parochial and piecemeal at this time. The interval AG 972-6 (AD 660-4) is covered only by a Maronite chronicle;[53] since Dionysius of Tel-Mahrē (on whom see Part Two), not knowing the

---

[49] 'Chronicon Edessenum' in *Chronica Minora* I, pp. 1-14; text No. 2 below.

[50] Michael, p. 378 (10.21, scholion), quoting Dionysius of Tel-Mahrē.

[51] Text No. 12 below; examining the *Chronicle of 846*, Brooks, 'The Sources of Theophanes and the Syriac Chroniclers', detects writers active around 728, 746 and 785.

[52] Note the present tense: 'As for this Leo, he *is* a courageous, strong and warlike man; and he *is* by origin a Syrian from these borderlands' (text No. 10, AG 1028).

[53] Text No. 4 and see Chronological Table 3; the comment of this chronicler that, since the raid of 664 (AG 975), 'the Arabs have not attacked again up to the present day' suggests that he was active not long after this date.

latter, was obliged to turn to Arabic sources to plug the gap,[54] we may infer that there were at least no Jacobite sources available to him. Another scant period, that between AG 952 and 960 (AD 641-9), Dionysius fills with information on the lives of the Muslim rulers ᶜUmar and ᶜUthmān 'according to the Arabs' and with extracts from ecclesiastical writings.[55] One cannot but admire the diligence with which Dionysius strove to achieve his aim of providing a continuous historical narrative in which to couch his ecclesiastical history, but he really had to scrape the historiographical barrel in order to do so.

By contrast, a genre closely related to history-writing, apocalyptic, flourished in this period.[56] Just as the Byzantines increasingly turned from human to heavenly intercessors, so they came to dwell more on the intentions of God than the affairs of men. Using the *Book of Daniel's* scheme of four world-empires and the well-known Eusebian division of history into ages and millennia, West Syrian apocalyptic writers strove to inject order and meaning into the past, to elaborate a conception of history that would explain the traumatic situation in which they now found themselves and so to provide a model of hope for the future, extending the promise of deliverance to those who stood firm. In2 particular, the idea of a redeeming Christian Emperor who would oust the Arabs fired the eschatological imagination of the men

---

[54] From their detailed and anecdotal nature and concentration upon solely internal Arab affairs, one can surmise that §§ 102-12 of text No. 13 are derived from an Arabic account.

[55] Text No. 13, §§ 87-92. For Dionysius's use of Arabic sources see Hoyland, 'Arabic, Syriac and Greek historiography in the first Abbasid century'.

[56] Useful introductions to the genre are provided by J. Collins, *The Apocalyptic Imagination* (New York, 1984), esp. ch. 1; D. S. Russel, *The Method and Message of Jewish Apocalyptic* (London, 1964). C. Mango, *Byzantium: The Empire of New Rome*, ch. 11 gives an overview of the Byzantine variety; P. J. Alexander, *The Byzantine Apocalyptic Tradition* (California, 1985) gives examples and some discussion.

of this time.[57] Signs of the end were much in evidence in the seventh century: 'Here is a people against a people and a nation against a nation; here are famines, earthquakes and plagues; only one thing is missing for us: the advent of the Deceiver' wrote a Christian observer of the plague and famine of 686/7.[58] The tumultuous years of the Persian and Arab invasions inevitably elicited apocalyptic reactions,[59] as did those of the second Arab civil war (683-92) when many became convinced that the end of the world was nigh: Christians,[60] Mandaeans[61] and Arabs.[62] Then there was the siege of Constantinople with which this book ends; it fell on the eve of AH 100, the year in which began the messianic movement which would culminate in the ^cAbbāsid revolution;[63] the year in which Tiberius, the supposedly murdered son of the emperor Justinian II (685-95, 705-11), would appear and initiate the eschatological wars between the

---

[57] G. Reinink, 'Pseudo-Methodius und die Legende vom römischen Endkaiser'.

[58] A. Mingana, ed./tr., *Sources syriaques* (Leiden, 1907), p. 165/192-3; S. P. Brock, tr., 'North Mesopotamia in the Late Seventh Century. Book XV of John Bar Penkāyē's *Rīš Mellē*', *Jerusalem Studies in Arabic and Islam*, 9 (1987), p. 72; repr. in *id.*, *Studies in Syriac Christianity: History, Literature, Theology* (Collected Studies Series, 357; London, 1992), chapter II.

[59] Dagron, 'Juifs et Chrétiens', *TM*, 11 (1991), pp. 38-43 signals a number of them. There is also the pseudo-Ephrem apocalypse, ed./tr. H. Suermann, *Die geschichtstheologischer Reaktion auf die einfallenden Muslime* (Frankfurt, 1985), pp. 12-33; and possibly J.-B. Chabot, 'L'Apocalypse d'Esdras', *Revue Sémitique*, 2 (1894), pp. 242-50; 333-46.

[60] Text No. 14 and see H. J. W. Drijvers, 'The Gospel of the Twelve Apostles: a Syriac apocalypse from the early Islamic Period', in Cameron etc., *Byzantine and Early Islamic Near East I*, pp. 189-213.

[61] M. Lidzbarski, tr., *Ginza: der Schatz, oder das große Buch der Mandäer* (Göttingen, 1925), pp. 411-6, proposing that the end would come after 71 years of Arab rule; cf. Ibn Hishām, *Sīrat rasūl Allāh*, ed. F. Wüstenfeld (Göttingen, 1858-60), pp. 377-8.

[62] W. Madelung, '^cAbdallāh b. Zubayr and the Mahdī', *Journal of Near Eastern Studies*, 40 (1981), pp. 291-305; *idem*, 'Apocalyptic Prophecies in Hims in the Umayyad age', *JSS*, 31 (1986), pp. 141-86.

[63] Tabari, II, 1358.

Byzantine and Muslim realms;[64] the year in which, predicted Muhammad, there would be no one left alive on the face of the earth.[65]

(iii) *The Texts*

All surviving Syriac chronicles were compiled by Christians. They present themselves as objective annalists, but, according to the view proposed here, they compiled or composed their texts in retrospect to serve moral, religious and political purposes. The writers assumed that God was the steersman who determined the course of history and that natural phenomena and the chance of battle, far from being arbitrary factors, reflected his approval and disapproval of human actions and beliefs.[66] By careful selection and significant juxtaposition of events they led the reader to draw conclusions by his own intelligence, with a minimum of didactic intrusion on the author's part, though some authors did indulge in moralistic rhetoric.[67] There is a tension in the Syriac chronicles between two styles: factual reporting (usually

---

[64] Nu\(^c\)aym b. Hammād, *Kitāb al-Fitan* (BL Ms. Or. 9449), numerous versions - esp. f. 115.

[65] Mas\(^c\)ūdī, *Murūj al-dhahab*, ed. C. Pellat (Beirut, 1966-79), III, p. 38.

[66] Text No. 13 contains (in a note on § 140) a passage, which shows that the chronicler, whether Dionysius or another churchman, thought he had found a proof that scientific determinism was wrong and that natural phenomena are directly caused by the divine Will and can be read as statements with reference to human affairs.

[67] The passage referred to in the previous footnote is the exception which proves the rule: in general, clerical authors expected their readers to look for God's meaning in the events they record, even when this meaning is not signalled explicitly. A good example of moralization is to be found in a note on § 59 of text No. 13, where an Arab raid on civilians celebrating a religious festival is interpreted as a just punishment for the wrong behaviour of Christians in general, many of whom are alleged to attend such festivals for reasons of pleasure and society.

brief) on the one hand and emotionally coloured story-telling (often long) on the other. The chief models for the former were the annals of Edessa and the chronological tables of Eusebius and his continuators, whereas the latter style (as far as the Syrians were concerned) was mainly represented by the ecclesiastical historians.

The chronicles which stick to bare facts should be seen not so much as works of literature (they make dry reading), but more as handbooks to cite in the context of debate, or even oracles, providing the desired answers to those who approached them. These were most effective if they were composed in an 'objective' style. The authors who adopted a narrative style wrote essentially with a hortatory, as opposed to a polemical, purpose, presenting history as a morale-booster to the members of their own religious group and as a warning to disruptive members of the group. It is debatable whether any Syrian chronicler sought to rise above polemic and homiletic. But if anyone tried to extrapolate a coherent pattern from the complexities of the commemorated past and of his own experience, it was the ninth-century Jacobite patriarch, Dionysius of Tel-Mahrē, whose narrative of the seventh century, as preserved in two later chronicles, forms the central feature of this book. Indeed, readers without any background knowledge will find it useful to read Dionysius (Part Two = text No. 13) before tackling the disconnected bulletins of the minor chronicles (Part One).

Nevertheless it seemed better to present the sources in the order of their composition, so far as their dates can be determined. **Text No. 1** is quite exceptional, being apparently a memorial jotted down for posterity during the Arab invasion of Palestine in AD 637 by someone on the spot who realized that he was living in momentous times. **Text No. 2** is usually seen as a mindless assemblage of disjointed chronological oddments; it can be argued, however, that it is the work of a single man, the priest Thomas, with a single anti-Chalcedonian purpose, writing in northern Mesopotamia in the penultimate year of Heraclius's reign. According to this interpretation the whole chronicle, including the parts concerned with earlier times, is relevant to the seventh-century context.[68] **Text No. 3** is an extract from a chronicle which is derived from a lost text probably completed shortly after Heraclius's death in AD 641, by someone who agreed with his policy of imposing the decision of the Council of Chalcedon on all Byzantine subjects. Those Syrians who were not opposed to Chalcedon suffered an internal split towards and after the end of the period covered by this book. The two opposing camps were the Byzantine Conformists ('Melkites') and the dissident Maronites, formerly the champions of Chalcedon in Syria. The *Maronite Chronicle,* **text No. 4**, was written before this division, probably not long after AD 664. It keeps the annalistic framework, but uses it to present both brief factual bulletins and longer episodes which read as self-contained anecdotes.   It denigrates the Jacobites and highlights Byzantine successes against the Arabs, while playing down the more substantial Arab gains.

The next group of texts, **Nos. 5 to 9**, with the exception of text No. 7, have one thing in common: they all attempt to establish the chronology of the Arab caliphs, a problem bedevilled by the fact that the Arabs themselves counted in lunar years. Moreover, **text No. 5**, by Bishop James of Edessa, who enjoyed vast prestige as a chronographer by virtue of having emulated and even improved upon Eusebius, unfortunately gave Muhammad only seven years in power; his authority perpetuated this error. The most valuable of this group of sources for the purpose of dating the caliphs is **text No. 8**. This is the so-called *Liber calipharum*, which is found attached to the end of the manuscript of text No. 2. It was translated from a lost Arabic original. One advantage of the method of presentation adopted in this book is that the survival of this group of texts strikes the reader as potentially significant for Syrian attitudes around 700. Was it only

---

[68] The last folio of the manuscript is a completely separate work, incorporated in the course of producing a new copy. The separation of these two texts and the presentation of the former as a much earlier work may momentarily disorientate those readers to whom the whole manuscript is more familiar under the name of *Liber calipharum* or. *Chronicle of AD 724.*

then that it began to dawn on the Syrians that the Arab Conquest was not a temporary setback for Byzantium, but the beginning of a new empire to which they would continue to be subjected?

Texts Nos. 7, 10 and 12 are written in the annalistic form which we have encountered before, especially in text No. 2. The short chronicle of disasters dated AD 716 (**text No. 7**) was apparently written with a purely hortatory purpose, although some have seen it as apocalyptic. The *Chronicle of Zuqnīn*[69] (**text No. 10**) was put together by someone who had access to a considerable range of historical texts, but who rather went to pieces in the seventh century, because of the lack of a continuous narrative history on which to hang the incidental snippets of information he had obtained. A close analysis shows that he could have done it better, had he not been slipshod in his approach to chronology; it is amusing to find him retaliating defensively by labelling anyone who sets out to pick holes in his chronology as insufficiently devout. After all, history is there to teach us moral lessons, not to be argued over for its own sake! Fortunately it is quite easy to take the chronicle apart and so recover the valuable materials which this muddle-headed moralist had at his disposal. **Text No. 12** presents two related chronicles which go up to AD 819 and 846 respectively. Selective though they are, these chronicles seem to reproduce information in a straightforward way, except on the rare occasions when it suits them to 'improve upon' history slightly for the sake of pointing a moral.

Text No. 11 includes two late eighth-century inscriptions from a church on the Euphrates, which seem to confirm the connection between chronography and apocalyptic.

Text No. 13 contains extracts from two later chronicles, the *Chronicle of AD 1234* (main text) and (partially translated in the notes) the *Chronicle of Michael I* (Michael died AD 1199), the main usefulness of which lies in their complementary testimony to the text

---

69 Sometimes called 'the Chronicle of Pseudo-Dionysius of Tel-Mahrē'.

of the lost chronicle of Dionysius of Tel-Maḥrē. The *Chronicle of AD 1234* was on the whole more inclined to preserve the original wording and less inclined to paraphrase; above all it seems to have preserved the shape of Dionysius's narrative, which, except for the Church History, is lost in Michael. In the latter's chronicle, which is a compilation rather than a coherent whole, the author was in fact drawing on other sources as well, but the task of separating and identifying his sources for each episode is not attempted here. The introduction to text No. 13 does, however, try to construct a satisfactory picture of Dionysius's chronicle and to determine, so far as possible what were his sources. Dionysius should be ranked among the best historians, but his genius has never been sufficiently understood. The *Chronicle of AD 1234* is translated without significant omissions. To save space Michael has not been translated in full, but only where his text is in disagreement with the other chronicle, or adds to it something of substance. To place the fragments of Michael in their context, the reader can refer to Chabot's French translation. There he will find also virtually all that is preserved of Dionysius's History of the Church, composed on the Eusebian model around extensive quotations from the patriarchal archives. Since Dionysius saw the key to history in religion, his secular chronicle should be read together with his ecclesiastical history, which was in fact placed before it.

(iv) *Chronology*

Chronology is a complex subject. No attempt has been made to establish all the dates objectively. The first chronological table relates the Byzantine systems of dating by regnal years and by Indictions to the regnal years of the Persian shahs, to the Seleucid era used by the Syriac chronicles and to the Christian era familiar to most readers of English; separately, because of the complication caused by the lunar calculation, the same table relates the regnal years of the Muslim rulers and the era of Islam to the Christian era. The second table lists Roman emperors, Persian shahs, Arab caliphs and Syrian Orthodox patriarchs with their dates; this table gives some information which could not be fitted into Table 1. The third table displays the coverage of events by the minor chronographic texts here translated; it reveals concentrations and gaps which help in plotting the distribution and location of original sources through the period. The fourth table displays Dionysius's material and suggests some interesting reflections on his method and on his sources. These two tables are not intended to be used to plot established points in an historical narrative of the seventh century. They give the dates offered by the West-Syrian chronicles, which are not always reliable. Their purpose is to facilitate the study of those chronicles themselves. More work is necessary before we can be sure of the strengths and weaknesses of the chronology of text No. 13. As appears from the notes, some of the chronological mistakes in that text are evidently due to scribal error. This can occur easily, since Syriac often represents dates in abbreviated form. The overlapping chronologies used by Dionysius, the ultimate source of this text, make possible in theory a greater precision in months and even days. But it is not yet certain whether Dionysius actually worked with such accuracy. And he appears to have made an important error in numbering the regnal years of Heraclius (see Appendix I). Table 4 takes account of this error in recording the dates given by text No. 13.

The various dating systems used in this book need some introduction.

The Byzantine Indictions

The following extract from C. Mango, *Byzantium: The Empire of New Rome* (London, 1980), p. 189, explains the Byzantine system of tax-Indictions: 'The average Byzantine, like all other simple folk, had but a limited awareness of the succession of years. When he thought about such matters at all, he reckoned by the system of indictions. An indiction was a fifteen-year cycle initially introduced for the purpose of tax assessments, but when one referred, for example, to the fifth indiction, one meant the fifth year (starting on 1 September) of any given cycle, not the fifth cycle.' The Indictions are the bedrock on which the edifice of Byzantine chronology is built (see Ostrogorsky, 'Die Chronographie des Theophanes'). In our period the Indiction cycles began on 1 September AD 597, 612, 627, 642, 657, 672, 687, 702 and 717. These cycles are marked in Roman numerals to the right of the Roman emperors in Table 1.

The Seleucid era (AG)

This system is also based on the Julian calendar, beginning on 1 October, 312 BC. The years numbered according to the Seleucid or Greek era are sometimes referred to as the years of Alexander, the son of Philip of Macedon, whose name spelled the beginning of the Hellenistic period in Syria. This was the era used by all the Syriac chronographers. To convert an AG date into an AD date, one simply has to subtract 312 and count twelve Julian months forwards from 1 October. Thus AG 895 began on 1 October, AD 583, and ended on the last day of September, AD 584. A convenient shorthand is 'AD 583/84'. The succession of AG-years is listed to the right of the Persian shahs in Table 1.

The Islamic era (AH).

This system is based on a cycle of twelve lunar months, beginning with 16 July, AD 622. Every thirty-two years or so two lunar years have their beginning in the same solar year. For the Islamic years I have consulted the *Wüstenfeld-Mahler'sche Vergleichungstabellen zur muslimischen und iranischen Zeitrechnung* (Wiesbaden, 1961). The succession of 'AH'-years is listed to the right of the Arab caliphs in Table 1; the dates on which these years began and ended are noted to the right of the 'AD'-years in that table.

The Christian era (AD)

This system is based, for our period, on the Julian (solar) calendar, beginning with 1 January, AG 312. The succession of AD-years is listed in a column to the right of the AG-column (each equivalence running from 1 October of one AD-year to 30 September of the next, although the equivalence moves back to 1 September for the purpose of comparison with Byzantine regnal years and Indictions) and again to the right of the AH-column (each Islamic lunar year begins on a different date, as shown) in Table 1.

TABLE 1: CHRONOLOGY: BYZANTINE, PERSIAN, SELEUCID, ISLAMIC AND CHRISTIAN

N.B. The Byzantine year, beginning on 1 September, is equated here with the Seleucid year, which begins a month later, on 1 October. The Persian New Year fell in June during our period, but it is likely that text No. 13 counted Persian regnal years from a date not long after 15 September, perhaps 1 October (see Appendix I).

Byzantine rulers	Indictions	Persian rulers	AG	AD
Maurice 3	III	Hormizd IV 6	896	584/5
Maurice 4	IV	Hormizd IV 7	897	585/6
Maurice 5	V	Hormizd IV 8	898	586/7
Maurice 6	VI	Hormizd IV 9	899	587/8
Maurice 7	VII	Hormizd IV 10	900	588/9
Maurice 8	VIII	Hormizd IV 11	901	589/90
Maurice 9	IX	Chosroës II 1	902	590/1
Maurice 10	X	Chosroës II 2	903	591/2
Maurice 11	XI	Chosroës II 3	904	592/3
Maurice 12	XII	Chosroës II 4	905	593/4
Maurice 13	XIII	Chosroës II 5	906	594/5
Maurice 14	XIV	Chosroës II 6	907	595/6
Maurice 15	XV	Chosroës II 7	908	596/7
Maurice 16	I	Chosroës II 8	909	597/8
Maurice 17	II	Chosroës II 9	910	598/9
Maurice 18	III	Chosroës II 10	911	599/600
Maurice 19	IV	Chosroës II 11	912	600/1
Maurice 20	V	Chosroës II 12	913	601/2
Phocas 1	VI	Chosroës II 13	914	602/3
Phocas 2	VII	Chosroës II 14	915	603/4
Phocas 3	VIII	Chosroës II 15	916	604/5
Phocas 4	IX	Chosroës II 16	917	605/6
Phocas 5	X	Chosroës II 17	918	606/7
Phocas 6	XI	Chosroës II 18	919	607/8

Byzantine rulers	Indictions	Persian rulers	AG	AD
Phocas 7	XII	Chosroës II 19	920	608/9
Phocas 8	XIII	Chosroës II 20	921	609/10
Heraclius 1	XIV	Chosroës II 21	922	610/11
Heraclius 2	XV	Chosroës II 22	923	611/2
Heraclius 3	I	Chosroës II 23	924	612/3
Heraclius 4	II	Chosroës II 24	925	613/4
Heraclius 5	III	Chosroës II 25	926	614/5
Heraclius 6	IV	Chosroës II 26	927	615/6
Heraclius 7	V	Chosroës II 27	928	616/7
Heraclius 8	VI	Chosroës II 28	929	617/8
Heraclius 9	VII	Chosroës II 29	930	618/9
Heraclius 10	VIII	Chosroës II 30	931	19/20
Heraclius 11	IX	Chosroës II 31	932	620/1
Heraclius 12	X	Chosroës II 32	933	621/2
Heraclius 13	XI	Chosroës II 33	934	622/3
Heraclius 14	XII	Chosroës II 34	935	623/4
Heraclius 15	XIII	Chosroës II 35	936	624/5
Heraclius 16	XIV	Chosroës II 36	937	625/6
Heraclius 17	XV	Chosroës II 37	938	626/7
Heraclius 18	I	Chosroës II 38	939	627/8
Heraclius 19	II	Shīrōē 1	940	628/9
Heraclius 20	III	Ardashīr III 1	941	629/30
Heraclius 21	IV	Shahrvarāz 1	942	630/1
Heraclius 22	V	Bōrān 1	943	631/2
Heraclius 23	VI	Yazdgird III 1	944	632/3
Heraclius 24	VII	Yazdgird III 2	945	633/4
Heraclius 25	VIII	Yazdgird III 3	946	634/5
Heraclius 26	IX	Yazdgird III 4	947	635/6
Heraclius 27	X	Yazdgird III 5	948	636/7
Heraclius 28	XI	Yazdgird III 6	949	637/8
Heraclius 29	XII	Yazdgird III 7	950	638/9
Heraclius 30	XIII	Yazdgird III 8	951	639/40

Muslim rulers	AH	AD	from	to
Muḥammad b. ᶜAbd Allāh 1	1	622/3	16 July	4 July
Muḥammad b. ᶜAbd Allāh 2	2	623/4	5 July	23 June
Muḥammad b. ᶜAbd Allāh 3	3	624/5	24 June	12 June
Muḥammad b. ᶜAbd Allāh 4	4	625/6	13 June	1 June
Muḥammad b. ᶜAbd Allāh 5	5	626/7	2 June	22 May
Muḥammad b. ᶜAbd Allāh 6	6	627/8	23 May	10 May
Muḥammad b. ᶜAbd Allāh 7	7	628/9	11 May	30 Apr
Muḥammad b. ᶜAbd Allāh 8	8	629/30	1 May	19 Apr
Muḥammad b. ᶜAbd Allāh 9	9	630/1	20 Apr	8 Apr
Muḥammad b. ᶜAbd Allāh 10	10	631/2	9 Apr	28 Mar
Abū Bakr b. Abī Quhāfa 1	11	632/3	29 Mar	17 Mar
Abū Bakr b. Abī Quhāfa 2	12	633/4	18 Mar	6 Mar
Abū Bakr b. Abī Quhāfa 3	13	634/5	7 Mar	24 Feb
ᶜUmar I b. al-Khaṭṭāb 1	14	635/6	25 Feb	13 Feb
ᶜUmar I b. al-Khaṭṭāb 2	15	636/7	14 Feb	1 Feb
ᶜUmar I b. al-Khaṭṭāb 3	16	637/8	2 Feb	22 Jan
ᶜUmar I b. al-Khaṭṭāb 4	17	638/9	23 Jan	11 Jan
ᶜUmar I b. al-Khaṭṭāb 5	18	639/40	12 Jan	1 Jan

Byzantine rulers	Indictions	Persian rulers	AG	AD
Heraclius 31	XIV	Yazdgird III 9	952	640/1
Constans II 1	XV	Yazdgird III 10	953	641/2
Constans II 2	I	Yazdgird III 11	954	642/3
Constans II 3	II	Yazdgird III 12	955	643/4
Constans II 4	III	Yazdgird III 13	956	644/5
Constans II 5	IV	Yazdgird III 14	957	645/6
Constans II 6	V	Yazdgird III 15	958	646/7
Constans II 7	VI	Yazdgird III 16	959	647/8
Constans II 8	VII	Yazdgird III 17	960	648/9
Constans II 9	VIII	Yazdgird III 18	961	649/50
Constans II 10	IX	Yazdgird III 19	962	650/i
Constans II 11	X		963	651/2
Constans II 12	XI		964	652/3
Constans II 13	XII		965	653/4
Constans II 14	XIII		966	654/5
Constans II 15	XIV		967	655/6
Constans II 16	XV		968	656/7
Constans II 17	I		969	657/8
Constans II 18	II		970	658/9
Constans II 19	III		971	659/60
Constans II 20	IV		972	660/1
Constans II 21	V		973	661/2
Constans II 22	VI		974	662/3
Constans II 23	VII		975	663/4
Constans II 24	VIII		976	664/5
Constans II 25	IX		977	665/6
Constans II 26	X		978	666/7
Constans II 27	XI		979	667/8
Constantine IV 1	XII		980	668/9
Constantine IV 2	XIII		981	669/70
Constantine IV 3	XIV		982	670/1

Muslim rulers	AH	AD	from	to
^cUmar I b. al-Khaṭṭāb 6	19	640	2 Jan	20 Dec
^cUmar I b. al-Khaṭṭāb 7	20	640/1	21 Dec	9 Dec
^cUmar I b. al-Khaṭṭāb 8	21	641/2	10 Dec	29 Nov
^cUmar I b. al-Khaṭṭāb 9	22	642/3	30 Nov	18 Nov
^cUmar I b. al-Khaṭṭāb 10	23	643/4	19 Nov	6 Nov
^cUthmān b. ^cAffān 1	24	644/5	7 Nov	27 Oct
^cUthmān b. ^cAffān 2	25	645/6	28 Oct	16 Oct
^cUthmān b. ^cAffān 3	26	646/7	17 Oct	6 Oct
^cUthmān b. ^cAffān 4	27	647/8	7 Oct	24 Sept
^cUthmān b. ^cAffān 5	28	648/9	25 Sept	13 Sept
^cUthmān b. ^cAffān 6	29	649/50	14 Sept	3 Sept
^cUthmān b. ^cAffān 7	30	650/1	4 Sept	23 Aug
^cUthmān b. ^cAffān 8	31	651/2	24 Aug	11 Aug
^cUthmān b. ^cAffān 9	32	652/3	12 Aug	1 Aug
^cUthmān b. ^cAffān 10	33	653/4	2 Aug	21 July
^cUthmān b. ^cAffān 11	34	654/5	22 July	10 July
^cUthmān b. ^cAffān 12	35	655/6	11 July	29 June
Civil war 1	36	656/7	30 June	18 June
Civil war 2	37	657/8	19 June	8 June
Civil war 3	38	658/9	9 June	28 May
Civil war 4	39	659/60	29 May	16 May
Civil war 5	40	660/1	17 May	6 May
Mu^cāwiya b. Abī Sufyān 1	41	661/2	7 May	25 Apr
Mu^cāwiya b. Abī Sufyān 2	42	662/3	26 Apr	14 Apr
Mu^cāwiya b. Abī Sufyān 3	43	663/4	15 Apr	3 Apr
Mu^cāwiya b. Abī Sufyān 4	44	664/5	4 Apr	23 Mar
Mu^cāwiya b. Abī Sufyān 5	45	665/6	24 Mar	12 Mar
Mu^cāwiya b. Abī Sufyān 6	46	666/7	13 Mar	2 Mar
Mu^cāwiya b. Abī Sufyān 7	47	667/8	3 Mar	19 Feb
Mu^cāwiya b. Abī Sufyān 8	48	668/9	20 Feb	8 Feb
Mu^cāwiya b. Abī Sufyān 9	49	669/70	9 Feb	28 Jan
Mu^cāwiya b. Abī Sufyān 10	50	670/1	29 Jan	17 Jan

Byzantine rulers	Indictions	AG	AD
Constantine IV 4	XV	983	671/2
Constantine IV 5	I	984	672/3
Constantine IV 6	II	985	673/4
Constantine IV 7	III	986	674/5
Constantine IV 8	IV	987	675/6
Constantine IV 9	V	988	676/7
Constantine IV 10	VI	989	677/8
Constantine IV 11	VII	990	678/9
Constantine IV 12	VIII	991	679/80
Constantine IV 13	IX	992	680/1
Constantine IV 14	X	993	681/2
Constantine IV 15	XI	994	682/3
Constantine IV 16	XII	995	683/4
Constantine IV 17	XIII	996	684/5
Justinian II 1:1	XIV	997	685/6
Justinian II 1:2	XV	998	686/7
Justinian II 1:3	I	999	687/8
Justinian II 1:4	II	1000	688/9
Justinian II 1:5	III	1001	689/90
Justinian II 1:6	IV	1002	690/1
Justinian II 1:7	V	1003	691/2
Justinian II 1:8	VI	1004	692/3
Justinian II 1:9	VII	1005	693/4
Justinian II 1:10	VIII	1006	694/5
Leontius 1	IX	1007	695/6
Leontius 2	X	1008	696/7
Leontius 3	XI	1009	697/8
Tiberius III 1	XII	1010	698/9
Tiberius III 2	XIII	1011	699/700
Tiberius III 3	XIV	1012	700/01
Tiberius III 4	XV	1013	701/2

Muslim rulers	AH	AD	from	to
Mu^{c}āwiya b. Abī Sufyān 11	51	671/2	18 Jan	7 Jan
Mu^{c}āwiya b. Abī Sufyān 12	52	672	8 Jan	26 Dec
Mu^{c}āwiya b. Abī Sufyān 13	53	672/3	27 Dec	15 Dec
Mu^{c}āwiya b. Abī Sufyān 14	54	673/4	16 Dec	5 Dec
Mu^{c}āwiya b. Abī Sufyān 15	55	674/5	6 Dec	24 Nov
Mu^{c}āwiya b. Abī Sufyān 16	56	675/6	25 Nov	13 Nov
Mu^{c}āwiya b. Abī Sufyān 17	57	676/7	14 Nov	2 Nov
Mu^{c}āwiya b. Abī Sufyān 18	58	677/8	3 Nov	22 Oct
Mu^{c}āwiya b. Abī Sufyān 19	59	678/9	23 Oct	12 Oct
Mu^{c}āwiya b. Abī Sufyān 20	60	679/80	13 Oct	30 Sept
Yazīd b. Mu^{c}āwiya 1	61	680/1	1 Oct	19 Sept
Yazīd b. Mu^{c}āwiya 2	62	681/2	20 Sept	9 Sept
Yazīd b. Mu^{c}āwiya 3	63	682/3	10 Sept	29 Aug
Mu^{c}āwiya b.Yazīd 1	64	683/4	30 Aug	17 Aug
Marwān b. al-Hakam 1	65	684/5	18 Aug	7 Aug
^{c}Abd al-Malik b. Marwān 1	66	685/6	8 Aug	27 July
^{c}Abd al-Malik b. Marwān 2	67	686/7	28 July	17 July
^{c}Abd al-Malik b. Marwān 3	68	687/8	18 July	5 July
^{c}Abd al-Malik b. Marwān 4	69	688/9	6 July	24 June
^{c}Abd al-Malik b. Marwān 5	70	689/90	25 June	14 June
^{c}Abd al-Malik b. Marwān 6	71	690/1	15 June	3 June
^{c}Abd al-Malik b. Marwān 7	72	691/2	4 June	22 May
^{c}Abd al-Malik b. Marwān 8	73	692/3	23 May	12 May
^{c}Abd al-Malik b. Marwān 9	74	693/4	13 May	1 May
^{c}Abd al-Malik b. Marwān 10	75	694/5	2 May	20 Apr
^{c}Abd al-Malik b. Marwān 11	76	695/6	21 Apr	9 Apr
^{c}Abd al-Malik b. Marwān 12	77	696/7	10 Apr	29 Mar
^{c}Abd al-Malik b. Marwān 13	78	697/8	30 Mar	19 Mar
^{c}Abd al-Malik b. Marwān 14	79	698/9	20 Mar	8 Mar
^{c}Abd al-Malik b. Marwān 15	80	699/700	9 Mar	25 Feb
^{c}Abd al-Malik b. Marwān 16	81	700/1	26 Feb	14 Feb
^{c}Abd al-Malik b. Marwān 17	82	701/2	15 Feb	3 Feb

Byzantine rulers	Indictions	AG	AD
Tiberius III 5	I	1014	702/3
Tiberius III 6	II	1015	703/4
Tiberius III 7	III	1016	704/5
Justinian II 2:1	IV	1017	705/6
Justinian II 2:2	V	1018	706/7
Justinian II 2:3	VI	1019	707/8
Justinian II 2:4	VII	1020	708/9
Justinian II 2:5	VIII	1021	709/10
Justinian II 2:6	IX	1022	710/11
Philippicus 1	X	1023	711/2
Philippicus 2	XI	1024	712/3
Anastasius II 1	XII	1025	713/4
Anastasius II 2	XIII	1026	714/5
Theodosius III 1	XIV	1027	715/6
Theodosius III 2	XV	1028	716/7
Leo 1	I	1029	717/8
Leo 2	II	1030	718/9

Muslim rulers	AH	AD	from	to
ᶜAbd al-Malik b. Marwān 18	83	702/3	4 Feb	23 Feb
ᶜAbd al-Malik b. Marwān 19	84	703/4	24 Feb	13 Jan
ᶜAbd al-Malik b. Marwān 20	85	704/5	14 Jan	1 Jan
ᶜAbd al-Malik b. Marwān 21	86	705	2 Jan	22 Dec
Walīd b. ᶜAbd al-Malik 1	87	705/6	23 Dec	11 Dec
Walīd b. ᶜAbd al-Malik 2	88	706/7	12 Dec	30 Nov
Walīd b. ᶜAbd al-Malik 3	89	707/8	1 Dec	19 Nov
Walīd b. ᶜAbd al-Malik 4	90	708/9	20 Nov	18 Nov
Walīd b. ᶜAbd al-Malik 5	91	709/10	19 Nov	28 Oct
Walīd b. ᶜAbd al-Malik 6	92	710/11	29 Oct	18 Oct
Walīd b. ᶜAbd al-Malik 7	93	711/2	19 Oct	6 Oct
Walīd b. ᶜAbd al-Malik 8	94	712/3	7 Oct	25 Sept
Walīd b. ᶜAbd al-Malik 9	95	713/4	26 Sept	15 Sept
Walīd b. ᶜAbd al-Malik 10	96	714/5	16 Sept	4 Sept
Sulaymān b. ᶜAbd al-Malik 1	97	715/6	5 Sept	24 Aug
Sulaymān b. ᶜAbd al-Malik 2	98	716/7	25 Sept	13 Aug
ᶜUmar II b. ᶜAbd al-ᶜAzīz 1	99	717/8	14 Aug	2 Aug
ᶜUmar II b. ᶜAbd al-ᶜAzīz 2	100	718/9	3 Aug	23 July

TABLE 2: ROMAN, PERSIAN, ISLAMIC AND SYRIAN ORTHODOX LEADERS

Roman emperors (Sear)
>   Mauricius 582-602
>   Phocas 602-610
>   Heraclius 610-641
>   Constantine III 641
>   Heracleonas 641
>   Constans II 641-668
>   Constantinus IV 668-685
>   Justinianus II (first reign) 685-695
>   Leontius 695-698
>   Apsimar = Tiberius III 698-705
>   Justinianus II (second reign) 705-711
>   Bardanes = Philippicus 711-713
>   Artemius = Anastasius II 713-715
>   Theodosius III 715-717
>   Leo III 717-741

Persian shahs (Nöldeke)
>   Hormizd IV 579-590
>   Chosroës II (first reign) 590
>   Vahrām (usurper) 590
>   Chosroës II (second reign) 591-628
>   Shīrōē 628
>   Ardashīr III 629
>   Shahrvarāz 630
>   various contendents 630-631
>   Bōrān 631
>   Yazdgird III 632-651

Islamic rulers (Ostrogorsky)
>   Muhammad b. ᶜAbd Allāh died 632
>   Abū Bakr b. Abī Quhāfa 632-634

^{C}Umar I b. al-Khattāb 634-644
^{C}Uthmān b. ^{C}Affān 644-656
^{C}Alī b. Abī Tālib 656-661
Mu^{C}āwiya b. Abī Sufyān 661-680
Yazīd b. Mu^{C}āwiya 680-683
Mu^{C}āwiya b. Yazīd 683-684
Marwān b. al-Hakam 684-685
^{C}Abd al-Malik b. Marwān 685-705
Walīd b. ^{C}Abd al-Malik 705-715
Sulaymān b. ^{C}Abd al-Malik 715-717
^{C}Umar II b. ^{C}Abd al-^{C}Azīz b. Marwān 717-720

Syrian Orthodox patriarchs (Hage/Palmer: see Appendix I)
    Peter of Callinicum 584-591
    Julian I 592-593
    vacancy of nine years' duration
    Athanasius I, 'the Cameldriver' {Gammōlō} 603-631
    John I, 'the Composer of Prayers' {d-Sedraw(hy)} 632-648
    Theodore 649-667
    Severus II bar Mashqē 668-683
    Athanasius II 684-687
    Julian II, 'the Byzantine Soldier' {Rūmōyō} 688-708
    Elijah 709-724

TABLE 3: DATES GIVEN BY TEXTS NO. 2, 4, 7, 10 (see the commentary), 11 and 12

AD	Source	Short description of event
[582]	10	Emperor Maurice enthroned
591 April 22	2,12	Death of Patriarch Peter; Julian succeeds
590/1	2	Chosroës appeals to Maurice
595 July 9	2	Death of Patriarch Julian; no succession
598/9	2,12	Domitian persecutes Monophysites
601	10,12	Solar eclipse
[602]	10	Emperor Phocas enthroned
602/3	10,12	Narseh occupies Edessa and executes bp. Severus of Edessa
603 August 23	2	Assassination of Maurice
603 November 6	2,5,10	Patriarch Athanasius enthroned
603/4	2	Persians take back Dara
604/5	10	Edessa captured (by Phocas?)
604/5	12	Persians take fort of Ṭūr ʿAbdīn
608/9 winter	2	Euphrates blocked by ice
609 summer	2	Persians take Mardīn, Rhesaina
609 autumn	2	Persians take Edessa, Ḥarrān, Callinicum, Circesium
609/10 winter	2	Euphrates is the frontier between Romans and Persians
[610]	10	Emperor Heraclius enthroned
610 August 7	2	Zenobia first Persian conquest west of Euphrates
610/11	2	Persians occupy Emesa
611 summer	2	Romans and Persians fight at Emesa
612/3	2	Persians occupy Damascus
613/4	2	Persians take Jerusalem
614/5	12	Daniel, abbot of Qartmīn, made bishop of Dara
616/7	10	Imperial order to baptize Jews
616/7	10	Jerusalem Jews forcibly baptized
617/8	2	Jacobite Union with Damianite sect
618/9	2	Jacobite Union with sects of Conon and Eugenius
618/9	9,11	Muḥammad 'subdues the land'
619 June	2	Persians take Alexandria
620/1	5,10,12	Muḥammad's reign and the Muslim era begin
620/1	12	Muḥammad institutes the sacrifice
621/2	9	Muslim era begins
622/3	2	Slavs invade Crete and kill Jacobite monks
622/3	10	Cyriac of Amida dies; Thomas succeeds
625/6	2	Persians invade Rhodes
625/6	2	Heraclius marches to Persia
625/6	10	Stars shoot towards the north, presage of Arab Conquest
626/7	12	Edessenes deported to Persia
627 September 15	2	Simultaneous solar and lunar eclipse (!)
628 February	2 + 12	Chosroës murdered by Shīrōē, who succeeds him
628 September	2	Death of Shīrōē; accession of Ardashīr
628/9	10	Heraclius builds church at Amida
629 June	2	Persian evacuate Alexandria and Syria
629 June	2	Earthquake
629 July	2	Pact of Arabissus Tripotamus
630/1	12	Death of Muḥammad; Abū Bakr succeeds
631 July 28	2,12	Death of Patriarch Athanasius
631/2	2	Patriarch John enthroned
633/4	12	Death of Abū Bakr; ʿUmar succeeds

AD	Source	Short description of event
633/4	12	Gabriel becomes bishop at Qartmīn
634 February 4	2	Romans and Arabs fight near Gaza
635/6	2	Arabs invade Syria and raid monasteries near Mardīn
636/7	10	Arabs conquer Mesopotamia
640/1	10 (cf.12)	Arabs take Dara and Dwīn
[641]	10	Emperor Constantine enthroned
641/2	10	Arabs take Palestinian Caesarea
[642]	10	Emperor Constantine enthroned
643/4	12	ʿUmar killed by 'Indian' slave; ʿUthmān succeeds
643/4	10	Roman general Valentine marches to Syria
643/4	10	Procopius and Theodore sack Sᶜrūgh
648/9 (in 10: 649/50)	12	Death of Patriarch John
648/9	10	Arabs invade Cyprus, take Arwād
649/50	10	John of the Arabs and Simeon of Edessa die
650/1	10	Patriarch Theodore enthroned
651/2	10	Romans and Arabs fight at Tripolis
652/3	10	Ḥabīb invades Mesopotamia
652/3	10	Procopius makes treaty with Arabs
655/6	12	ʿUthmān killed; anarchy for 44 months
656/7	10,11	Battle of Ṣiffīn
657/8 (12:660/1; 10:661/2)	4	Assassination of ʿAlī at al-Ḥīra
658/9	4	Constans executes Theodosius and leaves Constantinople
659 June (7)	4	Earthquake in Palestine
659 June	4	Jacobites dispute with Maronites
659 June 9	4	Earthquake
659/60	12	ʿAlī killed; Muʿāwiya enthroned
659/60	4	Muʿāwiya acclaimed at Jerusalem
659/60	4	Earthquake in Palestine
660 or 661 July	4	Muʿāwiya's rule is established
662 April 13	4	White grapevines withered by frost
(662/3)	4	Arabs at walls of Constantinople
663/4	4	Ibn Khālid attacks Lake Scutarium
663/4	4	Amorium submits to Ibn Khālid
663/4	4	Synaus (or Synnada?) resists Arab siege
663/4	4	Arabs take Smyrna and other cities
664/5	10,12	Death of Patriarch Theodore; Severus succeeds
[669]	10	Emperor Constantine enthroned
GAP		
679 April 3	10 + 12	Earthquake in Sᶜrūgh and Edessa
679/80	12	Death of Muʿāwiya; Yazīd succeeds
682/3	10,12	Death of Patriarch Severus; 5 years' vacancy
682/3	12	Yazīd dies; Marwān succeeds
683/4	11	Severe famine
684/5	12	Marwān dies; ʿAbd al-Malik succeeds
684/5	12	Romans treat with ʿAbd al-Malik for peace
[685]	10	Emperor Justinian enthroned
687/8	10	Patriarch Athanasius enthroned
691/2	10	First Arab census in Mesopotamia

AD	Source	Short description of event
693/4	11	Solar eclipse
694/5	12	Dīnār defeats Romans at Antioch
[695]	10	Emperor Leontius enthroned
696/7	12	Arabs mint aniconic coinage
696/7	12	George becomes bishop of Sᶜrūgh
697/8	12	ᶜAṭiyya takes census of foreigners
[698]	10	Emperor Tiberius Apsimar enthroned
before 698/9	12	Simeon made bishop of Ḥarrān
698/9	12	Jacobite church built at Ḥarrān
699/700	12	Stylite George of Tarᶜēl dies; plague in Syria
703/4	12	Arabs rebuild Mopsuestia
703/4	12	All pigs killed
703/4	10	Death of Patriarch Athanasius; Julian succeeds
704/5	12	Death of Shabīb the Ḥarūrite
704/5	10	Plague in northern Mesopotamia
[705]	10	Emperor Justinian enthroned again
705 October 1	6+12	ᶜAbd al-Malik dies; Walīd succeeds
705/6	10	Synod of Shīlō Abbey
706/7	12	Jacobite church built at Nisibis
707/8	10,12	Death of Patriarch Julian; Elijah succeeds
708/9	12	Patriarch Elijah enthroned
708/9	10,12b	Second (?) Arab census in Mesopotamia
709/10	12	Maslama invades Roman Empire
709/10	10	James of Edessa dies; Ḥabīb succeeds
710/11	12	Third (?) Arab census in Mesopotamia
[711]	10	Emperor Philippicus enthroned
712 August 8	7	'Lance' in sky pointing south
712/3	10	Thomas of Amida dies; Theodotus succeeds
712-713 December-February	7	Plague
713 February 28	7,12	Earthquake in Syria
713-716	7	Earthquakes at Antioch, famine, locusts
713 May	7	Severe gales and hailstorms
[714]	10	Emperor Anastasius enthroned
715 February	7,12	Death of the caliph Walīd
715 April 27	7	Hailstorm
715/6	12	Caliph Sulaymān invades Roman Empire
[716]	10	Emperor Theodosius enthroned
716 April 20	7	Hailstorm
716/7	10	Maslama sets out to besiege Constantinople
[717]	10	Emperor Leo enthroned
716/7	12	Arab army under ᶜUbayda invades Thrace
717 September	12	Death of the caliph Sulaymān; ᶜUmar succeeds
718	10	Arab victory over Romans at Tyana

Remarks on the above table

 Historians always try to identify the primary sources behind the chronicles; this table suggests a way in which that goal can be approached.

 There is a gap between 665 and 678, when the texts represented in this table seem to have had no chronographic sources at all. We shall see in Table 4 that text No. 13 (the reconstructed Dionysius of Tel-Maḥrē) had a Byzantine, but no Syrian, source for the period 665-672 and that he, too, was bereft of sources for the period between 672/73 and 677.

 For the rest of the period we may assume at least five different authors contemporary with the events they describe:

1 One wrote after 636 and is represented in text No. 2.
2 One wrote after 656 and is represented in text No. 10.
3 One wrote after 664 and is represented in text No. 4.
4 One wrote after 716 and is represented in text No. 7.
5 One wrote after 718 and is represented in text No. 12.

TABLE 4: DATES GIVEN BY TEXT NO. 13 (ASTERISK INDICATES *CHRONICLE OF MICHAEL*)

terminus post quem or date	*terminus ante quem*	Event	Para.
601 October 1 -	602 September 1	Accession of Phocas	11
603 October 1 -	604 August 31	Invasion of Tūr ^cAbdīn	14*
604 Summer		Persians take Dara	14
605 October 1 -	606 September 1	Persians take Hesnō d-Kīfō	14*
606 October 1 -	607 September 1	Persians take Mardīn	14
608 October 1 -	609 September 1	Persians occupy the area east of the Euphrates	14*
609 October 1 -	610 September 1	Persians conquer Syria	20
610 September 1		Accession of Heraclius	23
610 September 1 -	611 August 31	Solar eclipse	10*
613 September 1 -	614 August 31	Persians take Damascus	23
616 September 20 -	617 August 31	Persians take Jerusalem 24,	44
616 September 1 -	617 August 31	Persians take Egypt, Alexandria, Libya, Chalcedon	24*
GAP	-	-	

622 July 16 -	623 July 4	Persians take Ankara	30*
622 September 1 -	622 October 1	Muhammad in Medina	25
625 June 13 -	625 August 31	Siege of Constantinople begins	33
627 September 1 -	628 February 9	Deportation of Edessa	32
627 May 23 -	627 September 31	Solar eclipse	32*
628 February 9		Death of Chosroēs	38
628 September 1 -	629 April	30 Accession of Shīrōē	38
629 October 1 -	630 April 19	Persians evacuate Syria	43
630 October 1 -	631 April 8	Death of Shahrvarāz	44
631 October 1 -	632 August 31	Death of Muhammad	45
	635 February 24	Death of Abū Bakr	57
634 March 7 -	635 February 24	Arabs take Damascus	63
635 October 1 -	636 February 13	Arabs weaken Persians	57*
636 October 1 -	637 February 1	ᶜUmar goes to Jerusalem	73
638 October 1 -	639 September 30	Muᶜāwiya takes Caesarea	83
639 October 1 -	640 September 30	Arabs invade Mesopotamia	78
639 October 1 -	640 September 30	Poll-tax on Christians	78*
(640 October 1 -	640 December 20 (sic)	Death of Heraclius	85)
	641 February 1	Death of Heraclius	85+23

642 October 1 -	643 September 30	Accession of Constans	85
642 October 1 -	643 September 30	Rebellion of Valentine	86
643 October 1 -	644 September 30	Arab invasion of Africa	86
		Destructive gale	86
[644] November 4		Death of ^cUmar	87
(643 October 1 -	644 September 30	Accession of ^cUthmān	87*)
GAP	-	-	
648 October 1 -	649 September 30	Arabs invade Cyprus	93
649 Spring		Arabs take Arwād	99
651 approximately		Death of Yazdgird	100
		Roman treaty with Arabs	100
652 approximately		Hostage of peace dies	100
653 October 1 -	654 September 30	Arabs take down colossus	101*
654 October 1 -	655 July 10 or		
655 July 11 -	655 August 31	Sea-battle near Lycia	101
655 October 1 -	656 June 29	Death of ^cUthmān	104*
GAP	-	-	
664 October 1 -	665 March 23	Confusion about Easter	114
665 March 24 -	666 March 12	Mu^cāwiya invades Egypt	114
667 September 1 -	668 August 31	Rebellion of	

		Shabuhr	115
667 November 4		Great flood at	
		Edessa	115
668 Summer		Roman treaty	
		with Arabs	115
668 October 1 -	669 February 8	First census of	
		labourers	110
668 October 1 -	669 September 30	Harsh winter	118*
669 February 9 -	669 August 31	Death of Constans	116
669 September 1 -	670 August 31	Accession of	
		Constantine	117
		Arabs invade	
		Africa	117
669 October 1 -	670 January 28	Roman victories	
		in Gaul	117*
671 December (7)		Solar eclipse	118*
672 September 1 -	673 August 31	Bow in sky at	
		night	118
GAP	-	-	
677 August 28 -	677 October 26	Comet	118*
677 September 1 -	678 August 31	'Mardaïtes' in	
		Lebanon	119
677 October 1 -	678 September 30	Rats eat crops in	
		Syria	118*
678 October 1 -	679 September 30	Locusts	118*
679 April 3		Earthquate at	
		S^{e}rūgh & Edessa	120
679 September 1 -	679 October 12	Death of	
		Mu^{c}āwiya	121
681 September 1 -	681 September 20	'Martyrdom' of	
		Senator Leo	122
		Emperor's brothers	
		deposed	123

682 September 10 - 683 August 29 (Jan.?)		Death of Yazīd	124
684 September 22 and 23		Battle among Arabs	124*
684 October 1 -	685 September 30	Death of Marwān	127
684 October 1 -	685 August 31	Death of Constantine	127
685 October 1 -	686 September 30	Roman treaty with Arabs	128
GAP	-	-	
690 October 1 -	691 September 30	Peace is broken	136
693 October (1)		Solar eclipse	120*
694 September 1 -	695 August 31	Justinian deposed	138
694 October 1 -	695 September 30	Arabs win near Antioch	136*
695 October 1 -	696 April 9	Usurper deposes Leontius	139
697 October 1 -	698 September 30	Census of foreigners	135*
GAP	-	-	
701 October 1 -	702 September 30	Arabs capture Mopsuestia	140*
		Arabs rebuild Mopsuestia	140
702 October 1 -	703 September 30	Armenian revolt crushed	140
		Justinian escapes exile	141
704 October 1 -	705 September 30	Arabs rebuild Mopsuestia	140*

704 1 September -	705 August 31	Justinian rules again	141
705 October 1 -	705 December 22	Death of ^cAbd al-Malik	143
705 October 1 -	706 September 30	Arabs fight on Tigris	140*
706 July 16		Stars shoot to north	140*
707 October 1 -	708 September 30	Arab siege of Tyana	144
		Greek forbidden in *dīwān*	145
709 September 1 -	710 September 30	Death of Justinian	148
710 October 1 -	711 September 30	Arab raids on Byzantium	147*
		Prisoners of war killed	148*
710 October 29 -	711 October 18	Census of Mesopotamia	147
710 October 1 -	711 September 30	Death of Philippicus	148
711 February		Earthquake at Antioch	149
GAP	-	-	
715 February		Death of Walīd	150
715 October 1 -	716 September 30	Deposition of Anastasius	151
716 Summer		Arab invasion	152
716 Autumn -	717 Spring	Arabs winter in Asia	153
716 October 1 -	717 September 30	Deposition of Theodosius	155
717 June		Arabs cross into	

		Europe	157
717 Autumn -	718 Spring	Famine in Arab camp	159
717 October		Death of Sulaymān	160
718 Spring		Arab survivors go back	162

Remarks on the above table

The regnal years of Heraclius have been altered, in accordance with the solution of Dionysius's discrepancies offered by Robert Hoyland, except where the regnal year is recorded independently of the Seleucid year (see Appendix I).

Here, as in the previous table, the gaps may be significant, though perhaps not those of under three years. Gaps longer than three years may indicate the end of one of Dionysius's sources and the beginning of another. Such gaps occur after 615, 644, 655, 672, 685, 697 and 711 and are marked as such in Table 4.

In the gap between 644 and 648 Dionysius placed three narratives of diverse origin, which might have been more at home in a history of the Church, as if he felt the need to fill a lacuna in secular history. Likewise he filled the gap between 655 and 664 with Arab anecdotes of indeterminate date. In the gap between 686 and 690 Dionysius placed, among other things, a digression on Athanasius bar Gūmōyē, which he attributes to a mid-eighth century author.

By contrast, the remaining gaps seem to have been left unfilled. That between 672/73 and 677 coincides with part of the empty period in Table 3, from 665 to 678. However, Dionysius had a Byzantine source unknown to the texts represented there, which covered the first part of this period. And we must remember that the original text of Dionysius has not yet been found.

SELECT BIBLIOGRAPHY OF WEST-SYRIAN CHRONICLES

N. B. **Texts No. 14 and No. 15**, which are apocalyptic, are separately introduced in Part Three by Sebastian Brock with their own bibliography. Robert Hoyland's notes to his section of the Introduction provide bibliographical references relating to the history of the period.

All publications cited in this book but not in the bibliography which follows this note can be located by the author's or the editor's name through the index.

F. M. Abel, 'L'Ere des Séleucides', *Revue Biblique*, 2 (1938), pp. 198-213.

R. Abramowski, *Dionysius von Tellmahre, jakobitischer Patriarch von 818-845: zur Geschichte der Kirche unter dem Islam* (Abhandlungen für die Kunde des Morgenlandes, 25,2; Leipzig 1940).

W. Adler, *Time Immemorial: Archaic History and its Sources in Christian Chronography from Julius Africanus to George Syncellus* (Dumbarton Oaks Studies, 26; Washington, D.C., 1989).

I. E. Barsawm, *Al-lu^lu^ al-manthūr fī ta^rikh al-ʿulūm wa 'l-ādab al-suryāniyya* [The Scattered Pearls in the History of Syriac Science and Literature] (1943; reprinted at the Barhebraeus Verlag, Glane, 1987).

[K.] A. Baumstark, *Geschichte der syrischen Literatur mit Ausschluß der christlich-palästinensischen Texte* (Bonn, 1922)

N. H. Baynes, 'The Restoration of the Cross at Jerusalem', *EHR*, 27 (1912), p. 294.

P. L. Bernhard, *Die Chronologie der Syrer* (Sitzungsberichte der Österreichischen Akademie der Wissenschaften, philosophisch-historischen Klasse, 264,3; Vienna, 1969).

S. P. Brock, 'Syriac Sources for Seventh-Century History', *Byzantine and Modern Greek Studies*, 2 (1976), pp. 17-36 (this and the following two articles are reprinted in S. P. Brock, *Syriac*

Perspectives on Late Antiquity (Collected Studies Series, 199; London, 1984), chapters VII, VIII and XII.

idem, 'Syriac Views of Emergent Islam', in *Studies on the First Century of Islamic Society*, ed. G. H. A. Juynboll (Carbondale and Edwardsville, 1982), pp. 9-21, 199-203.

idem, 'A Syriac Life of Maximus the Confessor', *Analecta Bollandiana*, 91 (1973), pp. 299-346.

idem, 'Syriac Historical Writing: A Survey of the Main Sources', *Journal of the Iraqi Academy (Syriac Corporation)*, 5 (1979-80), pp. 1-30; repr. in *id.*, *Studies in Syriac Christianity: History, Literature, Theology* (Collected Studies Series, 357; London, 1992), chapter I.

E. W. Brooks, 'The Sources of Theophanes and the Syriac Chroniclers', *BZ*, 15 (1906), pp. 578-87.

idem, 'The Chronological Canon of James of Edessa', *ZDMG*, 53 (1899), pp. 261-327.

idem, 'The Chronology of Theophanes, 607-775', *BZ*, 8 (1899), pp. 82-87.

idem, 'The Sicilian Expedition of Constantine IV', *BZ*, 17 (1908), pp. 455-59.

H. Buk, 'Zur ältesten christlichen Chronographie des Islam', *BZ*, 14 (1905), pp. 532-34.

Averil Cameron and Lawrence I. Conrad, eds., *The Byzantine and Early Islamic Near East (I): Problems in the Literary Source Material* (Studies in Late Antiquity and Early Islam, 1; Princeton, 1992).

J.-B. Chabot, *La Chronique de Michel le Syrien*, 4 vols. (Paris, 1899-1910; reprinted, including the *Introduction*, in 4 vols., Brussels, 1963).

idem, *Chronique de Michel le Syrien: Introduction* (Paris, 1924; reprinted in the reprint of the previous title).

L. I. Conrad, 'Theophanes and the Arabic Historical Tradition: Some Indications of Intercultural Transmission', *Byzantinische Forschungen*, 15 (1990), pp. 1-44.

idem, 'The Conquest of Arwād: A Source-Critical Study in the Historiography of the Early Medieval Near East' in Cameron etc.,

Byzantine and Early Islamic Near East I, pp. 317-401.

R. Duval, *La Littérature syriaque*, third edition (Paris, 1907; reprinted in Amsterdam, 1970).

M. J. de Goeje, *Mémoire sur la conquête de la Syrie* (Leiden, 1900).

V. Grumel, '*Theophánous enantiophaníai aphanizómenai*: l'année du monde dans la *Chronographie* de Théophane', *Echos d'Orient*, 33 (1934), pp. 396-408.

idem, *La Chronologie* (Traité d'études byzantines, 1; Paris, 1958).

W. Hage, *Die syrisch-jakobitische Kirche in frühislamischer Zeit nach orientalischen Quellen* (Wiesbaden, 1966).

A. de Halleux, 'La Chronique melkite abrégée du ms. Sinaï Syr. 10', *Le Muséon*, 19 (1978), pp. 5-44.

idem, 'Trois synodes impériaux du VIe s. dans une chronique syriaque inédite', in R. H. Fisher, ed., *A Tribute to Arthur Vööbus: Studies in Early Christian Literature and its Environment, Primarily in the Syrian East* (Chicago, 1977), pp. 295-307.

R. Hoyland, 'Arabic, Syriac and Greek historiography in the first Abbasid century: an inquiry into inter-cultural traffic', *Aram*, 3 (1991, pp. 217-239).

Walter Emil Kaegi, *Byzantium and the Early Islamic Conquests* (Cambridge, 1992).

C. Mango, 'Who wrote the Chronicle of Theophanes?', *Zbornik Radova Vizantinoloskoǧ Instituta*, 18 (1978), pp. 9-17; reprinted in C. Mango, *Byzantium and its Image* (Collected Studies Series, 191; London, 1984), chapter XI.

idem, 'Deux études sur Byzance et la Perse sassanide: II. Héraclius, Šahrvaraz et la Vraie Croix', *TM*, 9 (1985), pp. 105-18.

idem, 'The tradition of Byzantine chronography', *Harvard Ukrainian Studies*, 12/13 (1988/1989), pp. 360-71.

M. G. Morony, *Iraq After the Muslim Conquest* (Princeton, 1984), especially pp. 561-68.

F. Nau, 'Fragments d'une chronique syriaque inédite relatifs surtout à S. Pierre et à S. Paul (ms. syr. add. 14642 du Brit. Mus.)', *Revue de l'Orient Chrétien*, 1 (1896), pp. 396-405.

idem, 'Un colloque du patriarche Jean avec l'émir des Agaréens et faits divers des années 712 à 716 d'après le ms. du British Museum Add. 17193', *Journal Asiatique*, XI, 5 (1915), pp. 225-79 (253-56 text, 264-67 translation).

T. Nöldeke, 'Zur Geschichte der Araber im 1. Jahrhundert d. H. aus syrischen Quellen', *ZDMG*, 29 (1875), pp. 76-98.

idem, Geschichte der Perser und Araber zur Zeit der Sasaniden aus der arabischen Chronik des Tabari übersetzt und mit ausführlichen Erläuterungen und Ergänzungen versehen (Leiden, 1879; reprinted in Leiden, 1973).

G. Ostrogorsky, 'Die Chronologie des Theophanes im 7. und 8. Jahrhundert', *Byzantinisch-neugriechische Jahrbücher*, 7 (1930), pp. 1-56.

A. N. Palmer, '*Semper Vagus*: The Anatomy of a Mobile Monk', *Papers of the 1983 Oxford Patristics Conference* (Studia Patristica, XVIII, 2; Kalamazoo and Leuven, 1989), pp. 255-60.

idem, Monk and Mason on the Tigris Frontier: The Early History of Tur ʿAbdin (University of Cambridge Oriental Publications, 39; Cambridge, 1990).

idem, Review of Witakowski (1987), in *Abr-Nahrain*, 28 (1990), pp. 142-50.

idem, 'Who Wrote the Chronicle of Joshua the Stylite?', in R. Schulz and M. Görg, eds., *Lingua restituta orientalis: Festgabe für Julius Aßfalg* (Ägypten und altes Testament, 20; Wiesbaden, 1990), pp. 272-84.

idem, 'The Messiah and the Mahdi: History Presented as the Writing on the Wall', H. Hokwerda and E. Smits, eds., *Polyphonia Byzantina: Studies in Honour of Willem J. Aerts*, forthcoming in the series Mediaevalia Groningana (Groningen, 1993).

idem, 'De overwinning van het Kruis en het probleem van de christelijke nederlaag: Kruistochten en djihaad in Byzantijnse en Syrisch-orthodoxe ogen', H. Bakker and M. Gosman, eds., *Heilige Oorlogen: Een onderzoek naar historische en hedendaagse vormen van collectief religieus geweld* (Kampen, 1991), pp. 84-109.

idem, 'Une chronique syriaque contemporaine de la conquête arabe: essai d'interprétation théologique et politique', P. Canivet and J.-P.

Rey-Coquais, eds., *La Syrie de Byzance à l'Islam, VIIe-VIIIe siècles* (*Damascus*, 1992), pp. 31-46.

N. V. Pigulevskaya, 'Theophanes' *Chronographia* and the Syrian Chronicles', *Jahrbuch der Österreichischen Byzantinischen Gesellschaft*, 16 (1967), pp. 55-60.

A. S. Proudfoot, 'The Sources of Theophanes for the Heraclian Dynasty', *Byzantion*, 44 (1974), pp. 367-439.

G. J. Reinink, 'The beginnings of Syriac apologetic literature in response to Islam', *Oriens Christianus* (forthcoming)

E. Riad, *Studies in the Syriac Preface* (Studia Semitica Upsaliensia, 11; Uppsala, 1988).

J. B. Segal, 'Syriac Chronicles as Source Material for the History of Islamic Peoples', in P. M. Holt, ed., *Historians of the Middle East* (London, 1962), pp. 246-58.

A. N. Stratos, *Byzantium in the Seventh Century* (English tr.), 5 vols. (Amsterdam, 1968-1980).

H. Turtledove, *The Chronicle of Theophanes: An English Translation of A.M. 6095-6305 (A.D. 602-813), with an introduction and notes* (Philadelphia, 1982).

D. S. Wallace-Hadrill, *Christian Antioch: A Study of Early Christian Thought in the East* (Cambridge, 1982), especially ch. 3: 'Historiography in the Eastern Church'.

[L.] M. Whitby, *The Emperor Maurice and His Historian: Theophylact Simocatta on Persian and Balkan Warfare* (Oxford, 1988).

W. Witakowski, 'Chronicles of Edessa', *Orientalia Suecana*, 33/35 (1984/1986), pp. 487-98.

idem, The Syriac Chronicle of Pseudo-Dionysius of Tel-Mahrē: A Study in the History of Historiography (Studia Semitica Upsaliensia, 9; Uppsala, 1987).

idem, 'Sources of Pseudo-Dionysius for the Third Part of his *Chronicle*', *Orientalia Suecana*, 40 (1991), pp. 252-75.

W. Wright, *Catalogue of Syriac Manuscripts in the British Museum Acquired Since the Year 1838*, 3 vols., continuous pagination (London, 1870-72).

ABBREVIATIONS, BRACKETS ETC.

AD	=	ANNO DOMINI, i.e. of the Christian era
AG	=	ANNO GRAECORUM, i.e. of the Seleucid era
Agapius	=	Agapius of Menbij, 'kitāb al-ᶜunwān / Histoire universelle', pt. 2, ed. and tr. A. A. Vasiliev, *Patrologia Orientalis*, 8 (1912). Reference given to pages of text (add 360 for page numbers of journal).
AH	=	ANNO HEGIRAE, i.e. of the Islamic era
AJ	=	ANNO JACOBI, i.e. of the 'era' of James of Edessa
Ar.	=	Arabic
b.	=	son of, in Arab names (pronounce 'ibn')
BL Add.	=	British Library (Additional Manuscript Number).
BZ	=	*Byzantinische Zeitschrift*
CM	=	*Chronica Minora*, CSCO (Scriptores Syri) 1-6, eds. E. W. Brooks, I. Guidi, J.-B. Chabot (Paris, 1903-7)
Chr. Pasch.	=	*Chronicon Paschale*, ed. L. Dindorf (*Corpus Scriptorum Historiae Byzantinae*, 1832) / *Chronicon Paschale 284-628 AD*, translated with notes and introduction by M. and M. Whitby (Liverpool, 1989). Reference given first to the page of Dindorf's edition, then, after a slash, to the page of the Whitby translation.
CSCO	=	*Corpus Scriptorum Christianorum Orientalium*
DOP	=	*Dumbarton Oaks Papers*
EHR	=	*English Historical Review*
Gr.	=	Greek

JÖB	=	*Jahrbuch der Österreichischen Byzantinistik*
JSS	=	*Journal of Semitic Studies*
Lat.	=	Latin
Michael	=	*La Chronique de Michel le Syrien* (see the bibliography under Chabot). All references to Michael will be first to the page of the Syriac text, which is also printed between brackets in bold type in the French translation, followed by book, followed by chapter and, where applicable, column (a = secular history; b = natural disasters and miscellanea; c = ecclesiastical history) or scholion.
Nöldeke	=	T. Nöldeke, *Geschichte der Perser und Araber* (see the bibliography).
Ostrogorsky	=	G. Ostrogorsky, *History of the Byzantine State* (2nd ed., Oxford, 1968 = Eng. tr. of 3rd German ed., 1963).
PG	=	J.-P. Migne, *Patrologiae cursus completus*: *Series Graeca*
Sear	=	D. R. Sear, *The Emperors of Rome and Byzantium: Chronological and Genealogical Tables*, 2nd ed. (London, 1981).
Syr.	=	Syriac
Theophanes	=	*Chronographia*, ed. C. de Boor (Leipzig, 1883-5). Mango's forthcoming translation (like Turtledove's) will give de Boor's pagination, which is offered here.
TM	=	*Travaux et Mémoires: Collège de France: Centre de Recherche d'Histoire et Civilisation de Byzance*
ZDMG	=	*Zeitschrift der deutschen morgenländischen Gesellschaft*

ROUND BRACKETS	indicate a word inserted in translation because it makes the text easier to read; this may or may not be because words have been omitted by a copyist in transmitting the Syriac text.
SQUARE BRACKETS	indicate a word which cannot be read in the manuscript, though it must be what was written there before the manuscript was damaged.
DITTO, ENCLOSING THREE DOTS	indicate a passage is missing from the text, whether because the manuscript is damaged or because I have decided not to include it in the translation.
CURLY BRACKETS	indicate the word or words lying behind the translation, whether it is by origin Syr., Ar., Gr., Lat. or Pers(ian). N.B. Curly brackets in text No. 1 indicate traces of partially deleted Syriac words which have not yet been identified.
/p. 141/	indicates the beginning of a page in the edition of the Syriac text on which the translation is based.
/f. 128/	indicates the beginning of a folio (recto = a, verso = b) of the Syriac manuscript on which the translation is based.

PART ONE

MINOR WEST-SYRIAN CHRONOGRAPHY

1. A RECORD OF THE ARAB CONQUEST OF SYRIA, AD 637

INTRODUCTION

This much faded note appears to have been penned soon after the battle of Gabitha (AD 636), at which the Arabs inflicted a crushing defeat on the Byzantines. The words 'we saw' (line 13: the alternative reading is also in the first person plural) are positive evidence that the author was a contemporary. He speaks of olive oil, cattle (?) and ruined villages, aspects of the invasion important to a native of peasant stock, but never reported by the Arab sources. If he was a peasant who could write, he was probably a monk or a parish priest. His purpose in jotting this note in the book of the Gospels was probably purely commemorative. He seems to have realized how momentous the events of his time might be. The note is preserved on fol. 1 of BL Add. 14,461, a codex containing the *Gospel according to Matthew* and the *Gospel according to Mark*; it has been edited most recently by E. W. Brooks in *CM* 2, p. 75. The surviving traces are here indicated and annotated in a way that is avoided elsewhere in this book. In addition to the published observations of Nöldeke, 'Zur Geschichte der Araber', and Brooks, this translation draws on an improved reading of the text by S. P. Brock, which has not been published. Syriacists who want to check the translation must be enabled to do so; and, although the Syriac letters themselves leave non-Syriacists none the wiser, the overall impression that the text is very fragmentary and many of its readings disputable will serve the useful purpose of making them more cautious in formulating any argument they may base on it.

1   {Syr. ...T$^\circ$.DL...}

2   {Syr. ...T} M[uhammad[70]

3   [...] the p]riest Lord Elijah [...]

4   {Syr. ...Š...S...WT...$^\circ$} and they came

5   {Syr. ...W...BLYL$^\circ$}[71] and fr[om] Ba{Syr. ...$^\circ$}

6   [...] strong [...] month {Syr. ...N(final)} [...]

7   {Syr. ...$^\circ$} appeared {...Syr. WN(final)...} and the Romans [...][72]

8   {Syr. ...$^\circ$ ...} and in January they took the word for their lives,[73]

9   (did) [the sons of][74] Emesa, and many villages were ruined with killing by

10   [the Arabs of][75] Muhammad[76] and a great number of people were killed and captives

11   [were taken] from Galilee as far as Bēth[77] {Syr. ZK..WT$^\circ$}[78]

12   [...] and those Arabs pitched camp beside [Damascus?][79]

13   [...] and we saw[80] everywhe[re...] {Syr. $^\circ$ ...}

---

[70] Brock, who has reexamined the manuscript, finds this word 'very uncertain'; yet Brooks prints M[W]HMD, without showing that it is a doubtful reading.

[71] The last three letters are tentatively read by Brock.

[72] Brooks restores here the word 'fled', but Brock feels that this 'cannot be right: {Syr. W..^{c}QWN(final)} is what I read.'

[73] This phrase is used several times, with reference to the submission of Christians to the Arabs, by the author of text No. 13 (Part Two).

[74] {Syr. b^{e}nay}: conjectured by Palmer. Brooks conjectured {Syr. ^{c}ammō}, 'the people'.

[75] {Syr. tayyōyē d-}: conjectured by Hoyland (cf. line 12 and text 2, AG 945).

[76] {Syr. MWHMD}.

[77] Marked by Brooks as uncertain.

[78] The last three letters are tentatively identified by Brock.

[79] Conjectured by Nöldeke.

[80] Brock comments: 'could be {Syr. h^{e}dayn} "we rejoiced".'

14 and[81] o[l]ive oil which they brought and {Syr. NŠ...R} them. And on the t[wenty-

15 six]th[82] of May[83] went S[ac[ella]rius][84] {Syr. ...WN(final)}[85] cattle[86] [...]

16 [...] from the vicinity of Emesa,[87] and the Romans chased them [...][88]

17 {Syr. ...W. ᵓ ...N(final) ...} and on the tenth

18 [of August[89]] the Romans fled[90] from the vicinity of Damascus [...]

19 many [people], some 10,000. And at the turn

20 [of the ye]ar the Romans[91] came; on the twentieth of August in the year n[ine hundred

21 and forty]-seven there gathered in Gabitha [...]

22 [...] the Romans and a great many people were ki[lled of]

23 [the R]omans, [s]ome fifty thousand [...]

---

[81] On this line Brock comments: 'Most of this (especially the end) is very uncertain. {Syr. Dᵓ YTYW} "which they brought" could just be {Syr. ...Rᵓ YTBW} "... they settled".'

[82] The only number which will fit the space.

[83] Brock comments: 'Could just be {Syr. BᵓB} "of August".'

[84] Nöldeke (supported cautiously by Brock) could read more than Brooks; it is possible that we should translate: 'the Sacellarius'.

[85] 'and raided', the conjecture of Nöldeke, requires the ending -BWWN. Brock finds even Brooks's ending -BWN unlikely: '{Syr. ...QᶜWN(final)} or {Syr. ...NKWN(final)} are possible.'

[86] Brock comments: 'This word might be {Syr. BᶜYDᵓ} "as usual".'

[87] Brock comments: ' "Emesa" needs a lot of faith to read: it is just possible, but so are other restorations (only very faint traces).'

[88] cf. Theophanes, p. 337: 'The Emperor...dispatched the sakellarios Theodore with a large force against the Arabs. Theodore met a host of Saracens near Emesa; he killed some of them, and chased the rest with their commander as far as Damascus.' [R.H.]

[89] Nöldeke's conjecture.

[90] This reading is confirmed by Brock.

[91] This word is written above the line.

24 [...] in the year nine hundred[92] and for[ty-eight]
25 {Syr. ... LH ... ⁻Q ... B ...}

DISCUSSION

The 'turn of the year' (lines 19-20) signifies that the beginning of the note refers to the year 634/5. First the Emesenes 'took the word for their lives', a 'technical' expression for surrendering on terms of tolerance, confirmed by oaths {Ar. sulh}. Then there was a battle (one infers) in Palestine, as a result of which many villages were ruined and many people from the region between Galilee and (perhaps) Beth Sacharya, 20 km south-west of Jerusalem, were taken captive. Then the Arabs laid siege to Damascus (if Nöldeke's supplement is right). In May, AD 635, a Byzantine general of the rank of *sakellarios* was in the region of Emesa. (His name, according to the Byzantine sources, was Theodore.) Apparently, however, he was unable to lift the siege of Damascus. The note dates the next battle (at Gabitha) to 20 August, AG 947 = AD 636, which agrees with the best Arab date for the battle of the river Yarmūk.[93] Gabitha is a town to the north of the river Yarmūk in the Golan massif.

---

[92] Brock: ' "Nine hundred" is very uncertain.'

[93] For further discussion see Nöldeke, 'Zur Geschichte der Araber', pp. 79-82; F. M. Donner, *The Early Islamic Conquests* (Princeton, 1981), pp. 142-6. De Goeje, *Mémoire*, pp. 89ff., 119ff. tries to reconcile this fragment with other sources. [R.H.]

2. EXTRACT FROM A CHRONICLE COMPOSED ABOUT AD 640

INTRODUCTION

There are, so far as I can see, two possible assessments of the manuscript from which text No. 2 is taken. Either it is a rag-bag of geographical and historical information (and misinformation), put together, with a total disregard for coherence and even, towards the end, for chronological order, by a scribe who had no intelligence, only a hoarding instinct comparable to that of a squirrel. Or else there is method in its madness. The scholarly consensus seems to be the former; here, for the first time in English,[94] arguments for the latter are adduced. As a result, this introduction is disproportionately long. But the reader of my translation has a right to know what is at issue here. It would be misleading to extract the notices with an explicit bearing on our period from their original literary context, if there are weighty arguments against reading them in isolation.

One thing, at least, is agreed: the last folio of the manuscript stands apart from the rest. This is a list of caliphs, translated from the Arabic (= text No. 8), after which Land, the first editor, dubbed the whole manuscript 'liber calipharum' (Book of the Caliphs); and it contains the date AD 724, from which the most recent editor derived his title 'chronicon miscellaneum ad annum domini 724 pertinens' (Miscellaneous Chronicle up to AD 724). Nothing else in the manuscript need have been written after AD 640. Indeed, the scribe marked the last folio off as a new beginning by placing the rubric: 'It is finished' at the end of what preceded it.

The date AD 640 is implied by the note (on p. 139 of Brooks's edition) which gives Heraclius 30 years. Heraclius reigned for 31 years and died in AD 641. One might conjecture that 30 years represents approximately the total of 31 and that this information was added after

---

[94] Palmer, 'Une chronique syriaque' develops them at length, but less maturely than the present discussion.

Heraclius's death. But then why, if he lived later, did the scribe listing Roman emperors not refer to Heraclius's successors? It makes more sense to assume that this passage was written about 640, some months before Heraclius's death. After mentioning Heraclius in this way, the author goes on to say: 'And in the days of Heraclius, in the 940th year of Alexander (AD 629), during one night in June, the earth shook violently.' He then reports a pact made between Heraclius and the Persian Shahrvarāz in July of the same year.

Who is this author? The answer seems to be: the same as the author of an almost identical notice on the same earthquake and the same pact, which comes in a series of early seventh-century events a little further on in the manuscript (on p. 147 of Brooks's edition). This repeated notice is followed in that series by two others, one on the year AG 945 (AD 633/4) and one on the year AG 947 (AD 635/6). The latter reads as follows: 'The Arabs invaded the whole of Syria and went down to Persia and conquered it; the Arabs climbed the mountain of Mardīn and killed many monks there in (the monasteries of) Qedar and Bᵉnōthō. There died the blessed man Simon, doorkeeper of Qedar, brother of Thomas the priest.' After this the seventh-century series stops and a new series on the Early Church begins, going back to the foundation of the church in Antioch by Simon Cephas.

Most scholars would see this notice as the signature of an author contemporary with Heraclius, the priest Thomas, who probably lived near the Mountain of Mardīn, in the region of Rhesaina.[95] But they would say that Thomas was the author of the seventh-century series and perhaps of some of the sixth-century notices which precede

---

[95] Apart from the fact that his brother was at Qedar, near Rhesaina (see text No. 13, § 57), Thomas's omission of the Byzantine Indictions from AD 609/10 until after the total recovery of Mesopotamia by the Byzantines in AD 629 helps to pinpoint his home. Mardīn and Rhesaina were taken by the Persians in AD 609; Syria west of the Euphrates was conquered in AD 610 and the following years. If Thomas was from the Rhesaina region, his omission of the years of the Byzantine tax-cycle dates from the year in which Byzantium ceased to raise taxes in his homeland. His resumption of Indictions coincides with the reincorporation of Mesopotamia in the Byzantine Empire.

it in chronological order, but not of any other part of the manuscript. The fact, however, that the first of these two notices on Heraclius forms the culmination of a previous series in the manuscript, the culmination, in fact, of a concatenation of series covering world history in sequence, though in uneven detail, up to the time of Heraclius, needs explaining. One scholar, the Syrian Orthodox patriarch Barsawm, concludes from this passage that it was the priest Thomas who compiled the whole manuscript, though he does not explain why Thomas should have compiled it in such a strange way. Land, Baumstark, Brooks, Witakowski and others simply postulate a lack of intelligence on the part of the compiler: Land calls him 'stultissimus homo' (a total idiot) and Baumstark uses equally disdainful language, betraying the exasperation of a philologist baffled by an unusual literary form.[96] But it is implausible to suggest that the priest Thomas, whose series of bulletins on the early seventh century give evidence of considerable intelligence, may have displayed such 'stupidity' in compiling the whole manuscript.

Evidence for method in the compiler's madness is given by the words appearing at the head of 'Rubric 6', a chapter of seeming miscellany. The original words {Syr. sukkōlō da -shnayyō d-mawd^{c}ōn: mettūl sebwōtō saggiyyōtō: qadmōyat ^{c}al zaw^{c}ō da-hwō hwō b-antiōkiyya} represent literally the following: 'Elucidation of years which give information concerning many matters, first about an earthquake that had occurred in Antioch.' The range of concepts covered by the first word is evoked by the following English equivalents: 'intelligence', 'understanding', 'thought', 'explanation', 'knowledge', 'erudition', 'elucidation', 'scholium', 'idea', 'purpose', 'sense', 'point', 'signification'. For example, the Syriac poet Narsai

---

[96] Baumstark, *Geschichte der syrischen Literatur*, p. 274: 'ziemlich unwissend und historisch ungeschult [with reference to text No. 9] ... Noch tiefer [with reference to the present text] ... Auf jeden Versuch, aus diesem buntscheckigen Stoff etwas wie eine literarische Einheit zu gestalten, ist völlig verzichtet. ... Eine den dürftigsten Schichten dieser Kompilation "literarisch" verwandte Chronik [with reference to text No. 11] ...'

uses the word in the following sentence: 'Now let us go back and explain the deeper meaning ({Syr. ḤYL SWKLᵓ}, 'burden of significance') which is veiled behind these words (*sc.* of Holy Scripture).' In our chronicle 'elucidation of years which give information' can hardly been interpreted as 'record of years which are worthy of notice' (Chabot translates the rubric 'notitia annorum qui notandi sunt propter res varias. et primum de terrae motu qui Antiochiae accidit.') {Syr. SWKLᵓ} is in any case not attested with the sense of 'record', for which {Syr. ᶜWHDNᵓ} might rather be expected. Nor are the years themselves to be 'elucidated' or 'explained'. The best way is then to understand 'of' as meaning 'consisting of'; in which case the 'elucidation' must apply to something else, most obviously to the text under which the note stands. This justifies my translation of {Syr. sukkōlō} as 'explanatory note', in the extract printed below.

This rubric, then, thus translated, is evidence that the compiler intended the miscellany to be read as a significant sequence, having a bearing on the interpretation of what goes before it. It is necessary first to describe the concatenation of texts to which this 'elucidation' is appended, then to see if we can 'explain the deeper meaning which is hidden behind the words' of the 'elucidation' itself. Syrian Christians were used to being told in church that they should always look for the allegorical meaning of a scriptural text and should never be satisfied with the surface meaning. They may well have applied this rule of thumb to history, which resembles the Bible in many ways.

The compilation appears to have begun, to judge by the fragmentary opening of the surviving part of the codex, with a geographical treatise. We may call this 'Rubric 1'. Then comes 'Rubric 2': a genealogy beginning with Adam, the First Man, and reaching down to the Twelve Patriarchs, the sons of Jacob. 'Rubric 3' suggests that we may be dealing with a history of the world in the tradition of Christian chronography. Under the catch-all title 'A record of various matters' (the first actual red-ink title preserved in the damaged codex) the editor reveals himself in the following words: 'I have put into tabular form {Gr. kanónes} the names of the heathen kings from Abraham until the twentieth year of Constantine and the events which occurred in their reigns and I have written a narrative to show how they were subjected to the Romans.' In what follows he is concerned above all to tie in the personalities of the Old Testament with secular history so as to prove that Moses was a contemporary of Cecrops, king of Athens, and that his Law thus antedates all Greek religion. He also represents the Romans as heirs to a God-given crown which has been passed on from one empire to another in a unique succession, beginning with Sīkūn, the semi-divine chief of the giants. Before this he has a list of the prophets, in which he names also the kings under whom they prophesied. The promised narrative concerning the subjection to the Romans mainly concerns the sack of Jerusalem. The author makes calculations backwards and forwards and establishes relative chronologies, referring to various sources, Hebrew, Greek and Syriac. The Syriac source is an allegedly infallible chronographic compilation in the archives of Edessa, where the date AG 309 (3/2 BC) is given for the Epiphany {Syr. denhō} of Christ (p. 97f.).[97]

'Rubric 4' makes a good companion to the previous one. It is an epitome of the *Chronicle* of Eusebius of Caesarea.[98] The heading, on p. 98, reads as follows: 'The beginning of the chronological tables from Abraham and Ninus, king of the Assyrians, until the twentieth year of Constantine, the victorious king.' That means, of course, that there is a large overlap between 'Rubrics' 3 and 4, but 'Rubric 3' was schematic and intended to prove a chronographic point, whereas 'Rubric 4' leaves chronography, for the most part, aside and presents instead a sequence of undated events. Where 'Rubric 3' concentrates

---

[97] This may mean that the Conception of Christ occurred on 25 March, 2 BC, because the chronicler has stated on p. 95 that Christ's Nativity was in AG 310 (2/1 BC), i.e. on 25 December, 2 BC (cf. text No. 11, below). On the other hand the author may have failed to harmonize all his sources. That he is fallible is shown by his statement that Christ stayed on earth for thirty-three years, followed by the statement that he ascended into heaven on 4 June, AG 339 (AD 28).

[98] Oddly enough, the chronicler does not acknowledge his debt to Eusebius, although he describes that bishop's literary output in 'Rubric 5'; nor does he explain at the end of 'Rubric 3' that Eusebius differed from the Edessene tradition concerning the date of Christ's Nativity.

on Old Testament times, 'Rubric 4' has much more about the New Testament and the history of the Church. The chronicler adds to Eusebius by inserting a note on the Ishmaelites, whom he also calls Hagarenes and Ṭayyōyē, and two apocryphal stories associated with Christ's Nativity. The note on the Ishmaelites is unlikely to antedate the Arab Conquest and it may be evidence of a seventh-century compiler's hand, in which case the priest Thomas is a candidate.

The heading of 'Rubric 4' justifies us in placing a caesura at the end of Constantine's twentieth year, after the words 'and henceforth peace in plenty' on p. 129, although the scribe has marked no division there, and calling what follows 'Rubric 5'. 'Rubric 5', so defined, is the continuation of Eusebius up to the thirtieth year of Heraclius, with great detail in the mid-fourth century and very little detail in the fifth. The end of 'Rubric 5' is translated below.

What follows, 'Rubric 6' (translated in full below), is a patchwork of date-sequences interspersed with theological and church-political comments. The dates range between AD 31 and AD 636, but they are not placed in overall chronological order and the separate sequences are partly overlapping. Nevertheless, the scribe has copied these fragments one after the other without separate rubrics or divisions; and the heading 'Explanatory Note' shows (so, at least, I have argued above) that the reader is expected to find order in the apparent chaos. After 'Rubric 6' comes 'Rubric 7', with the following heading: 'At what dates and under which kings the synods were held' (p. 150). This rubric ends in a resounding condemnation of the Council of Chalcedon (AD 451) and was plainly written by a Jacobite clergyman.

Since the work closes here, it is reasonable to assume that this is part of the key to the compilation, if it is to be seen as a whole. The condemnation of Chalcedon and Chalcedonian emperors at the end of 'Rubric 5' could help to confirm this and it is consistent with Barsawm's theory, because Thomas was evidently a Jacobite priest. A theory may now be formulated as follows: one man put together all seven 'Rubrics', placing a geographical treatise at the beginning, where we should expect an account of the Creation, and ordering his extracts from other sources according to the framework of a World Chronicle updated to the time of Heraclius. He also added a series of date-sequences intended to suggest an explanation of recent history consonant with anti-Chalcedonian propaganda. For some reason he did not integrate the separate elements of his compilation into a fully coherent unity, but left them standing loosely one beside the other.

The sources used in this compilation included a Greek geographer also known to the authors of the *Chronicon Paschale* and the *Chronicon Barbari*; the fourth-century Syriac writer Aphrahat; the Greek chronicle of Eusebius of Caesarea; an unidentified (Syriac) chronographic compilation at Edessa; an Antiochene chronicler of the mid-fifth century; and sources at the monastery of Qēnneshrē, on the east bank of the Euphrates, a great centre of learning in the seventh century, where Greek was studied at an advanced level by the Syrian Jacobites. The connection with Qēnneshrē is shown by some passages in the chronicle composed by the priest Thomas himself. Qēnneshrē lay near a busy trade-route between Thomas's home country, the Rhesaina region, and Antioch.

Before the first reference to the Council of Chalcedon there is nothing specifically Jacobite about this codex, so it is legitimate to concentrate on the part beginning with that first reference and ending with the condemnation of Chalcedon at the end of the work. This is the part which is translated below. The author who condemns the dogma of Chalcedon in Rubric 5 goes on immediately to represent the history of Byzantium thereafter and until the thirtieth year of Heraclius as a period of heretical domination, interrupted by the tolerant reigns of Zeno and Anastasius (AD 474-518). By giving the length of the period of Orthodox domination which preceded Chalcedon, he implicitly compares the Chalcedonian emperors to the Arian Valens (AD 367-78), who expelled the Orthodox from their churches.

The events recorded under the Seleucid year 940 should be seen as a focus around which the rest of the composition clusters. This appears from the starkly detached position of the record at the culmination of world history; from the sharp caesura made after it; from the fact that what follows is described as an 'explanatory note'; and from the repetition of the passage in the course of 'Rubric 6', with minor changes.

For the purpose of introducing the text, it is necessary only to register a conclusion from what has been said. It is reasonable to see the codex as a copy of a composition by Thomas, a Syrian priest from Mesopotamia, dated to the thirtieth year of Heraclius and written directly after the Arab Conquest of Mesopotamia in AD 639-40. The last folio is an addition by the early eighth-century copyist. Thomas disapproved of Heraclius's Chalcedonian church politics (this emperor persecuted Jacobites who would not change their Faith) and gave the pact between Heraclius and the Persian Shahrvarāz a pivotal position in his history of the world.

Text No. 2, whose author I shall refer to as 'the priest Thomas', is preserved in BL Add. 14,643, VIIIth century, and edited in *CM* 2, pp. 76-154 (called in the Latin translation *Chronicon miscellaneum ad annum domini 724 pertinens*).

[END OF 'RUBRIC 5'] /p. 138/ After Theodosius II reigned Marcian, for 7 years. He assembled a synod in Chalcedon and they confessed openly two natures and made confusion in the Church of God. Before this for 62 years the Orthodox had been in possession, from Theodosius I until Theodosius II. Then the heretics had possession of the churches for 23 years, since the reign of Marcian's successor, Leo, lasted 16 years. Leo was succeeded by Zeno, who reigned 18 years and made union in the Church of God. After him came Anastasius, who reigned for 27 years. So for 45 years the Orthodox were again in possession of the churches. Anastasius was succeeded /p. 139/ by Justinian, who introduced the Synod of Chalcedon into the Church a second time, the husband of the faithful Theodora. In this period the successive bishops in Constantinople were: Gennadius, Acacius, Phrabitas, Anthimus, and Menas the xenodocharius, a heretic.[99] The bishop of Alexandria was Theodosius and he of Antioch was Severus. After that Justinian reigned for 40 years; and after him Justin, for 14 years; Tiberius, 4 years; Maurice, 22 years; Phocas, 8 years; Heraclius, 30 years. And in the days of Heraclius, in the 940th year of Alexander, during one night in June, the earth shook violently. And in July of that year, Heraclius, king of the Romans, and the patríkios Shahrvaräz met each other at a certain pass in the north named Arabissus Tripotamus. There they negotiated the terms of peace and the Euphrates was recognized between them as the frontier. Thus they made peace with each other and they built a church there and named it Eirēnē.[100]

['RUBRIC 6'] *Explanatory note consisting of annalistic information on a wide range of subjects, beginning with an earthquake which occurred*

---

[99] The period from Gennadius's accession to Menas's death is AD 458-552; between Phrabitas {Syr. FLBYTS} (died 490) and Anthimus (536) five patriarchs have been omitted.

[100] Eirēnē is the Greek for 'peace' and we know other churches dedicated to Hagia Eirēnē; but a Syrian without Greek would read this word as 'aryōnō' = 'leper', or as 'aryānō' = 'Arian'.

at Antioch.[101]

['SECTION 1']

AG 767, year 506 in the era of Antioch: On Saturday, 14 September, in the middle of the night there was a fearful earthquake. /p. 140/ All of a sudden buildings collided with one another and collapsed and fell on those who lived in them. The suffering was widespread and terrible. Two of the parts (i.e. two thirds?) of the great and famous city of Antioch collapsed and fell by the anger of God. [There follows an extended description (nearly two pages of the Syriac text) of the consequences of the earthquake, in which the bishop, Acacius, plays a praiseworthy role.] /p. 141/ [...]

AG 771, year 507 in the era of Antioch: On 19 June in the evening, at the time that the service ends in church, wrath was sent of a sudden from God and there was a noise like a roar and the earth quaked and shuddered. [There follows another extended description (about one page of Syriac text) of the earthquake, which concentrates on the evidence of God's mercy mingled with his chastisement.] /p. 142, 143/

['SECTION 2']

AG 814: Kawad went up into Roman territory.

AG 851: Chosroēs went up for the first time.

AG 853: Chosroēs went up for the second time.

AG 830: Al-Mundhir went up for the first time.

AG 865: Al-Mundhir died in June.

AG 843: The Indians came in December.[102]

AG 854:[103] The first outbreak of the plague.

AG 855: The earth quaked and the cities were inundated.

---

[101] For the translation of this rubric, see the introduction to this text.

[102] For 'Indians', read 'Huns'. The manuscript does not say in which of the two winter months they came; it can be corrected from *CM* I, 12.

[103] Corrected in the manuscript by a second hand to AG 855.

AG 873: Outbreak of a plague[104] in April.

['SECTION 3']

AG 881: There was a contention about Lent throughout Syria. The people were divided, some recognizing Lent from 17 February and some from 24 February. But all the people celebrated the Paschal feast together. The same year, on the Thursday of the Ascension, al-Mundhir declared war. God helped al-Mundhir to defeat Qābūs and the Cross was victorious.

The next year, the earth quaked in November and there was a great tremor, in which all Antioch collapsed, save a small part, and Seleucia, too, with both Cilicias,[105] fifty-eight years after Severus left his see.

['SECTION 4']

The centurion who guarded our Lord on the Cross was Longinus. He pierced our Lord's side, but at the end he believed and died a martyr.

['SECTION 5']

The patriarch Severus of Antioch was consecrated in November, indiction V, AG 823. He was from Sozopolis[106] of Pisidia, the son of a bishop of that place. This bishop had been one of those who deposed /p. 144/ Nestorius in the reign of Theodosius the son of Arcadius. Severus remained six years in his see, then was expelled on 29 September, AG 829, indiction XII. He lived in exile for 19 years, three of which he spent at Constantinople. He departed from this world on 8 February. In that same year died also Lord John of Tella, the son of Crassus, on 9 February. At this time lived Lord Jacob the Teacher, who died AG 830.

['SECTION 6']

AG 876, indiction XIII: Death of the patriarch Theodosius of Alexandria on 22 July.

---

[104] The manuscript names the plague as {Syr. shar^cūtō}.

[105] Brooks regards this passage as corrupt.

[106] The manuscript has 'Shizpolis'.

AG 888, indiction XI: Death of Bishop Jacob, of Psīlthō, on 31 July.

AG 901,[107] indiction IX: Death of the patriarch Peter, 22 April.

AG 906: Death of the Patriarch Lord Julian, 9 July.

AG 915: Consecration of Lord Athanasius, on 6 November, and he died in AG 942, indiction IV, on 28 July.

At this time the people emigrated from the area east of the Euphrates.

AG 943,[108] indiction V: Consecration of Lord John as patriarch.

AG 678: Death of Lord Julian the Ancient on 15 February.

AG 684: Death of Lord Ephraem the Teacher on 18 June.

AG 673: Nisibis was taken by the Persians from the Romans. /p. 145/

AG 746: Death of Lord Rabbūlō, bishop of Edessa, on 7 August.

AG 730: Lord Symeon mounted the pillar.

AG 770: Death of the same on 2 September.

['SECTION 7']

AG 871: Chosroēs went up with his army to Antioch and took it by siege. He destroyed it and led its inhabitants into slavery. He laid many cities waste and took a vast number of captives, then he went down to his own country and built a city for the captives whom he had led down from Antioch. He named it: 'Chosroēs's Antioch'.

AG 884: Chosroēs went up again with his army and besieged Dara and he sent his general {Pers. marzbān} Adarmahān[109] up to Antioch and he set fire to Amos (?) and the Sanctuary of Lord Julian. Then he went to Seleucia and took it by siege. Then he went to Apamea, which surrendered to him of its own accord, yet he set fire to it and took its inhabitants away with him as captives. While he was going down to join his lord, he[110] took Dara by siege and led its inhabitants into captivity, giving the empty city to some settlers of their own Persian race.

---

[107] Read '902'.

[108] Literally, 'the next year'.

[109] In the manuscript stands MZLDRHMN; but the name is known from other writers.

[110] i.e. Chosroēs.

AG 902, indiction IX: Chosroēs went up into Roman territory while still a young man;[111] he was received in great honour and the Romans escorted him home and seated him upon his throne.

AG 910, indiction II: Domitian persecuted the faithful.

AG 914, indiction VI: On 23 August the Romans slew Maurice and his sons.

AG 915, indiction IX:[112] Dara was taken this second time. /p. 146/

AG 920, indiction X:[113] There was a great deal of snow everywhere and it was so cold that the entire Euphrates froze on the night of Epiphany and rafts of ice were floating on it for six days so that ferries could not cross it. A large number of fish died and olive trees were withered everywhere.

During this year Mardīn was taken and in the same year Rhesaina was taken, in the summer.

AG 921: Edessa, Harrān, Callinicum, and Circesium and every remaining city to the east of the Euphrates was taken. That winter the Euphrates was the frontier.

On 7 August of the same year Shahrvarāz crossed to Zenobia and took it; this was the first city west of the Euphrates to be taken.

AG 922: The Persians entered Emesa, where they found many people of eastern origin and these they sent away from there, each to his own country.

In the summer of the same year the Romans and Persians fought a battle at the sanctuary of St Thomas in Emesa.

AG 924: The Persians entered Damascus.

AG 925: Jerusalem was captured.

AG 929: Union with the Damianites.

AG 930: Union with the members of the sect of Conon and Eugenius.

In June of the same year Alexandria was captured, only to be

---

[111] {Syr. talyō}, which can also mean 'child'.
[112] Incorrect synchronism.
[113] Incorrect synchronism.

evacuated in June, 940, together with all the cities of Syria, not under human compulsion but at God's command. /p. 147/

AG 934: The Slavs invaded Crete and the other islands. There some blessed men[114] of Qēnneshrē were taken captive and some twenty of them were killed.

AG 934:[115] The Persians invaded Rhodes, made the general {Gr. stratēgós} in that place their prisoner and took back captives from the island to Persia.

That year the King Heraclius left his residence and led a large army down to Persia; he laid the area waste and took many captives.

AG 938: On 15 September the sun and moon were darkened.

AG 939: Chosroēs died in February. He had subdued the whole earth and reigned for forty years. His son Shīrōē succeeded him; he reigned for seven months and died at the end of the same year. After him reigned his (Shīrōē's) son, whose name was Ardashīr.

AG 940: During one night in June, the earth shook violently.

In July of the same year Heraclius, king of the Romans, and Shahrvarāz, the patríkios of the Persians, met each other at a pass {Gr. kleisoûra} in the north named Arabissus Tripotamus and they built a church there and named it ᵓRYNW.[116] There they negotiated the terms of peace and the Euphrates was recognized as the frontier between them. Thus they made peace with each other.

AG 945, indiction VII: On Friday, 4 February,[117] at the ninth hour, there was a battle between the Romans and the Arabs of

---

114 {Syr. tūbbōnē}: a term usually applied to saints and monks; its use here and at AG 947, below, may suggest that the dead men should be seen as martyrs.

115 The last digit should probably be a seven, which is easily confused with a four in Syriac.

116 See above, 'Rubric 5', last part, where this detail is sensibly placed after the conclusion of the peace treaty; ᵓRYNW cannot, like ᵓRYNᵓ there, be read as 'Eirēnē' or indeed as 'leper', but only as 'Arians'.

117 4 Feb., AD 634, was indeed a Friday.

Muhammad in Palestine twelve 'miles'[118] east of Gaza. The Romans fled, leaving behind the patríkios the Son of YRDN {Syr. BRYRDN},[119] whom the Arabs killed. Some /p. 148/ 4,000 poor village people of Palestine were killed there, Christians, Jews and Samaritans. The Arabs ravaged the whole region.

AG 947, indiction IX: The Arabs invaded the whole of Syria and went down to Persia and conquered it; the Arabs climbed the mountain of Mardīn and killed many monks there in (the monasteries of) Qedar and B^{e}nōthō. There died the blessed man Simon, doorkeeper of Qedar, brother of Thomas the priest.

['SECTION 8']

AG 343: Simon Cephas[120] laid the foundations of the church at Antioch.

AG 344: Stephen the martyr was stoned by the Jews in Jerusalem.

AG 345:[121] Paul began his ministry.

AG 375: Nero killed Paul and Peter in Rome.

---

[118] Compare text No. 13, § 99, with the note there, and §§ 164-5.

[119] Land, *AS*, 1.116 and M. Gil, *A History of Palestine 634-1099* (Cambridge, 1992), pp. 38-9 suggest 'in Jordan'; this seems most implausible, geographically and etymologically. One could possibly read Wārdan {Armenian: Vardan?}, a Byzantine commander who led and was killed at the battle of Ajnādayn (Azdī, p. 88; Pseudo-Wāqidī, pp. 102-25). Modern scholars, however, following De Goeje, *Mémoire*, pp. 30-4, usually associate this entry with a battle at Dāthin, described by Balādhurī (p. 109) as 'one of the villages of Gaza', and with a battle lost by Sergius, patríkios of Caesarea (Theophanes, p. 336; text No. 13, §§ 49-50). Rather than force disparate accounts to apply to one incident, it might be better to postulate separate encounters. One could identify Dāthin and neighbouring ^{c}Araba, where the Byzantines regroup after an initial defeat at Dāthin (Balādhurī, p. 109; Tabarī, I, p. 2108), with biblical Dothan (*Genesis* 37.17) and ^{c}Araboth, c. 20 miles east of Caesarea and 3 miles apart, which would make better sense of the account in Theophanes and Dionysius (= text No. 13) of the battle which Sergius apparently waged near Caesarea. But the suggestion remains tentative. [R.H.]

[120] The second name means 'the Rock'.

[121] Literally, 'the next year'.

AG 376: Jerusalem was destroyed by Vespasian and his son Titus and in this same war the chronicler Josephus was killed.

AG 383: A pestilence broke out in Rome such that one thousand people died.

AG 420: Death of Lord John the Evangelist.

AG 415: A great persecution of Christians was unleashed by the wicked emperor Trajan, in which Simon the son of Cleophas, bishop of Jerusalem, was signally martyred.

AG 419: Trajan made Armenia into a province. In the same year Ignatius, who had been a disciple of John the Evangelist, was martyred at Antioch. /p. 149/

AG 448: Marcion and Montanus became known as the initiators of heresies in Phrygia.

AG 479: Bardaysōn, who propagated the doctrine of Valentinus, became known.

AG 543: Martyrdom of Sergius and Bacchus.

AG 552: The end of the Romans' millennium.[122]

AG 560: Valentinus, the Arian emperor, initiated a persecution of the Christians [*sic*].

AG 563: Shabuhr, king of Persia, laid Syria and Cappadocia waste and in the same year the barbarians crossed the river Danube and laid the islands waste.

AG 500:[123] Paul of Samosata arose.

AG 573: Mani the deceiver arose.

AG 583: The emperor Aurelian unleashed a persecution, but God struck him with a thunderbolt and he died.

AG 611: The churches were uprooted by the evil Diocletian and Peter, bishop of Alexandria, was martyred.

AG 619: The victorious Constantine became emperor.

AG 720:[124] Constantine transferred his throne from Rome to

---

[122] The Syriac has an unfinished sentence, which the editor (Brooks) completes.

[123] Read, with Brooks, '560'.

[124] Read '620'.

Constantinople.

AG 26:*125* Constantine gave freedom to the Christians and honoured and magnified the churches of Christ.   .

AG 636: The synod of 318 bishops was held.

AG 648: Death of Constantine the Great.

AG 670: Beginning of the celebrity of Lord Ephraem the Teacher.

['SECTION 9']

AG 814: Amida was taken by siege on 24 December.

AG 820: Dara was built. /p. 150/

AG 824: Armenia rebelled and the emperor Anastasius sent an army and forced it into submission. The same emperor issued coins of 40 nummi and of 20, 10 and 5.

AG 830: The bishops were persecuted by Justin [*sic*] the husband of the empress Theodora.

AG 835: Edessa was flooded.

AG 840: Zuraq, the Persian general, went up into Roman territory and fought the Romans on the river Euphrates and the majority of the Romans were drowned in the Euphrates.

['RUBRIC 7'] *At what dates and under which kings the synods were held.*

[Summary of pp. 150, line 12, to 154, line 4:

'AG 427 = AD 117:*126* Council of Ancyra under Hadrian, against the opinion that the Trinity is one Person, present in the eucharistic elements.

'AG 530 = AD 220: Council of Antioch under Severus, against the opinion that Jesus was just a righteous man.

'AG 640 = AD 330: Council of Gangra under Julian on the question of clerical abstinence from meat and sex.

---

125 Read '626'.

126 The dates AD are those of the manuscript, not editorial calculations; the facts are distorted, but it is not helpful to repeat the word '*sic*' throughout.

'AG 636 = AD 326: Council of Nicaea under Constantine, against Arius.

'AG 691 = AD 380: Council of Constantinople under Theodosius I, against Macedonius.

'AG 740 = AD 430: Council of Ephesus under Theodosius II, against Nestorius.

'AG 760 = AD 450: Second Council of Ephesus under the same, against those who condemned Eutyches for not confessing two natures in Christ.

'AG 763 = AD 453: Council of Chalcedon under Marcian, undoing the work of Ephesus II.'

[The text continues as follows:]

/p. 154/ These men (he has just listed a number of bishops) had been with Flavian in Constantinople at the deposition of Eutyches. But when they saw that Flavian had been defeated, they changed their mind and signed the manifesto[127] of the second synod of Ephesus, anathematizing their former opinion and gaining recognition there. After they had arrived at Chalcedon, however, they saw that everything that was being done was in contradiction with the second synod of Ephesus and its resolution; then they returned to their original vomit[128] and went back on what they had performed at the second synod of Ephesus, saying that they were doing[129] these things against their will and moreover under compulsion. Now the opinion they had sustained at Constantinople was that Eutyches should be deposed and that we should confess two natures in Christ, precisely the opinion that was anathematized at the second synod of Ephesus. When they were assembled at Chalcedon, they first deposed the great and holy confessor Dioscorus, then they were required by the representatives of civil authority and the senators who were included in the assembly to

---

[127] {Lat. libellus}.

[128] An allusion to *Proverbs* 26:11: 'Like a dog returning to his vomit is a stupid man who repeats his folly.'

[129] By an unnecessary emendation the editor makes this: 'we did'.

make a statement defining the Faith. They, however, began to cry out, 'We are not permitted to do this. We would not presume! We would not dare! The law itself prevents us from doing this.' Yet, though they repeated this many times, the authorities did not give way and they were compelled to yield to the authorities. By this transgression of their own anathemas they made themselves the object of those thirty-five curses they had pronounced against anyone who says that there are two natures in Christ after the Union.

It is finished.

DISCUSSION

If the arguments presented in the introduction to this text are accepted, the general conclusion may be drawn that chronography was mingled with homiletic by certain Syrian clerics and distorted wildly in the process. The connections which would be made explicit in a sermon are sometimes left unwritten, presumably as a challenge to the reader to puzzle the message out for himself. On a much smaller scale, the epigraphic chronicle on the south wall of the church of St Sergius at Ehnesh (text No. 11) is another example of this. There is a connection between text No. 2 and the monastery of Qēnneshrē and Ehnesh is connected with the same monastery by a short stretch of the Euphrates. Considering the importance of Qēnneshrē in the chronographic tradition, it is reasonable to attribute the similarity between texts No. 2 and No. 11 to this common connection.

Instead of giving a full commentary, I leave the reader to puzzle out for himself what significance the priest Thomas saw in most of the sequences of historical facts which he lists. My own interpretation can be found in Palmer, 'Une chronique syriaque'. I add here just two points to supplement what was said in the introduction.

One point which fits in with the anti-Heraclian tenor of the text is Thomas's account of the Persian conquests west of the Euphrates. He avoids mentioning the Persian evacuation of Egypt and Syria in AD

628/9, presumably in order that no one should connect it, to Heraclius's credit, with the peace treaty of the same year. Instead he slips it in at a much earlier point in the chronological account and he plays down the fact that Syria, the homeland of his readers, also benefited from Heraclius's reconquest, by making the whole event a footnote to the Persian conquest of Egypt. In case any reader should nevertheless try to make the connection and to see something positive in Heraclius's achievement, he adds that the Persians went home 'not under human compulsion but at God's command'.

Not only earthquakes are significant for our author. A bad winter followed on the second capture of Dara in AG 915 (the fact that it followed five years later is played down by a direct juxtaposition); the sun and the moon were eclipsed simultaneously (*sic*) near the end of the year preceding AG 939, when Chosroēs died after a reign of 40 years (magic, quasi-eternal number; it actually lasted 38 years) in which he had subdued 'all the earth'. Incidentally, this eclipse occurred in China and was not visible in Syria; news of it must have travelled to Syria along the silk-route. In the process, the date was misunderstood, since calculations show that it happened on 15 October, not 15 September.

3. EXTRACT FROM THE *MELKITE CHRONICLE* (AFTER AD 642)

INTRODUCTION

Text No. 2, on my interpretation, shows that theology can be of central importance for a Syrian cleric who turns his hand from writing sermons to writing history. It is therefore important to establish the religious denomination of the several historians writing in Syriac. There is a so-called 'Melkite' chronicle of which a small fragment refers to our period. This offers an opportunity to introduce the terms 'Melkite' and 'Maronite' (cf. text No. 4).

'Melkite' designates not merely the Chalcedonians among the Syrian Christians, but specifically those who followed the dyothelete dogma laid down by the Sixth Ecumenical Council of AD 680/1 (that Christ's volition *qua* man is to be distinguished clearly from his volition *qua* God, although the two volitions were never at variance). In doing so they distanced themselves from what was probably then the main body of opinion in Syria, where, in intensive debates with Jacobites (cf. text No. 4), the Chalcedonians had come to lay stress on their teaching that Christ was double with regard to his nature, but single with regard to his person and his will. This compromise had long before been suggested to the patriarch Athanasius 'the Cameldriver' by the emperor Heraclius himself (Michael, pp. 405-8, 11.2c, translated in a note on § 44 of text No. 13). The leading controversialists among these 'monothelete' Syrian Chalcedonians came from a monastery on the Orontes near Apamea called after Maron, a holy man. Already in the sixth century they had made a name for themselves as opponents of the Jacobites and the 'Maron-ites' are known long before any 'Byzantine Conformist' party was distinguished from them (for that is what Melkite, 'malkōyō' = imperial, means). Probably the Byzantine Conformists only became prominent in Syria in the eighth century, as a result of imperially inspired efforts in AD 727 to use an influx of Byzantine captives to make the customs of the Chalcedonians in Syria conform to those of Constantinople.

The dispute concerned not only the Sixth Council, but also the

Trisagion.   The Trisagion is a prayer like the thrice-holy of the
Seraphim, which plays a prominent part in all Orthodox liturgies. The
Orthodox see the consecrated Mysteries on the altar as Christ seated on
his throne in heaven, so that the sanctuary is transformed momentarily
into the place where the Seraphim continually sing.   In Syria both
Chalcedonians and Jacobites used a longer form of the prayer than was
current in Constantinople. Because this Syrian form had been forced
upon the Constantinopolitans by the emperor Anastasius, who ended by
supporting the anti-Chalcedonian patriarch Severus, Constantinople had
come to identify it, wrongly, as a badge of opposition to Chalcedon.
Anastasius's attempt to introduce the long form in Constantinople had
led to riots; conversely, the introduction by Sergius, son of Mansūr (cf.
text No. 13, § 134), of the shorter form in Aleppo occasioned such
disorderly conduct that the Muslim authorities were obliged to
intervene. The Byzantine Conformists labelled the others as 'Severans'
(after Severus of Antioch), 'Jacobites' and 'Theopaschites', insinuating
that their use of the longer Trisagion and their refusal to accept the
Sixth Council (at which there had been hardly any Oriental
representatives) were part and parcel of a kind of Syrian separatist
disease which they had caught from the anti-Chalcedonians; the
non-conformists, led on by the monks of 'the House of Maron',
retaliated with shouts of 'Maximians' (after the theologian Maximus
Confessor), 'Nestorians' and 'Jews'.

The significant thing about this event is that the Arab emir of Aleppo
divided the cathedral of that city half-way down the nave, so as to keep
the parties separate; but the ones to whom he accorded the main altar
as of right were the Maronites and their supporters, whereas the
Byzantine Conformists, like intruders, were obliged to build a wooden
altar against the partition wall.   They celebrated the Eucharist in an
area which the women of the Maronite party took pleasure in treating
as unconsecrated (women were normally excluded from the sanctuary).
Assuming that the emir was trying to see fair play, this arrangement
would imply that the main body of Alepine Christians at that date were
of the Maronite party. Subsequent events led to the domination of the
cities by the Melkites and to the retreat of the Maronites into the

Lebanon, where the modern Maronites live.[130]

The name of the *Melkite Chronicle* is thus not truly applicable to this chronicle, which was written shortly after Heraclius's death.[131] It presents world history in a compendium from the Chalcedonian point of view. The text is preserved in a Sinaï manuscript edited by de Halleux, 'La Chronique Melkite abrégée'. The following extract from pp. 40-42 begins with an account of the last recorded anti-Severan council of the sixth century in AD 571.[132] In fact, the latter part of the chronicle is designed, as de Halleux says, to give 'Monophysitism' its place in the history of heresy by treating this one subject at length with reference to Severus and other leaders of the movement, while reducing the rest of history to the barest skeleton.

After Justinian had reigned for thirty-nine years he ended his life and Justin, his sister's son, succeeded to his throne.

22   Now seeing that those who had come to be embroiled in the unclean doctrine of Severus would not consent to cease (from controversy), the King summoned once more a council in Constantinople and once again Severus and those who shared his ideas were anathematized at Constantinople. Present were the bishop of that city, John, John of Jerusalem, John of Alexandria, Anastasius of

---

[130] This account is based on a part of Dionysius's Ecclesiastical History preserved in Michael (pp. 457-61, 11.20a) and on the open-minded approach of Brock, in his article 'An Early Syriac Life of Maximus', especially pp. 343-5. According to an older perspective still found in the handbooks, the Maronites were a splinter-group by origin.

[131] De Halleux argues that this chronicle is a summary of a longer original and it is this original that he would date between Heraclius's death and AD 680, probably in 642 or shortly after. It is also possible that the longer original is of the late sixth century and that the present composition brought it up to date with the regnal years of the emperors up to Heraclius.

[132] De Halleux, 'Trois synodes impériaux': the text translated here is unique in preserving an extract from the lost Acts of this council.

Antioch and the legates of John of Rome.

23 *John's anathema of Severus*: 'Since Severus expelled himself from the Holy Church and incurred the penalty of his own accord, as is evident and as everybody knows, we, following the direction given by the Divine Canons and the Holy Fathers, lay down that this man is an outsider, who was long ago condemned by the Divine Canons for his wicked blasphemies, and we, too, anathematize him.'

24   As for Justin, he reigned 13 years; Tiberius, 4; Maurice, 20; Phocas, 8; Heraclius, 30 and 6 months.

DISCUSSION

The 'Melkite Chronicle' is preserved in a Sinaï manuscript in a codex which also contains anti-Jacobite polemic. It retells in a short compass the history of the world, concentrating on the Chalcedonian version of the Ecumenical councils, with a clear statement of the errors of Arius and of Nestorius; and, of all the individuals it refers to, it describes the lives of Philoxenus of Mabbugh and Severus of Antioch in most detail. The 'Melkite' Chronicle's clear statement as to the errors of Philoxenus and of Severus could be read as a negation of Thomas's proposition (see the beginning of text No. 2) that Byzantine doctrinal policy had been wrong ever since the deposition of Severus.

4. EXTRACT FROM THE *MARONITE CHRONICLE*

INTRODUCTION

This chronicle goes up to AD 664 and was probably written by someone who was alive then. The writer is clearly one of the Maronites and a supporter of the Romans, i.e. the Byzantines; that makes it likely that he was writing before the Sixth Council (AD 680/1), which the Maronites rejected, and certain that he wrote before the disputes of AD 727. The accuracy of this chronicle as to weekdays makes it likely that it was compiled during and immediately after the events. Like the other West-Syrian chronicles, it seems to favour Mu^{c}āwiya, rather than ^{c}Alī. The chronicler describes in tendentious terms the {Ar. dhimma} (denoting the 'protection' accorded to the {Ar. ahl al-kitāb}, the People of the Book), by which the Jacobite patriarch had entered into a special relationship with the caliph and paid him a yearly tribute in return for the liberty to run the affairs of his own Church and the backing of the State for his authority. The inference that the Maronites were not so successful as the Jacobites in adapting to the new political system seems to be justified. The Maronite author uses a few success-stories from the Byzantine defence of Asia Minor to boost the morale of his readers, who would have liked to see the Byzantines back in Syria. The Jacobites only wanted the Byzantines back if they would reject Chalcedon; but if the Arab conquest had not convinced them of their error, what could? At this date the Jacobites were perhaps already accommodating themselves to what they saw as a situation that would continue.

The text of the *Maronite Chronicle* is preserved, with some lacunas, in BL Add. 17,216 (VIIIth or IXth century), fol. 12a, and edited in *CM* 2, pp. 43-74. The narrative of the earlier seventh century is lost and the chronicle resumes after the lacuna as follows:

/p. 69/...Mu^{c}āwiya, Ḥudhayfa, the son of his sister, and Mu^{c}āwiya gave orders that he be put to death.

^{C}Alī, too, threatened to go up once again against Mu^{c}āwiya, but they struck him while he was at prayer in al-Hīra[133] /p. 70/ and killed him.[134] Mu^{c}āwiya (then) went down to al-Hīra, where all the Arab forces there proffered their right hand to him,[135] whereupon he returned to Damascus.

In AG 970, the 17th year of Constans, on a Friday in June,[136] at the second hour, there was a violent earthquake in Palestine, and many places there collapsed.

In the same month the bishops of the Jacobites, Theodore and Sabūkht[137] came to Damascus and held an inquiry into the Faith with the Maronites[138] in the presence of Mu^{c}āwiya. When the Jacobites were defeated, Mu^{c}āwiya ordered them to pay 20,000 denarii and commanded them to be silent. Thus there arose the custom that the Jacobite bishops should pay that sum of gold every year to Mu^{c}āwiya, so that he would not withdraw his protection and let them be persecuted by the members of the (Orthodox) Church. The person called 'patriarch' by the Jacobites fixed the financial burden that all the convents of monks and nuns should contribute each year towards the payment in gold and he did the same with all the adherents of his faith.

---

[133] Arabic sources say he was killed at a mosque in Kūfa; ^{C}Alī is, however, described as governor of al-Hīra by a Palestinian Christian writing c.680 (Brock, 'An early Syriac Life', p. 313/319). [R.H.]

[134] Arabic sources are generally agreed that ^{C}Alī was killed in Ramadān 40 (January 661 = AG 972). Our chronicler may have been misled by the fact that 'the Syrians acknowledged Mu^{c}āwiya as caliph in Dhū 'l-Qa^{c}da 37 (April 658 = 969)' (Tabarī, II, p. 199), or he may be better informed than we. Theophanes, p. 347 also places ^{C}Alī's death earlier than the accepted date, in 659/60. [R.H.]

[135] By this is probably meant the glancing gesture of right palm against right palm by which Arabs today seal a contract; see text No. 10, under AG 967.

[136] 7 June, AD 659.

[137] {Syr. SBKWT}.

[138] Literally: 'those of the House of Lord Maron.'

He bequeathed his estate to Mu^{c}āwiya,[139] so that out of fear of that man all the Jacobites would be obedient to him.

On the ninth of the same month in which the disputation with the Jacobites took place, on a Sunday at the eighth hour, there was an earthquake.[140]

In the same year King Constans ordered his brother Theodosius to be put to death - quite unjustly and without any fault on his part, according to what many people said. Many were grieved at his violent end and they say that the citizens chanted slogans {Gr. phōnás} against the King, calling him a second Cain, murderer of his brother. In great anger he left his son Constantine on /p. 71/ his throne and himself set out for the north, taking the queen and the whole Roman fighting force with him, against foreign peoples.

In AG 971, Constans's 18th year, many Arabs gathered at Jerusalem and made Mu^{c}āwiya king[141] and he went up and sat down on Golgotha; he prayed there, and went to Gethsemane and went down to the tomb of the blessed Mary to pray in it. In those days, when the Arabs were assembled there with Mu^{c}āwiya, there was an earthquake and a violent tremor and the greater part of Jericho fell, including all its churches, and of the House of Lord John at the site of our Saviour's baptism in the Jordan every stone above the ground was overthrown, together with the entire monastery. The monastery of Abba Euthymius,

---

[139] Literally: he made himself a legator of Mu^{c}āwiya {Syr. wa-^{c}bad napšēh mawr^{e}tōnō d-Mu^{c}āwiya}.

[140] 9 June, AD 659, was indeed a Sunday.

[141] Allegiance was rendered to Mu^{c}āwiya in Jerusalem after the death of ^{c}Alī in the year 40 (February 661=972: Tabarī, II, p. 4); 'the people as a whole' recognized him after ^{c}Alī's son, Hasan 'had made peace with him and turned matters over to him in the year 41, five days before the end of the month of Rabī^c I (31 July 661=972)' (Tabarī, II, p. 199). Again, our chronicler may have inside information, but one suspects that he has brought forward Mu^{c}āwiya's accession and tour in Jerusalem to coincide with the earthquake of 659, the latter being in his mind an evident indication of God's disapproval of the former event. Note that the entry for 'the following year', a severe frost, falls in 662, not 660. [R.H.]

as well as many convents of monks and solitaries and many other places also collapsed in this (earthquake).

In July of the same year the emirs and many Arabs gathered and proffered their right hand to Mu^{c}āwiya. Then an order went out that he should be proclaimed king in all the villages and cities of his dominion and that they should make acclamations and invocations {Gr. phōnás, klēseis} to him. He also minted gold and silver, but it was not accepted, because it had no cross on it. Furthermore, Mu^{c}āwiya did not wear a crown like other kings in the world. He placed his throne in Damascus and refused to go to Muhammad's throne.

The following year there was frost in the early morning of Wednesday, 13 April, and the white grapevines were withered by it.[142]

When Mu^{c}āwiya had acquired the power which he had aimed at and was at rest from the (civil) wars of his people, he broke the peace settlement with the Romans and refused to accept peace from them any longer. Rather he said, 'If the Romans want /p. 72/ peace, let them surrender their weapons, and pay the tax {Ar. jizya}.'

[one folio missing]

... of the year, Yazīd b. Mu^{c}āwiya went up again with a large army.[143]   While they were encamped in Thrace, the Arabs scattered for the purpose of plunder, leaving their hirelings and their sons to pasture the cattle and to snatch anything that should come their

---

[142] The weekday shows that this was AD 662.

[143] Theophanes, p. 351 and Tabarī, II, p. 86 place 'the raid of Yazīd b. Mu^{c}āwiya against the Byzantines' in 668=980. The campaign of Busr b. Abī Artat of the year 43 (663=974), which possibly reached as far as Constantinople (Tabarī, II, p. 27), may be meant here (Agapius, p. 228, recording this raid, says the Greeks fled as far as Constantinople); otherwise, our chronicler is either confused or better informed than we. See Nöldeke, 'Zur Geschichte der Araber', pp. 86-8; M. Canard, 'Les expéditions des Arabes contre Constantinople dans l'histoire et dans la légende', *Journal Asiatique*, 208 (1926), pp. 67-8. [R.H.]

way. When those who were standing on the wall (saw) this, they went out and fell upon them and (killed) a great many young men[144] and hirelings and some of the Arabs too. Then they snatched up the booty and went in (to the City). The next day, all the young men[145] of the City[146] grouped together, along with some of those who had come in to take refuge there and a few of the Romans and said, 'Let us make a sortie against them'. But Constantine told them, 'Do not make a sortie. It is not as if you had engaged in a battle and won. All you have done is a bit of common thieving.' But they refused to listen to him. Instead, a large number of people went out armed, carrying banners and streamers {Gr. bánda, phlámoula} on high as is the Roman custom. As soon as they had gone out, all the gates {Lat. portae} were closed. The King had a tent erected on the wall, where he sat watching. The Saracens drew (them) after them, retreating a good long way away from the wall, so that they would not be able to escape quickly when put to flight. So they went out and squatted in tribal formation. When the others reached them, they leapt to their feet and cried out in the way of their language, 'God is great!'. Immediately the others turned tail in flight, chased by the Saracens, who fell on them, killing and making captives right up to the point where they came within range of the catapults {Lat. ballistrae} on the wall. In his fury with them Constantine /p. 73/ was barely willing to open (the gates) for them. Many of them fell and others were wounded by arrows.

In AG 975, the 22nd of Constans and 7th[147] of Mu͏ᶜāwiya, (ᶜAbd al-Rahmān) b. Khālid, commander of the Arabs of Emesa, the capital of Phoenicia, went up with an army against Roman territory. He came and pitched camp by the lake called Scutarium;[148] and

---

144 {Syr. tᵉlōyē}: the word is more usual in the sense of 'children'.
145 See previous note.
146 viz Constantinople.
147 Read 4th; see the note on the date AG 934 in text No. 2
148 {Syr. ᵓSQDRYN}; 'Scutarium' is my unsupported guess.

when he saw that a large number of people were dwelling in it, he wanted to take it. So he made rafts and boats and embarked a force on them and sent them towards the middle (of the lake). The lake-dwellers, seeing this, ran away and hid from them. When the Arabs got into the harbour, they disembarked and tied up the boats, then made off towards the interior to attack the people. At that moment the men who were in hiding got up and ran to the boats, cut off their moorings and rowed out onto the deep water. Thus the Arabs were left on shore in the harbour, penned in by deep water and mud. The inhabitants then grouped together against them, surrounding them from all sides, fell upon them with slings, stones and arrows and killed them all. Their companions stood watching from the opposite shore, unable to come to their aid. The Arabs have not attacked that lake again up to the present day.

Ibn Khālid then set off from there and came to the city of Amorium and gave it the word.[149] When they opened (their gates) to him he stationed an Arab garrison there and left that place. He then came to the great fortress of SYLWS,[150] because a master-carpenter from Paphlagonia had played a trick on him. This man had said to him, 'If you give me and my household your word (that our lives will be spared), I will make you a catapult {Gr. manganikē} capable of taking this fortress.' Ibn Khālid gave him (his word) and gave orders for some long logs[151] to be brought; and so he made a catapult {Gr. manganikē} such as they had never seen before. They went up and installed it opposite the gateway {Lat. porta} /p. 74/ of the fortress. The men defending the fortress, trusting to its impregnability, let them get quite close. Ibn Khālid's men then drew back their catapult; a rock rose up in the air and hit the gate {Syr. tar^{c}ō̄} of the fortress. They then shot another rock and it fell a little short; then they shot a third rock, which fell shorter than the other two. The men above jeered and

---

149 i.e. a pact or {Ar. ṣulḥ}; cf. text No. 1, line 8.
150 Synaus or, more likely, Synnada?
151 {Syr. BLDʾ}: the word, unknown to the lexica, is translated *ad sensum*.

cried out, 'Pull your weight, Khālid's men, you are drawing badly'. They wasted no time in using their own catapult to propel a huge rock down onto Ibn Khālid's catapult from above, hitting it and wrecking it. In the process of rolling away, the boulder killed a large number of men.

Ibn Khālid went on from there and took the fortresses of Pessinus, Cius and Pergamum,[152] and also the city of Smyrna.

DISCUSSION

The successes of the Arabs are recorded very briefly, as if even the capture of Amorium and of Smyrna was insignificant. The anecdotal character of this chronicle contrasts strongly with the Jacobite chronicles of the seventh century, such as text No. 2 and text No. 5; but Sergius of Edessa, a scion of the Jacobite family of Rusafōyō, was one of the sources of Dionysius of Tel-Maḥrē and, from what we know of Dionysius (see Part Two, *introduction*), Sergius appears to have written a very colourful memoir.

Note the unusual number of Latin and Greek loan-words, probably due to the close relationship between the Maronites and the Byzantines at this date.

Like the priest Thomas, this text uses earthquakes as sign-posts of God's disapproval, first of the Jacobites, then of Mu^cāwiya. In the latter case the chronicler may have brought forward an event by one year to make it coincide with an earthquake.

---

[152] {Syr. PYRYMWS}, giving Y for the soft G of mediaeval Greek.

5. FRAGMENT OF THE CHARTS OF JAMES OF EDESSA, AD 691/2

INTRODUCTION

There was one Syrian writer in the seventh century who appeared to have a scientific approach to chronography: James of Edessa. His chronological charts made it possible to see at a glance at what interval from one another events occurred. Using this form it was more difficult, though still of course possible, to edit history selectively in order to produce a pattern to suit one's own doctrinal book. It is lucky indeed that the Syrians produced an expert in the science of chronology within two generations from the Hijra; and even luckier that James's correspondent, John of Litarba, was able to correct James's charts on the exact chronology of Muhammad. That this is due to John seems evident from two facts: the first evidence of the Syrians' knowledge that Muhammad reigned for ten years (less three months) is dated AD 724 (text No. 8), before John finished his chronicle in 726; and Dionysius of Tel-Mahrē, who quotes only James and John as specialists in this kind of chronography (Michael, p. 378, 10.21, scholion), does not follow James in giving Muhammad seven years.

The text is preserved in BL Add. 14,685, Xth or XIth century, f. 23, pp. 324-27, and edited in *CM* 3, pp. 261-330.

/p. 324/ [Chart I (on the recto)]

Total years	Of the Romans	Of the Persians	Of the Arabs
AJ (= AG)	Maurice	Chosroēs	-
277 (= 913)	20	12	-
No. 53 (of the Roman kings): Phocas, 7 years, 8 months			
278 (= 914)	1	13	-
279 (= 915)	2	14	-
280 (= 916)	3	15	-

Total years	Of the Romans	Of the Persians	Of the Arabs

OLYMPIAD 346:

Total years	Of the Romans	Of the Persians	Of the Arabs
281 (= 917)	4	16	-
282 (= 918)	5	17	-
283 (= 919)	6	18	-
284 (= 920)	7	19	-

OLYMPIAD 347:

Total years	Of the Romans	Of the Persians	Of the Arabs
285 (= 921)	8	20	-

No. 54 (of the Roman kings): Heraclius, 32 years /p. 325/

Total years	Of the Romans	Of the Persians	Of the Arabs
286 (= 922)	1	21	-
287 (= 923)	2	22	-
288 (= 924)	3	23	-

OLYMPIAD 348:

Total years	Of the Romans	Of the Persians	Of the Arabs
289 (= 925)	4	24	-
290 (= 926)	5	25	-
291 (= 927)	6	26	-
292 (= 928)	7	27	-

OLYMPIAD 349:

/p. 326/ [Chart 2 (on the verso)]

Total years	Of the Romans	Of the Persians	Of the Arabs
293 (= 929)	8	28	-
294 (= 930)	9	29	-
295 (= 931)	10	30	-
296 (= 932)	11	31	-

Muhammad, the first king of the Arabs, began to reign, 7 years

OLYMPIAD 350:

Total years	Of the Romans	Of the Persians	Of the Arabs
297 (= 933)	12	32	1
298 (= 934)	13	33	2
299 (= 935)	14	34	3
300 (= 936)	15	35	4

OLYMPIAD 351:

Total years	Of the Romans	Of the Persians	Of the Arabs
301 (= 937)	16	36	5
302 (= 938)	17	37	6 /p. 327/
303 (= 939)	18	38	7

No. 21 (of the Persian kings): Shīrōē, son of Chosroēs, 9 months

Total years	Of the Romans	Of the Persians	Of the Arabs
No. 2 of the Arabs: Abū Bakr, 2 years, 7 months			
304 (= 940)	19	1	1
No. 22 of the Persians: Ardashīr, son of Shīröē, 1 year, 10 months			
OLYMPIAD 352			
305 (= 941)	[20]	[1]	2
306 (= 942)	[21]	[2]	3

NOTICES TO THE RIGHT OF CHART 1:

/p. 324/ Bishop Severus of Edessa was stoned (to death).

The faithful in the east made Athanasius their archbishop (i.e. patriarch).

Paul became bishop of the faithful in Edessa.

As for the Chalcedonians they appointed for themselves Theodosius.

The bishops of the eastern region took flight to Egypt, and (the) monks and many people (went) with them, (to escape) from the Persian advance.

In Alexandria Cyrus began to reign as bishop of the Chalcedonians.

The [Un]ion of the Faithful, /p. 325/ [wh]ich (was cemented) in Alexandria.

The [Chalcedonian?] bishops are expelled [by] the Persians from [the east?] ... to take ... of the Romans ... the east. And there came ... [l]ittle ...

NOTICES TO THE LEFT OF CHART 1:

/p. 324/ [When] Maurice [is] killed [with] al[l] his [s]ons, the peace is broken between the Romans and the Persians.

Narseh revolted against Phocas and came to Edessa and seized it and shut himself up in it.

The Persians conquered the city of Dara.

The Persians took the Castle of Tūr ^cAbdīn.

The Persians took the city of Amida and Tella and Rhesaina.

AG 920. /p. 325/

The Romans kill Phocas and make Heracl[ius] their king.

The Persians conquered Edessa.

The Persians subjected all Syria, Phoenicia and Pa[lestine].

Heraclius promoted his son Constantine to (the rank of) [Augustus].

The Persians conquered [Egypt] and subjected [Libya].[153]

NOTICES TO THE RIGHT OF CHART 2:

/p. 326/ Isaiah is sent from Persian territory to be bishop in Edessa.

The faithful in Alexandria made Andronicus (their) bishop.

Benjamin began to reign as bishop of the faithful in Alexandria.

At the command of Chosroës, (the population of) Edessa was deported.

AJ 304 = AG 940

Cyrus launched an offensive against the faithful in Alexandria.

The faithful in the east made John their archbishop (i.e. patriarch). /p. 327/

The years of Shahrvarāz and of Bōrān and of Chosroës [and of] Pērōz and of Āzarmēdukht [and of Ho]rmizd are approximately two in all. (cf. text No. 13, § 44)

NOTICES TO THE LEFT OF CHART 2:

/p. 326/ [...]

and Muḥammad goes down on commercial business to the lands of Palestine and of the Arabias and of Phoenicia of the Tyrians.

There was a solar eclipse.

The Persians took captives and wasted all the land of the Romans up to Bithynia and (Western) Asia (Minor) and as far as the Sea of Pontus.

Beginning of the kingdom of the Arabs whom we call Ṭayyōyē, while Heraclius, king of the Romans, was having his eleventh year and while Chosroës, king of the Persians, was having his thirty-first year.

The Arabs began to carry out raids in the land of Palestine.

/p. 327/ The Persians killed Chos[roës] and made Shīrōē king for nine [months].

---

[153] For the supplements, cf. text No. 13, § 24 with note.

As many of the Edessenes as had surv[ived] returned from [captivity].
Heraclius made a pact with Shahrvarāz and it was agreed that the
Persians should ev[acuate Roman territo]ry and go b[ack to their
country.]
The Je[ws ...]

DISCUSSION

These notices correspond to the charts they are placed beside and are
in the correct separate sequences, but the placing opposite years in the
charts (if this was ever exact) has been lost in the process of manuscript
transmission. This is presumably why so many of the notices in the
chronicle of Michael, who incorporated all of James's work in his own,
begin: 'At the same time'.[154] At the end we have the beginning
of what must have been a notice about Heraclius's expulsion of the
Jews from the Byzantine empire (see Michael, p. 413, 11.4a, translated
in the note on text No. 13, § 51).

---

[154] The notes to text No. 13 contain passages from Michael's
Chronicle which supplement the narrative of that text. Some of these
notices must have been found by Michael in James's time-charts. The
style of the fragment quoted above gives us a certain criterion for
judging how much of Michael's material comes from James.

Like the other chroniclers, James is sparing with eclipses of the sun
(see Appendix II). In the period covered by our extract he records one
solar eclipse immediately after Muhammad's first appearance as a trader
in Syria and Phoenicia. The fact that the eclipse is listed opposite the
chart beginning with AD 618 under one or more previous events, with
one notice intervening after it before the beginning of the Islamic era
(dated by James AD 620/1), suggests that it was dated by James in AD
620. There was indeed a total eclipse on 2 September, 620, which
might have been visible as a partial one in Syria. There were also
eclipses in 604, 606, 613 and 616, during the last of which the apex of
the lunar cone-shadow passed right over northern Syria on 21 May.
All of these fall within the period covered by our fragment. James
does not appear to mention any of them, although those of 613 and 616
might have been recorded in the lacuna on p. 325. This is unlikely,
however, seeing that Michael does not have any eclipses for the dates
in question, while he claims to have incorporated all of James's notices
in his chronicle (see Part Two).

This claim of Michael's comes in a long scholion in appreciation of
James (Michael, p. 450), whose charts Michael continued from where
they left off in AG 1021 (AD 709/10), two years after James's death.
He did not find any continuation of them after this date. Clearly
Michael did not know the Nestorian Elijah of Nisibis, the greatest
exponent of the art of pure chronology among the Syrians (eleventh
century). Elijah tells us (f. 88a of BL Add. 7197, the sole surviving
and partly autograph manuscript) that James wrote his chronicle in AG
1003 (AD 691/2). That means that the last eighteen years must have
been added by a continuator, perhaps by a disciple of James's. The
fact that Elijah was unknown to Michael is eloquent testimony to the
independence of the West Syrian chronographical tradition; I underline
that here because it justifies the decision to concentrate in this book on
one of the two traditions.

Brooks ('The Chronological Canon') has warned that the fragments
translated here may belong to a concise edition of James's work. Be
that as it may, Abramowski is right to say that James must have

followed Eusebius's example in providing laconic notices, not reports or descriptions, let alone anecdotes. Accuracy (if we except the length of Muhammad's reign) may be a virtue of James, but it is tempered by the extreme selectivity his medium imposes. James dates the consecration of the patriarch Athanasius after AD 602 and after the stoning of Severus of Edessa, which other chroniclers date to the first years of the reign of Phocas (602-10). This supports the date AG 915 = AD 603, which is given by the priest Thomas (text No. 2, rubric 6, section 6), a source which has considerable authority, since it was composed about 640. My other reasons for rejecting Michael's date, AD 594, are given in Appendix I.

6. A LIST OF CALIPHS COMPOSED AFTER AD 705

INTRODUCTION

After James the Syrians start doing for the Arab caliphs what Greek chroniclers had been doing for centuries with other 'kings', namely making lists of them to establish how long each had reigned. These lists were useful for discussions of the past, because people could remember or easily transmit the knowledge in which year of which caliph's reign an event had occurred. In the list which follows here we read that it was followed by a list (now missing) of territorial conquests. This of course was also a useful instrument for debate, since it was necessary to be able to say which parts of the world had at a given time been under the caliph's control. Text No. 6 is preserved in BL Add. 17,193, IX century?, fol. 17a (AS 2, p. 11 of the Addenda).

Again a report giving information about the kingdom of the Arabs and how many kings they produced and how much land each of them held after his predecessor previous to his death.

Muhammad came upon the earth in 932 of Alexander son of Philip the Macedonian; he reigned for seven years.

After him Abū Bakr reigned for two years.

After him ^CUmar reigned for twelve years.

After him ^CUthmān reigned for twelve years.

They were without a leader during the war of Siffin for five and a half years.

After this Mu^Cāwiya reigned for twenty years.

After him Yazīd b. Mu^Cāwiya reigned for three and a half years.

(In margin: 'After Yazīd they were without a leader for one year').

After him ^CAbd al-Malik reigned for twenty-one years.

After him his son Walīd came to the throne in AG 1017, at the beginning of October.

DISCUSSION

The information about the territory governed by each successive caliph
was presumably compiled separately and has now been lost. We may
assume that the list was made between AD 705 and 715, while Walīd
was caliph. The text makes Muhammad 'come to the earth' in AG 932
= AD 620/1; but it is only if we count his seven years from the year
after that, AG 933, which actually was the year of the Hijra, that we
come, thanks to the marginal addition of one empty year after Yazīd,
to AG 1017 (933 + 84 = 1017). The seven years for Muhammad's
reign are presumably derived from James (see text No. 5). ᶜUmar
actually reigned for ten years (like Muhammad), not for twelve. The
caliphate of ᶜAlī is here described as a period of anarchy. The caliphs
between Yazīd and ᶜAbd al-Malik are ignored.

7. A CHRONICLE OF DISASTERS DATED AD 716

INTRODUCTION

A short notice, concerning various natural disasters which occurred between the years AD 712 and 716, is to be found in a manuscript dated AD 874, where it follows an account of the meeting between the Syrian Orthodox Patriarch, John I, Composer of Prayers (AD 632-48), and an unnamed emir, on 9 May of an unspecified year (see Reinink, 'Syriac apologetic literature'). The text (translated by S. P. Brock) helps to make the transition from the chronicles to the apocalyptic texts, No. 14 and No. 15. The author of the historical note would appear to have been a contemporary of the events he describes; his openness about the significance with which his beliefs endowed them is useful in understanding those texts in which we have to try to read between the lines. The text was edited, with a French translation, by Nau, 'Un colloque'.

Next, the various afflictions which came to the land in the year 1024 according to the numeration of Alexander, and [in the years] following:

When the kingdom of the Ishmaelites held sway, its control spread over the whole land, in the days of Walīd b. ͨAbd al-Malik b. Marwān who was reigning at that time, and the patriarch of the apostolic faith of the Orthodox, Elijah, was recognized throughout the whole land of Syria - he was from the monastery of Gubbō Barrōyō, called 'in the desert': in the year 1023 according to the reckoning of the Greeks, on 8 August, a sign was seen in the sky, in the shape of a long lance, wide at the upper tip. It was in the northern part of the sky, facing and inclined towards the southern part, and it appeared in the evening, about the second hour [of the night].

In the following year, 1024, from December to February, there occurred [as] a judgment a great plague in the land, and many people perished in it, mercilessly. During this aforesaid act of judgment, before it had yet come to an end, on 28 February of that same year, in the middle of the night before Tuesday, there occurred a great earthquake, so that houses in the villages, churches, and many large towns collapsed on top of the people living there, bringing death to them in various and many terrible ways: in some cases houses, villages and towns caved in; some people were suffocated, while others were crushed; many others were left alive, with their homes made into graves; others were rescued. All these things occurred in accordance with the just, inscrutable and astonishing judgments of God.

This in particular happened, the story and account reaching us by way of people who were actually involved and who saw it. In what is now called the 'western region', I mean the city of Antioch and the area of Seleucia (?) and KSYWT, and the whole coast, this earthquake lasted from 28 February until the year 1027, so that the inhabitants of the villages and towns everywhere spent all this time with any of their property that remained, camping out and living away from their homes, in the fields, on the hills, on threshing floors, in orchards, making themselves tents and shelters. Many others (fled), their work left under the open sky without protection, out of fear and terror at the terrible judgment that had been brought upon the land and all who live in it because of our sins and iniquities. While these two terrible afflictions were still running their course together without any relaxation or end, God sent to the land a third affliction, known as the bubonic plague; countless people were buried without pity in all sorts of places.

Alongside the aforementioned affliction God also sent upon the land a dearth of rain, and locusts that destroyed vineyards, sown fields and plants. All this was ordained and done by God for the providence of mankind.

Along with all this, on Saturday, 20 May,[155] there arose a violent gale, with the result that trees were uprooted and houses collapsed, while people were barely able to stand up on the ground. After this there was heavy hail in various regions, damaging vineyards and plants.

---

[155] The weekday shows that AD 713 is meant.

All these various frightful and intolerable afflictions, all occurring together, took place so that the survivors who had acted wickedly should be rebuked and repent in fear from their sins, trembling at what is written. Christ, too, the Word of God and the Father spoke to the stubborn and crass-hearted people of the Jews: 'Do you think that those upon whom the tower at Shiloh fell were more sinful than you? Indeed I tell you, that unless you repent, you shall perish as they did.'[156]

Again, in the year 1026, in February, the king Walīd died and his brother Sulaymān rose after him as king. He judged and enslaved the satraps, nobles and money-changers under him, plundering them, collecting great quantities of gold and silver from them. He assembled all the treasure of the Saracens, hoarding it and putting it into a single treasury in Jerusalem, the holy city, which people say is the centre of the earth.

Again, after all this, in April 1026, on the 27th, there was rain, or, rather, heavy and dreadful hail, killing quite a quantity of animals, drowning them in the torrents it created. In this human beings also perished, together with pack-animals such as camels and donkeys.

Again, on 20 April (10)27, on Monday,[157] there was dreadfully heavy hail, with the result that plants and seedlings, as well as a quantity of birds, were destroyed in it.

DISCUSSION

More clearly than most of the chronicles here collected, this text shows how history could be read as a catalogue of divine punishments or of the warnings given by God to mankind. There are passages in the New Testament (e.g. *Matthew*, chapter 24) which suggest that a time of

---

[156] *Luke* 13:4.
[157] 20 April, AD 716, was indeed a Monday.

concentrated and various disasters is a warning that the end of the world might be close. Our chronicle has been described as apocalyptic, both because of the apparent reminiscence of such passages and because of the presence in the narrative of a passage on the obstinacy of the Jews (Saint Paul had predicted that all Jews would become Christians before the end of the world). The reference to Jerusalem as the centre of the world is also reminiscent of apocalyptic literature. But there is nevertheless no clear indication that the author was representing his time as the end of the world.

Some Syrian contemporaries would appear to have looked earnestly for apocalyptic clues in what the Arabs did at Jerusalem. The chronicles make much of the prophetic simplicity of ^{C}Umar, contrasting his proud poverty with the fastidiousness of the Chalcedonian bishop Sophronius. It is true that he arrived there riding a camel, rather than a donkey; but he spent his spare time weaving palm-leaves to make fans, which is suggestive of the children waving palm-branches on the day of Jesus's entrance into Jerusalem.[158] He is supposed to have banished the Jews from the city; and his construction of a mosque on the site of the temple of Solomon is sometimes described as 'rebuilding' that temple.[159] When Mu^{C}āwiya went to Jerusalem he 'sat down on Golgotha',[160] a phrase strangely like that of Pseudo-Methodius XIV.2,[161] where he says that the king of the Greeks will climb up Golgotha. However, the author of text No. 7 must have been more preoccupied with the Dome of the Rock, which was completed by ^{C}Abd al-Malik only a few years previously, in 690/1.

---

[158] Text No. 13, §§ 74-5; cf. *John* 12:13.
[159] Text No. 13, § 86.
[160] Text No. 4, AG 971.
[161] Text No. 14, below.

8. A LIST OF CALIPHS TRANSLATED FROM AN ARABIC SOURCE OF AD 724

INTRODUCTION

This list was made on the last folio of the manuscript containing text No. 2, which is the reason why the chronicle of the priest Thomas goes under the misnomer of the *Chronicle of AD 724*. This text shows that the fact that Muhammad had reigned for ten years was known to Syriac chronography from at least AD 724. As was claimed in the comment introducing James of Edessa's charts, it is almost certain that we have John of Litarba to thank for putting the Syrians right on this matter. The present list, or one like it, might have been his source for this knowledge.

The Syriac text is preserved in BL Add. 14,643, VIIIth century, last folio, and edited in *CM* 2, p. 155 (the Arabic source is not extant):

A notice of the life of Muhammad, the Me[ssenge]r[162] of God, after he had entered his city and before he entered it three months, from his first year; and how long each king who subsequently arose over the Hagarenes[163] lived once they had come to power; and for how long there was dissension between them:

Three months before Muhammad came.

And Muhammad lived (another) ten years.

And Abū Bakr b. Abī Quhāfa, 2 years, 6 months.

And ᶜUmar b. al-Khattāb, 10 years, 3 months.

And ᶜUthmān b. ᶜAffān, 12 years.

And dissension following ᶜUthmān, 5 years, 4 months.

And Muᶜāwiya b. Abī Sufyān, 19 years, 2 months.

---

[162] {Ar. ra[sūl]}, with a Syriac ending; the word has been erased.
[163] {Syr. mᵉhaggᵉrōyē} related to {Ar. muhājirūn}. See S. Griffith, 'Free Will in Christian *Kalām*: Mōshē bar Kēphā against the teachings of the Muslims', *Le Muséon*, 100 (1987), pp. 151-4. [R.H.]

And Yazīd b. Mu^{c}āwiya, 3 years, 8 months.
And dissension following Yazīd, 9 months.
And Marwān b. al-Ḥakam, 9 months.
And ^{c}Abd al-Malik b. Marwān, 21 years, 1 month.
Walīd b. ^{c}Abd al-Malik, 9 years, 8 months.
Sulaymān b. ^{c}Abd al-Malik, 2 years, 9 months.
^{c}Umar b. ^{c}Abd al-^{c}Azīz, 2 years, 5 months.
Yazīd b. ^{c}Abd al-Malik, 4 years, 1 month and 2 days.
All this amounts to 104 years, 5 months and 2 days.

DISCUSSION

We may assume that the list was made between AD 724 and 743, during the reign of Hishām, probably shortly after the death of Yazīd in 724. But there is something wrong with the arithmetic: 104 years and 5 months after Muhammad's arrival in Medina (24 September, AD 622), brings us to the end of February, AD 727, three years after Yazīd's death. Yazīd is supposed to have died in AH 105, which suggests that this list is dealing in lunar months and years. AH 1 began, according to the Julian calendar, on 16 July. That is the best part of three lunar months before Muhammad's arrival in Medina on 24 September. Moreover, the introduction looks as if it were translated from an Arabic original intended for Muslims. {Syr. rasūlō d-allōhō} represents {Ar. rasūl Allāh}, without going so far as to equate Muhammad with the Christian Apostles by making him {Syr. sh^{e}līhō}; nevertheless, one later reader was scandalized and tried to rub this word out.

It may be significant that the scribe did not take the trouble to bring his reader up to date on the Byzantine empire, even to the extent of obtaining an up-to-date list of emperors since Heraclius, which would not have been difficult. This would mean that he either did not think of Byzantium as relevant to Syrian history any more, or else he no longer wished to continue the pretence that a return of Byzantine power in Syria was just around the corner.

9. EXTRACT FROM AN 'ACCOUNT OF THE GENERATIONS, RACES, AND YEARS, FROM ADAM DOWN TO THE PRESENT DAY', WRITTEN IN AD 775

Text preserved in BL Add. 14,683, Xth century, fol. 93a-102a (fol. 101a) = *CM* 3, pp. 337-49 (p. 348):

Tiberius: 6 years and 5 months;
Maurice: 27 years and 6 months;
Phocas: 8 years;
Heraclius: 24 years.
In 930 of Alexander (AG 930) Heraclius and the Romans entered Constantinople and Muhammad went forth from the south and entered the land and subdued it.[164]
The years of the Hagarenes[165] and the time when they entered Syria and took control, from the year 933 of Alexander, each by name, as follows:
Muḥammad: 10 years;
Abū Bakr: 1 year;
^cUmar: 12 years;
^cUthmān: 12 years;
No king: 5 years;
Mu^cāwiya: 20 years;
Yazīd, his son: 3 years;
No king: 9 months;
Marwān: 9 months;
^cAbd al-Malik: 21 years;
Walīd, his son: 9 years;

---

[164] It is unclear what event lies behind this comment. Text no. 11 has the Arabs 'enter the land' in 930; and in some Muslim sources, Muhammad is given 13 years at Medina which, if his death-date of 632=943 is to be kept, again makes 930 significant (see H. Lammens, 'L'Âge de Mahomet et la Chronologie de la Sîra', *Journal Asiatique*, ser. x, 17 [1911], p. 215). [R.H.]
[165] {Syr. m^ehagg^erōyē}.

Sulaymān: 2 years and 7 months;
ᶜUmar: 2 years and 7 months;
Yazīd: 4 years, 10 months and 10 days.

DISCUSSION

This list is full of oddities. Of the Byzantine emperors only Phocas reigned for a period approximately equivalent to that shown here. Of the Arab caliphs Abū Bakr is curtailed and ᶜUmar I is prolonged. Most of the odd months recorded in text No. 8 are omitted and where months or days are given they differ from the record in text No. 8. The total of regnal years and months brings us into the seventh month of AG 1037 (April, AD 726), at least two years after the death of Yazīd II, though here again (in spite of the mixture with Seleucid dates) we may possibly be dealing with lunar years.

The most striking aspect of the list is that it treats the Arab caliphs as 'successors' to Heraclius and his predecessors, glossing over the fact that Muhammad and Heraclius were contemporaries. It is almost as if the Syrian author was thinking in terms of a transference of legitimate authority ('translatio imperii') from the Romans to the Arabs.

10. EXTRACT FROM THE CHRONICLE OF ZUQNĪN (AD 775)

INTRODUCTION

After the puzzling list in text No. 9 we return to chronography of a more meaty kind. The following extract is from a writer whose chronicle was written in the year AD 775. The anonymous chronicler of Zuqnīn has been tentatively identified by Nau as the stylite Joshua.[166] Joshua was the scribe of the manuscript in which it is preserved; but both Tisserant and Chabot have declared that this manuscript is not the eighth-century autograph. If they are right, then Nau's identification is wrong, and *vice-versa*. We have seen that another Syrian stylite, John of Litarba, was engaged in chronography earlier in the eighth century. However, the author of our chronicle claims to 'have travelled to many places' (p. 146f), an exaggerated claim, it would seem, but one which implies at least a time when he was not on a pillar. Zuqnīn was the name of a monastery near Amida (Diyarbakir on the Tigris in the south-east of modern Turkey). There is a recent extended study of this chronicle by Witold Witakowski (*The Syriac Chronicle of Pseudo-Dionysius*), which concentrates on the tradition, intentions and historical vision of the author and makes no claim to establish 'source dependencies and the reliability of the information it offers'. Witakowski thinks the author was the steward of the monastery of Zuqnīn, because of his interest in food-prices. On the other hand, this characteristic might be due rather to the influence of one of his sources, the early sixth-century chronicle that has erroneously been attributed to Joshua the Stylite since the eighteenth century (see Palmer, 'Who Wrote the Chronicle of Joshua the Stylite?').

The text is preserved in Vatican Syriac MS 162, *Incerti auctoris chronicon anonymum pseudo-Dionysianum vulgo dictum*, II, ed. J.-B.

---

[166] In my review of Witakowski (see the Bibliography) I accepted this identification.

Chabot (*CSCO* 104, 1933). There is a French translation of this part by R. Hespel in vol. 507 of the same series, *Chronicon anonymum Pseudo-Dionysianum vulgo dictum* (Louvain, 1989). Our extract begins with the preface to the fourth part of the chronicle, the part composed by the eighth-century author, who in parts one to three has leaned very heavily on previous authors:[167]

/p. 147/ If anyone who reads this is of a mind to despise it, he should reflect that, just as affairs and doings of various kinds do not occur in one place alone, nor in a single kingdom, nor a single part of the world, so it is here also. If he has consulted a history which does not match this one, he should realize that not even the authors of former times agree with each other. One gives a low figure, another gives a high figure, this one writes on the Church, that one writes on other matters. It causes no injury to the discerning and the god-fearing if a date is one or two years out either way. It should be enough for the god-fearing to see the castigation of former generations and themselves to turn away from wickedness, lest they too should have to endure such castigation. Watch out, then, and fear thy God, lest I bring (*sic*) upon you this castigation!

I begin then with the year 898:

AG 898: Death of King Justinian. Beginning of the (joint) reign of Justinian IV (*sic*) and Tiberius Caesar.

AG 901: Death of this Justinian; the kingdom passed to Tiberius.

AG 902: Death of the holy (Peter), patriarch of Antioch. /p. 148/

AG 905: Death of Tiberius; his successor was Maurice: eight years.

AG 912: There was a great darkness at midday, and the stars came out and were visible as by night; they stayed for about three hours, then

---

[167] See Witakowski, 'Sources of Ps.-Dionysius'. Riad, *Studies in the Syriac Preface*, 100-2, treats one of this author's editorial intrusions (on p. 337 of the text), but not this, a passage with a better title to be regarded as a preface. The true preface of the chronicle (now fragmentary) was, however, where one would expect it: at the beginning.

that darkness was drawn back and normal daylight reappeared as before. The same year Maurice died. There reigned another Maurice and Theodosius his son for 12 years.

AG 914: Narseh, the general of the Persians, captured Edessa and entered it. He seized Severus, the bishop of the city, and stoned him to death.

AG 915: The holy Athanasius became patriarch of Antioch.

AG 916: Edessa was captured.[168]

AG 924: Maurice and Theodosius his son were killed; Phocas then reigned for eight years.

AG 928: King Phocas ordered that all the Jews under his rule should receive baptism; he sent the prefect {Gr. húparkhos} George to Jerusalem and all of Palestine to compel all the Jews to receive baptism. On arrival this man assembled all the Jews who were in Jerusalem and its vicinity; when their rabbis[169] had entered his presence he asked them: 'Are you the King's servants?' to which they replied 'Yes'. He went on: 'The Lord of the Earth bids you receive baptism.' They, however, were silent and did not give him any reply at all. 'Why do you not /p. 149/ answer?' he asked. One of the leaders amongst them, whose name was Jonah, replied, saying: 'Everything the Lord of the Earth commands we will do and assent to, but this particular command we cannot carry out, for the day of holy baptism has not yet arrived.' On hearing this the prefect became extremely angry; getting up he struck Jonah on the face and said: 'If you are servants, will you not obey your Lord?' Thereupon he gave orders that they be baptized. Thus he had them all baptized, whether they wanted it or not.[170]

At this time the following were famous: Jacob the Jew, Athanasius patriarch of Antioch, John, bishop of the (Christian) Arabs {Syr. ᶜarabōyē}, Simeon of Harrān and Cyriac of Amida.

---

[168] {Syr. etpattᵉhat}, which also means 'opened'; cf. {Ar. fataha}.
[169] Or 'their leaders' {Syr. rabbōnayhūn}.
[170] Compare the 'Doctrina Jacobi Nuper Baptizati', ed. Déroche, *TM*, 11 (1991).

AG 932: The Arabs conquered the land of Palestine right up to the river Euphrates, while the Romans fled, crossing over to the east of the Euphrates, and there (i.e. in Palestine) the Arabs established their rule. [...][171] as their first king a man of their own number whose name was Muhammad. This man they called a prophet as well, because he had turned them away from all sorts of cults and had told them that there is a single God, Maker of the Creation. He had also laid down laws for them, since they had been much addicted to the worship of demons and the cult of idols, especially the cult of trees. So, because he had shown them the one God and they had conquered the Romans in war under his (Muhammad's) direction[172] and he had also provided them with the kind of laws they desired, they called him Prophet and Messenger[173] of God. They are a very libidinous and carnal people, and any law framed for them (by) Muhammad or by some other God-fearing person which is not framed to appease their own desires they have ignored and set aside. But any law which fulfils their own wishes /p. 150/ and desires, even though it be framed by the most contemptible of their number, they pledge allegiance[174] to it and say, 'This was framed by the Prophet, the Messenger of God, and, what is more, he framed it at God's command.' So he governed them for seven years.

AG 933: Phocas, king of the Romans, died. Heraclius, his successor, reigned for 31 years.

AG 934: Cyriac, bishop of Amida, died; he was succeeded by Thomas.

AG 937: The stars of heaven fell in such a way that they all shot like

---

[171] I conjecture a lacuna here, caused perhaps by a scribe skipping the part between identical words {Syr. tayyōyē} in consecutive lines; the sense required is: 'And in the same year the Arabs enthroned over themselves ...'.

[172] {Syr. b^{e}yad m^{e}dabb^{e}rōnūteh}; this could also formally be read as 'by virtue of His [God's] purpose (cf. {Gr. oikonomía})'; but this seems unlikely.

[173] {Ar. rasūl}, with a Syriac ending; cf. text No. 8.

[174] {Syr. m^{e}bayy^{c}ūn}, on which compare the note on AG 967 below.

arrows towards the north. They provided the Romans with a dire
presage of defeat and of the conquest of their territory by the Arabs.
This in fact happened to them shortly afterwards and did not take
long.

AG 938: Muḥammad, king of the Arabs, or rather their prophet, died.
Abū Bakr ruled them for five years.

AG 940: Heraclius, king of the Romans, began to build the great
church of Amida.

AG 943: Abū Bakr, king of the Arabs, died. ᶜUmar, his successor,
ruled for twelve years.

AG 944: Heraclius, king of the Romans, went down to Edessa and the
battle of Gabitha {Ar. al-jābiya} took place; the Persians were routed
and left Mesopotamia.

AG 948: The Arabs crossed to northern Mesopotamia {Ar. al-jazīra}
and the Romans were routed. ᶜIyāḍ entered Edessa.

AG 952: The Arabs laid siege to /p. 151/ Dara and attacked it. A
great many people were slain on both sides, but especially among the
Arabs. In the end they made an agreement and they conquered the
city. From that moment onwards no human being was killed.

The same year they laid seige to Adavīn {Armenian: dwīn}, and
in this city a large number of people were killed, as many as 1200
of the Armenians.

AG 953: The Arabs captured Caesarea in Palestine.

AG 955: The patríkios Valentine, the Roman general, came to make
war on the Arabs, but he became afraid at their approach and ran
away, leaving behind all the money he had with him for the Arabs
to take.

The same year Procopius and Theodore marched out and invaded
Batnōn da-Sᵉrūgh in a great fury; they pillaged and plundered it,
taking as many captives as they wanted before returning to their own
territory.

Athanasius was succeeded as patriarch by his disciple, the holy John.
At this time the following were famous: the holy John patriarch of
Antioch, John, bishop of the (Christian) Arabs {Syr. ᶜarabōyē},
Simeon of Edessa, Matthew of Aleppo, from the holy monastery of

Zuqnīn, and Lord Thomas, bishop of Amida, from the same monastery.

AG 956: ^{c}Umar king of the Arabs died; his successor was ^{c}Uthmān, who reigned 12 years.

AG 960: Mu^{c}āwiya invaded Cyprus. In the very same year Aradus {Ar. arwād} was taken.

AG 961: The holy Lord John, patriarch of Antioch, died. He was entombed in Amida, in the holy temple of Lord Z^{ec}ūrō. In the /p. 152/ same year the holy Lord John, bishop of the (Christian) Arabs {Syr. ^{c}arabōyē} died; he was entombed in the shrine of Lord John the Baptist, in the same city of Amida. In the same year the holy Lord Simeon of Edessa also died, again in Amida; he was entombed in the shrine of Lord Z^{ec}ūrō.

AG 962: Theodore became patriarch of Antioch; in Edessa Cyriac[175] became (bishop).

AG 963: There was a battle between the Arabs and Romans at Tripolis.

AG 964: Habīb invaded northern Mesopotamia {Ar. al-jazīra} and Procopius came to make peace with the Arabs.

AG 965: Heraclius king of the Romans died, having reigned for 31 years. He was succeeded by Constantine II, for one year.

AG 966: Constantine died. He was succeeded by another Constantine (viz Constans II), for 27 (years).

AG 967: ^{c}Uthmān king of the Arabs died. People took sides in a civil war and the land was in turmoil; the Arab people were in confusion and there were many evils in the land. They committed a great deal of bloodshed amongst their own number, because they refused to submit to the authority of a single leader. Rather, every one of them made a bid for leadership, because each wanted himself to be the ruler. The general who was in the western region, whose name was Mu^{c}āwiya, wanted to reign; the westerners furthermore liked him,

---

[175] The name was added later in the margin.

pledged allegiance to him[176] and submitted to his authority. The eastern region and northern Mesopotamia {Ar. al-jazīra}, however, rejected this man and submitted to the authority of another general, called al-^{c}Abbās[177] and paid homage to him /p. 153/ as king. That is why, from this time on, there began to be wars and blood-letting between them. Not only did they shed each other's blood, they saturated the earth with each other's blood. The numerous battles they fought with each other in every region spanned a period of some five years, a time of dispute and conflict.

AG 968: The battle of Siffīn, between al-^{c}Abbās and Mu^{c}āwiya, took place. A great deal of blood was shed on both sides.

AG 973: Al-^{c}Abbās was killed by his nobles in a conspiracy; it was at the time of prayer on a Friday, while he was kneeling down in prayer. Mu^{c}āwiya then held rule by himself for 21 years, including those five years of civil war and turmoil between himself and al-^{c}Abbās.

AG 976: The holy Lord Theodore, the patriarch of Antioch, died. In his place there arose the holy Lord Severus Bar Mashqē.[178]

At this time Aaron, the Persian exegete, was famous.

AG 988: Mu^{c}āwiya, king of the Arabs, died. He was succeeded by

---

[176] {Syr. bayy^{ec}ū(h)y}: {Syr. bayya^c} means 'impeded', but this is the Arabic verb {Ar. ba^{c}a}, which in the third derived stem means 'make a contract', 'pay homage', 'acknowledge as leader', 'pledge allegiance'. It is used again a few lines further on. For this insight I am indebted to R. G. Khoury; Q. Twair showed me the glancing gesture of palm against palm which seals such a contract. Possibly this is what the Maronite chronicle (text No. 4) means by 'they proffered him their right hand'. If that is so it would suggest that the chronicle of Zuqnīn chose to use the Arabic word because it went together with this distinctively Arab gesture, which was somewhat awkward to describe in Syriac. Note that the Zuqnīn chronicler uses a Syriac phrase for the same relationship of allegiance on both occasions that he uses the Arabic word.

[177] The paternal uncle of Muhammad; we expect, of course, his son-in-law, ^{c}Alī b. Abī Tālib.

[178] In the margin: 'In Edessa, Lord James in place of Cyriac'.

Yazīd, for three and a half years.

AG 990: On Sunday 3 April, there was a great and violent earthquake in which Batnōn da-S^{e}rūgh collapsed, and the old church of Edessa, in which a great many people died.

AG 992: Yazīd, king of the Arabs, died and Marwān reigned for one year. In the same year Constantine, king of the Romans, also died. /p. 154/ He was succeeded by another Constantine, for 16 years.

AG 993: Marwān, king of the Arabs, died; he was succeeded by ^{c}Abd al-Malik who reigned for 21 (years). In his time people took sides in a civil war for nine years because the Arabs did not want to be subject to a single head. During these nine years they did not cease from wars and evils.

AG 994: The holy Lord Severus Bar Mashqē died. As a result of a dispute among the bishops the patriarchal see remained without a head for 5 years.

AG 999: The holy Athanasius became patriarch.

AG 1002: There was peace and the entire land submitted to the authority of ^{c}Abd al-Malik and he was established on the throne.

AG 1003: ^{c}Abd al-Malik made a census {Ar. ta^{c}dīl} among the Syrians, issuing strict orders that everyone should go to his own country and village and to his father's house, and that everyone should be registered by his own name and that of his father, together with his vineyard, olives, cattle, sons and everything that belonged to him. From this time the poll-tax {Ar. jizya} began to be levied on the skulls of adult males. From this all (sorts of) evils began to well up against the Christian nation. Previously rulers had levied the tax {Syr. maddātō} on land and not from adult males. From this point onwards the Sons of Hagar began to subject the Sons of Aram to Egyptian slavery. But it is our own fault: because we sinned, slaves have become our masters. This was the first assessment that the Arabs made. /p. 155/

AG 1014: ^{c}Abd al-Malik, king of the Arabs, died, having reigned 21 years, including those 9 years of civil war. In his stead reigned Walīd for 9 years.

AG 1015: The holy Athanasius, patriarch of Antioch, died; he was succeeded by the holy Lord Julian.

AG 1016: There was a great and virulent pestilence in the land, so devastating that the people were not equal to the task of burying their fellow human-beings. It was particularly strong in the region of S^{e}rūgh. During this plague 72 people from the monastery of Lord Shīlō died.

AG 1008: Constantine, king of the Romans, died. Justinian, his successor, reigned for 10 years.[179]

AG 1017: A synod gathered at the monastery of Lord Shīlō. Its principal members were the patriarch Julian, Thomas of Amida, and James of Edessa, Interpreter of the Scriptures. This holy Lord James, bishop of Edessa, was famous (at this time).

AG 1018: Justinian, king of the Romans, died. He was succeeded by Leontius who reigned for years.[180]

AG 1019: The holy Julian, patriarch of Antioch, died; he was succeeded by Elijah.

AG 1020: There was a census {Ar. ta^{c}dīl} which was based on[181] the first one, but it added much to the evils.

AG 1021: The holy Lord /p. 156/ James, bishop of Edessa, died; he was succeeded by Habīb.

At this time the holy Thomas, the Stylite of Tella, was famous.

AG 1022: Leontius, King of the Romans, died; he was succeeded by Tiberius Apsimar, (who reigned for) seven years.

AG 1023: Walīd, king of the Arabs, died; he was succeeded by Sulaymān, (who reigned for) two and a half years.

AG 1024: The holy Lord Thomas, bishop of Amida, died; he was succeeded by Lord Theodotus.

---

[179] On the anomalous position of this entry see Witakowski, *The Syriac Chronicle of Pseudo-Dionysius*, p. 123.

[180] Number missing.

[181] {Syr. ^{c}al}; this word is printed in Chabot's first edition, but not in the second.

After Apsimar, king of the Romans, Justinian ruled for six years; and after him Philippicus ruled for three years; and after him again Anastasius ruled for two years; and after him Theodosius Constantine ruled for one year, the king who was on the throne when Maslama invaded Roman territory.[182] The total period of these remaining kings of the Romans is twelve years. I have anticipated in writing this, because one (source) gives a low figure and another gives a high figure. As for the Arabs, they do not even count months like the Syrians, but only moons. Even the writers themselves mention as a rule only the periods when a king sat on the throne and omit the periods of anarchy, although I myself have noted them. Lest the mind of the reader be confused I have reconstructed the sequence of them in this way.

AG 1028: Maslama invaded the Roman empire. When a great and innumerable army of Arabs gathered and surged forwards to invade Roman territory, /p. 157/ all the regions of Asia and Cappadocia fled from them, as did the whole area from the sea and by the Black Mountain and Lebanon as far as Melitene and by the river Arsenias as far as Inner Armenia. All this territory had been graced by the habitations of a numerous population and thickly planted with vineyards and grain and every kind of gorgeous tree; but since that time it has been deserted and these regions have not been resettled.

When the (Roman) king saw that a great company had invaded (his empire) and that his own general, Leo, had made a pact with them, his heart beat faster and his hands began to shake. He abdicated from the kingdom and they relieved him of his crown; then he shaved his head. For there is a custom among them that if a king abdicates he shaves his head and stays at home; and from that time on he has nobody with him at all. This is what this king did. Even when the general Leo himself wrote to him, 'Pull yourself together! Do not be afraid!', he was obdurate and persisted resolutely in his abdication.

As for this Leo, he is a courageous, strong and warlike man;

---

[182] This is the next entry in the chronicle, under AG 1028.

moreover, he is by origin a Syrian from these borderlands. For his strength he was made a general. This man used his wisdom to spare (his) territory from drinking the blood of human beings by making a pact with Maslama to get him into Constantinople without a battle. He (Maslama), putting faith in his promise, did not attack anyone nor take any captives; instead, he made his way resolutely towards Constantinople, invaded (Europe) and attacked the City. As for Leo, once he had entered it /p. 158/ and had seen that the Romans' hands were shaking and that the King had abdicated, he encouraged the Romans, saying, 'Have no fear!' When they saw his courage and reflected how little confidence they could place in the man who had been their king, they took him and made him their king. As soon as he had clasped the imperial crown (upon his brow), he was invested with might and heroism. He reinforced the wall of the City itself and sent an army to cut off the routes by which supplies were brought to the (Arab) army from Syria. He also demolished the ships which formed the pontoon-bridge (over the Bosphorus), cutting it, so that the Arabs and their whole army were caught as in a prison. At this point Maslama ordered his men to plant a vineyard. They suffered cruelly from a terrible hunger, such that no bread was to be seen in the whole of their encampment; they actually consumed their own pack-animals and their horses.

When Maslama protested to Leo, 'Where is that oath which you swore to me in God's name, that you would enable me to enter Constantinople without a battle?', Leo replied soothingly, 'Wait a few more days. Give me time to obtain the consent of the chief men of the kingdom.' By such words the situation was prolonged, the Arabs waiting outside and the Romans inside, with no battles fought, for about three years.[183] The famine among the Arabs became so severe that they resorted to eating their sandals and even the flesh of dead men. They went so far as to attack each other, so that a man was afraid to walk alone. And while Maslama was protesting daily to Leo,

---

[183] Three months would be closer to the mark.

'Either give me what you promised, or I will make war!', they received the news that Sulaymān, the king of the Arabs, was dead, and that ᶜUmar ruled as his successor. This ᶜUmar, moreover, sent them a letter, /p. 159/ (telling them,) 'Leave that place, lest you and all that are with you should die of hunger!' When they received this letter, Maslama asked Leo to bring him into the City that he might have an interview with him. He entered it with thirty horsemen and toured it for three days, admiring the monuments of the kings; and afterwards they were dismissed and left the City with nothing accomplished.

When they reached a certain city called Tyana and the governor of that city saw how starved and pale and thin they were, he considered them of little significance and despatched a message to Leo, saying, 'Send me an army so that I can make a surprise attack on them!' Nevertheless, the ambush did not take them by surprise. When they discovered that there was an army on their heels, al-ᶜAbbās, one of the generals, a well-known man in the kingdom,[184] said to Maslama, 'Give me an army to go and confront them, before they arrive and surround us and send us up (?) from the earth; for then our end would be worse than all that has befallen us on this campaign.' He took a great army and went to meet them; and while they were advancing in loose formation and were not even as yet prepared for battle, not even knowing that an Arab army was on its way to meet them, al-ᶜAbbās descended onto an extensive grazing area, where the Romans were intending to pitch camp that day, and he positioned his whole army in hideouts and in ravines and on the reed-islands that are there. When the Romans arrived and descended into the meadowlands, neither knowing nor guessing what the Arabs had done, they pitched camp and even sent their animals out to graze, as an army usually does. /p. 160/ At this point the Arabs came up out of their ambushes and the crannies all around that meadow where they had lain hidden, obeying the signal on which they had agreed, and they descended upon them, surrounded

---

184 This is al-ᶜAbbās b. al-Walīd, son of the caliph Walīd I. Theophanes, p. 377 places the capture of Tyana in 709/10, Ṭabarī (II, pp. 1191-2) in Jumādā II, AH 88 (May 707). [R.H.]

them and slaughtered them all with the blades of their swords; and there were no survivors from that army, which had numbered about 60,000 men. Then the Arabs pillaged the dead and returned to their companions. A second army of Romans had gone out after the first; but when they heard what had happened to them, they turned back in fear. As for the Arabs, they took captives and plundered everything which they came across and so came out and arrived back in Syria.

DISCUSSION

The note which this author placed between AG 1024 and AG 1028 suggests a method by which we can repair the damaged chronology of this chronicle and so save some valuable information. First we must extract the lists of Byzantine and Arab rulers. That of the Byzantine rulers ended with Leo, like that used by text No. 12b (see the last entry in the extract below). The two texts can hardly have been identical, since the former was attached to a version of the invasion of AD 717-18 which is totally different from the account of that invasion in text No. 12b.[185] The Zuqnīn chronicler's list read as follows: Maurice: 8 years; Maurice and his son Theodosius: 12 years; Phocas: 8 years; Heraclius: 31 years; Constantine II (i.e. Constantine III): 1 year; Constantine III (i.e. Constans II): 27 years; Constantine (IV): 16 years; Justinian (i.e. Justinian II): 10 years; Leontius: ? years (actually 3); Tiberius (II) Apsimar: 7 years; Justinian (i.e. Justinian II, *bis*): 6 years; Philippicus: 3 years; Anastasius: 2 years; Theodosius (III) Constantine: 1 year (he actually reigned from AD 715-17), in whose time occurred an event dated AD 717; and, finally, Leo (III), whose reign began in AD 717. This list is likely to stem from the author of the description of the emir Maslama's campaign against Byzantium in 717-18, as can be inferred from the editorial intrusion which precedes it. The confusion between the Justinians shows that it was written in Syriac; and the panegyrical words applied to the emperor Leo III

---

[185] Most of the relevant portion of this text is lost.

suggest that it was written in his lifetime and by a Chalcedonian countryman of his from Germaniceia (Mar^cash) or another city on that border.[186]   By plotting the dates backwards from AD 717 the author could have got back (assuming the loss of Leontius's regnal years is due to a copyist) to AD 582 for the accession of Maurice, which is correct, although the distrubtion of years is not quite right. But he made the mistake of plotting the regnal years forwards from a false date for the death of Justinian, namely AD 586/7 (actually 565); in order to make matters a little better, he gives Justinian IV (*sic;* i.e. Justin II) three regnal years instead of thirteen. To Tiberius (II) he gives four, correctly. But the calculations are still eleven years out. His reason for beginning with 586/7 is unclear.

The list of Arab rulers ran as follows: Muhammad: 7 years; Abū Bakr: 5 years; ^cUmar (I): 12 years; Mu^cāwiya: 21 years, of which the first five were spent in civil war; Yazīd: 3 years and 6 months; Marwān: 1 year; ^cAbd al-Malik: 21 years, of which the first nine were spent in civil war; Walīd: 9 years; Sulaymān: 2 years and 6 months; ^cUmar (II) etc. As regards the caliph ^cAlī, the *Chronicle of Zuqnīn* is the first text in our collection explicitly to speak of Mu^cāwiya's rival as a king; but oddly it calls him al-^cAbbās.

We have only to look back at texts No. 5, 6, 8 and 9 to see how right the author was to say of his sources that 'one gives a low figure and another gives a high figure'. He also hints at one probable cause of this confusion by saying that the Arab months are lunar. The logical consequence of this observation would have been to equate one Arab year with twelve lunar months. But this is too difficult for our chronicler, who has little patience with chronology (he claims at the beginning of our extract that it distracts the reader from the moral, which is the essence of history): he equates the regnal years of the caliphs with whole solar years. He squares his figures approximately by giving to Mu^cāwiya the five years of 'anarchy' after ^cUthmān's

---

[186] Especially when we compare the Jacobite view of Leo III conveyed by text No. 12.

death and by occasionally making the year in which a caliph dies the
first regnal year of his successor. By such means he manages to land
Sulaymān's death in AD 715 (actually 717).

Another list which can be extracted is that of the Jacobite patriarchs.
For our period this ran as follows: Peter: died AD 590/1; Athanasius
(I): 603/4-c.643/4; John: c.643/4-649/50; Theodore: 650/1-664/5;
Severus: 664/5-682/3; vacancy: 5 years; Athanasius (II): 687/8-703/4;
Julian (II): 703/4-707/8; Elijah: consecrated in 707/8. This list omits
the patriarch Julian I, who succeeded Peter, but it has the priest
Thomas's dates for Peter's death and Athanasius I's consecration (see
Appendix I). The date for John's consecration is left vague and is
probably a guess. Theodore's and Severus's dates nearly coincide with
those adopted by Hage. But the five years' vacancy comes in the place
of Athanasius's reign, for which room then has to be found in the first
five years of Julian II's. The date for this Julian's death is that
generally accepted. It looks as if our writer overreached himself in the
matter on which he particularly prides himself: his care in recording the
periods of anarchy. He posited a period of anarchy in the Church
analogous to that which followed the caliph ͨUthmān's death in the
regnal sequence of the Arabs, assuming that his source did not mention
it because it was limited to regnal years. Somehow he read the year of
Athanasius II's death as that of his consecration. Perhaps the date he
gives for Julian's consecration is derived from a synchronization with
some ruler whom he dates too late.

Finally there are incomplete lists of the bishops of Edessa and Amida
which may be of some value.[187] As for the *floruits*, these may
perhaps be derived from hagiographical sources (this would explain
their extreme inexactitude).

Having extracted the lists of rulers, of patriarchs and of bishops and
the *floruits*, one is left with a relatively short list of notices, as follows:

---

[187] Theodotus, however, is dated wrongly; his reliable biographer (I
am editing the *Vita*) gives 698.

AD 603: Narseh occupies Edessa and stones bishop Severus.

AD 605: Edessa captured (*sc.* by forces loyal to Phocas).

AD 617: At the emperor's command the prefect George forcibly baptizes Jews in Jerusalem.

AD 621: The Arabs conquer Palestine.

AD 626: Shooting stars, a presage of Arab conquests in Asia Minor.

AD 629: Heraclius builds the cathedral at Amida.

AG 633: a) Heraclius goes to Edessa.

　　　　　b) The battle of Gabitha.

　　　　　c) The Persians leave Mesopotamia.

AD 637: The Arabs conquer Mesopotamia.

AD 641: The Arabs take Dara and Dwīn.

AD 642: The Arabs take Caesarea in Palestine.

AD 644: Two Byzantine campaigns in Syria, under Valentine and under Procopius and Theodore.

AD 649: Arab invasion of Cyprus, conquest of Arwād.

AD 652: Battle of Tripolis.

AD 653: Habīb invades Mesopotamia and Procopius makes peace with the Arabs.

AD 657: Battle of Siffīn.

AD 679: Earthquake destroys S^{e}rūgh and damages cathedral of Edessa.

AD 692: First Arab census in Mesopotamia.

AD 705: Plague in northern Mesopotamia.

AD 706: Synod of Shīlō Abbey.

AD 709: Second census.

AD 716/7: Arab invasion under Maslama and unsuccessful siege of Constantinople.

On the whole, if we except the group under AD 633 (the real dates are probably 629, 636 and 630, respectively), these dates are respectable. We may have considerable confidence in those emanating from the region where the chronicle was written, although 637 is two years before the complete conquest of Mesopotamia. That leaves only 617, 621, perhaps 626 (although this could have been a local record), 633b(!), 642, 644, 649, 652, 653. Many of these point to a source near the Mediterranean coast, perhaps in Phoenicia or Palestine (if our chronicler knew that his source lived in Palestine that would explain his assumption that the Caesarea conquered in 642 was the capital of that country, whereas it was probably Cappadocian Caesarea). The source in question may have been Chalcedonian, if it gave the names of lesser known Byzantine generals. It was probably written shortly after 653. We may be dealing with a concise version of the apparently contemporary source from which Dionysius of Tel-Mahrē's account of the events of 649 was derived (text no. 13, §§ 93-99).

The chronicler of Zuqnīn has been misunderstood on the question of his sources. Here is what he actually says (p. 146; I emend what I take to be a text corrupted by a scribe who was confused by the cognates here transliterated): 'From that point (AD 574) up to the present year (AD 775) [...] I have not found (supply: a history {Syr. makt^{e}bōnūtō}) concerning actions which is composed (emend {Syr. d-makt^{e}bōnūtō} to {Syr. d-makt^{e}bō}) on such solid foundations {Syr. hattī tōi t} as the former ones (by which he means the authorities he has named for the earlier period: Eusebius, Socrates, John of Ephesus).' (For an alternative translation, see Witakowski, *The Syriac Chronicle of Pseudo-Dionysius*, p. 125.) A little further on (p. 147) he says: 'Although I have travelled to many places, I have not found anything that was soundly {Syr. hattī tōi t} composed, but just a detail here and there, besides what I have heard from old men who were witnesses etc.'. What the author means is that there was no well-structured chronological framework (cf. Eusebius) or connected narrative history (cf. the Church historians) of the period available, only date-lists ('just a detail here and there').

A notice such as that for 679 may derive from James of Edessa, but it does not look as if our author had the full benefit of James; this makes it doubtful, in spite of his boast, that he travelled even as far as Edessa, though I suppose he went to Shīlō Abbey, which may have been to the south of Mardīn.[188] Apart from the western Syrian source and a selection from the annals of Edessa, he used the lists we have extracted and some sparse archive of Amidene events, perhaps entered on the fly-leaf of a Gospel Book at the monastery of Zuqnīn. In addition he used an Armenian record (or perhaps merely a tradition, brought to Amida by a merchant) from Dwīn, north of Lake Van, concerning the Arab conquest of that city. He also had access to a library (probably that of the monastery of Zuqnīn) containing Eusebius, Socrates, John of Ephesus and the so-called *Chronicle of Joshua the Stylite*, as well as other works which were tributaries to the 'main stream' {Syr. m^{e}lū^{ꝗ}ō} of his chronography.

---

[188] See Palmer, *Monk and Mason*, microfiche supplement 2, Gazetteer.

11. TWO INSCRIPTIONS ON A CHURCH AT EHNESH

INTRODUCTION

These inscriptions are published by me at greater length with a full commentary elsewhere.[189] The first inscription is chiselled on three limestone blocks on the south wall of the church of St Sergius at Ehnesh (Turkish: Gümüşgün) on the Euphrates, about 25 kilometres north of modern Nizip. It was first published badly, by J.-B. Chabot, then, competently, by H. Pognon, although the latter's translation is wrong on some important points. In the translation as published here no attention is paid to the line-divisions. The dates are Seleucid:

In the year 309 the Messiah came to the world[190]
and in the year 930 the Arabs came to the land [191]
and in the year 968 a battle occurred at Siffīn[192]
and in the year [9]95 a great famine occurred[193]
and in the year 1005 a darkness occurred[194]
and in the year 1088 the vale of Mar^cash entered into captivity in the territory of the Romans on account of our sins
and in the year 342, on 24 March, the 6th day, the Messiah suffered
and in the year 1091 the Commander of the Faithful, al-Mahdī,[195] came and entered as far as Gihon and he returned and ordered the churches to be torn down and the Banū Tanūkh to adopt Islam.

---

189 Palmer, 'The Messiah and the Mahdi'
190 cf. the introduction to text No. 2.
191 cf. text No. 9.
192 cf. text No. 10.
193 cf. text No. 13, § 124, note.
194 cf. text No. 13, § 130, note.
195 This word was added, on a separate course of stone, as an afterthought or was omitted to begin with by accident.

The second inscription had been noticed by Chabot and by Pognon, but the former printed the name of the prophet Mani as part of it, and treated it as part of the first inscription, whereas the latter dismissed it as a graffito. It is engraved on the east wall of the same building, one line horizontally, with a cross of five overlapping circles above it, and five lines vertically beneath it. The whole composition may imitate the form of the Byzantine *labarum*, a cross-shaped standard with pendents on either arm. It is badly eroded and the surface of the limestone has flaked, but it can still be seen that the letter-forms are identical with those of the first inscription. Both inscriptions were intricately decorated with non-functional drill-holes, which I have not seen elsewhere and which were not imitated by those who added graffiti to the inscriptions at Ehnesh.

Horizontal:
... wrote (third person masculine singular). [196]

Vertical:
1. Through Thee we shall beat down our enemies;
2. and for Thy Name's sake we shall trample on those that hate us. (Ps. 44:5, both halves.)
3. [Look] towards Him and hope on Him;
4. [and] your faces shall not blush with shame! (Ps. 34:6, both halves.)
5. They shall be [fat and con]tented. (Ps. 92:15, second half.) [197]

DISCUSSION

The East Wall Inscription contains verses associated with the power of the Cross for victory. Psalm 44 wrestles with the problem of the defeat

---

[196] Presumably this line contained the author's name and title.
[197] The restoration of this line is still in doubt.

of God's chosen people and calls on the Lord to support them in war against their enemies. Psalm 34 blesses the Lord for protecting the faithful against their enemies. Psalm 92 speaks of the wicked flourishing in the present, but doomed in eternity, and of the faithful being saved and rewarded. A long period of Muslim rule could lead Christian subjects of the Muslims to reinterpret this victory in terms of the mere survival of their religious community, or to interiorize it. But so long as the Christian Empire of Byzantium could hold its own in war with the Muslims, Christian subjects of the Muslims near the border with Byzantium must have wondered whether the victory of the Cross should be envisaged in literal, military terms.[198]

The obscurity of these inscriptions is surely intentional: the reader was meant to puzzle over them long and hard.[199] The East Wall Inscription not only requires a good knowledge of the psalter, but also makes the reader work at finding the correct order in which to read the symmetrically arranged lines (far-right, far-left, right-of-centre, left-of-centre, centre). Moreover, both visually and by the liturgical associations of the psalm-verses quoted, it suggests a connection with the 'victory of the Cross', which is surely intended to provoke thought in the context of al-Mahdī's reign. As for the South Wall Inscription, in which al-Mahdī is named, our survey of the Syriac chronographic genre gives us some important clues. The famine and the eclipse are there because they are signs of God's wrath. The suffering of Christ is recorded between two events of recent history to invest them with sacred significance.[200] The eight events recorded are somehow to

---

[198] See Palmer, 'De overwinning van het Kruis'.

[199] Baumstark, *Geschichte der syrischen Literatur*, p. 274, note 3, has no patience with the South Wall Inscription at all; compare his dismissive attitude to text No. 2 (quoted in a note on the introduction to that text), which, as he admits, has features in common with the chronographic inscription at Ehnesh.

[200] cf. the insertion of a reference to the Crucifixion in the sixth-century narrative of text No. 2, rubric 6, section 4, just after a passage about a military victory attributed to the power of the Cross.

be connected. The coming of the Messiah, of Muhammad ('the Arabs') and of al-Mahdī form a significant series, cutting 'diagonally' through the rest of history. The Battle of Siffīn, the famine and the eclipse form another. The 'entry' of the people of Marᶜash into slavery is parallel to the 'entry' of al-Mahdī ' as far as Gīhōn' and both stand in some relationship of meaning with 'our sins' and the suffering of the Messiah, which are placed between them. Oddly, the caliph is referred to not as 'king of the Arabs' (the usual Syriac term for him) but as 'Commander of the Faithful', a title which only Muslims could consistently accept and use. Yet the inscription was certainly not made by a Muslim, for it mentions the suffering of Christ. The inscription ends on a black note, with the destruction of churches and the forced conversion of a tribe of Jacobite Bedouin to Islam. Yet much of the language is reminiscent of chapter 24 of the *Gospel according to Matthew*, an apocalyptic prophecy. The irony implicit in the phrase 'Commander of the Faithful' may have been intended to suggest that al-Mahdī was the Antichrist.

12. EXTRACTS FROM THE CHRONICLES OF AD 819 AND AD 846

INTRODUCTION

This collection of short chronicles closes with a couple from the early ninth century. It is clear that one of them, that of AD 846, derived several of its notices on the seventh century from the other, which was written shortly after AD 819. This borrowing suggests that the chronicle of AD 846 was not simply built up of superimposed strata from chronicles up to *c.*728, *c.*746 and *c.*785 by a compiler who simply appended a brief list of rulers up to 846, as Brooks suggested ('The Sources of Theophanes and the Syriac Chroniclers'). The compiler disturbed the 'strata' to add certain notices from the chronicle of 819. These two chronicles can therefore conveniently be considered together.

N.B. Many entries in these two chronicles coincide nearly or completely; where the coincidence is complete I have italicized the text in the chronicle of AD 819 and have added '= X' to the date in the chronicle of AD 846 to avoid reduplicating the text. Where the coincidence is incomplete, I have used italics in both chronicles to indicate which words they have in common.

a) EXTRACT FROM THE CHRONICLE OF AD 819

Transmitted in a manuscript once kept at the village of Bēth S^{e}vīrīnō in Ṭūr ^{c}Abdīn, and possibly destroyed about AD 1915. On the basis of a transcript made by Barsawm, which may perhaps be preserved in France, it was published as *Chronicon anonymum ad annum Domini 819* pertinens, prefixed to *Anonymi auctoris chronicon ad annum Christi 1234 pertinens*, 1, ed. J.-B. Chabot (*CSCO* 81, 1920), pp. 3-22 (cf. Barsawm, *al-lu^{ᵓ}lu^ᵓ al-manthūr*, pp. 331-2). It clearly used the archives of the Abbey of Qartmīn, a monastery near Bēth S^{e}vīrīnō, as can be seen in our extract from the passages marked with an asterisk.

/p. 10/ AG 902: Lord Peter, the patriarch of Antioch, died; he was succeeded by his disciple Lord Julian and this man was succeeded by Lord Athanasius.

AG 910: Domitian, the Chalcedonian bishop, came and persecuted the faithful, forcing them to receive communion from him.

AG 912: There was darkness over the whole earth and the stars could be seen at midday.

The following year Narseh entered Edessa and held it; he stoned there the bishop Severus.

AG 916: The fortress of Tūr ^cAbdīn was subdued by the Persians and there was a great fight between them and the Arabs.*

AG 926: Lord Daniel ^cUzzōyō, abbot of Qartmīn, became metropolitan over four districts, Tella, Mardīn, Dara and Tūr ^cAbdīn.* /p. 11/

AG 932: Muhammad began to reign, the first king from the Arabs. He made the first sacrifice and caused the Arabs to eat it against their custom. From this point their enumeration of the years begins.

AG 938: (The population of) Edessa was deported and king Chosroēs was murdered by his son Shīrōē.

AG 942: There died the patriarch Athanasius and Muhammad, king of the Arabs; after him there reigned Abū Bakr for three years and three months.

AG 945: Abū Bakr died, and there reigned after him ^cUmar b. al-Khattāb, for 11 years. In the same year Lord Daniel ^cUzzōyō <died> and Lord Gabriel of Qustīn became bishop and abbot of Qartmīn after him. He it was who during his lifetime revived a dead man and performed other wonderful miracles.*

This year the Arabs entered Syria and took Damascus.

AG 947: The Romans and the Arabs fought a battle by the river Yarmūk[201] and the Romans were utterly defeated. ^cUmar took

---

[201] {Syr. yarmūkō}: this is the first place in the West-Syrian chronicles where this river is mentioned.

all the cities of Mesopotamia.   The first of their leaders to enter Edessa and Ḥarrān was Abū Badr; and the one who invaded Dara, Amida, Tella and Rhesaina was ᶜIyāḍ.

AG 954: Caesarea of Cappadocia was taken. And it was the last year ?...^{202}

And in the year nine ? ...

And in the following year, in the days of Lord Gabriel bishop of Dara and abbot of Qartmīn, the burial chamber of the monastery of Qartmīn was cleared out and 82 skulls^{203} were found there.* /p. 12/

AG 955: King ᶜUmar was killed by the Indian slave of one of the Quraysh, as he was praying in the mosque.^{204} After him ᶜUthmān b. ᶜAffān reigned eleven and a half years.

AG 960: Lord John, the Composer of Prayers, the patriarch, and Lord Simeon, bishop of Edessa, died.

AG 967: ᶜUthmān was killed and the Arabs were without a king for 3 years and 8 months.   The head of the Arabs in the west was Muᶜāwiya b. Abī Sufyān and the head of those in the east was ᶜAlī b. Abī Ṭālib.^{205}

AG 971: ᶜAlī was killed and Muᶜāwiya reigned for 20 years.   He made peace with the Romans and sent the general ᶜAbd al-Rahman (b. Khālid) to Roman territory, where he remained for two years.

AG 976: Lord Theodore, patriarch of Antioch, died.   The same year there was snow and a heavy frost; the olives and all kinds of plants generally were withered.

AG 990: There was a violent earthquake, destroying many settlements in Syria; *Batnōn da-Sᵉrūgh fell and was left in complete ruins and likewise one side of the old church of Edessa, on the Sunday of the*

---

^{202} With two intervening years before AG 955, this event should have been dated in AG 952; text No. 10 dates it to AG 953.

^{203} In the margin: 800 (*sc.* and two?).

^{204} Cf. text No. 13, § 87, where the slave is a Roman.

^{205} This is the first explicit reference to ᶜAlī's reign in a Syrian Orthodox chronicle.

Resurrection, *at the third hour.*

AG 991: Mu^cāwiya died and Yazīd his son reigned after him for 3 years and five *months.*

AG 994: Lord Severus Bar Mashqē, the patriarch, died. The same year Yazīd b. Mu^cāwiya died and Marwān b. al-Ḥakam reigned for a year and a half. /p. 13/

AG 996: Marwān died and ^cAbd al-Malik, his son, reigned after him for 21 years. He made peace with the Romans for three years, providing them with a daily tribute of 1000 dinars and an Arab horse.

AG 999: Lord Julian became the patriarch in the monastery of Lord Jacob of Cyrrhus and Lord George (became) bishop of the (Christian Arab) Tribes.

AG 1006: The Roman armies went out to the vale of Antioch. They were met by Dīnār b. Dīnār who massacred them and only a few of them escaped, returning to the Roman empire in disgrace. The same year the Romans rebelled against Justinian their king, cutting off his nose and banishing him. They brought Leontius out of prison and they made him their king.

AG 1008: The Arabs minted silver pieces {Syr. zūzē} and denarii without any images on them, only writing. In the following year ^cAṭiyya made a census of foreigners. Lord George, from the monastery of Lord Shīlō, became bishop of S^crūgh and the White Region.

AG 1010: The blessed Lord Thomas of Tella died. It was in his time that the catholic church of the Jacobites was built in Ḥarrān.

AG 1011: Lord George, the Stylite of Tar^cēl, died. There was a plague {Syr. šar^cūtō} in all the regions of Syria. This same year Lord Simeon, from the monastery of Qartmīn, was consecrated bishop of Ḥarrān.*

AG 1015: ^cAbd Allāh b. /p. 14/ *^cAbd al-Malik led a large army on an invasion, taking workmen with him, and rebuilt Mopsuestia in Cilicia.*

The same year the order went out that all pigs should be killed.

AG 1016: ^cAbd al-Malik died, and Walīd, his son, reigned after him for 9 years. He was a crafty man, who multiplied exactions and oppression more than all his predecessors. He completely wiped out all deserters (?)[206] *and bandits. He also built a city and named it ʿAyn Gērō.*[207] *The same year Shabīb the Harūrite, a renowned horseman and a mighty champion, was drowned in the Euphrates.*

AG 1018: Lord Simeon, bishop of Ḥarrān, built and completed the church of the Orthodox in Nisibis, all the necessary expenses and outlay for it being provided by the same bishop out of the monastery of Qartmīn. He built it three times over, for what he built during the day, the Nestorians and Jews tore down by night, with the result that the church was barely completed. *Lord Julian the patriarch consecrated it* along with Lord Simeon.*

At this time Lord James, the Interpreter of the Scriptures, was famous.

AG 1019: Lord Julian the patriarch and Lord James [the Interpreter] died.

AG 1020: Consecration of the patriarch Lord Elijah from the monastery of Gubbō Barrōyō.

AG 1021: Muhammad b. Marwān was deposed from (the governorship) of northern Mesopotamia {Ar. al-jazīra} and replaced by Maslama b. ʿAbd al-Malik, who gathered an army and invaded the Roman empire. He besieged the fortress of Ṭūranda and the cities of MWSYᵓ and MWSTYᵓ[208] *and he destroyed them and led all who were in them away as captives.* /p. 15/

AG 1022: Maslama sent officers throughout northern Mesopotamia {Ar. al-jazīra}, to measure lands, make a census of vineyards, plantations, livestock and people and hang leaden seals on everyone's neck.

---

[206] {Syr. līpūrē}; cf. chronicle of Michael, p. 437, 11.13a, translated in a footnote to text No. 13, § 119.

[207] The modern Majdal ʿAnjar.

[208] Phrygian Mosyna and Lydian Mostene, perhaps?

AG 1024: On Monday evening, 28 February, there was a violent[209] tremor in all the lands of Syria, which crushed and buried innumerable people. Moreover, there was a fatal epidemic and locusts without end.

AG 1026: King Walīd died and Sulaymān reigned after him for two and a half years.

AG 1027: Sulaymān mustered an army of soldiers and workmen and they set sail and encamped in Asia, capturing two cities, Sardis and Pergamum, as well as other fortresses. They killed many and took many captive. As for the Syrians who had been exiled there, he set them free in safety.

AG 1028: Once again Sulaymān mustered his armies, at the Meadow of Dābiq, and he sent a great army with ᶜUbayda as its general to the Roman empire. They invaded Thrace and encamped in that region. ᶜUbayda invaded the country of Bulgaria, but most of his army was destroyed by the Bulgars. Those who were left were oppressed by Leo, the sly king of the Romans,[210] to the point of having to eat the flesh and the dung of their horses. In that same year the fortress of Antigon (?) was taken by Dawūd, Sulaymān's son. Sulaymān himself died at the Meadow of Dābiq in September and ᶜUmar b. ᶜAbd al-ᶜAzīz b. Marwān reigned after him for two years and seven months, (a good man) and a king more merciful than [all those] who had preceded him.

b) SUPPLEMENTARY MATERIAL FROM THE CHRONICLE OF AD 846

The unique manuscript is BL Add. 14,642, fol. 1-36a, 40, 41, a palimpsest. The present text, dating from the first part of Xth century, is written on erased folia from five different Greek manuscripts. Edited as *Chronicon anonymum ad annum Christi 846 pertinens* in *CM* 2, pp.

---

[209] *Chron. 846* omits the word 'violent'.
[210] *Chron. 846* adds a short clause here.

157-238. See also Nau, 'Fragments'.

/p. 230/ [..] whom Phocas killed, r[eigned] after him; and Rhesaina was captured.

AG 912 and 914 = X (except that X seems to put Narseh's rebellion in 913).

AG 921: [Phocas, king of the Romans,] died. After him Hera[clius reigned] . . . and came . . . [several folios lost]

AG 992: [A synod met at Constantinople] and anathematized everyone who says there is one will and one energy in the incarnate Christ.[211] The monk Maximus was evidently victorious there. Justinian then reigned for 27 years and he upheld the synod which his father Constantine had assembled. He expelled from the church and prevented from celebrating (the Eucharist in) the sanctuary (all those /p. 231/ who did not accept) the dogma. The Romans rose up against him, cut off his nose and exiled him; they set up as king in his place the patríkios Leontius. After he had reigned for three years, they deposed him and made Apsimar king. After he had reigned for three years, Justinian returned from exile with a large army and killed all the leaders of the Romans. They rose up against him and killed him and his son Tiberius, making Philippicus king for one and a half (years). Because he wanted to gather a synod and re-establish the heresy of the Maronites, the Romans rose up against him, blinded him and made Anastasius king. When he had reigned for three years they deposed him and made Theodosius king. After two years they deposed him and made Leo king over them.

Previous to all this, in the time of Justinian and Constantine - in whose time the heresy of the Maronites came into being - *in AG 990* on 30 (read 3) April *on the Sunday* of Unleavened Bread *at the third hour, there was a great earthquake in which Batnōn da-Sᵉrūgh*

---

[211] {Syr. mᵉdabbᵉrōnūtō}, lit. 'the Dispensation' = {Gr. oikonomía}, but often used as a synonym for the life of Christ.

*collapsed, as well as the old church of Edessa. A great many people
died.*

AG 991: *Mu^cāwiya the king of the Arabs died. After him his son
Yazīd reigned for three years and six months.*

AG 994 = X

AG 995: Lord Athanasius became patriarch.

AG 996 = X; /p. 232/ 999 = X; 1006 = X (adding: These things we
have noted already, when we noted the names of the kings of the
Romans in sequence up to Leo).

AG 1008 = X; 1010 = X; 1015 = X; 1016 = X /p. 233/

*AG 1018: Lord Simeon, bishop of Ḥarrān, who was from the
monastery of Qartmīn, built and completed the church which is in
Nisibis. It was consecrated by Lord Julian the patriarch.* In the
same year a synod had been convoked in the abbey of Lord Shīlō
in the time of Lord Julian the patriarch.

At that time Abbās *Lord James, the Interpreter of the Scriptures, was
famous.* He was constrained by the synod to receive back the see [of
Edessa. After four months he set off to the west to collect his books
and he died at the monasterly of Tel ^cAddē.[212]

AG 1020: (for the first part, see above) And in the same year the
order went out that everyone should have his name written down by
going to his country and the home of his parents.

AG 1021 = X; 1022 = X;

AG 1024 = X; 1026 = X;

AG 1027 = X

AG 1028 = X, adding after 'Leo, the sly king of the Romans' the
following: 'whose name we have written above as the last in the list
of Roman emperors.'

---

[212] The supplement is an abbreviated version of the last part of
Michael, p. 446, 11.15c. In *Monk and Mason* I vocalized this name:
Tel ^cEda. The monastery has just been rebuilt by the Syrian Orthodox
Metropolitan of Aleppo.

DISCUSSION

On these two chronicles I have written in *Monk and Mason*, pp. 8-13. Here I wish to add the conjecture that the last compiler of the *Chronicle of AD 846* was Bishop David of Harrān, the twenty-sixth bishop consecrated by the patriarch John III (846-73). The reason for this conjecture is that the *Chronicle of 846* seems to have been written in Harrān, by someone with access to inside information from Tūr ᶜAbdīn, especially from the monastery of Qartmīn; and the manuscript from which Barsawm transcribed the *Chronicle of 819* was written by a certain Severus for his uncle David, bishop of Harrān and was certainly quite a bit older than AD 1095, before which date there is only one David, bishop of Harrān. Severus is unlikely to have been responsible himself for the compilation of the *Chronicle of 819*, because if he was, why did he not add anything after that date? But whoever composed it, he worked at the monastery of Qartmīn and this explains the Tūrᶜabdīnian elements in the *Chronicle of 846*. To sum up, David may have commissioned a copy of the Qartmīn chronicle in order to use it, together with other material in which the name of Harrān figured largely, to compile the *Chronicle of AD 846*.

The author of the *Chronicle of 819* had access to a brief continuous account of the caliphs to ᶜAbd Allāh al-Ma⁾mūn. The fact that the author of this account (the source of the *Chronicle of 846*) ignores the rebels Yazīd III and Ibrāhīm may mean that he wrote in the region of al-Jazīra (northern Mesopotamia), because these caliphs were not recognized there (*Chronicle of Zuqnīn, ad annum* AG 1055).

The *Chronicle of AD 846* gives a world history from Jacob to 846, whereby the surviving portion which contains original material begins in 679 with Byzantine, Arab and ecclesiastical history (679-728), then adds an ecclesiastical history with a few short notices relating to the caliphs from 737 to 784; and lastly a mere list of caliphs and patriarchs from 784-846 (Brooks, 'A Syriac Chronicle of the Year 846'). The part which betrays Harrānite authorship need have nothing to do with David, it is true; yet the geographical coincidence is suggestive. David might have found in Harrān the older chronicle and have copied it out, not only adding a brief supplement at the end, but also interpolating new material in the body of the chronicle from his Qartmīnite source, the *Chronicle of AD 819.*

It is striking that both chronicles regard Leo III as an untrustworthy monarch and that both give ᶜUmar II a very good character. Chalcedonian Byzantine policy sometimes involved the banishment of Jacobite Syrians to remote parts of the Byzantine empire, such as Asia (as here) or Thrace (see text No. 11 with my commentary in 'The Messiah and the Mahdi') and the Arabs treated such exiles well when they encountered them and set them free. This is acknowledged gratefully by text No. 12. Knowledge of such details helps us to understand the pro-Arab attitude of these chroniclers.

An Arab source close to Sharāhīl b. ᶜUbayda (for 'ᶜUbayda' in the text read 'Ibn ᶜUbayda') was probably used for the campaign of AD 717-18. The parallel account in text No. 13, §§ 159 and 160 shows that such a source could have considered the campaign against the Bulgars the main thing; but in any case, an Arab source might have suppressed the fact that the intention had been to take Constantinople. The references to the Meadow of Dābiq, a grassy plain to the north of Aleppo where many horses could gather to graze, could be paralleled from a Muslim writer; but I have never seen it in another Syriac source.

The *Chronicle of AD 819* differs from almost all the other texts in this book in that it ignores Heraclius altogether.

PART TWO

THE SECULAR HISTORY OF DIONYSIUS OF TEL-MAHRĒ

INTRODUCTION

The Church History and the Secular History

With the two chronicles of text No. 12 we have arrived in the ninth century and precisely in the lifetime of the greatest Syriac historian, Dionysius of Tel-Mahrē, who was Jacobite (or Syrian Orthodox) patriarch from AD 818 to 845. Little has survived of his work, except for what has been incorporated in other chronicles. Dionysius wrote, as we know from Michael I (Jacobite patriarch, AD 1166-99), a history of the period AD 582-842[213] in two parts {Syr. palgw^eōtō}, one devoted to the Church and one to the World, in that order.[214]

Michael does not mention the order of the two parts of Dionysius's history, but we know from § 44 in the extract translated below and from other cross-references that the Church History came first. The Syriac Chronicles of AD 1234 (divided into secular and ecclesiastical from the time of Constantine onwards: I, p. 137f) and of Gregory

---

[213] A. P. Diakonov, *Cyrus of Batnan* (St Petersburg, 1912), pp. 12-13, stated that the work of Cyrus of Batnae, which Dionysius continued, left off in the seventh century, perhaps as late as 631, presumably because he, like Chabot at one time, identified Cyrus with Gūryō. 'Gūryō wrote from Justinian to Heraclius, and about the entry of the Turks (*sic*) into the land of the Syrians, which happened in the time of Heraclius' (Michael, Preface to the *Chronicle*). However, Michael himself implicitly negates this identification in saying that Dionysius began with Maurice, because Dionysius's Preface expresses the intention to start where Cyrus left off. In his *Introduction*, p. xxxi, Chabot sensibly abandons the identification with Gūryō. The confusion of the two names is improbable.

[214] Michael, p. 544, 12.21, scholion, translated in full below; I shall refer to the second part sometimes as the 'World History' and sometimes as the 'Secular History'.

Barhebraeus (died AD 1286) began with the secular history. But the fact that all the internal references in the *Chronicle of AD 1234* to an already written ecclesiastical history come in Dionysius's period and that the only internal reference to a secular history comes in the late twelfth century (II, p. 338) makes it abundantly clear that this was an innovation of the latter period. That fact in itself is significant. In the chronicle of Michael the new priorities are already implicit in the lay-out of the page. The central column is given to secular history, so that natural disasters etc. (on the one side) and church history (on the other side) appeared as the 'handmaidens' of secular history.

It was methodologically unsound of Abramowski, therefore, in his great study of Dionysius, to put the two the other way around; though a churchman himself, he seems to have assumed that history proper is secular history, putting ecclesiastical history in a category of its own. Dionysius, by contrast, established a structural balance between the Church and the World, whereby Church history is both more important in itself and essential as a preparation for World history, to which, in a sense, it is the key. This applies to the overall philosophy of the work; for example, the point in the Church History from which Dionysius considers it useless to continue to mention the Chalcedonian bishops at Rome and at Constantinople, because they had become so corrupt through heresy, corresponds to the great caesura in the Secular History after the second Arab siege of Constantinople, where an excursus on the foundation of Constantinople and on Constantine the Great suggests, against the theological background, that the siege was allowed by God to show how low, in comparison with their divinely inspired origins, the Byzantines had sunk in His eyes.

It also applies to the work as a literary whole, the second part of which is written on the assumption that the first has been read and remembered. One example in our extract is the invasion of David the Armenian (text No. 13, §§ 79-82). The reader coming to this from the Church History will already know that the Syrian Orthodox patriarch Julian the Byzantine Soldier was so called because he and his father took part in the invasion of David the Armenian. After that, Julian, who had grown up in the army, was entrusted by his father to the monastery of Qēnneshrē, where he studied the Attic language and the art of writing. 'He loved the chaste life of monasticism and devoted himself to it, so that he was gifted with all kinds of virtue above the average. He surpassed everyone in his physical beauty, to such a degree that people said that, by the criterion of looks, he was worthy to be king' (Michael, p. 447, 11.16c). When one reads of the atrocities committed by David's men at Bēth Ma^{c}dē, one has difficulty imagining Julian among the torturers, hoard-hunters and rapists; it is satisfying, then, to discover that the Syrian contingent, under Titus, kept themselves aloof from all this and that Titus, by threatening to tell the Emperor, persuaded David to restrain his men. No doubt their innocence as well as their superior bravery guaranteed the survival of the Syrians and their safe arrival at Amida; at least, that was what Dionysius intended us to think. But in telling the story of David he never once referred (so far as we can tell) to the connection with the Patriarch Julian. The apologetic tone which would have resulted from that might have made the purpose of the story too obvious, awakening the suspicion that the role of Titus was invented to exculpate Julian.

Each of the two parts of Dionysius's history was divided into eight books, making sixteen books in all. Occasionally we learn from which book a quotation was taken; for our purposes here it is the second part, the Secular History, which is of primary interest, although in the footnotes some passages from the Church History are quoted to explain the World History. Abramowski thought that Books One and Two of the Secular History contained a survey of the whole period AD 582-842, after which, presumably, Dionysius would have gone back over it in more detail. But considering the length at which he told the episode of Īwannis Rusafōyō and his wife, which we know to have been in Book Two, this is unlikely; in any case the Syrians have never written history in that way, neither before nor after Dionysius.

What made Abramowski think this was the fact, mentioned by Michael, that Dionysius referred to the siege of Amorium (AD 838) in Book Two (Michael, p. 568, 14.1). In fact this is likely to have been a reference forward to the last book, like the reference he makes at the end of his account of the Rusafōyō family (§ 19 in the extract translated below) to the discovery of buried treasure in Edessa in AD 801/2. In the corresponding paragraph from Book Eight (Michael, p. 485, 12.4b), one can read how Dionysius picked this up again: 'In Book Two we related ...' Clearly he liked to bind his history together in this way. Besides, it was a good way of capturing the reader's attention at the beginning of a long and complex story which would cover 260 years.[215]   Dionysius used the same device when describing the Sixth Ecumenical Council of AD 680/1: 'And is it not so still today, 125 years after this wicked synod?' (Michael, p. 435, 11.12c). This passage, incidentally, shows that Dionysius was already writing his Church History in AD 805-6. The Rusafōyō episode belongs formally in the reign of Maurice, so one would expect it to come in Book One, because Michael says that Dionysius began with the reign of Maurice (582-602). Yet we know that it was built into the narrative of Book Two as a 'flash-back' from the year in which Edessa fell to Chosroēs. This is further evidence of careful composition and interweaving.

The second Arab siege of Constantinople and the accompanying excursus on the foundation of Constantinople, with which our extract ends, seem to form together a major caesura in the Secular History. As far as one can tell, Dionysius introduced no other excursus into the history of the period before his own and no other description of a city so discursive and so complete. I think it likely that this description closed the fourth book and so marked the middle of the Secular History. If that is right, then the period covered by the present collection, AD 582-718, which is 136 years, filled four books of Dionysius's history. From Maurice's accession to the Persian conquest of Edessa, AD 582-609, is 27 years. That is the maximum period that can have been covered by Book One, because the 'flash-back' following the conquest of Edessa was in Book Two (probably at the beginning, because it is so readable and involves such a jump in time). That means that books 2-4, on my theory, covered 109 years, an average of

---

[215] It is interesting to note that the Syrians could call this period 'six generations' {Syr. dōrē} (Michael, p. 409, 11.3b).

just over 36 years per book.[216] The theory would be strengthened if possible major caesurae could be found at the appropiate intervals in the narrative, about AD 645 and about AD 681. The dates suggest, to begin with, that there may have been a certain symmetry with the Church History, since the first corresponds to the point at which Dionysius explained the origin of the 'heresy' of Maximus and the second is the date of the Sixth Ecumenical Council. A caesura at the former date may in some way help to explain the intrusion of ecclesiastical history into the secular part of the *Chronicle of AD 1234* at this point (§§ 91 and 92). In the light of the interrelatedness between the ecclesiastical and secular parts, Book Three may have ended with Constantine's deposition of his two brothers in September of AD 681, because of the parallel drawn between the trinity of emperors and the Trinity in heaven (§§ 122 and 123).[217]

Michael adds that the books were subdivided into chapters; these chapters could probably be reconstructed. For instance, the Rusafōyō episode in §§ 15-19 was certainly a chapter, so were 25-29, on Muhammad and the origins of Islam; therefore the narrative connecting these two chapters must have formed a chapter, too. From these three examples we can get an idea of what Dionysius's chapters were like and this should help us to make correct decisions even when the content allows of alternative divisions. Unfortunately we cannot be sure how much of the text has been omitted in the course of being incorporated in other chronicles; nor can we be sure that the chapters were of approximately equal length.

---

[216] That is longer than Book One, but Book One may have included a long introduction.

[217] The substitution of an unworthy son for the two equal brothers might be seen as an allegory of Arian theology. Text No. 2 seemed to assume that Chalcedon was a different manifestation of the old Arian tendency in the Church. Compare Dionysius's comment on the development of Byzantine theology in the aftermath of the Fourth and the Sixth Councils (see the second extended quotation below, from Michael 11.18c): 'instead of one Christ they confessed Him as two.'

The author's programme

Our main source for Dionysius's History is the *Chronicle of AD 1234*, which is translated below, beginning with the reign of Maurice; supplementary material from the *Chronicle of Michael I* is added in footnotes appended to the several paragraphs of this translation. The first of these two chronicles clearly retains the narrative structure of the original; yet there are places where Michael, who usually excerpts and abbreviates Dionysius, has clearly copied him out in full and sometimes it seems that the *Chronicle of AD 1234* has the shorter version of a particular passage. Moreover, it is Michael who preserves the position of Dionysius's excursus on the foundation of Constantinople, whereas the *Chronicle of AD 1234* transports it back to the narrative concerning Constantine the Great.

One of Michael's extracts from Dionysius is the Preface to his History. This is essential for the understanding of his work. It is only paraphrased and briefly commented on by Riad in her *Studies in the Syriac Preface*, pp. 107-9, and so is translated here in full (Michael, p. 378, 10.21, scholion):

'Since your soul is set insatiably and with an unbridled desire upon the accumulation of wisdom, you, who are dearer than any to me, my spiritual son Īwannis, metropolitan of Dara; and since divine learning is not enough for you, nor the dogmas of Orthodoxy, in which you have been trained from the softness of your fingernails until the silvering of your hair, so that one might say that you are like a river, causing the water of life to flow and rejoicing the City of God, which is the holy Church; unerring as you are where the Truth is concerned, I perceive you are so enflamed with the desire to accumulate wisdom, that you must also muse upon the texts containing narratives of the events that have occurred in the world. But should you not be taking the trouble necessary to supply your own entertainment? Should you not gather the provender with which to still your own hunger, instead of burdening my feeble shoulders with this load, never pausing to consider that my white head is quite impotent at times in such matters as this and that my wretched soul is set about with worries, those ecclesiastical anxieties which do not allow me to breathe in the air with enjoyment, and that I do not even have quiet and repose in one place, but must go from village to village and travel from country to country, and the long and arduous journeys and the standings and the grovellings at the gates of the powerful and the contempt and the insults which go with all that? Yet, because I have been coerced by the force of your zest to remember that I, too, if the truth be told, used to feel that urge, so much so that I once communicated to many people my enthusiasm to see what has happened and is happening in our times written down for the generations to come - but they declined to do so - I have at last made up my mind to shoulder this burden also, however far it exceeds my paltry strength, and so, casting my hope upon God, I set about beginning my causal exposition.[218]

'Whereas wise men have written about the earliest times, from the beginning of the Creation until the time of Constantine, the believing King, and have told about the fashioning of the world and the making of the creatures and the succession of generations since Adam and the number of their years and about the kings who have ruled and the size of their territories, yet their writings are not termed "ecclesiastical histories", but "chronographies", that is time-writings {Syr. makt^{e}vōnūt zavnē}, such as those made by Josephus, Andronicus, Africanus, Annianus, George of Raggath, John of Antioch[219] and finally Eusebius, son of Pamphilus.

'The first to write ecclesiastical history, on the other hand, was the same Eusebius, who was followed by Socrates, Sozomen,[220] Theodoret, Zechariah,[221] Elijah,[222] John of Asia[223] and, last of

---

[218] Dionysius uses the Greek word 'pragmateia', which has had since Polybius, 1.1,4 and 1.3,1, the special sense of a grand scheme for making sense of the past.

[219] Malalas, not the other John of Antioch.

[220] The manuscript has 'Zosimus'.

[221] Ps.-Zacharias Rhetor?

all, the priest Cyrus of Batnae.

'Other men, however, charted the succession of the years, I mean James of Edessa and John, the Stylite of Litarba.

'Narratives resembling ecclesiastical history have been written by Daniel, son of Moses of Tūr ᶜAbdīn, another John, son of Samuel, of the western region (of Syria), a certain Theophilus, and Theodore, metropolitan of Edessa.[224] But those whom we have just mentioned made their narratives in a compartmentalized and fragmentary way, without preserving either chronological exactitude or the interrelatedness of events. One of these writers was Theophilus of Edessa, a Chalcedonian who regarded it as his birthright to loathe the Orthodox. His presentation of all events which involved one of our number is fraudulent.

'So, while we shall follow traditional practice and start where Cyrus of Batnae left off, we shall (start at the same point in World History and) take from the writings of this man (*sc.* Theophilus) some details here and there from those parts which are reliable and do not deviate from the truth.'

I suspect that the latter part of the Preface has been abridged by Michael or by his copyists, since it is neither clear nor rounded off, both of which would be surprising in such an accomplished stylist as Dionysius. That makes it all the more important to understand him correctly. Firstly, he is not explicitly listing here his sources, although some of the writers may happen also to be sources for his period; his purpose here is to review the genres of historiography, whereby he

---

222 Conceivably the biographer of John of Tella, although Chabot reads this name as a scribal corruption of Zechariah's Syriac epithet, *mlīlō,* 'the Eloquent'; the Arabic translation, however, has both this epithet and the name Elijah.

223 Or 'of Ephesus,' as he is usually known.

224 This was Dionysius's brother. Daniel, with whom the list begins, was his maternal grandfather: see Michael, p. 449, 11.16b, reading 'Moses' for 'Samuel'.

seems to be resisting a tendency to identify narrative history as 'ecclesiastical', regardless of the fact that the contents may be secular. This is due to the example of Eusebius, whose *Chronicle* resembled that of James and was not a connected narrative, whereas his *History of the Church* had a grand scheme ('*pragmateia*'), like the *History* of Polybius, and used a connected narrative to make sense of the past.

Daniel, son of Moses of Ṭūr ͨAbdīn was quoted by Dionysius as the source for at least one anecdote about secular history, namely the story of Athanasius Bar Gūmōyē, the seventh-century Edessene tycoon (see text No. 13, below, §§ 132-4). This shows what Dionysius must mean by 'narratives resembling ecclesiastical history', *viz* prose narratives, telling a story, as opposed to staccato bulletins. It is this recently developed genre of discursive, but fragmented memoirs that Dionysius wanted to use as a precedent for writing secular history in a narrative style; but he considered a clear chronological framework essential and demanded also that not only spotlighted events, but the connections between those events, be treated in such a history. That he succeeded in this original attempt to write an almost modern kind of history, we can tell from the extracts below.

There is another editorial passage (Michael, pp. 452-4, 11.18, inner column) describing Dionysius's method and aims. It was probably placed at the end of the first half of the Church History or at the beginning of the second.

'Up to this time one may find in our country in the books[225] of this (Syriac) literature of ours the names of the archbishops of the four chief sees, Rome, Alexandria, Constantinople and Antioch, /p. 453/ those of the Roman and the Greek nation and tongue, respectively, even though they were Chalcedonians from the time of the Synod of Chalcedon. But from this time onwards the names of the Chalcedonian incumbents or archbishops at Rome and at

---

[225] The manuscript printed by Chabot has the singular.

Constantinople are not mentioned anywhere in our literature,[226] only those Orthodox archbishops of our people and of the Copts at the two sees of Alexandria and of Antioch. This seems to be for two reasons. One is that the Arab empire has obtained control of Syria and of Egypt, the regions where our people and that of the Copts reside, so that they have had neither opportunity nor need to interest themselves in the Chalcedonians at all, seeing that they hate and persecute the Orthodox. The other is that the Chalcedonians have become even more corrupt under the influence of the additional heresies which they have acquired, as I have shown (above) and as I shall show again (hereafter).

'When the holy fathers who have been the writers in our Church saw that they (the Chalcedonians) had been corrupted not only by the doctrine of two natures, but also by that of two volitions and energic substances and forms and properties, and that instead of one Christ /p. 454/ they confessed Him as two, they turned right away from them for this reason and did not even use their language and their literature as in former times, nor did any Orthodox scholars remain in their regions. All this explains the fact that the names of their bishops are not included in any of our books, except here and there in a piecemeal fashion, where it was absolutely indispensable in some way.

'With God's help, therefore, I, too, shall collect from their (i.e. the Greek Chalcedonians') writings whatever items of information are well attested and these will be translated[227] with great care and accuracy from those books of theirs which can be found in our country. For, weak as I am, my aim is as follows: To collect with the help of God whatever information I can find and to put it all in

---

[226] The manuscript has 'my', which would involve translating the following word as 'book' rather than 'literature'; in any case, Syriac authors normally use the first person plural in referring to their own books.

[227] The passive is perhaps used because Dionysius would have the Greek translated by a good Greek scholar, such as his brother, Theodore, the metropolitan of Edessa.

this book in good order, selecting the most reliable version of events attested by the majority of trustworthy witnesses and writing them down here in the correct sequence.'

Sources used by Dionysius

As Dionysius states, in the passage just quoted, he made some use of Byzantine Greek sources. We know from Michael, p. 489, 12.5a that Dionysius referred to a Chalcedonian writer who 'levelled accusations against'[228] Nicephorus I (802-11). The author who best fits this description is George Syncellus, a Palestinian monk who moved to Constantinople around 780 and wrote history there, completing a chronicle from Creation to Diocletian and leaving extensive notes for a continuation up to his own time. These provisional materials were used by the Byzantine chronicler Theophanes, as he tells us in his Preface.[229] It seems possible that Dionysius may have known some writings of George on the seventh century, without having had recourse to Theophanes.[230]

This possibility suggests a new perspective on the old question of the historical information shared by the contemporary Greek and Syriac chronicles of Theophanes and Dionysius.[231] This question is

---

[228] {Syr. qatreg}; no further information about the writer in question can be extracted from this passage.

[229] Theophanes 'shows a pathological hatred' of Nicephorus I, 'whom he denigrates more than any previous ruler, except perhaps Constantine V'. But Mango shows that George Syncellus is much more likely to have been the one who hated Nicephorus than Theophanes himself (Mango, 'Who wrote the Chronicle of Theophanes?', pp. 14-16).

[230] In his Preface, Dionysius names an otherwise unknown chronographer called George *ragtōyō* ('of Raggath'?), who stood in the tradition of Africanus. George Syncellus definitely stood in that tradition (he is the major source for the Greek text of Africanus's chronicle). There is a place in Palestine, the country of his birth, called Raggath/Rakkat.

[231] For many years the authoritative statement of this problem was Brooks, 'The Sources of Theophanes and the Syriac Chroniclers'.

further complicated by the fact that Agapius, a later Chalcedonian chronicler writing in Arabic, also shares some information with each of the other chroniclers. Agapius advertises Theophilus of Edessa as a source, a Chalcedonian writer whom Dionysius had also acknowledged (in his Preface), though the latter claims to have used him with discrimination.[232]

[It is difficult to come to any definite conclusion about the common source of Dionysius, Theophanes and Agapius, so here I simply give a number of observations which I have arrived at from a comparison of the three works yields the following observations:

(i)   it will be clear from the frequency with which Theophanes (= T) and Agapius (= A) are underlined in the notes (indicating similar wording) that these two writers share a common source (= CS) with Dionysius (= D), beginning with Muhammad (§ 28) and stopping (so far as we can tell) at the year 751 (see Hoyland, 'Arabic, Syriac and Greek historiography');[233]

(ii)   furthermore, it will be noticed that a number of correspondences between T and A are found at places where the Chronicle of AD 1234 (= C) is supplemented from that of Michael (= M; e.g. § 118);

(iii)   likewise, M at times abbreviates an account which C narrates in detail (e.g. §§ 93-8);

(iv)   from (ii) and (iii) we may conclude that both C and M at times condense D, whose Secular History must therefore have been more detailed than either;

---

[232] The following paragraphs are based on Robert Hoyland's research into the interrelationship of Theophanes, Dionysius and Agapius.

[233] A and D do share a few notices before the arrival of Muhammad. It is possible that these are from CS and are omitted by T because his own sources are very full at this point. More probably, however, A and D have another source in common here. A at first has notices up to AD 668, becoming very brief towards the end. Then he breaks off and gives a computation of the years until his own time, continuing: 'We shall now relate the years of the Arabs' (p. 196). He starts again with Muhammad and repeats many of the notices he had given before, usually in greater detail. The implication is that he has switched to a different source. This might be CS.

(v)   T usually has the most compressed account, while A and D are more extended and often so close to each other as to show textual correspondence (D is generally longer than A, whereas A is only occasionally longer than D);

(vi)   even when relating the same episode, T, D and A will often omit elements included by one or more of the others;

(vii)   from (v) and (vi) we may deduce that T, D and A are all excerpting from CS, which was more comprehensive than any one of them;

(viii)   however, from the following three sub-points it is clear that T, A and D also have sources which they do not share with each other:

a)   T draws chiefly on Greek sources and only has recourse to CS when the former fail (e.g. for the reign of Constans II, 641-68)

b)   A draws more heavily on CS, but again has sources of his own (cf. his account of the first Arab civil war, which has a very different focus from that of D and slightly conflicts with him)

c)   D adduces a number of additional sources, Syriac, Arabic and Greek;[234]

(ix)   in the midst of his account of the ᶜAbbāsid Revolution, A cites Theophilus of Edessa, the Chalcedonian also mentioned by D, as a source, without, however, making it clear whether he also uses him at other points in his history;

(x)   the conclusion has been drawn from (ix) that Theophilus himself should perhaps be identified as CS (see Conrad, 'The Conquest of Arwad'[235]);

(xi)   Theophilus was astrologer to the caliph al-Mahdī (AD 775-85), so he might be expected to have been familiar with Arabic, and yet CS, as reconstructed from T, A and D, betrays no knowledge of Arabic sources;

---

[234] On these, see Andrew Palmer's continuation below.

[235] The same author's 'Theophanes' is also relevant to the question of the common source.

(xii)   while (xi) is not a crucial objection to Conrad's thesis,[236] it nevertheless encourages us to consider alternative identifications, such as CS = George Syncellus, though in that case one would have expected some correspondence between T and D for the period 750-80.[237]]

From the pattern of local coverage and significant gaps in the minor chronicles (see Chronological Table 4), one may infer that there was a series of Syriac chroniclers writing in the period treated in this book. Some of these are likely to have been used by Theophilus of Edessa, but there is no reason to think that Dionysius would not have consulted them independently.   Text No. 13, §§ 32-57, for example, makes it likely that Dionysius knew and used the priest Thomas (text No. 2). He follows his chronology faithfully, reporting the solar eclipse dated by Thomas to AD 627, even though the eclipse, as we know from the calculations of modern astronomers, was not visible in Syria, only in China (§ 32).   And he records the minor raid on the monasteries above Rhesaina, which was a major event for Thomas, because it involved the killing of his own brother.   However, Dionysius is a writer who selects and combines material from several sources; we should not be surprised that he does not include everything from the chronicle of Thomas, nor agree with him on every point.

A neglected passage, § 32, with the supplement in the note, makes it clear that Sergius, son of Īwannis Rusafōyō, was used by Dionysius as a source.[238]   The writer uses the first person plural: 'the governor [...] decided not to have us deported all at once'.   §§ 13-19, 31-32, and 40-41, with the supplements in the notes, give us a good idea of the memoir written by this Sergius, who is not mentioned in

---

[236] Theophilus may have written his history before his employment at the Muslim court, which would explain why CS cannot be shown to have passed the year 751, see (i).

[237] But see Andrew Palmer's remarks above; at this point Robert Hoyland's intervention ends.

[238] That this has never been noticed before is due to Chabot's mistranslation (repeated by Abramowski) of the crucial verb: {Syr. mettaytyō}, 'is derived', 'is quoted'.

any book on the history of Syriac literature.[239] The characteristics of Sergius appear to have been an intense interest in the affairs of the Edessene aristocracy, a gift for telling a vivid and psychologically convincing story and an astringent personal judgment. Dionysius may have learned from Sergius to spice his narrative with criticisms and praise. Here are some examples of this aspect of Sergius's writing. He says of his father that vanity was his consuming obsession. He condemns the baseness of the opponents of Cyrus the governor of Edessa and blames them more than Cyrus for the loss of the church treasures. He calls the Persian who was responsible for his own deportation 'a mild and pleasant man of a humane disposition', whereas the metropolitan bishop Isaiah of Edessa is 'zealous to a fault or rather, to tell the truth, an uneducated idiot' and is to blame for turning Heraclius's conciliatory stance into confrontation and enmity.[240]

Late in the eighth century the house of Sergius Rusafōyō had fallen to the inheritance of the Tel-Mahrōyō family, to which Dionysius belonged. This family in turn allied itself by marriage with another Edessene family which had not yet been counted among the great by Sergius: the Gūmōyē.[241] Since the adult male involved in this alliance was a Gūmōyō, the house became the property of that family. The most famous ancestor of the Gūmōyē was the late seventh-century

---

[239] Fiey does make his father, Īwannis, an author, though without sufficient reason: CSCO 354, p. 2 and p. 294.

[240] Dionysius inherited both the fair-mindedness and the plain speaking of Sergius. In the passage immediately following the end of our extract he describes ᶜUmar b. ᶜAbd al-ᶜAzīz as 'a good and a merciful man, a lover of truth and justice and one who avoided evil; but in his enmity towards the Christians he outdid all his predecessors.' (Compare text No. 12, AG 1028.) In his Church History, he told how the patriarch Cyriac rashly banned a certain doctrinally doubtful phrase from the liturgy, although a rebellious party in the Church threatened to treat it as a kind of badge of allegiance: 'and he did not reflect how George [his predecessor] had given way on this point, for fear of causing a schism in the Church.'

[241] cf. § 41 and Michael, p. 485, 12.4b.

millionaire Athanasius.[242]   What Dionysius tells us about him
comes from the historical work of Daniel, son of Moses, of Anhel in
Ṭūr ᶜAbdīn, a man whose daughter married into the Tel-Mahrōyō
family in Edessa.   This daughter was the mother of Dionysius.
Daniel's father had written some history, too, of which, however, little
is known.   From the two anecdotes explicitly attributed to Daniel by
Dionysius, it seems likely that he had a taste for tales of
intrigue.[243]   Compared with Sergius, Daniel is rather silly.   He is
inclined to exaggerate and his explanations are anything but convincing.

Another intriguing 'unknown quantity' is John, son of Samuel, from
'the western region', by which I suppose western Syria is intended (cf.
text No. 7, AG 1024).   His name has been mentioned in connection
with the 'Common Source' (Brooks, 'The Sources of Theophanes and
the Syriac Chroniclers'), but we have too little to go on.

Clearly more work must be done on these sources, before the basis
of Dionysius's account of the seventh century can be properly assessed.
What I hope to have shown is that Dionysius is an exception from the
rule that Syriac chronographers simply copied their predecessors and
added a section of their own on recent history.   In fact, the commentary
on texts No. 2, No. 9 and No. 12, above, suggests that this view of
Syriac chronography as consisting of superimposed strata, whereby the
older strata are left undisturbed, is altogether too simplistic.   Even the
rather incompetent author of text No. 9 interpolated and rearranged
some of his sources for the period before the death of Justinian
I,[244] and tried, clumsily enough, to amalgamate a number of
disparate sources in his account of the period covered by this book.

Dionysius was an enterprising historian, both as regards his own time
and in dealing with the more distant past.   He made use, for example,
of a visit to Egypt in his capacity as patriarch both to study the way the
Egyptians measured the Nile floods and to consult histories of the

---

[242] See text No. 13, §§ 132-4.

[243] See my discussion of Daniel in *Monk and Mason*, p. 169ff.

[244] See Palmer, review of Witakowski 1987, and *idem*, 'Who Wrote
the Chronicle of Joshua the Stylite?'.

seventh century written by Coptic Christians.[245] He certainly used Arabic as well as Greek sources.[246] He amalgamated sources with consummate skill and produced a virtually seamless narrative, flagged by references backwards and forwards, with a strong, yet discreetly revealed, chronological framework and very likely an overall structure which placed developments in ecclesiastical history in a significant parallel relationship with events in secular history. The dominating anti-Chalcedonian theme may have led to a certain distortion, but the *parti pris* of the author is not without nuance, whether he is talking about the Byzantines or the Arabs,[247] and it is set off by remarkable moments of objectivity.

We may not forget, in assessing Dionysius, that we do not possess his work as he presented it, only as it has been excerpted, abbreviated, corrupted and handed down by others. Michael knows of a number of set-backs suffered by the Arabs in their wars against the Byzantines and the annalistic chronicles, especially the *Maronite Chronicle* (text No. 4), add others; the *Chronicle of AD 1234* (text No. 13), by contrast, does not mention a single Arab defeat, although it does tell how the Arabs were foiled in their attempt to capture Constantinople. Did Dionysius sustain his objectivity here, so that the one-sidedness must be attributed to a later editor? Or was it Dionysius himself who took care to present an almost untarnished picture of Arab success? This would make sense if he was using history to prove that Byzantine Christianity took a wrong turning at Chalcedon and never retrieved itself, but only made God more angry by persecuting those who stayed in the path of the truth. And the fact that the eighth-century Edessene writer Theophilus had written a Chalcedonian history of the same

---

[245] See text No. 13, § 69.

[246] §§ 102-112 is an example of a passage which must be based on mainly Arabic sources; most of the following paragraphs, up to § 118, appear to be based on a source available to Theophanes, but not to the minor Syriac chroniclers translated in Part One. On Dionysius's knowledge of Arabic sources, see now R. Hoyland, 'Arabic, Syriac and Greek historiography'.

[247] See Palmer, 'De overwinning van het Kruis'.

events, in which the Jacobites were certainly pilloried, and probably given the blame for the Arab conquest, might have prompted him to write a polemical history of this kind. But we do not really know; nor shall we know, until, perhaps, a manuscript of Dionysius himself is rediscovered. Then, at last, the greatest of the Syriac historians may receive the honour which is his due.

In what follows I assume that the *Chronicle of AD 1234* preserves Dionysius faithfully, barring omissions and scribal corruptions. In the notes are translated those passages of the Syriac *Chronicle of Michael* (late twelfth century) which supplement the account of the *Chronicle of AD 1234*. New studies of Dionysius and of Michael are needed. However, Abramowski's monograph is still good on the context in which Dionysius wrote his history and Chabot's *Introduction* is good on Michael's sources. Michael, it is clear, was using more sources than we have today; but in order to use him properly we have to try to undo his painstaking work of compilation, just as, in order to recover the original form of John of Ephesus's *Ecclesiastical History*, we would have to retangle (if this were possible) skeins which Michael has laboriously unravelled. Fortunately, however, Michael did not suppress the disagreements between his sources; for instance, he tells us on one page two different dates for the accession of Maurice. Where Michael has material absent from the *Chronicle of AD 1234*, the following criteria should be applied:

a. if the addition looks as if it belongs to an unabridged version of the narrative in the *Chronicle of AD 1234*, it probably comes from Dionysius;

b. if the addition is a laconic factual notice without an exact date it probably comes from the chronological tables of James of Edessa or of John of Litarba, although it may come from an annalistic chronicle, in which case Michael has omitted to give it the date which its original position sufficiently indicated;

c. a short, crisply dated entry probably comes from an annalistic chronicle like texts No. 9 and No. 10;

d. a lengthy narrative entry not represented even in abridged form in the *Chronicle of AD 1234* has to be judged as Dionysian or otherwise by comparison with the Dionysius that we know;

e. a narrative entry judged to be non-Dionysian, whether on stylistic grounds or because it conflicts with what the *Chronicle of AD 1234* says, must be attributed to a discursive annalist such as text No. 4, to an anecdotalist such as Daniel of Ṭūr ᶜAbdīn, or to another source (possibly Byzantine) preserved for Michael by Ignatius of Melitene.

The text of the *Chronicle of AD 1234* was or is preserved in a unique manuscript of the early fourteenth century. This belonged once to Peter Fehim, who inherited it from his father, Paul, a native of Gargar, bishop of Edessa 1883-7 and thereafter of Constantinople. Fehim was likewise resident in Istanbul around the beginning of this century, but the present whereabouts of the manuscript are unknown to me. About two thirds of the text (up to fol. 352r) were published rather hastily by Rahmānī (*Chronicon civile et ecclesiasticum anonymi auctoris, quod ex unico codice edesseno primo edidit Ignatius Ephraem II Rahmani, patriarcha antiochenus Syrorum*, I, II, unfinished, Charfet-Beirut, 1904, 1911) then Barsawm collated the published text of it meticulously with the original and made a photographic reproduction of volume 2 for the use of J.-B. Chabot (Barsawm, *al-luᵓluᵓ al-manthūr*, p. 404). Chabot (in the *Praefatio* of vol. II of the text, p. v) describes the copy he received as Barsawm's own meticulous transcription. Perhaps he thought the photographic reproduction was made from a copy by Barsawm. Chabot published the full text of both volumes with a Latin translation of volume 1 (1920, 1916; 1937); an introduction and an index, with a French translation of volume 2 by A. Abouna, were published by J. M. Fiey (1974): *Anonymi auctoris chronicon ad annum Christi 1234 pertinens*, I, II: text; I, II: translation (CSCO 81, 82; 109, 354).

The text of the *Chronicle of Michael* is published as *Chronique de Michel le Syrien, patriarche jacobite d'Antioche (1166-1199), éditée pour la première fois et traduite en français par J.-B. Chabot*, 4 vols., *Introduction* and *Table générale* (Paris, 1899-1924; reprinted Brussels, 1963); Chabot printed a facsimile of the copy (now perhaps preserved in France) which was made at his request by two different scribes working from an older original at Urfa (ancient Edessa). This is the manuscript kept in the church of St George in Ḥayy al-Suryān in Aleppo, a church built by immigrants from Urfa who abandoned that city after the Syrian Orthodox patriarch left Turkey in the 1920s. The Syrian Orthodox bishop of Aleppo, Mor Gregorius Yuḥannōn Ibrāhī m, is publishing an Arabic translation made from the manuscript at Aleppo; the first volume is forthcoming in 1992. He also plans to publish a facsimile of the manuscript itself.

CONCORDANCE OF THE CONTENTS

The divisions of the text shown by the manuscript do not reflect the divisions of the original composition, but were imposed arbitrarily and rather carelessly on a text in which all divisions had been suppressed. The rubrics of the manuscript have therefore been extracted and listed separately. An asterisk has been placed in the text where a rubric, numbered or unnumbered, has been extracted. After removing the divisions of the manuscript a new division into paragraphs numbered from 1 to 165 was made, beginning at the point where, as Michael tells us, Dionysius began. A blank line between groups of paragraphs marks a caesura which might have come at the end of a chapter in Dionysius's original work. For general purposes the best system of reference is to the page-numbers of the Syriac text, vol. 1, which are given here between slashes /thus/. Reference to the translation published here should be given by paragraph of the translation and by page-number of the Syriac text. The numbering of the rubrics in the manuscript is not suitable for reference, because not every rubric has a number there. A concordance of the rubrics, numbered or unnumbered, which are found in the manuscript with, in the left column, the numbers of the paragraphs from which they have been extracted is not only useful for comparison with the Syriac, but will also serve as a rough-and-ready list of contents.

§ 1 = 76: On the reign of Maurice.

§ 2 = 77: On General Priscus's descent to Persia.

§ 4 = 78: How the Persians took the city of Mayperqat.

§ 5 = 79: How Maurice caused the pagans of Ḥarrān to be persecuted.

§ 6 = 80: How Chosroēs, the Persian king's son, became son-in-law to Maurice.

§ 7 = 81: How Chosroēs was summoned by the king of the Romans.

§ 9 = 82: How Maurice persecuted the Orthodox.

§ 11 = 83: On the assassination of King Maurice.

ibid. 84:   The reign of Phocas.

§ 12 = --:   On Philippicus, the brother-in-law of Maurice.

§ 13 = 85:   How the general Narseh rebelled against Phocas and how Severus, the Chalcedonian bishop of Edessa, was killed.

§ 14 = 86:   What Chosroës did when he heard of the assassination of Maurice.

ibid.   87:   On Īwannis Ruṣafōyō and how his wife was deported to Persia in the year nine hundred and nineteen [AD 607/8].

§ 20 = 88:   How Mesopotamia and all of Syria were conquered by the Persians in the year nine hundred and twenty-two [AD 610/11].

§ 21 = 89:   How the Chalcedonian bishops were expelled from the churches of northern Mesopotamia {Ar. al-jazīra}.

§ 22 = 90:   On the assassination of King Phocas.

§ 23 = 91:   The reign of King Heraclius.

ibid.   92:   How the Persians subjected Syria.

§ 24 = 93:   The Persian conquest of Jerusalem.

§ 25 = 94:   On the beginning of the kingdom of the Arabs and on Muhammad, their leader, who is called by them 'the Prophet and the Apostle of God'.

§ 27 = 95:   On their religion and their customs.

§ 30 = 96:   On what happened in the world in this year of Muhammad's coming.

§ 32 = 97:   On Chosroës's decree that Edessa should be deported into captivity.

§ 33 = 98:   On the Persian siege of Constantinople.

§ 37 = 99:   Heraclius's descent into Persia.

§ 38 = 100:   How Chosroës was murdered and how his son became king.

§ 39 = 101:   On the coming of Theodoric to Edessa.

§ 40 = 102:   On the coming of Heraclius to Edessa.

§ 43 = 103:   On the death of Shīrōē and the assassination of his son;

& §   44   and how Shahrvarāz became king; and on the venerable Wood of the Crucifixion.

ibid.   104:   On the assassination of Shahrvarāz and events at that time.

§ 45 = 105:   On the death of Muḥammad, the leader and the first king of the Hagarenes.

§ 46 = 106:   On the reign of Abū Bakr.

§ 48 = 107:   On the deeds of the Arabs when they went out and on the coming of Heraclius to Antioch.

§ 49 = 108:   On the defeat of the Romans by the Arabs in Palestine.

[There is no chapter numbered 109]

§ 52 = 110:   How the King's brother, Theodoric, went up against the Arabs.

§ 54   ---:   How another general called Baanēs was sent against the Arabs.

§ 55 = 111:   On the siege of Damascus and its capture and on the death of Abū Bakr and the succession of ᶜUmar.

§ 57 = 112:   On the death of Abū Bakr and the reign of ᶜUmar b. al-Khaṭṭāb.

§ 59 = 113:   On the end of the kingdom of the Persians.

§ 63 = 114:   On the conquest of Damascus.

§ 64 = 115:   The expedition of the Arabs against the regions of Phoenicia and the conquest of Emesa and other places.

§ 65 = 116:   On the army which was sent out by King Heraclius from Antioch against the Arabs and their defeat on the river Yarmūk.

§ 68 = 117:   On the departure of Heraclius from Syria.

§ 69 = 118:   How Egypt was conquered and betrayed to the Arabs by the agency of the patriarch Benjamin.

§ 72 = 119:   The conquest of Aleppo and other places by the Arabs.

§ 73 = 120:   On the siege of Jerusalem and its submission to ᶜUmar b. al-Khaṭṭāb.

§ 77 = 121:   On the conquest of Mesopotamia and of Antioch.

§ 79 = 122:   The expedition of David the Armenian and his followers into Mesopotamia.

§ 81 = 123:   On the coming of the Arabs and the defeat and destruction of David the Armenian.

§ 83 = 124:   On the conquest and destruction of Caesarea and of Euchaita.

§ 85 = 125:   On the death of Heraclius.

ibid.   126:   The reign of Constans, the grandson of King Heraclius.

§ 87 = 127:   On the assassination of ^CUmar, king of the Arabs, and on the reign of ^CUthmān b. ^CAffān, the son-in-law of Muhammad.

§ 89 = 128:   On the decree of ^CAmr b. Sa^Cd to take down the crosses from the churches.

§ 90 = 129:   How the patriarch John was commanded by the emir ^CAmr to translate the Gospel from the Syriac language into Arabic.

§ 91 = 130:   On the origin of the heresy of the Maximians, which holds the field today in the churches of the Chalcedonians. [This paragraph is not translated here.]

§ 92 = 131:   How some monks in the monastery of Qēnneshrē became diseased.

§ 93 = ---:   On Mu^Cāwiya's invasion of Cyprus and how he conquered it and led its population into captivity.

§ 98 = 132:   The second Arab invasion of Cyprus.

§ 99 = ---:   How Aradus, a fortified city in the sea, was conquered.

§ 100 = 133:   On the assassination of King Yazdgird and the definitive end of the kingdom of the Persians.

§ 101 = 134:   On the fleet of ships which Mu^Cāwiya equipped to send and besiege the Royal City and on the sea battle between the Arabs and the Romans.

§ 102 = 135:   On the assassination of ^CUthmān b. ^CAffān, king of the Arabs.

§ 105 = 136:   The reign of ^CAlī and the civil war which broke out between him and Mu^Cāwiya.

§ 109 = ---:   On the assassination of ^CAlī.

§ 112 = ---:   On the massacre of the people of Ḥarrān.

§ 113 = 137:   On King Constans's intention to move the seat of government to Rome, as in former times.

§ 115 = 138:   On the rebellion against Constans, king of the Romans.

§ 116 = 139:   On the death of Constans and on Mizīzī the Armenian, who became king for nothing.

§ 117 = 140:   The reign of Constantine the son of Constans.

§ 118 = 141:   On what happened in the days of Constantine: about the Mardaïtes, who came and established themselves in Mount Lebanon.

§ 121 = 142:   On the death of Muʿāwiya and how Constantine deposed his brothers from the throne, because he wanted his son to be king.

§ 124 = 143:   On the death of Yazīd and the confusion which reigned in the kingdom of the Arabs after his death.

§ 125 = 144:   On the reign of Marwān b. al-Hakam.

§ 127 = 145:   On the death of Marwān b. al-Ḥakam and the reign of his son, ʿAbd al-Malik.

ibid.   ---:   On the death of Constantine.

§ 128 = 146:   The reign of the arrogant Justinian.

§ 129 = 147:   On what happened in the kingdom of the Arabs in the days of ʿAbd al-Malik.

§ 131 = 148:   On the evil deeds of al-Ḥajjāj and of Muhammad b. Marwān in their provinces.

§ 132 = 149:   On Athanasius bar Gūmōyē, who became great and famous in the time of ʿAbd al-Malik.

§ 135 = 150:   On the renewal of hostilities between the Romans and the Arabs.

§ 138 = 151:   On the rebellion against Justinian and the reign of the patríkios Leontius.

§ 141 = 152:   How Justinian came into his kingdom once more.

§ 143 = 153:   On the death of ʿAbd al-Malik and the reign of his son Walīd.

§ 148 = 154:   On the death of Justinian and the insurrectious reign of Philippicus.

§ 149 = 155:　The reign of Anastasius and what happened in his days.

§ 151 = 156:　The reign of Theodosius and how they deposed Anastasius.

ibid.　　157:　The expedition of the Arabs and their siege of Constantinople.

§ 156 = 158:　The reign of Leo and Theodosius's fall from the throne.

§§ 158 = 159:　The coming of Maslama and his siege of
- 160　　　　　Constantinople.

§§ 160 = 161:　How God provided a way out and a solution for both
- 161　　　　　sides.

§§ 161 = 161:　The death of Sulaymān and the reign of his paternal
- 163　　　　　cousin, ᶜUmar.

§ 164　　---:　On the first foundation and the construction of the city of Byzantium.

§ 165　　---:　On the construction and the extension (of the City) in the reign of Constantine.

13. EXTRACT FROM THE ANONYMOUS *CHRONICLE OF AD 1234*, WITH SUPPLEMENTARY MATERIAL IN THE NOTES FROM THE CHRONICLE OF THE JACOBITE PATRIARCH MICHAEL (DIED AD 1199) [248]

§ 1*.[249]/p. 212/ After the death of Tiberius Caesar, king of the Romans, which occurred in AG 894, Maurice, from the city of Arabissus, came to the throne by virtue of his being the son-in-law of the King, since Tiberius himself had made him crown-prince while he lived by giving away his daughter Augusta to him in marriage. He sent for his parents and his brother[250] and sisters and they came to the Royal City, where he showered them with wealth. To his father, an old man, whose name was Paul, and to his brother, Peter, and his two sisters he gave great palaces and magnificent clothes (and) gold and silver. Little by little he enriched his whole family and raised their status, until they attained power through high and conspicuous appointments. He elevated his father above the whole senate and made him head of all the patricians, whereas he made his brother commander of all the forces /p. 213/ in the east and Domitian, one of his family, metropolitan of Melitene. Maurice found the palace swept clean as with a broom and the royal treasury emptied by Tiberius. Wealth unlimited had been accumulated since the time of Anastasius and the

---

[248] To facilitate source analysis, the text is cross-referenced to other texts in this book, and to Theophanes, Agapius, *Chr. Pasch.* and Nikephoros (*Short History*, ed. and tr. C. Mango [Washington: Dumbarton Oaks, 1990]). References to Theophanes and Agapius are underlined when it seems clear that they share a common source with Dionysius (whether in *Chronicle of AD 1234* or Michael). Where they occur together not underlined, it is still likely they are drawing on the common source, but the notices are too compressed to be sure. [R.H.]

[249] An asterisk indicates the fact that a rubric was at one time interpolated into the text; the rubrics have here been extracted, for the most part, and are translated in the concordance of paragraphs which precedes this translation.

[250] The text has 'brothers'.

three Justinians,[251] but all this Tiberius had squandered through his generosity in giving. So Maurice was obliged to tighten his fist [...] and so he got a name for being a miser.[252]

§ 2*. In year 6 of Maurice, Priscus, the Roman general, went down to Persia with a sizeable army. He was a difficult man and the cavalry, not being able to endure his character, complained of him to the King,

---

[251] Justin I, Justinian I and Justin II.

[252] Michael, p. 379:7-13, 10.21a: 'The reign of Maurice began on 5 August, AG 893, and he was confirmed in his rule on 4 August, 894. That same day Augusta bore him a son, Theodosius, who was born on the purple (bedclothes) of royalty.' (Dionysius apparently counted 895 as Maurice's first regnal year, so this would seem to be from another source.) Michael, p. 379:14-380:3, 10.21a, adds the following: 'At this time the Romans were in revolt against the king and they put themselves under the leadership of a general called Germanus. When he received this intelligence, Hormizd, king of Persia, sent them promises by his ambassadors to make them join an alliance with him; but they, despising his offer, made war on him instead and killed many of the Persians. They sent 3,000 captives as slaves to Maurice in Romania (that is, the Roman Empire) and returned of their own will to the obedience of the King, who magnanimously accepted them, to the extent of offering Germanus gifts and honours. At this time Maurice commanded that his native city, Arabissus, which is one of the cities of the province of Armenia III, be rebuilt. After it had been completely rebuilt with splendid edifices, it collapsed in the devastation (i.e. devastating earthquake) which occurred in AG 898. At the King's renewed command it was rebuilt a second time, even better than before, under the personal and intensive supervision of Maurice himself. Then there was another, more violent tremor and every stone above the ground was overturned.'
(I omit the column 10.21b on pp. 378-82, which concerns: (a) a fortress built by Maurice in Sophanene; (b) the capture and loss of the Persian fort at Oqba (= ᶜUkbarā ?) in AG 894; (c) the slaughter of Roman prisoners-of-war in Persia; (d) the attacks of the Avars and their vassals, the Slavs and the Langobards; (e) the construction of land-walls in Thrace to protect Constantinople; (f) the pillaging of churches by the Slavs and the alliance between Byzantium and the Antes; (g) the sacking of Anchialus by the Slavs; (h) the grant by Maurice of land in Upper and Lower Moesia and in Dacia to the Bulgars, who were seen as a buffer against the Avars, and the establishment of the related peoples of the Pugurians and the Khazars to the east of the Black Sea. All of these records (except the last) were derived from John of Ephesus, *Ecclesiastical History*, Book III; cf. Whitby, p. 111.)

who appointed in his place a certain Germanus. After the forces had done with making war on the Persians, they wintered in the environs of Antioch and mutinied against the King. At this time there was a harsh winter and a violent tremor occurred when the earth quaked in the early morning of Tuesday, 29 December,[253] and the greater part of Antioch collapsed.[254] The King sent his brother-in-law, Philippicus, to take over command of the army and the patriarch of Antioch reconciled the troops with the King. This general Philippicus was successful as a field-commander.[255]

§ 3. Now when Maurice had assumed power, he had sent al-Mundhir into exile. As for his son, Nu^cmān, he brazenly announced himself at court and was received. Maurice swore to him that, if he was successful in making war on the Persians, his father would be recalled. He was also told to partake of the Eucharist in the Royal City, but he declined, saying, 'All the (Christian) Arab tribes are Jacobites. If they come to hear of it, they will kill me.' For this reason he was not obliged to receive the Sacrament from the Chalcedonians. /p. 214/

§ 4*. Sittas, a Roman, was the guardian of the city of Mayperqaṭ. The Persians in Nisibis bribed this man with many gifts to betray the city to them. For this reason Sittas made continual expeditions to the environs of Nisibis with the Roman cavalry stationed at Mayperqaṭ, during which he made prisoner Persian men of powerful physique who had been primed to come out of Nisibis. In this way he brought enough of the Persians into Mayperqaṭ as prisoners of war to enable

---

[253] This is incompatible with year 6 of Maurice, but 'at this time' gives a certain latitude; in AD 582, 593 and 599, 29 December fell on a Tuesday. Agapius, p. 180 has 29 October, year 6 of Maurice (not a Tuesday).

[254] Evagrius, *Ecclesiastical History*, 6.8, ed. Bidez and Parmentier, 1898, pp. 227-8, records an earthquake which severely damaged Antioch in AD 588, so perhaps it is the weekday which is wrong; in AD 588, year 6 of Maurice, 29 December fell on a Wednesday, 29 October on a Friday.

[255] Michael, p. 380:12-13, 10.21a: 'Philippicus, who was the king's brother-in-law,' (not Germanus) was sent to replace Priscus.

them to carry out the underhand stratagem which he was preparing. At his signal the Persian general in Nisibis came with his forces to lay siege to Mayperqat. Then Sittas let loose the prisoners and gave them weapons; they leapt out onto the city, killing many people, and opened the gates, letting in those who were outside, who killed and pillaged and took captives and made themselves at home in the city. When Philippicus, the Roman general, heard of this, he forced a march from Antioch to Mayperqat and pitched camp outside the city. He persevered with vehement assaults until he had retaken it, then he killed every Persian whom he found there, stationed a garrison in the city and departed.[256]

§ 5*. At this time Maurice commanded Stephen, the bishop of Harrān, to initiate a persecution of the pagans there. When this bishop received the order, he began to persecute them. Many became Christians; and as for those who refused, he would cut them in half with a sword and hang their sides along the streets of Harrān. The governor[257] of Harrān at that time was a man called /p. 215/ Acindynus; in name he was a Christian, but in secret a pagan. He was betrayed to the bishop by his scribe, a young person called Honorius and they impaled him on the tell in Harrān. Honorius himself replaced him as city-governor.[258]

---

[256] Michael, p. 381:3-22, 10.21a: 'On his way back (from Mayperqat) Philippicus passed through Zeugma, where he commissioned a temple dedicated to the Mother of God. They say that on her feast-day they used to shut the doors of this temple and although they secured them with bolts, they would open suddenly of their own accord; and they used to claim that it was the Mother of God herself who opened them. But that is just a rumour put into circulation by those Chalcedonians; the true facts of the matter are unknown. There were some who said that they were opened by a certain device operated by the priests of the temple.'

[257] {Syr. shallīṭō}; in Michael: {Syr. hīgmūnō = Gr. hēgemōn}.

[258] Michael, p. 388:26-28, 43, 10.24b: 'His name was Iyarius (probably correct; Honorius being a corruption), the eponymous founder of the family of Iyār, an orphan abandoned by his parents in the *colonia* of Armenia I, in (one of) the villages of Nicopolis. There he had learned to write and had become a secretary. When he came to

§ 6*. In year 8 of Maurice the Persians revolted against their king, Hormizd; when they got their hands on him they gouged out his eyes. Shortly after their king Hormizd had been blinded, the Persians appointed his son Chosroës to rule over them in place of his father. Now this Chosroës was called Parwēz. However, one of his generals, who had been campaigning with an army in the east, was returning in glorious victory when he came to hear of what the Persians had done to Hormizd and how they had raised up his son as his successor. In the arrogance of his success he dismissed Chosroës as a mere child and showed his contempt by leading the army he had with him directly in revolt against him. Now the name of this rebel was Vahrām. As for Chosroës, when he heard of the audacious aggression of Vahrām, he panicked and was at a loss what he should do, because the majority of the Persians were at one with Vahrām. Chosroës decided to seek asylum with the king of the Romans. He sent for the Arab general who dwelt at Rusāfa as a subject of the Romans, a zealous Christian man called Abū Jafna Nuᶜmān b. al-Mundhir. When he arrived he gave him a letter to take to King Maurice. He sped to Maurice, gave him the letter from Chosroës and described to him exactly how dramatic the situation was and that Chosroës was standing ready to come to the King as soon as he should have his leave to do so. As for /p. 216/ Maurice, when he had read Chosroës's letter and understood its contents, he granted his request and sent him word to come to him, promising that he would help him. Abū Jafna conveyed this message back to Chosroës. When the latter heard what Maurice had promised, he left his palace, taking care to avoid being observed, and rode like a wild warrior across the border out of Persia, until he reached Mesopotamia and the city of Edessa. There he tarried, awaiting orders from Maurice, and was received as a guest in the house of Īwannis[259]

Harrān, he entered the service of Acindynus, the governor who [...] was executed.'

[259] In Syriac this 'Greek' form of the name John is a name distinct from Yuhannōn, the Syriac form. When I use the English form for a Syrian, this represents the Syriac form of the name, so I do not call

Rusafōyō, a leading citizen of Edessa, who accorded him the highest
honours, truly royal honours past compare. As for the recompense
which Chosroēs had in store for Īwannis, we shall relate that later, if
God gives us strength.[260]

§ 7*. While he was in Edessa a letter came to him from Maurice,
instructing him to direct his steps to Mabbūgh and to wait there for his
reply. Chosroēs wrote the King a letter of supplication, calling him
'father' and 'lord' and telling him about his situation. He wrote, 'It
befits me to find my end, if I am destined to die, at your hands, not at
the hands of my blood-relatives.' And he urged him to come to his
aid, promising him that he would be his son and slave and would make
all the people in his kingdom obedient to him. When Maurice received
Chosroēs's missive, he convoked an assembly of outstanding Romans
and ordered the letter of Chosroēs to be read out loud. Then he sent
John, the general of the Thracian division,[261] with an army of
20,000 and the general Anastasius with 20,000 men from the Armenian
and the Bucellarian (divisions);[262] he also sent him 40 centenaria
of gold denarii[263] for his expenses. When these reached Chosroēs
he set off on the march to his country.[264]

§ 8. As for the rebel Vahrām, after Chosroēs had left, /p. 217/ he

---

Īwannis 'John'. However, where {Syr. Īwannis} represents {Gr.
iōánnēs}, as a native Greek name, as in the next paragraph, I write
'John', because there is no need to distinguish it from another form of
the name in Greek.

[260] *Chr. Pasch.*, p. 691/140; text No. 2, section 7, AG 902; Agapius,
pp. 181-3; Michael, p. 381:27-29, 36, 10.21a: Exact date of
Chosroēs's accession: 'At the end of ten months (after the death of
Hormizd), in year 9 of Maurice, [...] AG 902.' This probably comes
from the same source as the extract above on the accession of Maurice;
certainly it is not from Dionysius, because it counts AG 894 as
Maurice's first year.

[261] {Gr. tágma thrakēsíōn}.

[262] {Gr. armeniakōn, boukellaríōn}.

[263] {Syr. drēkūnē}.

[264] Agapius, p. 183; Michael, p. 386:3-7, 10.23a: 'The emperor
Maurice invested his son Theodosius as Caesar and gave in his honour
a splendid banquet. The patriarch clasped the crown upon his head.'

came to Ctesiphon, seized the kingdom and the royal treasury and burned down the royal palaces, having taken from them all the loot he could find. When he heard of Chosroēs's return, he made ready to do battle with him. When Chosroēs reached Persian territory, the general Rōmēzān joined him, adding his 10,000 Persians to the army of the Romans, and became his ally. The battle with Vahrām was bitterly fought, but the rebels were routed; many were slaughtered and the rest were subjected to Chosroēs. Thus he recovered his kingdom. When he had established his position, he granted to the Romans everything they had pillaged and snatched from the Persian army in the battle and gave them in addition 400 silver pieces[265] for each mounted soldier. After this he dismissed them and they returned to Roman territory. To Maurice he sent many gifts, precious stones and garments of every kind, and he returned to him the city of Dara, which had been captured from the Romans. He also asked Maurice to give away his daughter Maria to him in marriage and Maurice was delighted to give his consent to this request. He gave away his daughter to him and she was escorted on her mission with great honour. Maurice sent bishops and clergy with her and, at the command of Chosroēs, two temples[266] were built for his bride, one dedicated to Saint Sergius, the other to the Mother of God; Anastasius, the patriarch of Antioch, was sent to consecrate them. There was profound peace between the Persians and the Romans and Chosroēs treated Maurice with the respect due to a father.[267]

§ 9*. AG 910 = year 17 of the reign of Maurice. Maurice decided to imitate the kings who had preceded him, so he summoned Domitian,

---

[265] {Syr. zūzē}.

[266] {Syr. hayklē}; 'churches' would suggest {Syr. ᶜīdōtō}, so I retain a distinction in translation, in case this reflects a difference in the type of churches.

[267] Agapius, pp. 184-7; Michael, p. 387:19-20, 25-26, 29-31, 10.23a: '(Chosroēs) returned Dara and Rhesaina to the Romans. [...] (Chosroēs) built three great churches [...] one to the Mother of God, one to the Apostles and one to Lord Sergius, the martyr.'

the metropolitan of Melitene, who was /p. 218/ the son of his brother Peter, and he gave him authority to persecute the followers of Severus[268] and to expel them from their churches. When he had arrived in Mesopotamia and had set the persecution in motion, he came to Edessa and began to exercize great pressure on the Orthodox. He summoned the monks from the Abbey of the Orientals and did his utmost to deflect them from Orthodoxy by playing on their emotions, but they would have nothing of it. He tried threats instead, but they were impervious to fear. So then he ordered the commander of the troops whom the King had sent with him, whose name was Sakellarios, to take them out to the ditch outside the southern gate, which was called the Bēth Shemesh[269] Gate and he slaughtered them all in a single pool of blood. In number they were four hundred men.[270]

§ 10. At this time there was a great outbreak of the plague in the Royal City which claimed 380,000 victims. In the same year there was

---

[268] Patriarch of Antioch, consecrated in 512; this is one name for the Jacobites.

[269] 'House of the sun', perhaps meaning 'Temple of the Sun'.

[270] Text No. 2, section 7, AG 910; text No. 12, AG 910; Michael, p. 386:10-15, 386:30-387:1-3, 10.23b: 'They say this (persecution) was provoked by that accursed bishop, who was gnawed by jealousy on account of the conversions to (Jacobite Orthodoxy) in Melitene and environs. He departed like a beast of prey for Mesopotamia [...] (There were 400 martyrs.) The faithful collected them and buried them where they had been crowned (a euphemism for martyrdom) and there they built a temple. As for that wicked man, he continued his persecutions for a long time, putting the Orthodox under pressure to receive communion from him even after they had eaten. Many of the Orthodox stood their ground sturdily in this combat and did not consent to accept the evil heresy of the Dyophysites. They reviled the King and Domitian, and the soldier called Spatharios (actually a title) used this as a pretext, saying that he had heard the monks insulting /p. 387/ the King and his nephew and that he had killed them for this reason. Many people were expelled from their churches.' (The extract in the next footnote but one follows without a break.)

a great earthquake in Syria on Monday, 19 January,[271] and many cities were left in ruins. At this time Peter, the patriarch of the Orthodox, died and Julian was consecrated.[272]

§ 11*. In year 20 of Maurice his army mutinied against him because he would not give them their stipends and gifts, as is the custom for kings to do, for he felt certain that he had no enemy left. A large number of soldiers held a meeting together. They conveyed to him the following message: 'God has given peace in your days; but peace does not feed the cavalry, unless they receive their due. So give us our due as is the custom and we will be your servants. If you do not, we will be your enemies.' King Maurice was like Rehoboam the son of Solomon: he did not take this warning to heart, but scorned the soldiers. So they approached Peter, their general, who was the King's brother, and asked him to become their king instead; /p. 219/ but Peter refused. He went to the King and told him of the soldiers' discontent and of their request that he should become their king. At this Maurice fled in fear to Chalcedon. When the Roman army arrived at the Royal City they found that Maurice had gone, but they followed him to Chalcedon and tracked him down; then they took him back to Constantinople and butchered his sons in his sight before putting his own life to an end. One consequence of this was that al-Mundhir, the king of the Arabs, was released and sent back to his country. Then* - AG 914 = year 13 of Chosroës - the army got hold of a contemptible

---

[271] The dated weekday points to AD 593 or 598; Agapius, p. 187 places it in year 17 of Maurice, so 598 is indicated.

[272] Texts No. 2, section 6, AG 901, and Nos. 10 and 12, AG 902. Michael, p. 387:3-14, 10.23b: 'On the same day there was a solar eclipse and it went dark on 10 March from the third hour until the sixth (Agapius, p. 187; there was in fact a total solar eclipse in Syria on 10 March, AD 601) and everyone said that the sun had been darkened because of the murder of those monks who served Christ. On 2 April there was a violent earthquake and many cities and settlements collapsed, inhuming their inhabitants. The earth boiled and was torn open.' See Appendix I on this deceptive 'synchronism'.

Roman called Phocas and made him king.[273]

§ 12*. After Phocas became king, the brother-in-law of Maurice, Philippicus, presented himself at court and tried to ingratiate himself by maligning his late brother-in-law. Claiming that he was responsible for the fall of Maurice, he requested the King to tell him what honourable position he might enjoy as his reward. To this Phocas replied, 'So you are prepared to be our friend, Philippicus?' 'Yes, my lord,' said Philippicus. Then the King continued, 'But how can you be a friend to us without deceit, when you were not even good to your own brother-in-law? Get out! One who does not keep faith with a brother-in-law will not keep an agreement with a friend, either.' Disappointed, Philippicus shaved his head and entered a monastery.[274]

§ 13*. /p. 220/ There was a certain Narseh, patríkios of Syria, who refused to acknowledge Phocas at his accession. When he learned that the King had sent a task-force to arrest him, this Narseh left Antioch with a part of his army, and made for Edessa. The impregnable walls of Edessa made it a suitable city for a rebel to hold out in. Now the Chalcedonians of Edessa had a bishop called Severus, the builder of the Palace[275] in Edessa, which is by the river, and of the street called 'The New Portico'; certain persons of Edessa denounced this bishop to Narseh on his arrival as a friend of Phocas. At the orders of the general he was brought to the palace of Marinus, where Narseh had

---

[273] Chr. Pasch., pp. 693-4/142-4; text No. 2, section 5, AG 914; text No. 5, to the left of the first chart; text No. 10, AG 924; Agapius, p. 188; Michael, p. 388:18-24, 388:44-389:1, 6-8, 10.24a: 'When the Bulgars began to lay waste the Thracian countryside, the Romans marched against them with Philippicus, defeated them and returned; but even so the King did not consider that they had earned their salary. [...] A contemptible old man called Phocas. [...] This was the fifty-third king of the Romans, the third of the Greek kings, of whom Tiberius was the first.'

[274] Michael, 10.25b. A similar story is told of Heraclius, Phocas's successor, and Phocas's son-in-law Crispus (or rather Priscus) by Nikephoros, in ch. 2.

[275] {Lat. palatium}.

taken up residence, and interrogated. Then Narseh made them take him out of the city by a postern and gave his sentence from the Gate of the Cave-Tombs,[276] so as to avoid causing a riot in the city when he was executed. They stoned him near the head of the spring, in the place called Kynēgion. The people of Edessa, meanwhile, were all standing around the palace of Marinus and did not realize that he was being stoned until it was over. Then John arrived - the general sent by Phocas - and laid siege to Edessa; however, he succeeded in capturing Narseh by a cunning trick, so there was no need to fight. He pardoned the Edessenes for their share in the rebellion, all except Thomas Bardōyō, who had insulted him from the wall; for this man he decreed the death penalty.[277]

§ 14*. When Chosroēs, the Persian king, heard that Maurice had been murdered, he was filled with grief and fury. He mourned for him in black clothes as for a father. Then he delivered a speech before his assembled soldiers about Maurice's benefits to him, especially in enabling him /p. 221/ to recover his kingdom; and he commanded the whole army to wear mourning. When the time of mourning was past he reassembled the army and distributed gifts to them, then declared himself ready to exact vengeance from the Romans: 'Which of you splendid generals and lords of the Persians is ready to serve my purpose?' To this Rōmēzān, a powerful, dedicated man with considerable experience in combat, replied, 'I am ready to carry out your purpose and battle with the Romans is something I can cope with.

---

[276] Chabot: 'et reduxerunt per portam Cryptarum'. The lexica attest {Syr. ahpek ^{c}al} with the sense 'gave a hostile response to' - hence 'gave his sentence' in my translation; Chabot gives no account of the preposition {Syr. ^{c}al}. As for the name of the gate, {Syr. tar^{c}ō d-kappē}, 'gate of the apses, niches,' it refers to the west gate of Edessa, which is opposite a hillside covered with ancient cave-tombs. {Syr. kappē} also means 'scales', so it is just possible that there is a connection between the name of the gate and the judiciary activity which is performed at it in this passage.

[277] Text No. 5, to right and left of the first chart; text No. 10, AG 914, 916; text No. 12, AG 913, 914; Theophanes, pp. 291-3; Michael, 10.23c and 10.25b.

I flinch from nothing, never stoop to compassion, pity no one, and I know neither respect nor regret for the aged and the infants.' Overjoyed, Chosroës exclaimed, 'Then your name is not Rōmēzān but Shahrvarāz, the Wild Boar!' So Shahrvarāz invaded the Roman empire at the head of the army with Chosroës following after him. The first city he besieged was Dara; after nine months it fell to his greater strength. Mardīn,* that inaccessible rock, held out for two and a half years, before it fell to the Persians in AG 919[278] = year 5 of Phocas = year 17 of Chosroës. In this way Persia conquered the cities of Mesopotamia and exacted tribute from them; and since Chosroës now ruled Edessa as well, he ordered the wife of Īwannis Rusafōyō to be deported to Persia. The reason for this was as follows.[279]

§ 15. Once upon a time when Chosroës had passed through Edessa on his way to see Maurice - as I have already related - he had stayed a number of days in the city as the guest of Marinus the Chalcedonian, in the palace next to that of Īwannis Rusafōyō. Both Īwannis and

---

[278] Read '918', as in Michael, translated in the note below; the date was perhaps altered under the influence of the false synchronism at § 23 (see the note there and Appendix I).

[279] Text No. 2, section 7, AG 915; text No. 5, to the left of the first chart; text No. 10, AG 916, 924; text No. 12, AG 916; Theophanes, pp. 292-3; Michael, p. 390:26-391:15, 10.25a: 'AG 915 = year 2 of Phocas: The Persians took Dara and invaded Tūr ᶜAbdīn. For two years they besieged Hesnō d-Kīfō, harming no one but the Romans, whom they slaughtered wherever they found them. When the Romans who were at Mardīn heard that Hesnō d-Kīfō had been surrendered, they abandoned the castle and ran away. But the monks flocked to the castle and occupied it, ready for the Persian attack. They were all priests and they sent to ask Basil, the bishop of Kafar Tūthō, whether they were permitted to kill the Persians. AG 918: Mardīn, that inaccessible fortress, was surrendered to the Persians. In the same year the Persians took Amida. In this year there was so much snow and ice that the rivers froze over, including even the Euphrates, and crops and (fruit-)trees were shrivelled by the frost. In the same year the Blues and the Greens declared war on each other; the cities were deserted and Phocas sent a general to Syria, who massacred a large number of people. In year 7 of Phocas the Persians came up and occupied all Roman territories east of the Euphrates.'

Marinus had a certain status in the civil hierarchy /p. 222/ of the Roman empire; but Marinus had always been jealous of Īwannis, not only because of the high esteem in which the emperor held him, but also because his estates were more lucrative than those of Marinus. On one of the days of his sojourn in Edessa Chosroēs looked out of one of Marinus's chambers and gazed in wonder at the beautiful buildings of Rusafōyō's palace. At that moment he conceived the desire to visit that palace and see what was in it. Īwannis came to hear of the King's desire and he prepared a great banquet, to which he invited all the leading men and the elders of the city. The honour which he gave to Chosroēs was breathtaking; the King himself remarked that he had never seen anything like it, not even in the kingdom of his fathers. But with Īwannis, vanity was a consuming obsession. He wanted to let Chosroēs know how much richer he was than Marinus. So he got out the complete service of gold and silver implements, tables, plates, serving-dishes, spoons, dessert-dishes, drinking-goblets, wine-jars, pitchers, flagons, basins and vessels of every kind, all of silver and of gold.

§ 16. Once Chosroēs had eaten and drunk he was in an extremely good mood. He called Rusafōyō and said, 'The honour you have shown me does you credit. But when a king of Persia condescends to enter the house of one of his lords, he invariably expects the wife of that man to come out and mix one goblet for him and hand it to him to drink. If you intend to do me perfect honour, set the seal on it with this.' Īwannis was hideously embarrassed, but he had no intention of offending the King by answering back. He left it to his wife to find a way out of the awkward situation, trusting in her excellent good sense. He summoned one of the maidservants /p. 223/ and sent her to tell his wife of Chosroēs's request. She greeted the proposal with a snort of disdain, but when she went in to give her answer she kept her true thoughts to herself: 'O King, in our eyes you are indeed a great man and it is a cause of much rejoicing that you have come under our roof. But the traditions and conventions of the Roman empire forbid a free-born woman to mix the wine for a man.'

§ 17. To this the King said nothing in reply. But when the company had broken up and Chosroēs had retired to his apartments, an informer told him what the wife of Rusafōyō had said afterwards: 'Did you see how I outfaced that flea-ridden monarch-in-exile?' When Chosroēs heard this he was livid; he swore by all his gods that if this land ever came beneath his sway, he would repay the wife of Rusafōyō for her insults: 'I will not let her alone until I have made her a stranger to her own country and have given her flesh as fodder to the fleas!'

§ 18. And that is why, when he conquered Edessa, he sent for this woman and had her deported to Persia, together with her son Sergius, Rusafōyō's only heir. Her he threw into a dungeon with orders that neither soap nor water should touch her body and that her clothes should never be washed or changed; but she was to be given enough bread and water to survive. The King's command was carried out. She died a prisoner after living in agony for a long time; for shortly after her imprisonment she became infested with fleas. As for Sergius, her son, the King treated him with honour and made him one of the companions of his table, in remembrance of his father's hospitality.

§ 19. After a while Sergius begged the King to allow him to go back and inspect his estates. Permission was granted on condition that he would return. But when Sergius got to Edessa he found his house empty /p. 224/ of all the gold, silver, slaves and possessions. Nothing was left except villages, orchards, mills and shops. Unbeknown to Sergius, his mother had buried the gold and silver implements in the ground. The location of the treasure remained unknown until AG 1113, two hundred years afterwards; and we shall tell in good time, God willing, how it was found and by whom. As for Sergius, he never went back to Chosroēs. Instead he got married, begat some sons and took possession of his ancestral property.[280]

---

[280] For this chapter (from § 15 to here), cf. Michael, 10.25b.

§ 20*. AG 922 = year 8 of Phocas = year 2 of Chosroës:[281] The Persians crossed the Euphrates and subjected all Syria. The Romans were expelled from it with Shahrvarāz at their heels all the way, cutting them down wherever he caught up with them. Those whom he did not kill he made captive and sent in chains to Chosroës. Thus he passed through the regions of Cappadocia and Galatia and reached the vicinity of Constantinople. Was there any region which rose up against him without him devastating and destroying it, killing the men and taking the women and children captive? And while the Persians were thus damaging the territory of the Romans, Phocas was outdoing them from within by his lack of clemency, killing the leaders of the Romans until his kingdom was bereft of powerful men.[282]

§ 21*. When Chosroës conquered Mesopotamia and expelled the Romans from it, he ordered at the same time the Chalcedonian bishops to be expelled from their churches and those churches to be given to the Jacobites; /p. 225/ for they had possessed them since the time of Maurice, but for the last ten years they had been ousted from them as a result of the persecution by Domitian of Melitene. So the (liturgical) commemoration of the Synod of Chalcedon was utterly abolished east of the Euphrates. Chosroës sent for bishops from the east and installed them in the cities. One of these was Isaiah of Edessa and another was

---

[281] This synchronism should read: AG 921 = year 8 of Phocas = year 20 of Chosroës. The Seleucid year was probably altered under the influence of the false synchronism at § 23 (see the note there and Appendix I and compare § 14). In certain circumstances it is possible to mistake the number 20 for the number 2 in Syriac.

[282] *Chr. Pasch.*, p. 696/145-6; text No. 2, section 7, AG 921; text No. 5, to the left of the first chart; Nikephoros, ch. 1; Theophanes, pp. 294-6; Michael, p. 391:16-20, 391:44-392:6, 10.25a: 'AG 921 = year 8 of Phocas: The Persians crossed the Euphrates and took Mabbūgh, Qēnneshrīn, Beroea (that is, Aleppo) and Antioch. [...] The Persians pillaged all Syria, Phoenicia, Armenia, Cappadocia and Palestine. They took Galatia and Paphlagonia, right up to Chalcedon. The Romans replied by shedding the blood of patriarchs and by murdering each other. The Jews of Antioch stirred up trouble and killed many people, including the Chalcedonian patriarch, Anastasius, himself. This same year there was a frost such that the water froze on the sea-shore.'

Samuel of Amida, who succeeded Cyriac, an eloquent man of outstanding talent, famous both for his way of life and for his learning. The latter had been one of those who had previously left their sees.[283]

§ 22*. When they saw that the Roman empire was plagued with disasters not only by the Persians but also, and above all, by King Phocas himself and when they heard of Phocas's disgusting acts and abominable crimes against the army, two men of patrician rank who were posted in Africa decided to organize a rebellion against him. One was called Gregory, the other Heraclius; both were advanced in years and sage in understanding. There was none better than them in the

---

[283] Text No. 5, to the right of the first chart; Michael, p. 389:30-390:1, 391:11-42, 10.25c: 'When the peace between the kingdoms had been broken by the murder of Maurice and the Persians had conquered Mesopotamia and Syria, Chosroës sent bishops from the east to take possession of the cities of Syria. To Edessa came at first the Nestorian, Ahīshmō; but he was not accepted by the faithful. Subsequently the Orthodox bishop Jonah came and when he was accepted, Chosroës ordered all Chalcedonian bishops to be expelled from the whole land of Mesopotamia and Syria. [...] The commemoration of the Chalcedonians was abolished east of the Euphrates. Thus the Lord brought their crimes back on their own head: what they had done by the agency of the Roman monarchy was paid back to them by the agency of the Persian kings of Assyria. At this time flourished Thomas Harqlōyō, from the monastery of Tar^{c}ēl, the bishop of Mabbūgh. In his youth he had studied Greek at Qēnneshrē. When he became a bishop he was persecuted by Domitian of Melitene in the reign of Maurice and went with the other persecuted bishops to Egypt, where he lodged at the Ennaton of Alexandria. There, with the most praiseworthy diligence, he revised the holy book of the Gospels and all the other books of the New Testament, making a more critical and exact translation which superseded the earlier interpretation which was made at Mabbūgh in the reign of Bishop Philoxenus and on his commission. At this time the bishops of Syria, who had been expelled by the Chalcedonians and had taken refuge in Egypt, returned to their sees in Syria at the command of Chosroës.' Michael, 10.23b, tells the story of this persecution, which he dates to AG 910 = year 17 of Maurice. No chronicler explains why, after a first mention in the passage just quoted, Bishop Jonah of Edessa is never referred to again, but Barhebraeus conjectures that 'he went back to his country'.

whole senate. Gregory had a son called Nicetas and Heraclius had a son called after his father - Heraclius. A sense of outrage prompted these men to send their sons with their own armies to make war on Phocas; and they had come to an agreement with each other: if Nicetas got to Constantinople before Heraclius, he was to be king of the Romans, but if Heraclius got there first, the empire was to be his. Nicetas would set off by land, Heraclius would sail by sea. After their departure Heraclius's journey was favoured by a following wind, the sea was calm and there were no impediments; so he and those with him arrived at one of the harbours of the Royal City well in advance /p. 226/ of Nicetas. The entire city went out to greet him and to fête his entrance, senate and people together. Thus, eight years after becoming king, Phocas was assassinated and Heraclius was seated on the throne.[284]

§ 23*. On September 1, AG 922 = year 21 of Chosroēs, Heraclius ascended the throne[285] and sent messengers to Chosroēs to sue for peace. But he, far from granting their suit, uttered warnings and threats against the Romans. On* October 8 of the following year the Persians took Antioch. On October 15 they took Apamea and marched on Phoenician Emesa, which surrendered on the strength of an amnesty.[286] In the same year a Roman army joined battle with the Persians in Syria and the Romans came off much the worse; and the Persian general Vahrām besieged Cappadocian Caesarea - some of the inhabitants were killed, but most went back with Vahrām as captives.

---

[284] Chr. Pasch., pp. 699-701/150-2; text No. 5, to the left of the first chart; text No. 10, AG 933; Nikephoros, ch. 1; Theophanes, pp. 295-6, 298; Agapius, 189; Michael, 10.25a.

[285] Dionysius has made Heraclius's reign begin at the end of AG 922 instead of at the end of AG 921, perhaps because his source had synchronized the Seleucid New Year with the Indiction (John of Ephesus, for example, sometimes does this). As a result, it is necessary to add one to the figure given for Heraclius's regnal year throughout the text, although this probably does not apply where the regnal year is the only date given, as at the end of the present paragraph, § 23, and in the note there (see Appendix I).

[286] Lit. 'they gave it the/a word (of pardon?) and it was subjected.'

In year 4 of Heraclius Shahrvarāz subjugated Damascus to the Persians and the Damascenes received an amnesty in return for the payment of tribute.[287]

§ 24*. In year 6 of Heraclius[288] = 27 of Chosroës, Shahrvarāz battered at the walls of Jerusalem and took it by the sword, slaughtering 90,000 Christians in it. The Jews in their hatred actually bought Christians at a low price for the privilege of killing them. As for Zechariah, the Chalcedonian bishop of Jerusalem, Shahrvarāz took him captive and sent him down to Chosroës in Persia, /p. 227/ together with the venerable Wood of the Cross and the gold and silver treasure. He also banished the Jews from Jerusalem. The following year Shahrvarāz invaded Egypt and, with much bloodshed, subjected it with Alexandria to the Persians.[289]

---

[287] Text No. 2, section 7, AG 922, 924; Theophanes, pp. 299-300; Agapius, 190; Michael, p. 403:11-19, 36-40, 11.1a: 'When Heraclius came to the throne he sent envoys to Chosroës seeking peace, saying, "Because Phocas had your friend, King Maurice, murdered, we have executed him." He hoped by such flattery to make reconciliation possible. [...] In year 4 of Heraclius Shahrvarāz subjected Damascus to the Persians and the following year he conquered Galilee and the region of (the) Jordan.'

[288] Read 'year 7' (see Appendix I).

[289] *Chr. Pasch.*, pp. 704-5/156 (giving year 4 of Heraclius = 614 for the sack of Jerusalem); text No. 2, section 7, AG 925 (= 614; Jerusalem), 930 (Alexandria); text No. 5, to the left of the first chart; Theophanes, p. 301; Michael, p. 404:13-24, 34-37, 11.1a: 'The next year (year 7 of Heraclius) Shahrvarāz invaded Egypt and conquered it. He conquered Alexandria and killed many people there. He also subjected Libya to the Persians, as far as the borders of Ethiopia (lit. 'of the Cushites'). In the same year the Persian Shāhīn besieged Chalcedon and took it by force; he cruelly massacred the entire population and returned unscathed. [...] At this time Heraclius proclaimed his son Constantine Augustus in order to send him at the head of an army to fight the Persians who had occupied all Roman territories from Pontic coast to the east.' See also Michael, p. 403:5-19, 11.1b: 'The first year of Heraclius's reign, there was a solar eclipse lasting four hours. There was also such a drought that all the crops failed, not only the wheat, with the result that there was a serious food-shortage. In the same year a party of Arabs came up from Arabia into Syria, capturing people and booty, wasting many regions and

§ 25*. AG 933 = year 12 of Heraclius = year 33 of Chosroës:[290] In Yathrib[291] Muhammad, a member of the tribe of Quraysh, became known by his claim to be a prophet. At this point it is necessary to insert a note on the Arabs {Syr. ṭayyōyē}, whose collective name {Syr. arabōyē} is derived from the general designation of their homeland as Fertile Arabia (Arabia Felix). This region extends north-south [from the river Euphrates to the Southern Sea][292] and west-east from the Red Sea to the gulf of the Persian Sea. The Arabs also have a great many specific appellations corresponding to their ancestral tribes. The said Muhammad had begun as a young man to go up and down from his own city of Yathrib to Palestine for reasons of commerce, both buying and selling. That is how he became familiar with that country; and the monotheist religion which he had observed there had met with his approval. Back at home he would expound this religion to his tribesmen, a few of whom were convinced and became his followers. When speaking to them of these matters he used also to extol the quality of the land in Palestine and he maintained that it was 'because they confessed that unique God' /p. 228/ that such a good and fertile land had been given to them. Then he would add, 'If you listen to me, you too will have a good land, flowing with milk and honey, as a gift from God.' To back up this claim, he gathered those who were amenable into a band and began to lead them up to raid the land of Palestine, returning unscathed with a load of captives and booty. He

---

committing numerous massacres and acts of arson without the slightest compunction.'

[290] If we correct to year 13 of Heraclius, the synchronism with AG 933 pinpoints the month September; this is probably an indication that Dionysius's synchronisms were intended to be accurate as to months, since Muslim tradition puts Muhammad's arrival in Medina at a date corresponding to September 24, 622.

[291] Here and elsewhere in the Syriac sources the old name of Medina is used.

[292] Supplemented from Michael, p. 405:12.

had given them his word; and he did not let them down.[293]

§ 26. Acquisitiveness is habit-forming. One raiding expedition to Palestine and back was naturally followed by another. And of course, when the uncommitted ones saw Muhammad's disciples enriching themselves so royally, they did not need to be press-ganged into his service; they flocked to him. Later, when his followers had grown into a great army of men and when he himself occupied the seat of honour in his own city of Yathrib, he no longer permitted them to carry out (mere) raids.[294] Nor could little Palestine be satisfaction enough for long, once forces of this kind had been unleashed. They ranged much further afield, killing openly, taking captives, laying waste and plundering. And even so it was not enough for them, unless they had reduced the population to subjects who were obliged to pay regular tribute. In this way they grew by degrees in strength and extended their territory, until they were powerful enough to conquer all but a few of the Roman territories and the Persian empire as well. From this hegemony was born an established empire with one ruler following another in regular succession. And God, whose purpose was to chastise

---

[293] Text No. 5, to the left of the second chart; text No. 10, AG 932; text No. 12, AG 932; Agapius, 191, 196-7; Michael, p. 405:3-6, 17-21, 11.2a: 'They are called Arabs {Syr. tayyōyē}, but also Ishmaelites and Hagarenes {Syr. HGRYɔ} after Hagar and Ishmael, and Saracens {Syr. SRQYɔ} after Sarah, and Medyanōyē, (the Armenian translation adds: 'after Midian') the son of Cetura. [...] Muhammad had learned through conversation with the Jews of their belief in a single God. Seeing that his tribesmen worshipped stones, wood and other created things he became an adept of Judaism, which he admired.'

[294] Michael, p. 405:43-406:3, 11.2a: 'When many had sworn allegiance to him, he no longer went up in person as leader of those who went up to plunder, but he sent others at the head of his armies, while remaining himself in his city on the seat of honour.' Chabot translates the Chronicle of 1234 as if it meant the same: 'Et postea, cum ipsi adhaerebant viri multi, ingens exercitus, non amplius deduxit eos in depraedationem, sed Iathrippis, in sua civitate, honorifice sedebat.' This involves reading 'no longer led them out' where the Syriac of our only manuscript clearly has 'no longer permitted'. My translation respects the transmitted text and lays the emphasis instead on the difference between raiding expeditions and wars of conquest.

us for our sins, nodded in assent while this empire waxed in power.[295]

§ 27*. So much for the cause and origin of the movement of Muhammad, the first king of the Arabs. Now we may turn to the laws and commandments which, as he claimed, he was inspired by God to impose upon them. To begin with, he taught them /p. 229/ to confess one God, the Creator of everything. He eschewed the names of Father, Son and Spirit and affirmed instead that the Divinity was unique in His Person and unique in His Being, a Being neither begotten nor begetting, and having no companion. He recognizes Moses and his book and he even recognizes the Gospel, though he declines to confess that Christ was crucified. As to Christ himself, Muhammad considers Him a just man and the most honoured of the prophets, born of a virgin without intercourse, formed, as Adam out of earth, by the creative power of God's Word. He admits that He worked miracles and raised the dead, but not that He was crucified; for he maintains that when the Jews 'laid hands on Him,' they actually crucified someone else who appeared to them identical with Him, whereas Christ Himself was raised up, alive, to the fourth heaven. There He will stay until the end, when He will come a second time to the earth. At God's command He will be the Judge of mankind on the Day of Resurrection. They also confess the resurrection and the requital of deeds.[296]

---

[295] Michael, p. 406:3-6, 11.2a: 'Whoever did not accept his doctrine was made to conform, not by persuasion, but by the sword; those who refused he killed.'

[296] Michael, p. 406:20-31, 38-41, 407:3-11, 11.2a: 'He affirms that there is one Divinity, unique in His Person and unique in His Being, neither begotten nor begetting, and having neither son, nor associate, nor companion. He accepts the books of Moses and of the Prophets and even something of the Gospel, but of this latter he rejects the greater part and accepts only a fraction. As for Christ, he agrees that He is the one whose coming was predicted by the prophets, but says that He was merely a just man and a prophet like the others, not God, nor the Son of God, as we Christians confess Him to be. [...] they call Him sometimes the Word of God or His Spirit, alleging that He is the work and the creation of the Word of God. [...] They say that the holy virgin Mary was the sister of Moses and Aaron. They do not all admit

§ 28. As for Muḥammad's conception of Paradise, it is sensual and crude in the extreme. He envisages food and drink, copulation with glamorous courtesans, beds of gold to lie upon with mattresses of coral and of topaz, and rivers of milk and honey. They also maintain that there will be an end to torment. Their view is that every man suffers torments commensurate with the sins he has committed, then comes out of that Place into Paradise.[297]

§ 29. Muḥammad emancipates the man and permits him legally to marry as many freeborn women as he wishes - and he is permitted as many concubines as he can cope with. He may divorce his wife by giving her a letter of annulment, just as in the Law of Moses. He also taught them to pray five times a day and he made it an absolute obligation to wash themselves before prayer. Thirty days of the year, constituting a special month called Ramaḍān, are set aside for fasting. They fast by day, but are permitted to eat all night. They practise circumcision of both the males /p. 230/ and the females of their number. Their prostrations at prayer-time are directed to the south. A document was drawn up of which Muḥammad said that a copy had been transferred[298] onto his mind by God himself through the mediation of an angel and that he, Muḥammad, had used his own language to render it comprehensible to human ears. This they call the Divine Book.[299]

---

that Christ was crucified by the Jews, but claim that one of His disciples, to whom He lent His likeness, was crucified and died, whereas Christ, who had gone into hiding, was snatched up and taken by God into the Garden.'

[297] Agapius, p. 197; Theophanes, p. 334.

[298] {Syr. etn^{e}sek}, 'poured', as molten metal, but also 'written'.

[299] Michael, p. 407:19-408:4, 11.2a: 'They use the concepts of fate, luck and divine predestination. They take up to four freeborn wives and as many concubines as they wish. Whoever divorces his wife with oaths may not take her back, which would involve breaking his oaths, unless he first give her to another man; for then he is released from his oaths and may take her back. They pray five times a day and make four prostrations with each prayer. They believe that the dead will rise and be judged and that each individual will be rewarded according to

§ 30*. In this year Shahrvarāz took Ankara in Galatia and many islands in the sea and caused the massacre of vast numbers of his victims. Chosroēs became harsh, arrogant and overweening as a result of his victories. Who is there now to compose lamentations (as Jeremiah did) about the distress and the loss of life that people suffered at this time? Who can count the tragic deportations, the pillagings and depredations, the cruel requisitions, the harsh taxations? How many blocks of stone, slabs and pillars of marble and pedestals of gold and silver from the churches were carried off to Persia?[300]

§ 31. At this time all the silver with which the Great Church of Edessa was adorned was stripped and sent off to the emperor Chosroēs in Persia, because of the enmity which had arisen between Cyrus, the governor of Edessa, and the people of the city. Certain uncouth citizens who envied him denounced him with characteristic baseness to Chosroēs. As a result he took all the treasure of all the temples of Edessa, including that of the Great Church itself, and he stripped off the silver plate from the ciborium[301] above the altar and from its four pillars, from all the pillars in front of the altar and from the ambo[302] in the centre of the church. The total weight of the silver

---

his deeds. They are given over to the love of the world and to physical urges, eating, drinking, dressing up and promiscuous copulation, both with freeborn wives and with concubines. There is nothing to impede them from divorcing one wife in order to marry another. They have a day-time fast lasting thirty days, i.e. one lunar month in the year; but they eat all night until the dawn. Before praying they wash with water even their excretory members. When they have been to bed with a woman or had a wet dream, they wash their whole body and afterwards they pray. Their worship is directed towards the Ka^{c}ba; wherever they are they turn towards that place to worship. They practise circumcision of males and females; yet they do not observe the Law of Moses, which prescribes that circumcision should take place on the eighth day, for they circumcize at any age.'

[300] Text No. 2, section 7, AG 934; Agapius, pp. 191, 197; Theophanes, pp. 302, 314; Michael, p. 408:13-16, 11.3a: 'In the first year of Muhammad the Persian Shahrvarāz took Ankara, then Rhodes.'

[301] {Gr. naós}.

[302] {Gr. bēma}.

was established as one hundred and twelve thousand pounds; and all this he sent to Chosroës.[303]

§ 32*. In year 18 of Heraclius[304] Chosroës commanded /p. 231/ that the inhabitants of Edessa be deported to Persia. The letter he wrote to the governor[305] in charge of Edessa urged him to act swiftly; but the governor, who was a mild and pleasant man of a humane disposition, decided not to have us[306] deported all at once, but little by little, because he expected a reprieve to come from the King. So he started to send them off street by street. When news arrived of Heraclius's expedition against Persia, Edessa was spared for this reason from deportation, except for two streets, the inhabitants of which had already been floated down the Euphrates as far as Dastgird.[307] Some of the leading men in the city had gone down

---

[303] Michael, p. 403:43-404:, 11.1b: 'A man called Cyrus, one of the nobles of the city, was appointed by Chosroës as governor {Gr. arkhōn}. The Edessenes accused him of many things out of envy, but Chosroës ignored them. Then they turned to Cyrus and pretended that they had had a change of heart. He believed them and did not nurse a grievance. They asked him to go to Chosroës to petition him for a diminution of the tribute. This he did and he obtained the desired edict in their favour. But when he was about to return he met two uncouth men who had been sent by the Edessenes to make false accusations against him in the presence of Chosroës. Realizing what was afoot, he went back to Chosroës, who let them speak as much evil against him as Satan gave them strength for. Then, once they had been dismissed, Cyrus spoke to Chosroës of the great affluence which was to be found at Edessa. Chosroës had all the silver of the Edessenes, from the temples and the aristocratic houses and everywhere else, collected and brought to Persia. The total weight of it was 120,000 pounds.'

[304] This regnal year cannot be altered to 'Heraclius 19' (beginning in September, AD 628), because Chosroës died in February of that year. On the strength of this, and of § 38, I have left Heraclius's regnal years unaltered where they are not synchronized with the Seleucid era (see Appendix I).

[305] {Pers. marzbān}.

[306] The first person pronoun derives from the original memoir by Sergius Rusafōyō, from which this passage was drawn: see the introduction to this text.

[307] {Syr. sōqartō}.

with them, including Sergius the son of Īwannis Rusafōyō, who had been deported once before, together with his mother, as we have told. In this year the sun was darkened and lost the light of half its orb. It remained so from October until June, so that people began to say it would never regain its full orb.[308]

§ 33*. AG 936 = year 14 of Heraclius = year 35 of Chosroës = year 3 of Muhammad:[309]   Chosroës sent Shahrvarāz and Kardīgān, the Persian generals, with a great force and an arsenal of military equipment and they laid siege to the city of Constantinople from the west. For nine months the Persians maintained their guard on the City and brought the emperor Heraclius, who was within, under great pressure. But after that the Persians rebelled against their king and made peace with Heraclius. How this happened we shall now explain.[310]

---

[308] Text No. 5, to the right of the second chart; text No. 12, AG 938; Agapius, pp. 200-1; Michael, p. 409:1-17, 11.3b: 'From this important citizen Sergius is derived {Syr. mettayt^eyō} the chronicle of the patriarch Dionysius of Tel-Mahrē (which extends) over six generations {Syr. dōrē} (i.e. Sergius is one of Dionysius's earliest sources; perhaps the words 'a part of' have fallen out of the text before 'the chronicle'). AG 938 = year 17 (read '18'; see Appendix I) of Heraclius = year 37 of Chosroës = year 6 of Muhammad: the light of one half of the orb of the sun was extinguished and there was darkness from October until June, so that people said that the orb of the sun would never again be restored. In this year an epidemic of pestilence {Syr. shar^cūtō} struck in the land of Palestine and many tens of thousands of people died there.'

[309] Read 'year 15 of Heraclius' and 'year 4 of Muhammad' (see Appendix I).

[310] Michael, p. 408:23-34, 11.3a: 'AG 936 = year 15 (correct, through 'intelligent corruption'; see Appendix I) of Heraclius = year 35 of Chosroës = year 4 of Muhammad: Shahrvarāz and Kardīgān laid siege to Constantinople and conveyed their forces into Thrace, where some of them besieged (it from) the west side; the City had been under continuous siege for one year and was in such straits that hope was abandoned, when, all of a sudden, relief appeared in the following manner.' The siege of Constantinople is dated to 626 by Theophanes, p. 316 and by the contemporary Constantinopolitan Chr. Pasch., pp.

§ 34. The general Shahrvarāz was denounced for insulting the King. He was supposed to have accused him of arrogance and depravity, and of 'hogging the credit for other men's victories'. As a result Chosroēs sent Kardīgān, the other general, written instructions for the arrest and decapitation of Shahrvarāz. /p. 232/ The bearer of this missive together with the escort responsible for his safe arrival fell into the hands of the Romans in Galatia and were sent as prisoners to Heraclius. The messenger entered the Royal City unnoticed by the Persians who had it under surveillance. When Heraclius learned from the envoy what he had been sent for and why, he sent a secret summons to Shahrvarāz, assuring him under oath that it was in his own interest to come. Shahrvarāz was accordingly smuggled in and Heraclius showed him what Chosroēs had written to Kardīgān. The envoy was brought in and made to stand in front of Shahrvarāz, who recognized him immediately. After reading the letter and interrogating the envoy as to certain details, he took his leave of Heraclius and returned to the camp, where he pondered what it was expedient for him to do.[311]

§ 35. The scheme which his intelligence devised was both admirable in its cunning and effective in its execution. For the letter he substituted another, altered version, adding instructions to the effect that such and such leading Persians of outstanding reputation, three hundred in all, should be executed along with Shahrvarāz. Having placed a seal on this letter to authenticate it, he summoned the leaders of the Persians, including Kardīgān, to a meeting. After the letter had been read out aloud to the assembled chiefs, Shahrvarāz asked Kardīgān, 'What do you say? Are you prepared to execute this order? What do you say, my lords?' The lords were furious and began to abuse Chosroēs and revile his name. Between them they decided to make peace with Heraclius, agreeing to his terms, so that he might be their accomplice in encompassing the downfall of Chosroēs. Their

---

715-26/168-81. See also Michael, p. 410:34-36, 11.3a: 'Those of the Edessenes who survived in captivity came back from Persia.'

[311] Theophanes, pp. 323-4; <u>Agapius</u>, pp. 201-2; Michael, 11.3a.

envoys reached a settlement with Heraclius, under the terms of which they gave him hostages as a guarantee of the agreement between them. It was for the King to select his hostages among the sons and the brothers of the Persians; he chose, amongst others, /p. 233/ the son of Shahrvarāz. It was agreed that the Persians would strike camp and depart from the City and that Heraclius would lead a Roman army to make war on Chosroës. Accordingly the Persians evacuated Europe and returned to Asia. Heraclius meanwhile sent word to the King of the Khazars, bidding him despatch an auxiliary force of forty thousand men from the Caspian region. Khagan the King replied by his envoy: 'I am sending them to join up with you wherever you wish.' Heraclius promised (in return) to give Khagan his daughter, Eudocia, in marriage.[312]

§ 36. About this time Heraclius, rabid with the lust of the flesh and flouting the laws of God, the Church and Nature itself, took Martina, his brother's daughter, to wife. She bore him an illegitimate son, Heraclonas, to set beside the sons born to him by his first wife.[313]

§ 37*. Heraclius then set off from the Royal City with a great army and marched against Armenia. In every city which he passed he re-established Roman sovereignty and expelled the Persians. When Chosroës heard of the general mutiny led by Shahrvarāz and of Heraclius's expedition, he was alarmed and disheartened. Most of his forces were scattered throughout Syria, Palestine, Egypt and the other western countries. He mustered as many as he could and ordered a certain Rōzvēhān to lead them into battle with Heraclius. Rōzvēhān set out accordingly to meet Heraclius in Assyria. On his passage through their country Heraclius had attracted many Armenians to his standards and he had met up with the Persian and Khazar auxiliaries sent by Khagan. /p. 234/ Now they descended upon the Median lands in the region of Azerbaijan and pillaged them. Rōzvēhān had to force a

---

[312] Theophanes, p. 324; <u>Agapius</u>, pp. 202-3; Michael, 11.3a.
[313] Theophanes, pp. 300-1; Michael, 11.3a.

march to meet him in Assyria; and after a stalwart fight near the river
Zāb the Persians took to their heels. Most were killed, including
Rōzvēhān; and the Romans siezed their camp. When Chosroēs was
informed, he abandoned the Royal City with all his granaries and
treasure. He had built a fort called Dastgird[314] about five and a
half kilometres[315] to the east of Ctesiphon and thither Heraclius
pursued him. He penetrated his defences, seized and plundered
everything in the royal palaces and left the fort itself in flames. He
similarly pillaged and sacked the whole of Bēth Ōrōmōyē.[316]

§ 38*. Shīrōē, son of Chosroēs, had been thrown into gaol by his
father; but when he learned that Heraclius was on Chosroēs's track, he
escaped and hunted down and killed his father. That was on February
9; Chosroēs had reigned for thirty-eight years. He was succeeded by
his son. Heraclius meanwhile was wintering between Assyria and
Armenia. He intended to return in pursuit of Chosroēs, for he had not
yet heard of his assassination. This he learned from the new king's
messenger, after Shīrōē had assumed the kingship. Under the terms
of the treaty that was drawn up between them, all territories which had
formerly belonged to the Romans were to be surrendered to Heraclius,
by which action Persia would retreat within its traditional boundaries.
All Persian forces in the west were to be transferred back to Persia. /p.
235/ This was in year 19 of Heraclius = year 7 of Muhammad,[317]
the year that Shīrōē became king of the Persians. After this Heraclius
marched towards Syria and his brother Theodoric went ahead to eject
the Persians from the cities as agreed in the earlier pact with Shahrvarāz

---

[314] {Syr. sōqartō}.

[315] 'Two parasangs'.

[316] Text No. 2, section 7, AG 934; Theophanes, pp. 303-27;
Agapius, pp. 203-4; Michael, 11.3a.

[317] Year 19 of Heraclius was year 7 of Muhammad, but Shīrōē
became king on 25 February while Heraclius was still in his 18th year.
This confirms the rule that Heraclius's regnal year should not be
corrected upwards in the absence of a Seleucid date, for here it should
be corrected downwards, if at all (see Appendix I).

and as confirmed by the recent treaty with Shīrōē.[318]

§ 39*. So Theodoric began to make the rounds of the Mesopotamian cities, informing the Persian garrisons of their duty to return to their country. In fact they had already been informed of the treaty in letters from Shahrvarāz and from Shīrōē. Close on his brother's heels the King advanced, establishing governors and Roman garrisons in the cities. When Theodoric reached Edessa, however, the Persians there turned a deaf ear to his proclamation. Their reply was, 'We do not know Shīrōē and we will not surrender the city to the Romans'. The Jews of Edessa were standing there on the wall with the Persians. Partly out of hatred for the Christians, but also in order to ingratiate themselves with the Persians, they began to insult the Romans and Theodoric was obliged to hear their sarcastic taunts against himself. This provoked him to an all-out attack on the city, which he subjected with his catapults to a hail of rocks. The Persian resistance was crushed and they accepted an amnesty[319] to return to their country. A certain Jew called Joseph, anticipating a pogrom,[320] scaled down the wall and sped off to find Heraclius in Tella.[321] He was admitted to the Royal Presence, where he urged the King to forgive his fellow-Jews /p. 236/ the insults to which they had subjected Theodoric and to send an envoy to restrain his brother from exacting vengeance. Meanwhile Theodoric had entered Edessa and taken over control. After expelling the Persians and sending them off home, he had sent his men out to herd together all the Jews who had insulted him. He had already begun to kill them and to plunder their houses, when Joseph arrived with a letter from the King, by which he forbade his brother to harm

---

[318] *Chr. Pasch.*, pp. 727-8/182-3; text No. 2, section 7, AG 939; text No. 5, to the left of the second chart; text No. 12, AG 938; Theophanes, pp. 326-7; Agapius, pp. 192, 204; Michael, 11.3a.

[319] Lit. 'the word of a pact'.

[320] Lit. 'the destruction of his people'.

[321] {Syr. tellō d-mawz^elat}.

them.[322]

§ 40*. At about the time that Theodoric, who had left Edessa and crossed the Euphrates, arrived at Mabbūgh and set about expelling the Persians from Syria and Phoenicia, Heraclius himself arrived in Edessa and took up residence in the palace at the head of the source. One day, he set out to receive communion in the Great Church; but he was intercepted by Isaiah, the metropolitan of Edessa, who refused to give him communion. This man was zealous to a fault or rather, to tell the truth, an uneducated idiot. He said, 'Unless you first anathematize the Synod of Chalcedon and the Tome of Leo in writing, I will not give you communion.' At this the King flared up in anger and expelled the bishop from his church, handing it over instead to his own co-religionaries, the Chalcedonians.[323]

§ 41. At this time the chief dignitaries of Edessa were descended in the following great lines: the Rusafōyō family, the Tel-Mahrōyō family, the family of Cosmas, son of Araby, and the family of Nōlar. These and their ancestors had endowed the Great Church with all its treasure of gold and silver, together with gardens, mills, shops and public baths. On this occasion they were unable to oppose the King's command. Nevertheless they expected to return with their bishop to

---

[322] Theophanes, p. 327; Agapius, p. 206; Michael, 11.3a.

[323] Agapius, pp. 206-7; Michael, p. 408:28-409:14, 11.3c: 'When the power of Persia was removed and the Romans regained the mastery and possession of the cities of Syria and Mesopotamia, Heraclius came to Syria and arrived in Edessa. The people, the priests and the monks came out to greet him. He admired and praised the great multitude of monks; then, when he learned about their Faith, he said to some of those accompanying him, "How can it be right to exclude so admirable a group of people from our own company?" And so he entered the city, anxious to make peace between the two parties. Then, when a feast-day came round, the King went down to the church belonging to us Orthodox and distributed great largesse to the whole people. When the Office and the divine Sacrifice were finished, the King approached to communicate in the Holy Mysteries, as is the custom of Christian kings. But Isaiah, the metropolitan of the city, in the fervour of his zeal, prevented the King from taking the Sacrament'; cf. Michael, 11.3a.

the church and to repossess it after the King had gone back to the heartlands of Byzantium.

§ 42. However, God, who exacts his due /p. 237/ and who determines sovereignty among people on the earth, will give power to whom He chooses. He may appoint even the dregs of mankind to be their rulers. When He saw that the measure of the Romans' sins was overflowing and that they were committing every sort of crime against our people and our churches, bringing our Confession to the verge of extinction, He stirred up the Sons of Ishmael and enticed them hither from their southern land. This had been the most despised and disregarded of the peoples of the earth, if indeed they were known at all. Yet it was by bargaining with them that we secured our deliverance. This was no small gain, to be rescued from Roman imperial oppression.[324] Yet we suffered a loss as well. The cathedral churches which had been unjustly confiscated from our people by Heraclius and given to his co-religionaries, the Chalcedonians, have continued to languish in their possession until the present day.[325] For at the time when they were conquered and made subject to the Arabs the cities agreed to terms of surrender,[326] under which each confession had assigned to it those temples[327] which were found in its possession. In this way the Orthodox were robbed of the Great Church of Edessa and that of Ḥarrān; and this process continued throughout the west, as far as Jerusalem. The remaining cities of Mesopotamia escaped this fate, however, because the persecution had its origin in Edessa, as we have shown.[328]

§ 43*. Heraclius had now departed from Edessa and crossed the Euphrates. He advanced to Jerusalem and then to Antioch, whence he

---

[324] Lit. 'from the tyrannical kingdom of the Romans.'

[325] That is, presumably, the early 840s, when Dionysius wrote.

[326] Lit. 'accepted the word'.

[327] {Syr. hayklē} here seems to include all places of worship.

[328] Michael, 11.3c.

returned to Mabbūgh. At this moment Shīrōē, the Persian king, died. His son, whose name was Ardashīr, was chosen to succeed him. But he had hardly begun to reign when he lost his life to the usurper Shahrvarāz, who confirmed by letters his sworn agreement with the Romans and the command to the Persians in Egypt and Palestine to evacuate these regions /p. 238/ and return to Persia. By AG 941 = year 19 of Heraclius[329] = year 8 of Muhammad, the last Persian had gone back across the Euphrates.[330]

§ 44. At this point civil war broke out in Persia between the supporters of Shahrvarāz and those of Kardīgān. Heraclius sent Roman auxiliaries at the request of Shahrvarāz. The latter killed Kardīgān in battle and was left undisputed king of the Persians. Then Heraclius requested Shahrvarāz to return the Wood of the Cross, which he had taken from Jerusalem - captured by him in year 6 of Heraclius[331] - and Shahrvarāz did so gladly and with great ceremony. Heraclius came out from Mabbūgh to greet the Cross on its arrival and he took possession of it with due solemnity. At this time the patriarch Athanasius was summoned to Mabbūgh for an interview with Heraclius; he and twelve bishops entered the King's Presence, with the consequences we have described in our History of the Church.[332]

---

[329] Read 'year 20 of Heraclius' (see Appendix I).

[330] Text No. 2, section 7, AG 939; text No. 5, to the left of the second chart; Agapius, p. 207; Michael, p. 410:14-16, 11.3a: 'AG 940: Shīrōē the Persian died after a reign of nine months. His son Ardashīr reigned after him for one year and ten months.'

[331] This regnal year should be altered to '7', although it is not directly coupled to a Seleucid date, because it is derived from § 24, not from an independent source (an exception to the rule outlined in Appendix I).

[332] Theophanes, p. 329; Michael, 11.1c, 11.2b, and especially p. 409:34-410:29, 11.3c: 'The King having removed to Mabbūgh, the patriarch Athanasius entered his presence with twelve bishops: Thomas of Palmyra {Syr. tadmur}, Basil of Emesa, Sergius of ᶜUrd (apparently a fortress in the desert between Palmyra and Rusāfa, no doubt the 'see' of a bishop responsible for bedouin Christians), John of Cyrrhus, Thomas of Mabbūgh, Daniel of Harrān, Isaiah of Edessa, Severus of Qenneshrīn, Athanasius of Arabïssus, Cosmas of Cilician Epiphania

AG 942* = year 20 of Heraclius[333] = year 9 of Muhammad: Shahrvarāz was assassinated by one of the relatives of Chosroēs, and Bōrān, daughter of Chosroēs, became queen of the Persians. She died shortly afterwards and was succeeded by her sister Āzarmēdukht. In this year the patriarch Athanasius died. Two years later commotion struck the Persian people, for some of them wanted to crown Yazdgird, the son[334] of Chosroēs, as their king, while others were committed to a man whose name was Hormizd. But the boy Yazdgird was crowned and shared power with his sister Āzarmēdukht.[335]

---

and Severus of Samosata. They remained in his presence for twelve days, debating. He required from them a written statement {Lat. libellus} of their belief and they gave him the document reproduced above (11.2b; cf. also 11.1c, a letter from Heraclius to the 'Doubters' {Gr. diakrinómenoi}). When he had read it, he praised their Faith and asked them to give him Communion and to accept the charter which he had drawn up, confessing two natures unified in Christ, one will and one energy, in accordance, so it was alleged, with Cyril (of Alexandria). When they saw that it was in agreement with Nestorius and Leo they did not accept it and Heraclius was angered. He circulated instructions throughout the empire that it was a duty to cut off the nose and the ears and to loot the house of anyone who was not a supporter of the Synod of Chalcedon. This persecution went on for a long time and many monks gave their support to the synod. The monks of the House of Maron, of Mabbūgh, of Emesa and (of) the southern region revealed their dastardliness: many of them, by accepting the synod, unjustly obtained possession of (these four words represent {Syr. htap}, 'snatched') the majority of churches and monasteries. Heraclius would not admit the Orthodox into his presence, nor would he allow them to present their case in the matter of the unjust transference of church-ownership (lit. 'the snatching of the churches'). And that is why [...]' (here follows a passage almost identical with § 42).

[333] Read 'year 21 of Heraclius' (see Appendix I).

[334] Actually grandson; probably {Syr. BR}, 'the son of', has been omitted before {Syr. BRH}, 'his son'.

[335] Text No. 5, to the right of the second chart; Theophanes, p. 335; Michael, p. 410:24-26, 11.3a: '[Shahrvarāz] reigned for one year and was killed by one of his relatives who had been a friend of Chosroēs.'

§ 45*. AG 943 = year 21 of Heraclius:[336] Muhammad, king of the Arabs, died, /p. 239/ after reigning for ten years. On his death-bed he had appointed Abū Bakr as his successor; this was the father of his wife, ᶜĀᵓisha. Muhammad himself was descended in the male line from Ishmael, who was the son of Abraham by Hagar. Now Ishmael begat the following sons: Nebayoth, his first-born, Qedar, Adbeel, Mibsam, Mishmaᶜ, Dumah, Massa, Hadar, Tema, Jetur,[337] Naphish, Qedemah, Aqīd[338] [...] ᶜAbd al-Muttalib begat ᶜAbd Allāh and his twelve brothers and ᶜAbd Allāh begat Muhammad, who became the first leader and king, as we have recorded.[339]

§ 46*. After the death of Muhammad Abū Bakr became king and sent an army of 30,000 Arabs to conquer Syria in the first year of his reign. For this army he appointed four generals: the first was Abū ᶜUbayda b. al-Jarrāh, i.e. ᶜUmar b. ᶜAbd Allāh b. al-Jarrāh; the second was ᶜAmr b. Saᶜīd b. al-ᶜĀs;[340] /p. 240/ the third was Shurahbīl b. Hasana; the fourth was Yazīd b. Abī Sufyān. With

---

[336] Read 'year 22 of Heraclius' (see Appendix I).

[337] Genesis 25:13-15 suggests that the Syriac should be emended where it substitutes 'R' for the similar 'D' in the names of Adbeel and Dumah; Jetur represents {Syr. NTWR}.

[338] There follows a genealogy of the descendants of Aqīd (according to Abū 'l-Feda, 'Kidār'), an 'extra', thirteenth son of Ishmael not known from Genesis, down to Muhammad in the twenty-eighth generation. Only the last three generations are given here.

[339] Text No. 10, AC 938; text No. 12, AG 942; Theophanes, p. 333; Michael, p. 410:32-34, 11.3a: 'Muhammad died after a reign of seven years. After him Abū Bakr reigned for two years and seven months.'

[340] This is the name of a famous Umayyad (Ibn Saᶜd, al-Tabaqāt al-kubrā, Beirut 1960, IV, pp. 100-1), not to be confused with the renowned general and right-hand man of Muᶜāwiya, ᶜAmr b. al-ᶜĀs, who was a Sahmī. The former's brother, Khālid b. Saᶜīd b. al-ᶜĀs (Ibn Saᶜd, IV, pp. 94-100), is often named as one of the first generals (Ibn ᶜAsākir, pp. 443-6; Tabarī, I, p. 2101), and it may be that Dionysius or his source has muddled Khālid and ᶜAmr b. al-ᶜĀs. [R.H.]

them he sent an army of 12,000 Yemenites with {Syr. ABWLKWLB}*341* at their head. On inspecting these forces outside the city Abū Bakr gave them the following exhortation:*342*

§ 47. 'In the land you will invade kill neither the aged, nor the little child, nor the woman.*343* Do not force the stylite from his high perch*344* and do not harass the solitary. They have devoted themselves to the service of God. Do not cut down any (fruit-)tree, neither damage any crop, neither maim any domestic animal, large or small. Wherever you are welcomed by a city or a people, make a solemn pact with them and give them reliable guarantees that they will be ruled according to their laws and according to the practices which obtained among them before our time. They will contract with you to pay in tribute whatever sum shall be settled between you, then they will be left alone in their confession and in their country. But as for those who do not welcome you, make war on them. Be careful to abide by all the just laws and commandments which have been given to you by God through our prophet, lest you excite the wrath of God.'

§ 48*. The forces sent out by Abū Bakr approached [Syria] by the desert route to the south of Damascus. When Heraclius was informed that they had invaded Moab, he summoned the forces of the Romans and the Christian Arabs to join him in Damascus and after impressing

---

341 This is probably Dhū 'l-Kalāᶜ; Azdī, pp. 9-10 likewise mentions him alongside Abū Bakr's appointment of four generals, and asserts that he came to Abū Bakr with 'a large number of the people of Yemen' (p. 16). [R.H.]

342 The theme of the appointment of four generals appears in Theophanes, pp. 335-6; Agapius, pp. 193-4, 208; and numerous Arabic sources (see Donner, *Early Islamic Conquests*, pp. 114-5). cf. also the 'four heads of chastisement' in text No. 14, XI.4, XI.8. [R.H.]

343 This paragraph is based on an Arabic original, which enjoyed wide circulation because of its relevance to the legal debate on the conduct of war; cf. Tabarī, I, p. 1850; Ibn ᶜAsākir, pp. 454-7 (further references and discussion given in R. Hoyland, 'Arabic, Syriac and Greek Historiography'). [R.H.]

344 Lit. 'cause the stylite to get down from his place.'

on them the imperative of guarding the cities, he sent them to meet the Arabs in battle and to expel them from /p. 241/ the country. He himself marched with a large army to Antioch. Of the four generals sent by Abū Bakr one came, as we have said, to the land of Moab *en route* for Palestine; the second went to Egypt and Alexandria; the third set out against the Persians; and the last attacked the Christian Arabs who were subject to the Romans.[345]

§ 49*. The opposite number of the general sent to Palestine was the patríkios Sergius, to whom Heraclius had committed Palestinian Caesarea and its region. When he learned of the Arab army's approach he assembled his own forces and sent for 5,000 Samaritan foot-soldiers to strengthen his arm in the coming encounter with the Arabs. When the Arabs heard about these preparations they concentrated their forces and laid an ambush by which to surprise and destroy the Romans.[346]

§ 50. Already the Romans were on the march. They had reached the place where the ambush had been laid. Unaware, as yet, of the presence of the Arabs, they requested permission from Sergius to rest a little and to lay down their burdens - for most of them were foot-soldiers. The Patríkios refused. He knew by this time that the enemy were close at hand. He ordered the trumpets to be sounded, the drums to be beaten. The Romans were just preparing to charge, when the Arabs, mightily armed, sprang out of their hiding-places and advanced on them with deafening, angry shouts. The first ranks to meet their onslaught were those of the Samaritans, for these had marched at the head of the column. Under the attack they collapsed and every one of them perished by the sword. The Patríkios saw this and began to flee headlong /p. 242/ to save his skin. The Arabs pursued the Romans, like harvesters scything a ripe field of corn. Sergius fell from his horse, but his attendants came to his aid and set

---

[345] Michael, 11.4a.

[346] For this and the following two paragraphs, cf. text No. 2, section 7, AG 945 (but see note thereto); text No. 10, AG 953; Theophanes, p. 336; Agapius, pp. 194, 209; Michael, 11.4a.

him back on again. He stayed briefly in the saddle, then fell again.
Again his companions held ranks and set him back on his mount. A
few steps further on he fell to the ground for the third time. They were
making as if to put him back in the saddle, when he said: 'Leave me!
Save yourselves! Otherwise you and I shall drink the cup of death
together.'

§ 51. So they left him behind; and indeed they had not gone far
before the pursuers swooped in on him and killed him on the spot.
They continued their pursuit and slaughter of the Romans until darkness
fell. A few got away by hiding in trees, behind stone walls and in
vineyards. And so the Arabs entered Caesarea.[347]

§ 52*. When Heraclius heard of the death of the patríkios Sergius
and of the defeat of the combined forces of the Romans and the
Samaritans, he gave his brother Theodoric orders to muster all the
Romans who were with him in northern Mesopotamia[348] and all
those on the west side of the Euphrates. With all present and ready and
the army at full strength, they marched off, swaggering with unbounded
arrogance and conceit, confident in their greater numbers and their
superior arms.[349] (At evening) every tent in the camp became a
place of dancing, rejoicing, drinking and song. And they shot out their
lips, and they wagged their heads, and they said: 'We will not give
those Arabs a second thought. They are dead dogs, no more, no

---

[347] Michael, p. 413:5-40, 11.4a, adds: 'AG 945: There was a violent
earthquake in the month of September and afterwards a portent in the
sky, resembling a sword stretched out from the south to the north. It
stayed there for thirty days and it seemed to many that it stood for the
coming of the Arabs. At this time Heraclius decreed that all Jews in
the Roman empire should be baptized and become Christians. For this
reason the Jews emigrated from Roman territory. They came first of
all to Edessa, but when they were assaulted there as well, they fled to
Persia. A great number of them received baptism and became
Christians.' (Compare text No. 10, AG 928.)

[348] {Ar. al-jazīra}.

[349] Lit. 'the pride of weapons'.

less.'*350*

§ 53. When they reached the village of al-Jūsiya in the region of Emesa,*351* Theodoric approached a stylite standing on /p. 243/ his pillar; the man was a Chalcedonian. At the end of the long conversation which ensued between them the stylite said to Theodoric, 'If you will only promise that on your safe and victorious return from the war you will wipe out the followers of Severus*352* and crush them with excruciating punishments ...'; to which the patríkios Theodoric replied, 'I had already decided to persecute the Severans without having heard your advice'. These words were overheard by an Orthodox soldier standing near by; though he smarted with indignation, respect for superior rank prevented him from speaking. So the Romans, still puffed up with conceit, left that place and approached the Arab positions. They pitched camp near the tents of the Arabs and from May until October the two armies were encamped side by side, menacing one another. Then, suddenly, they were ranged in opposing battle-lines. For one hour at the start it seemed that the Romans would be stronger. But then the Arabs turned on them - and they trembled. In that moment the spirit went out of them and they lost their nerve, turned tail and took to flight. Even so they could not escape alive, because divine Providence had abandoned them. They were trampled underfoot by their enemies, who put them all to the sword. No one was able to defend himself except for Theodoric, who escaped with a handful of men. That soldier who was a believer saw Theodoric on the point of losing consciousness - his eyes staring out into impenetrable darkness - and he found the courage to say to him, 'Well, /p. 244/ Theodoric? What has become of your stylite and his promises? This is a fine achievement to add to your successes. Will you bring the news of the victory to the King?' The Patríkios took this in but did not even answer back. So the whole Roman army was destroyed, while

---

350 Agapius, p. 194; Michael, 11.5a.

351 Yāqūt, ii, 154.

352 That is, the Jacobites.

Theodoric himself got away to the King. The Arabs switched their attention to the fortified camp of the Romans and secured for themselves more gold, silver, expensive clothing, slaves and slave-girls than they could count. Rich men they became that day and much wealth they acquired.[353]

§ 54*. Then Heraclius sent general Baanēs and the son of Shahrvarāz, who since his father's assassination had been the Romans' companion at arms, with Sacellarius, the patríkios of Edessa, to lead a great army towards Damascus and to prevent the Arabs from entering the cities. On reaching Emesa they encountered the Arab emir Khālid b. al-Walīd. The Romans were defeated and 40,000 of them were massacred, including both Baanēs and Sacellarius; but the son of Shahrvarāz escaped with his life and came to terms with the Arabs. They gave him an amnesty and settled him at Emesa.[354]

§ 55*. After the Arabs had distinguished themselves in battle against the Romans, they went to the region of Baalbek, destroying and sacking everything in their path; and Khālid b. al-Walīd, the emir, went with them. A certain Roman general who was called /p. 245/ ? {Syr. QYQL‾WS}[355] appeared with 20,000 men and attacked the Arabs at al-Ajnādayn. Many arrows fell upon the Arabs and a large number of them and of their horses died; but when the battle grew fiercer the Romans were defeated and the general was killed.

§ 56. Khālid b. al-Walīd then led the Arab army to besiege Damascus. He himself lodged in a monastery at the East Gate, Abū

---

[353] Michael, p. 414:40-41, 11.5a: 'the village called al-Jūsiya {Syr. GWSYT} (as in the text translated above) in the region of Antioch.'

[354] Michael, 11.6a. Theophanes, pp. 337-8, has a parallel account in which Baanēs and Sacellarius and 40,000 men die, but he equates it with the battle of Yarmūk (see §§ 65-7 below); cf. also Nikephoros, ch. 20. [R.H.]

[355] Tabarī, I, p. 2125 has QYQLĀS or QBQLĀR (the manuscript is corrupt), which would appear to intend the title Cubicularius (de Goeje, Mémoire, p. 62). It was usual for military officers to be designated by their rank, so one should not expect a name here. [R.H.].

^cUbayda lodged at the Gabitha³⁵⁶ Gate and Yazīd at the Gate of the Apostle Thomas. For the gates of the city were shut against them. The Arabs outside surrounded the wall and launched a determined attack on the city. The Damascenes were in a bad way and in great fear of the Arabs, when a Roman auxiliary force of 50,000 arrived and fought its way with set determination into the city. The Arabs, undeterred,³⁵⁷ continued fighting for all they were worth to capture Damascus.

§ 57*. While the Arab armies were besieging Damascus they received the news of Abū Bakr's death; he had reigned for two and a half years. The following king was ^cUmar b. al-Khattāb. He sent a detachment to that part of Arabia called al-Balqā^ɔ and it took Bostra³⁵⁸ and destroyed the rest of the villages and cities. He also sent Sa^cd b. (Abī) Waqqās against the Persians. On their way these Arabs went up into the Mardīn mountains and they killed there many monks and excellent ascetics, especially in the great and famous abbey on the mountain above Rhesaina, which is called 'The Abbey of B^enōthō', i.e. of the eggs.³⁵⁹

---

³⁵⁶ {Ar. al-jābiya}.

³⁵⁷ This word attempts to do justice to {Syr. w-kad}, 'and although', *vel sim.*, a conjunction which appears, however, often to be used superfluously in the text translated.

³⁵⁸ {Ar. busrā}. Theophanes, pp. 336-7; Agapius, p. 209.

³⁵⁹ Text No. 2, section 5, AG 947; text No. 10, AG 943; text No. 12, AG 945; Michael, p. 414:14-35, 11.5c: 'At this time the Arabs invaded Persian territory. They climbed up into the Mardīn hills, near Rhesaina, and killed many monks in the Monastery of Qedar and in the Monastery of B^enōthō, because they had been told that the monks were Persian spies. A few of the monks survived and made their way to the desert which lies to the east of the river {Syr. KLYH^ɔ} and, finding there a water-source, built an abbey near it, called 'the abbey of the house of Rishīr', because Rishīr was the name of the superior of the Monastery of B^enōthō. The Monastery of B^enōthō is so called because of the "b^enōthō" or eggs, of a bird, which were found by Jacob, the founder of the abbey.' Michael, p. 414:2-3; 9-22, 11.5a, adds: 'AG 946, year 24 (read '25'; see Appendix I) of Heraclius, AH 13 [...] The following year ^cUmar sent an army to Persia and found the Persians in uproar and in great strife and discord. Some wanted to make Yazdgird,

§ 58. At this time the son of Shahrvarāz - we have related how he came to an agreement with the Arabs and settled at Emesa - heard of ^cUmar's accession to the throne and wrote him the following letter: 'Give me command of a tribe of Arabs to go to Persia and fight /p. 246/ my enemies and I will make the whole country your subjects and tributaries.' When this letter reached ^cUmar, the daughter of Chosroēs and his son,[360] who came to hear of its contents, made bold to speak to ^cUmar as follows - for they had access to the King's ear: 'O King, do not be deceived by that lying son of Shahrvarāz! He intends to do the opposite of what he writes to you. He has no scruples about killing his fellow-countrymen and his lords as if they were foreigners. If he cannot keep faith with his own flesh and blood, is he going to keep faith with you? He just wants you to provide him with a pretext. As soon as he has seized power he will defy you and become your enemy.' ^cUmar was convinced. He sent word to Damascus that the son of Shahrvarāz should be impaled on (a stake of) wood. When this message arrived he was executed summarily at the gate of Emesa.

§ 59*. By now Sa^cd b. (Abī) Waqqās, whom ^cUmar had sent, as we have said, against the Persians, had reached the village of Qadash, which the Arabs today call al-Qādisiyya, on the edge of the desert of Qadash at about fourteen kilometres[361] remove from ^cAqūlō, i.e. al-Kūfa. There the Arabs pitched camp. The forces mustered by Yazdgird to oppose them established themselves on the bank of the Euphrates near al-Kūfa; and a spy was sent to check out the Arab camp. Being a Hīrtian,[362] he was, though a Persian subject, an Arab by race and fluent in their language; so he set out confidently

---

the (grand-)son of Chosroēs, their king, others wanted Hormizd. There was a battle in which the Arabs proved the stronger, the Persians were massacred and their kingdom was weakened. Afterwards Hormizd was killed and Yazdgird became king.'

[360] Michael, p. 416:16, 11.6a: 'the daughters of Chosroēs' (no son mentioned).

[361] 'Five parasangs.'

[362] i.e. from al-Hīra.

towards the Arab camp. When he reached the camp he saw one /p. 247/ of the Ma^cadd squatting outside to piss and using the time to eat some bread and to pick some lice out of his garment. When the Hīrtian saw the other Arab he asked him in their language, 'What do you think you are doing?' The answer he received was this: 'As you see, I am putting in the new, getting rid of the old and killing my enemies.' The Hīrtian was astute enough to see the hidden meaning of these words, and he grieved. 'So,' he sighed to himself, 'a new people is invading us and driving out the old and the Persians will be destroyed.'[363]

---

[363] For the classical ancestry of this motif, cf. S. P. Brock, *The Syriac Version of the Pseudo-Nonnos Mythological Scholia* (Cambridge, 1971), Invective I. 33, pp. 97-8 and *id.*, 'Syriac Views of Emergent Islam', p. 13. Michael, p. 417:4-23, 11.6a, adds the following anecdote: 'One of the Persians' champion fighters was running away, clad in a cuirass and armed to the teeth. His pursuer, one of the Ma^cadd, had none of those things; he was naked and carried a spear, nothing more. The Persian in flight reached a village, spotted a man in a field and begged him to show him a place where he could hide from his pursuer. The man, assuming that there were many men after him, hid him away. After a considerable delay a man with no battle-dress went past in pursuit of him, riding his horse in a nonchalant way. The farmer was amazed and astonished at his lack of the equipment that soldiers generally have. "How is it that a big man wearing a cuirass and armed with various weapons which give him a frightening appearance is now running away and trembling in front of this ragamuffin?" He found it so disgraceful that he began to tell the Persian off for running away and hiding from the Ma^cadd tribesman. The Persian answered, "Do not blame me! Wait, listen and see with your own eyes, then you will believe it!" He took an arrow and his bow, shot at an iron spade and made a hole in it. Then he said, "Several times I shot bolts like that one at this Ma^cadd tribesman whom you have seen, but he brushed away all the arrows with his hand, like so many flies. That is what convinced me that the Lord has accorded them the victory, so I turned tail and ran away." ' In the same place (p. 417:23-32) Michael has this report: 'Later, when the Arabs heard of the festival which took place at the monastery of St Symeon the Stylite in the region of Antioch, they appeared there and took captive a large number of men and women and innumerable boys and girls. The Christians who were left no longer knew what to believe. Some of them said, "Why does God allow this to happen?" But a discerning person will see that Justice permitted this because,

§ 60. He went straight back to the Persians and told them: 'I have seen a people that is hideous, unshod, naked and weak. But they have boundless confidence. The rest I leave up to you.' To the general, however, he revealed in private what he had seen and what he had heard, and the emotions which had tormented him. The Persians were unanimous. They marched to Qadash to do battle with the Arabs. But the Persians were routed and the Arabs pursued them right up to the gate of Ctesiphon.[364]

§ 61. Then the Persians gathered their strength for a second encounter. They cut the bridges on the Tigris so that the Arabs could not cross. But the Arabs leapt on their horses and shouted to each other with triumph in their voice: 'God helped us on land. God will protect us in the water.' Their horses took them down into the river, treading the Tigris with their hooves, crossing over to the other side. Not one of them was drowned, not even a single horse. Then they fell upon the Persians in their camp, pursuing them, cutting them down. At last they collected the booty from the camp, opened the gates of

---

instead of fasting, vigils and psalm-singing, the Christians used to yield to intemperance, drunkenness, dancing and other kinds of luxury and debauchery at the festivals of the martyrs, thus angering God. That is why, quite justly, he slapped and punished us, in order that we might improve our behaviour.'

[364] cf. Michael, 11.6a; Michael, p. 414:2-30, 11.5b, adds the following: 'At this time (c.AG 940) there was a great earthquake, that coincided with a solar eclipse. In this earthquake the Church of the Resurrection, that of Golgotha and many other places collapsed. Modestus, the Chalcedonian bishop, rebuilt them. While the Persians were still making war on the Romans, Isaiah of Edessa was expelled, together with all the Orthodox bishops, and the Chalcedonians invaded the churches. Soon afterwards the Arabs became masters of Mesopotamia. Cyrus, the Chalcedonian bishop, was expelled from Edessa, and all the Orthodox bishops returned to their sees throughout the kingdom of the Arabs. At this time there was a terrible epidemic throughout Syria and Phoenicia and a great comet could be seen which had the appearance of a lance. There was another earthquake at this time in the region of Armenia, which left many settlements in ruins.'

Ctesiphon,[365] took possession of its treasures, its granaries, and took captive the courtiers of the King and those of his noble lords.[366]

§ 62. Twice more Yazdgird rallied the Persians. Once at a place called Jalūlāʾ,[367] where the Arabs caught up with them, routed them and massacred them. /p. 248/ The last stand of the Persians was near a city called Nihāwand in the mountains of Media. Again the Arabs cut them to pieces. Within one year the Arabs had made themselves masters of Persia. Yazdgird fled to the land of Segestān. If God gives us strength we shall show later what happened to him there.[368]

§ 63*. But with God's help we shall now return to Damascus and tell how this and the rest of the cities were taken from the Romans. Seeing that the Arabs showed no sign of slacking in their struggle for the city, as we have shown above, and that there was no one who could save them, the inhabitants of Damascus lost their nerve and the fight went out of them. They surrendered on certain terms after receiving sworn assurances concerning (the preservation of) their laws from Khālid b. al-Walīd; and Khālid ordered a contract to be drawn up which respected all their wishes. Thus they themselves opened the city for the Arabs;[369] though on the west side one of the Arab emirs overpowered the defenders and forced an entrance through one of the gates, so that, in a sense, Damascus was also taken by the sword. Nevertheless Khālid b. al-Walīd confirmed the contract and the sworn

---

[365] Here and in several other places this text (like some others translated in this book) uses {Syr. PTH}, 'open', with a city as the object of the verb, probably from {Ar. fataha} which, though also meaning 'open', has the additional sense of 'conquer'.

[366] Michael, 11.7a.

[367] The manuscript has {Syr. GʾWLʾ}.

[368] Michael, 11.7a.

[369] Here {Syr. PTH} is used of the surrender of a city, not of its conquest; in the following sentence it is used in the passive, where the translation has 'it was taken'.

assurances and gave them the name of tributaries.[370] The mediator of this agreement was the deacon John, son of Sargūn, himself a Damascene, who was loved and well-known among the Arabs. So Damascus[371] was occupied in AH 13.[372]

§ 64*. Khālid b. al-Walīd then set out with an Arab army from Damascus for Jordan, al-Balqā⊃ and the land of Hawrān.[373] The Arabs wanted to take captives and to loot, but Abū ⊂Ubayda, at the command of king ⊂Umar, prevented them and made /p. 249/ the people tributaries instead. From there they went to Baalbek, Palmyra and Emesa. The Emesenes shut the gates against them and went up on the wall above the al-Rastan[374] Gate, outside which the Arabs were encamped, to parley with them. Their proposal to the Arabs was this: 'Go and engage the king of the Romans in battle. When you have defeated him we will be your subjects. If you do not we will not open the gates for you.' When the Arabs began to attack the city regardless, the Emesenes expected reinforcements to come and rescue them, but none came. Then they lost their will to fight and sued for peace. They asked the Arabs for an amnesty,[375] a pact and oaths; and they received, like the Damascenes, a written covenant granting them their own lives and possessions and churches and laws and requiring them to pay 110,000 denarii as the tribute of the city. So the Arabs gained control of Emesa. The emir who was put in charge of collecting the tribute from them was Habīb b. Maslama. As for the Palestinians and the inhabitants of the coastal settlements, they all congregated within the walls of Jerusalem.

---

[370] Lit. 'he named over them that give tribute', possibly corrupt, though the sense is clear.

[371] {Gr. damaskós}.

[372] Text No. 12, AG 945. This account of the capture of Damascus is almost certainly based on an Arabic version; cf. de Goeje, *Mémoire*, pp. 82-102 and note that Dionysius gives only an AH date for the event. [R.H.]

[373] {Syr. NWRN}, a copyist's error.

[374] The manuscript has {Syr. RSN}.

[375] Lit. 'a word'.

§ 65*. When Heraclius heard this news, he mustered more than 300,000 troops from Armenia, Syria and the Roman heartlands. He had them drawn up under three commanders, Krikor the Armenian, Buccinator {Syr. QNTRYS}[376] and Ardigān {Syr. ARDYGWN}.[377] Then they set out from Antioch to Emesa to confront the Arabs. The Arabs, however, dreaded a confrontation with them and even considered abandoning their hard-won cities and returning to their own country. They held counsel together and the gist of what they said to each other was this: 'How can we abandon such a rich land? /p. 250/ If we do, one thing is certain: we shall never get it back. We had better fight the Romans after all.' Abū ͨUbayda, whom ͨUmar had put in command of the Arabs, ordered Ḥabīb b. Maslama to return to the Emesenes the tribute which he had exacted from them with this message: 'We are both bound by our mutual oaths. Now we are going to do battle with the Romans. If we return, this tribute is ours; but if we are defeated and do not return, we are absolved of our oaths.' So they left Emesa for Damascus; and the emir

---

[376] Azdī, pp. 210, 217, 226 names an Ibn Qanātir as a general of this battle. He may be connected with the Ibn Qāṭur mentioned by Ibn ͨAsākir, p. 473 as governor of Jerusalem c.632ʿ (Bukhārī, al-Saḥīh, Beirut 1981, 1.6-7 has Ibn Nāṭūr) and/or with Buqantar, patríḱioś óf Tripolis c.645 (Tahdhīb taʾrīkh Ibn ͨAsākir, ed. ͨA.ʾ-Q. Badrān and A. ͨUbayd, Damascus 1911-32, pp. 183ff). Behind all this would appear to lie an official nicknamed Buccinator, whose sons killed the emir of Tripolis in the 650s (Theophanes, p. 345; Agapius, p. 223). [R.H.]

[377] Possibly a commander named Stephen, mentioned by Pseudo-Wāqidī, p. 109 as present at Ajnādayn and having the rank of Ardigān (or Ardihān); Azdī, pp. 81-2 names al-Drungār as chief of the Byzantines at a battle by Busrā, which very likely reflects the title Drungarius. This may also be what is intended by the appellation Artabūn applied to a general at Ajnādayn (de Goeje, Mémoire, pp. 61ː2, suggesting that it derives from the title Tribunus). A. Butler, The Arab Conquest of Egypt, (Oxford 1902), p. 215 reads Aretion. L. M. Whitby suggests: 'possibly Ferdigun or Kardīgān, Persian titles that would indicate this was one of the Iranian refugees at Heraclius's court?'; one would then have to suppose that Dionysius obtained this account from non-Syriac sources, since he is familiar with Persian titles (cf. § 35 above). [R.H.]

Abū ᶜUbayda ordered Saᶜīd[378] b. Kulthūm to return the tribute
to the Damascenes likewise; for as their governor he had been
responsible for exacting it. To them he said: 'If we return victorious
we shall take it back. But if we are defeated and prove powerless to
save you from the Romans, here is your tribute: keep it! We, for our
part, shall be absolved of the oaths which we have sworn to you.'

§ 66. So the Arabs left Damascus and pitched camp by the river
Yarmūk. As the Romans marched towards the Arab camp every city
and village on their way which had surrendered to the Arabs shouted
threats at them. As for the crimes the Romans committed on their
passage, they are unspeakable, and their unseemliness ought not even
to be brought to mind. For some days on that same river the two
camps confronted each other. They held peace-talks to put an end to
the conflict, but they could not agree to each other's demands. So they
made ready for battle; and amidst the preparations Abū Sufyān arrived
to reinforce the Arab army.

§ 67. Then they beat their drums and sounded their trumpets and
fought all day until the dark night came upon them and the Romans
were defeated. The Romans turned their backs to the Arabs and fled
headlong, mown down by Arab swords. They were disorientated and
did not know /p. 251/ in which direction to run. Many of them made
for the bright light of a shepherds' fire, pushing ahead so heedlessly
that many thousands - more than those who had been killed in the battle
- fell headlong from a steep cliff and were smashed to death. The
Arabs returned, elated with their great victory, to Damascus; and the
Damascenes greeted them outside the city and welcomed them joyfully
in, and all treaties and assurances were reaffirmed.[379]

---

[378] The manuscript has {Syr. SWYD}.
[379] Text No. 10, AG 944; text No. 12, AG 947; Theophanes, p. 338;
Agapius, p. 193; Michael, p. 416:11-12, 11.6a, adding: 'a large
number of them were drowned {Syr. ethᵉneq(w)} in the river Yarmūk.'

§ 68*. Heraclius was at Antioch when the news was broken to him. Not one of his soldiers had lived to tell the tale. The messenger was a Christian Arab. At this intelligence Heraclius left Syria in great sorrow for Constantinople. He is supposed to have said, as he took his leave, 'Sōzou, Syria', i.e. 'Farewell, Syria', as if he despaired of ever seeing her again. After that he raised the rod in his hand and gave his army leave to ravage indiscriminately, as if Syria was already enemy territory. He sent written instructions to Mesopotamia, Armenia, Egypt and the other countries where Romans remained, not to fight against the Arabs nor to stand against the decree of the Lord. He said that each should guard his post - whether city or region - until the matter surpassed his strength.[380]

§ 69*. While the Arabs were at the zenith of their strength ᶜAmr b. al-ᶜĀs set out with an army to invade Egypt. We have found in the tales and stories of the Egyptians that Benjamin, the patriarch of the Orthodox /p. 252/ in Egypt at that time, delivered the country to the Arab general ᶜAmr b. al-ᶜĀs out of antipathy, that is enmity, towards Cyrus, the Chalcedonian patriarch in Egypt. This Cyrus, they say, received from Heraclius not only the office of patriarch, but also command over all Egypt as its governor and had soldiers and armed men as his servants. To indicate that he enjoyed as bishop simultaneously also the rank of general he used to wear a red slipper on one foot and a monk's sandal on the other. He was a tyrant in all his ways and he did great harm to the Orthodox with the armed forces he had from the King. He barred the patriarch Benjamin from his own churches and appropriated them for himself. When Cyrus heard of the approach of ᶜAmr b. al-ᶜĀs he set out to meet him and agreed to pay him 200,000 denarii a year to keep the Arabs out of Egypt. At this, certain persons went and denounced him to Heraclius for taking gold from Egypt and giving it to the Arabs. Heraclius then wrote Cyrus a letter relieving him of the governorship of Egypt and sent a general of

---

[380] Michael, 11.7a.

Armenian birth, Manuel, to replace him.[381]

§ 70. A year later the Arab emissaries came as usual to collect the tribute. They found Manuel's camp at Babylōnē, which today is called Fustāt; they requested an audience and demanded their gold. He replied: 'I am not that Cyrus who used to give you gold. He did not wear armour, but a woollen tunic. But I, as you can see, am armed. Go away and do not come here again.' The messengers reported back to their emir that Cyrus was no longer /p. 253/ the governor of Egypt; but [c]Amr b. al-[c]Ās did not dare to launch an invasion.[382] Benjamin, however, the Orthodox patriarch, sought [c]Amr out and encouraged him to do so, promising that he would deliver all Egypt over to him on condition that all the churches were then transferred to his jurisdiction and that the Chalcedonians were wiped out. On his return, Benjamin told his co-religionaries what he had done and he gave them permission to have themselves circumcized, to provide them with a distinguishing mark which might prevent them being killed along with the Chalcedonians. He incited them to rebel against the Romans, deliver the country over to the Arabs and so make themselves free from their cruel oppression. For the Romans persecuted them tirelessly on account of their faith. Indeed, the Chalcedonians had sunk so low in their barbarity as to break in upon Eucharistic celebrations of the Orthodox and trample the Holy Mysteries on the ground. This is the reason for the institution of the custom, still observed in Egypt[383] today, that a deacon must stand at the east end at the time of the Mysteries, so as to be able to see if persecutors enter the church, and warn the priest in time for him to consume the Mysteries before they get into the sanctuary.

§ 71. The leading men of Alexandria and of Egypt made common cause with Benjamin. When [c]Amr arrived they surrendered the city to him. The Arabs, entering, fell upon the Romans and slaughtered them.

---

[381] §§ 69-71: <u>Theophanes</u>, pp. 338-9; <u>Agapius</u>, pp. 212-3; Michael, 11.7a.

[382] Lit. 'to come to Egypt'.

[383] Lit. 'in Egypt {Syr. mesrēn} and in Egypt {Gr. aíguptos}'.

As for Cyrus and Manuel, when they saw that the Arabs were winning, they took all they could lay their hands on of the gold and silver treasure belonging to the church, embarked in a small ship and fled to Constantinople, leaving Benjamin to assume patriarchal authority over the churches of Alexandria and all Egypt. Since that time the Chalcedonians have not raised their heads anywhere in that country,[384] though a remnant was left in the villages and towns along the coast.[385] /p. 254/

§ 72*. Khālid b. al-Walīd pitched his camp in front of the bolted gates of Aleppo, but the city was soon surrendered, once the Alepines had received sworn assurances and a covenant respecting all their wishes; and likewise Qēnneshrīn[386] and the rest of that region. Abū ʿUbayda, the Arab commander, sent Habīb, the emir of Emesa, to the region of Qēnneshrīn because it paid tribute together with Emesa. This remained so until the time of Yazīd b. Muʿāwiya, when Qēnneshrīn was separated from the authority of Emesa. Saʿīd b. Zayd was appointed emir of Damascus.

§ 73*. The Arab army, led by Abū ʿUbayda b. al-Jarrāh, then advanced to lay siege to Jerusalem. The people in the city came out, formed ranks and fought a battle with the Arabs, then went back within the walls. This episode was followed by a determined Arab assault. With no hope of being relieved, those within requested the Arab general Abū ʿUbayda to send for ʿUmar b. al-Khaṭṭāb, the King, to

---

[384] Lit. 'in all Egypt {Gr. aíguptos}'.

[385] Michael, p. 419:28-39, 11.7a: 'The Arabs occupied Egypt. When Heraclius learned this, he wrote to Bishop Cyrus that he should get the Arabs out of Egypt, if possible, by offering them twice the amount of gold that had been agreed the first time. Cyrus went to the Arab camp and explained that he had not been to blame for the offence which had been committed. He beseeched them eloquently to (let him) give them the gold, but ʿAmr replied, "I will not do what you ask. Now that we have occupied the country we will not give it up." With these words the Arab {Syr. ʿarabōyō} dismissed Cyrus, who went home crestfallen.'

[386] A city south of Aleppo, not to be confused with the monastery of that name on the Euphrates, also called Qēnneshrē.

negotiate a covenant with them for the surrender of the city. So the Arabs sent a letter to ^{C}Umar and he set off for Jerusalem AG 946 = year 26 of Heraclius = AH 15.^{387} A great many fighting men came with him and he was accompanied by the great and famous of the Quraysh, including al-^{C}Abbās b. ^{C}Abd al-Muttalib, the paternal uncle of Muhammad, the prophet of the Arabs. As his viceroy in Yathrib he left ^{C}Alī b. ^{C}Abī Tālib, Muhammad's son-in-law through marriage with the prophet's daughter, Fātima.^{388}

§ 74. This is how ^{C}Umar arrived at Jerusalem. He was riding on a camel with a coarse woollen saddle under him. In one of the saddle-bags was barley flour, in the other were dates, a jar of water and the stock of a vine. The Arab army came out /p. 255/ to meet him as a sign of welcome. Last of all came their commander, Abū ^{C}Ubayda. He and ^{C}Umar both dismounted to greet and to welcome one another in peace. Now the leaders of the city came out to meet the approaching King. One of them was the man the Arabs call Abū Ju^{C}aydid,^{389} the other was the bishop, Sophronius. They swore to a covenant^{390} and he wrote letters patent,^{391} as they desired, concerning their churches and their customs. They accepted the amnesty and the oaths concerning all Palestine. The stipulation was made that no Jew might live in Jerusalem. The covenant was set down in writing and endorsed by all parties. Then at last King ^{C}Umar

---

^{387} Given that we should read 'year 27 of Heraclius' (see Appendix I), the regnal year and the Islamic year agree, so the Seleucid year must have been corrupted. Dionysius therefore originally had AG 948 = AD 636 [the same date proposed by Theophanes, p. 339, for the surrender of Jerusalem: R.H.]. I cannot think how 948 was corrupted to 946.

^{388} Michael, 11.7a.

^{389} Abū Ju^{C}ayd ('Ju^{C}aydid' looks like an error) is well known in the Arabic sources for his part in the battle of Yarmūk and the surrender of Jerusalem. ^{C}Umar's visit is discussed in detail by H. Busse, "^{C}Omar b. al-Khattāb in Jerusalem', *Jerusalem Studies in Arabic and Islam*, 5 (1984), pp. 73-119. [R.H.]

^{390} Lit. 'they established a covenant and oaths'.

^{391} {Lat. sigilla}.

entered Jerusalem. His first action was to order a mosque, that is an Arab house of prayer, to be built on the site of the temple of Solomon.

§ 75. When Bishop Sophronius saw that King ᶜUmar was wearing dirty clothes, he offered him a robe and a loin-cloth as a personal gift. However, though he begged him to accept them, ᶜUmar steadfastly refused. 'I may take no thing from any man,' he said. ᶜUmar, you must know, spent all his time weaving fans from the leaves of the date-palm; out of the income from the sale of these fans he provided for his clothing. He even earned his daily bread with the work of his hands. When the bishop persisted in his entreaties, the King said, 'Since you insist and because I cherish your honour, do me the kindness of having them brought here to me. I will wear them while you take these clothes of mine and have them washed. When I get them back, your property will be returned to you.' That is just what happened: when the King got his clothes back from the wash, he dressed himself in them again and returned the bishop's clothes to him. And after staying a little longer in Jerusalem he went back to his own city, Yathrib.[392]

§ 76. AH 18: After ᶜUmar had gone back down to his city the pestilence[393] was unleashed throughout the land of Palestine. Abū ᶜUbayda, the Arab emir and general, contracted the disease and died /p. 256/ at Emmaus, a city of Palestine. His place was taken by Muᶜādh b. Jabal.[394]

§ 77*. The next year ᶜIyād b. Ghanm and his army of Arabs passed through the cities of Syria, giving them assurances,[395] and Syria became subject to the Arabs. John, who had been left behind by Heraclius to guard Mesopotamia, sought ᶜIyād b. Ghanm out at

---

[392] §§ 73-5: Theophanes, p. 339; Agapius, pp. 213-5; Michael, 11.7a.

[393] {Syr. sharᶜūtō}.

[394] Michael, p. 421:23-26, 11.8b: 'At this time (?) the pestilence raged and many people died in Syria and Mesopotamia.'

[395] Lit. 'the word'.

Qēnneshrīn and made with him a pact to give him 100,000 denarii[396] a year for the whole of Mesopotamia, if the Arabs would stay on the west bank of the Euphrates. Having ratified these terms John returned, exacted one year's tribute and sent it off. When Heraclius heard about this, he deposed John in anger at what he had done and appointed a certain Ptolemy instead; for God had removed His Hand from the kingdom of the Romans. A year later King ᶜUmar sent word and appointed Muᶜāwiya b. Abī Sufyān over all Syria. He took Antioch by siege and plundered the villages around, leading the people away as slaves. Then the Arabs sent a demand for the tribute of Mesopotamia.[397]

§ 78. AG 951: When Ptolemy refused to pay the tribute to the Arabs, they crossed over the Euphrates and made for Edessa. The Edessenes went out and secured assurances and a covenant, as did the Harrānites. The first Arab to rule in Edessa was Abū Badr. The Edessenes had also received an assurance with regard to Ptolemy and his Romans, so they returned to their country. But when ᶜIyād b. Ghanm came to Tella[398] the arrogant Romans in the city did not deign to accept assurances, so they were obliged to fight. In a determined assault ᶜIyād overwhelmed the city and killed the three hundred Romans who were there. Next he went to Dara, assaulted it likewise, took it /p. 257/ and killed every Roman in the city. But Rhesaina, Mardīn and Amida he took by amnesty and covenant and oaths. It was at Amida that ᶜIyād b. Ghanm died by violence and was buried.[399]

---

396 {Syr. drēkūnē}.

397 Theophanes, p. 340; Agapius, pp. 216-7; Michael, 11.7a.

398 {Syr. tellō d-mawzᵉlat}.

399 Text No. 10, AG 948, 952; text No. 12, AG 947; Theophanes, p. 340; Agapius, p. 217; Michael, p. 421:6-11, 11.7a, who adds: 'After subjecting all Mesopotamia, ᶜIyād b. Ghanm returned to Syria. ᶜUmar ordered all the countries of his kingdom to be registered for the poll-tax. The poll-tax was imposed on Christians in AG 951' (Theophanes, p. 341; Agapius, p. 218).

§ 79*. At this time David the Armenian, a Roman general, who was in communication with a certain Valentine in the west, launched a strategy which was supposed to annihilate the Arabs of Syria by a simultaneous invasion from the west and from the east. But the Arabs were forewarned. They took the initiative by attacking Valentine first and on him they inflicted a crushing defeat. When David arrived in Mesopotamia he was told there were no Arabs there. They had gone to help strip off spoils from the Romans of Valentine's company. So David pitched camp over against the village of Bēth Ma^{c}dē instead. His soldiers had no scruples at all about plundering the population down to their last possession. They also tortured men and women cruelly to discover where hoards of treasure had been buried underground. Above all the shouts, the complaints, the tears and the groans arose the screams of well-born women, the daughters of well-born men, with whom the soldiers were fornicating in lascivious adultery, openly, shamelessly, under the eyes of their own husbands and in the sight of all.[400]

§ 80. With them was a certain Titus, a Syrian by race, who commanded a company from one of the cities. When this man saw these atrocities being committed by the companions of David the Armenian he approached him and said, /p. 258/ 'It is not right that you, a Christian and the soldier of a Christian king, should draw your sword against other Christians and allow your own soldiers to ruin their lives. They have not sinned against the Roman state;[401] but the King will certainly not praise you when he hears of this.' David the Armenian then ordered that no harm should be done to the local population.[402]

---

[400] The style of this passage has been tightened a little in translation. Text No. 10, AG 955; Michael, p. 428:4-6, 23-27, 11.10b: 'At this time David the Armenian set off with a large force from the Royal City [...] They beat Christian men, poured vinegar and (the Syr. has 'of') ashes down their nostrils to make them show their valuables and their buried hoards.'

[401] {Gr. politeía}.

[402] Michael, 11.10b.

§ 81*. When ᶜIyād heard of David's expeditionary force he and his army left the region of Damascus and - according to witnesses who heard it from those very men - they did not change horses once until they reached the region of Edessa. The good-for-nothing Armenians were mightily alarmed at the news of the Arabs' arrival. They were hampered by all the booty, the captives and the livestock which they had plundered from Mesopotamia. That very night they abandoned everything and took to their heels. When the Arabs arrived they found the camps of the Armenians and began to make eyes at all that booty. But the emir bellowed: 'God's curse on you if you get held up by the booty! Pursue the enemy! When the Lord has delivered them into our hands, we can take the gold, the silver, the expensive clothes, the horses and the cattle which they have with them. After that we can come back for these things here.'[403]

§ 82. So they gave swift chase and caught up with them. They divided them into droves of fifty and a hundred, like so many sheep, and began to thrust at them pitilessly with swords and lances. As for Titus and his Syrians, they all stood off to one side. The Arabs tried attacking them, but when they realized what brave fighters they were, they went off to fight against David instead. That coward David shouted /p. 259/ to Titus: 'Now is your chance to prove your love for the Roman state by distinguishing yourself in battle.' 'If I help you,' came the retort, 'I shall get no help from God.' So Titus parted with David and was saved, while David and his army perished by the sword; and there were no survivors.[404]

§ 83*. AG 950: Muᶜāwiya besieged Caesarea with vigorous assaults, taking captives from the surrounding country and laying it

---

[403] Michael, p. 429:4-7, 11.10b: 'ᶜIyād heard while he was in Damascus about David the Urtian (i.e. from Bēth Urtōyē = Anzitene, a part of Armenia IV), he mustered his troops and came to Edessa.'

[404] Michael, p. 429:36-37, 11.10b: 'Titus escaped to Amida.' Michael, p. 429:42-430:1, 11.10b, adds: 'In these years (c.AG 958?) the people of ᶜAqūlō, i.e. the people of Baghdād (not yet founded at this date), moved from Harrān to Mabbūgh and thence to Hamath.'

waste. He sustained the hostilities by night and day for a long time until he conquered it by the sword. All those in the city, including the 7,000 Romans sent there to guard it, were put to death. The city was plundered of vast quantities of gold and silver and then abandoned to its grief. Those who settled there afterwards became tributaries of the Arabs.[405]

§ 84. Mu^{c}āwiya's next goal was the heartlands of the Romans, so he advanced to Euchaita, which is BLSTYN, leaving a trail of destruction behind him. No one sounded the alarm. The Euchaitans were scattered over the countryside, harvesting the crops and working in the vineyards. They had seen the aggressors all right; but they were under the impression that they were Christian Arabs, from one or other tribe allied with the Romans. So they saw no reason to alter their dispositions, let alone to run away. The Arabs found the gates of the unhappy city open and the people sitting around without the slightest fear. The next moment they were entering it, plundering it, piling up great mounds of booty. They seized the women, the boys and the girls to take back home as slaves. Even the city-governor[406] was taken prisoner. Euchaita lay ravaged and deserted, while the Arabs returned, exulting, to their country.[407] /p. 260/

§ 85*. AG 952 = AH 19 = year 7 of ^{c}Umar b. al-Khaṭṭāb: Heraclius died after a reign of thirty years and five months and was succeeded by his eldest son, Constantine.[408] Four months later

---

[405] Text No. 10, AG 953; text No. 12, AG 954; Theophanes, p. 341; Agapius, pp. 194, *218*.

[406] {Gr. árkhōn}.

[407] Michael, p. 423:19-23, 11.8a: 'The Arabs enslaved the entire population, men and women, boys and girls. They committed a great orgy in this unfortunate city, fornicating wickedly inside the churches.'

[408] Thirty years and five months, counted from 1 September, 610, gives a date in January or February of 641 for the death of Heraclius (actually January 11, 641). Although Dionysius was accurately informed as to the length of Heraclius's reign and the Seleucid year of his death (between October 1, 640, and September 30, 641), he failed to notice that the (correct) equation of AG 952 with year 31 of Heraclius clashes with the false synchronism in § 23, which put his

Constantine lay dead, poisoned by his own father's unlawful wife, Martina. The next king was Heraclonas, Heraclius's son by the same Martina. The senators took exception to this king and deposed him. He was succeeded by Heraclius's grandson, Constans, the son of Constantine - AG 954 [...].[409]

§ 86. A year later a rebellion led by the general Valentine was crushed by the King and the rebel leader killed.[410] The next year there was another rebellion, this time in Africa, just at the time when the Arab invasion of Africa occurred. The patríkios of Africa, Gregory, who had instigated the revolt, was defeated in battle by the Arabs. He himself escaped and gave himself up to the King.[411] In this year a violent gale uprooted great trees and toppled many columns of holy stylites. At the time of the gale the Arabs were building their temple in Jerusalem; the structure was damaged and it began to fall. When they asked why this was happening the filthy Jews told them: /p. 261/ 'Unless you take down that cross on the Mount of Olives opposite the temple, you will never succeed in building it.' They took the cross down and after that the structure was stabilized.[412]

---

count of Heraclius's regnal years out by one (see Appendix I). Instead, he read here, forgetting to count rigorously in his desire to continue consistently his tally of Heraclius's regnal years, the equation: AG 952 = Heraclius 30. And since he had dated the Hijra to Heraclius's year 12 (§ 25), he equated Heraclius 30 with AH 19 and with ᶜUmar's year 7, not realizing that this synchronism also contradicted the correct information in his source, by putting Heraclius's death before December 20, AD 640.

[409] The Syriac is longer by six whole lines containing no fresh information. Theophanes, p. 341; Agapius, pp. 194, 218; Michael, p. 421:14-15, 11.7a: 'Little Heraclius, who was called the new David.'

[410] Theophanes, p. 343.

[411] Theophanes, p. 343; Agapius, p. 219.

[412] Theophanes, p. 342; Agapius, p. 220; Michael, p. 421:26-29, 11.8b: 'At this time, when the Arabs were rebuilding the Temple of Solomon at Jerusalem, the structure began to collapse; then the Jews said [...].' Michael, p. 428:17-32, 36-39, 429:18-36, 11.10a, adds: 'Muᶜāwiya divided his troops into two armies. At the head of the first he placed a wicked Syrian called Habīb, whom he sent to Armenia in the month of October. When these troops arrived they found the

§ 87*. After a reign of twelve years[413] ^cUmar was killed on November 4, a Thursday.[414] The reason for his assassination was as follows. One of the Quraysh had a Roman slave whom he had several times sexually abused. The slave took his grievance to ^cUmar; but whether from absent-mindedness, or because he was too busy with the affairs of government, he did nothing about it. It was this slave who attacked ^cUmar while he was praying in the mosque. He ripped open his stomach with a knife and he died on the instant. He was succeeded by ^cUthmān b. ^cAffān, a very greedy man, whom the status of king made even greedier. He not only hoarded quantities of gold, but he departed from the modest ways made traditional by the kings

---

country deep in snow; but they craftily obtained some oxen and used them to plough through the snow in front of them. In this way they were able to press their invasion without hindrance. The Armenians were caught unawares, having never suspected this could happen. [...] The other army, under Mu^cāwiya himself, invaded the region of Cappadocian Caesarea [...] (the passage omitted adds that they forced the city, at the second attempt, to surrender on terms). When the Sons of Hagar entered the city and saw the beauty of the buildings, the churches, the monasteries and its great affluence, they regretted their oaths; but they could not go back on their word. So they took all they wanted, then invaded the country of Amorium. When they saw how beautiful the countryside was, like a veritable paradise, they caused no damage there, but made straight for the city, which they surrounded. However, recognizing that it was impregnable, they suggested to the inhabitants that they should treat for peace and open the gates. They refused. Then Mu^cāwiya sent his troops to ravage the countryside; when they went home, they took with them gold, silver and other wealth, like so much dust.'

[413] Text No. 10, AG 956; text No. 12, AG 955; <u>Theophanes</u>, p. 343 and <u>Agapius</u>, p. 219 also give ^cUmar a 12-year reign. But Michael, p. 422:6-7, 11.8a, writes: '^cUthmān began to reign in AG 955 (AD 643/4)'; and since Dionysius correctly dated Muhammad's death to AG 943 (§ 45) and gave his successor, Abū Bakr, two and a half years (§ 57), he contradicts Michael here. That does not necessarily mean he contradicted himself, since Michael might have got this information from the continuation of text No. 5, which he certainly knew. The question is discussed in more detail in Appendix I.

[414] Correct for AD 644, but not for the date given in the parallel passage in Michael, nor for the year implied by Dionysius's statement that ^cUmar reigned for twelve years.

before him, *viz* Muhammad, Abū Bakr and ᶜUmar. However, confronted by an assembly of Arabs with murder in their hearts, he repented and agreed to continue the tradition.

§ 88. ᶜUthmān was very well-read in Arabic[415] and had many worldly accomplishments. It was he, according to the Arabs, who collected and ordered the Qurʾān, that is their 'book which came down from heaven, the words of which are of God'. Everyone in possession of a fragment or a story from that 'book' heard by himself from Muhammad was commanded to bring it to the King. He then assembled the fragments into one book and ordered it to be called the Qurʾān. He used, so they say, to go into retreat for days at a time. When they asked him what he was doing, he replied that he was 'putting the Qurʾān in order'. /p. 262/ This ᶜUthmān was not from the tribe of Quraysh but from the tribe of the Umayyads.[416]

§ 89*. At this time the Arab general ᶜAmr b. Saᶜd[417] yielded to the influence of malicious advisers and began to treat the Christians in his province (Damascus) like enemies; for he resolved to humiliate them and to rob them of the symbol of their pride and glory. He ordered all crosses to be extirpated and effaced from walls and streets and places open to view and he forbade the standard of the Cross to be shown on days of feasting and supplication. When the King endorsed this command with menacing words, like a tyrant, the Jewish people were overjoyed. They began to run up the roofs of temples and

---

[415] {Syr. arabōyō}.

[416] The Umayyads were a clan of Quraysh. Dionysius obviously has information from Arabic sources (cf. his comment that ᶜUthmān collected the Qurʾān, almost axiomatic in Arabic accounts but not recorded in any other Syriac work), but this confusion over Quraysh suggests the information was obtained indirectly. [R.H.]

[417] This is most likely ᶜUmayr b. Saᶜd al-Ansārī, who was one of ᶜUmar I's right-hand men and at one point governor of Damascus, Emesa and northern Mesopotamia (Tabarī, I, pp. 2646, 2798; see P. Crone and M. Cook, *Hagarism*, Cambridge 1977, p. 162 n. 11). Balādhurī mentions him in connection with attempts to convert Christian Arabs (pp. 136, 182). [R.H.]

churches and to take down the venerable crosses; they also effaced those that were on the streets and walls. On account of this the Christians put on mourning. A certain well-known and god-fearing Christian who had access to the court of ^cAmr told him this: 'O good emir, it is unjust to make the accursed Jews, the enemies of our religion, superior to us and free to climb up onto our churches and to make a mockery of our Mysteries and of our crosses.' God put it into the emir's mind to reply: 'I merely commanded that the crosses which we always see when we pass through the streets should be effaced.' And he ordered one of his constant companions to go out and throw any Jew whom he should find on the roof of a church headlong to the ground. Now one Jew had climbed onto the roof of the great temple of John the Baptist and had broken off the cross. He was just coming down the stairs, when he met that general sent by the emir coming up. This man took the cross from him and brought it down on his head with bone-breaking force; /p. 263/ his brains spurted out of his nostrils and he fell down dead. After this all enthusiasm for carrying out the Arab threat evaporated.[418]

§ 90*. This emir Ibn Sa^cd hated the Christians and it may be that he wanted to stop them calling Christ God; but whatever his motives may have been, he summoned by letter the patriarch John. The interview was a very strange one; but the patriarch, helped by God's Grace, answered all the emir's devious questions. When the emir heard his spirited and fearless defence he said: 'Put that Gospel of yours into Arabic speech for me and do not change anything except the word GOD, where it is applied to Christ, the word BAPTISM and the word CROSS. These words you are to omit.' The Spirit strengthened John to answer bravely: 'May Christ, my God, forbid that I should take away one jot or one tittle from my Gospel, even if I must be pierced

---

[418] Michael, 11.8c; Michael, p. 422:31-38, 11.8b, adds: 'The Christians began (again their custom of) carrying crosses in procession at rogations, festivals and burials. However, at Emesa and at Damascus, they have never enjoyed this freedom since this decree of ^cAmr.'

by all the lances in your armoury. I would rather not write it at all.'
Impressed by this spirited protest and by John's manly character, the
emir told him to go and write as he wished. Then the patriarch sent for
pious people of the Banū Tanūkh[419] and from ᶜAqūlō and selected
those most fluent in both Arabic and Syriac and wh o knew how to
translate words elegantly from one language into another. When they
had, with great difficulty, interpreted the Gospel at his command and
collated it repeatedly, they produced immediately a final version in
elevated calligraphic style free from technical blemishes and most
skilfully illuminated with (gold and silver) leaf. /p. 264/ This they
then presented to the governor ᶜAmr b. Saᶜd.[420] [...][421]

§ 92*. AG 960: There is a village on the Euphrates in the district
of Sᵉrūgh with the name of Zōybōnō. Near this village some people
were digging a hole to obtain a supply of soil, when they discovered
a stone slab[422] inscribed with thirteen columns of Median
characters which no one could be found to read. Digging underneath
this slab they found a small bronze cauldron[423] with a bronze
figurine inside it; and the figurine had a chain around its neck.
Fortune-tellers and sorcerers were fetched, 'for surely,' people said, 'it
was sorcerers who buried this in days of old!' They whispered their

---

[419] A Christian Arab tribe (cf. text No. 11).

[420] Michael, p. 422:20-25, 11.8c: 'The patriarch gathered the bishops
and summoned certain of the Banū Tanūkh, the people of ᶜAqūlō and
the Tuᶜāyē, who knew both Arabic and Syriac, and ordered them to
translate the Gospel into Arabic.' For the alleged text of this interview
see Nau, 'Un Colloque'.

[421] The following paragraph (§ 91*) need not be translated here, since
it was translated by Brock in 'An Early Syriac Life of Maximus', pp.
337-40, with the parallel passage from Michael in the left-hand column.
Both that paragraph and this would be more at home in a history of the
Church than in a Secular History; but Dionysius may have used them
to plug a gap in his continuous narrative and, at the same time, to mark
a major division in his material (see the introduction to this text).

[422] A diminutive of {Gr. plax}.

[423] {Lat. calidarium}.

spells over the little idol until, as they alleged, it began to speak with
them. 'Sixty thousand demons are imprisoned in this figurine,' it said.
And the demons asked, 'What command do ye give us? Whither shall
we go?' At this the sorcerers undid the chain from the neck of the
figurine and said, 'Go! Enter into the monks of the monastery of
Qēnneshrē!' Just then the monks of that abbey began to suffer many
misfortunes and ailments. Many became possessed by demons. They
began to crow like cocks and to bleat like goats. They insulted the
icons of the saints, calling Peter 'Fool-Fisherman', Paul 'Flayed-Skull',
Thomas 'One-Ball', John the son of Aphtonia 'Bushy-Beard', Saint
Ephraem 'Shrivelled Bald-chin' and Saint Theodore 'Blind
Man';[424] nor was that by any means the end of the perverse
inventions of those monks. In the end, most of them threw themselves
into the river where it flows past the monastery and died by
drowning.[425]

---

[424] Note that the farmyard sounds suggest masculine vanity and
lasciviousness and that the nicknames of the saints reflect their lack of
these qualities: Peter was no scholar, although many monks of
Qēnneshrē were that; Paul was partially bald; Thomas, according to
legend, was opposed to marriage; John, the founder of the monastery,
had become a monk before his beard was even grown, but apparently
acquired a rather wild and unkempt one in the memory of posterity; as
for Ephraem, the great hymnographer, he evinced in his writings a
great sympathy for the qualities conventionally associated with the
female gender and identified male sexual desire with intellectual
arrogance and blasphemy, so he could be mocked as lacking in virility.
Which of the Theodores is meant I am uncertain.

[425] Michael, p. 420:27-421:19, 11.7c: 'In the time of Lord Daniel,
bishop of Edessa (AD 665-84), fiends took possession of certain
brothers in the monastery of Qēnneshrē. The abbot sent and called
upon Daniel to find some remedy for those poor boys. He told them
to go to Saint Jacob's (at Kayshūm) and fetch the body of Bishop
Severus (of Samosata). They (the monks of Kayshūm) did not want to
give him up, but under pressure they gave a part of him. When this
was brought near, the demons began to wail, "Alas for us! That
Broken One has come! He is not content to have driven us out of the
region of Samosata, but he must come here also!" The reason why the
demons said this was that the saint had once fallen from a beast of
burden and had been lamed in one foot. One of those possessed by a

§ 93*. /p. 268/ AG 960: In the nine hundred and sixtieth year of Alexander, the Sons of Hagar made up their minds to have the island of Cyprus. Emir Mu^{c}āwiya spread the word and before long innumerable ships and many smaller boats, which had hearkened to the summons, were moored along the coast. The field-commander at Alexandria also received a letter from Mu^{c}āwiya, bidding him to send ships bearing a numerous task-force from Egypt as reinforcements, which he promptly did.[426]

§ 94. Now the two fleets had mingled and the multitudinous masts had turned the sea into a floating forest, concealing a large area of the surface. They began hoisting their sails, like snow-clad mountains, and it was as if the abyss were being shaken to its very foundations. Then, all together, seventeen hundred ships weighed anchor and in a single massive movement the voyage was begun. Those watching from the shore were staggered at the size of the fleet, under which the waves of the sea were all but invisible. Brave and gallant were the marines who stood on the top-decks in the full finery of their fighting gear, boasting

---

fiend had formerly been a disciple of the Bishop. When they threatened the fiend in him, saying, "Now this man's master has come to drive you out!" the fiend answered, "I did not enter this man of my own free will, but under compulsion. He killed our Teacher's dog in the upper vineyard and for that reason he sent me to torment him; and my friends he sent to enter into these monks because they used to leave the church at the time of the Offering and go outside to swim and play in those pools of water outside the monastery." "Our Teacher" was the fiends' name for some sorcerer. But the moment the monks stood those boys in front of the right hand of the saint, the demons shrieked violently and came out of them. These stories about sorcerers and demons which were exorcized by saints cannot be doubted, because they are in the book of that truthful man, the patriarch Dionysius; but the reader should understand that sorcerers and fiends are not able to gain possession of people without the permission of God, as happened in the case of Righteous Job.'

[426] §§ 93-99: text No. 10, AG 960; Theophanes, pp. 343-4 and Agapius, pp. 220-1 appear to share a common source with the *Chronicle of 1234* but drastically abbreviate it. On the sources for the capture of Arwād, see Conrad, 'The Conquest of Arwād'. [R. H.]

that they were going to destroy the luxurious cities of the Cypriots,[427] which had never been the victims of a raid or the tributaries of a foreign power.

§ 95. They were already nearing their voyage's end, when Mu^{c}āwiya signalled to them to furl sails and put the ships ashore. He wanted to use clemency towards the lords of the island, so he gave them this chance to be subjected on the receipt of assurances instead of letting their country be ruined by enemy aggression. He positioned his own ship at the head of the whole fleet /p. 269/ and said to his friends, 'Let us stay here and wait for them to come to us. Will the Cypriots ask for an amnesty to save their lives[428] and so spare their country from ruin, or not?' One day passed, then another; but no one came to sue for peace or to beg them not to ruin the island. In Mu^{c}āwiya's mind a cruel doom of destruction took shape against the unfortunate population. Moreover, the Egyptian contingent put him under considerable pressure with their hostile recriminations and their angry insults because he had delayed and had held them back from an invasion of the island. At last he let the Alexandrians have their head and ordered them suddenly to leap the fence, as it were, and invade.

§ 96. The Cypriots lifted up their eyes and saw a large number of ships approaching. At first they thought they were Romans. When the Arabs reached the coast, they dropped anchor, moored their ships, armed themselves powerfully and came ashore. They scattered throughout the island, spoiling, enslaving, killing without pity. Mu^{c}āwiya himself with his captains and the company[429] under his personal leadership made straight for the famous city of Constantina, the capital of Cyprus, urged on by hot desire, and entered her there and then. They found her prosperously settled and provided with amenities, full to overflowing with people of every race under the sun. When Mu^{c}āwiya saw the affluence of her breath-taking palaces and the

---

[427] Lit. 'the paradisiacal city of Cyprus'.

[428] Lit. 'take the word for their lives'.

[429] {Gr. opsíkion = Lat. obsequium}.

abundance of her edifices, his heart swelled and his conceit knew no bounds, intoxicated by so many treasures and riches all won without a battle. The sword and the shackles soon put the city under his control. He took up residence with due ceremony in the bishop's palace [...]^{430} and after resting to his heart's /p. 270/ content, he used it as a place in which to fulfil his unlawful lust.

§ 97. Why did God allow this to occur? I think, because those who had held office in that place had been unworthy heirs and bad servants. These holy edifices had been erected in the time of Epiphanius, whose glory was his divine doctrine;^{431} but the priests, who were themselves the trustees of the law, were strangers to the Lord, and had departed from Epiphanius's faith and moral example. I forbear to go over one by one the crimes that had been committed there.^{432} [...] That is why the cup of God's wrath, which was filled to the brim with this ordure, was flung out over the deflowered city.

The barbarian force had scattered throughout the land, as I said before, to collect gold, slaves and expensive clothing and to bring it to Mu^{c}āwiya in Constantina, who was absolutely delighted, as were his companions, at the quantity of the accumulated loot and of the captives, male and female of every age.^{433} All this booty was divided into two portions, for which the two armies, that from Egypt and that from Syria, cast lots. After a few days, when they felt they had stayed long enough, they embarked their human loot in the ships. What misery and lamentation were seen then! Fathers were separated from their children, daughters from their mother, brother from brother, some destined for Alexandria, others for Syria. / p. 271/ The return passage

---

^{430} Glossed superfluously in the Syriac.

^{431} Bishop of Salamis/Constantina, and a prolific theologian; died AD 403.

^{432} There follow six lines in which these crimes are evoked in general terms.

^{433} cf. Theophanes, p. 344.

of the invaders was smooth and calm.[434]

§ 98*. Evidently the Lord had fixed this island with a baleful stare, not to do good there, but to make it a byword and a curse among all nations. Shortly afterwards he stirred the barbarians up to invade Cyprus again under a commander called Abū 'l-A^{C}war.[435] They had heard that it was already as full of people as ever and that a large force of Romans had taken up residence there. The vessels were ready, the Arab forces embarked, and the journey began on a halcyon sea.[436] Meanwhile, the Roman force on the island encouraged the populace, which had emerged from its hiding-places in the caves and mountains, to have confidence. 'Stay where you are!' they said, raising false hopes, 'Do not panic! There is no need to worry!' But when the Romans and the natives actually sighted the Arab ships on the horizon and saw their number, their courage deserted them and they took to flight. Some, being rich, possessed sailing vessels in which they escaped to Roman territory. Others attempted to avoid death or slavery by shutting themselves up in Lapethus, one of the cities on Cyprus. As for the Romans, on whom the islanders had depended, when they saw that their own lives were in danger, /p. 272/ they took to their own ships and saved themselves from Arab aggression. As soon as the ships were ashore, the invaders filled all the mountains and the plains, intent on plunder and slaves. They winkled the natives out of the cracks in the ground, like eggs abandoned in the nest. The general, Abū 'l-A^{C}war, went down to Constantina and stayed there for forty days, enslaving the population and eating the livestock head by head. At length, when they had had their way with the rest of the island, they

---

[434] The verbose style of this paragraph has been tightened in translation.

[435] {Syr. ꝯBWL^{C}WR}. This is very likely Abū 'l-A^{C}war b. Sufyān, governor of Jordan for Mu^{C}āwiya (Tabari, I, p. 3057). The article 'Kubrus' in Encyclopaedia of Islam, 2nd ed., gives Abū 'l-Anwār without any corroboration. [R.H.] Cf. Conrad, 'Arwād', p. 361f.

[436] Lit. 'and they began to sail by sea between the waves with all tranquillity and calm and stillness' - a good example of the pleonastic style of this paragraph and the one before.

all gathered against Lapethus. For several days they tried the effect of promises of peace, but finding the Cypriots unreceptive to these, they began eventually to bombard the city with catapults from all around. When the inhabitants saw that it was hopeless and that no help was on its way, they petitioned the general to proffer them his right hand in token of deliverance from death. He showed clemency readily and sent them the following instructions: 'The gold and silver and other assets which are in the city are mine. To you I give an amnesty and a solemn pact that those of you who so wish may go to Roman territory, and that those who wish to stay will neither be killed nor enslaved.' So the city was taken, its treasures were embarked on the ships with the rest of the booty and the Arabs sailed back to Syria in victory.

§ 99*. The city of Aradus,[437] which is called Arad Const[antini], is an off-shore island opposite Antaradus at a distance of three 'miles'.[438] Mu^{c}āwiya, finding it impossible to take by siege, sent a certain bishop to them, by the name of Thomas, with the demand that the inhabitants should leave the city and go their way unharmed. But on his admission to the city the bishop was taken prisoner and not allowed to return: Aradus did not surrender to Mu^{c}āwiya. After this Mu^{c}āwiya returned to Damascus,[439] because winter had come upon him, which made besieging Aradus an impractical option. When he came to renew the siege[440] in the spring, Mu^{c}āwiya's forces were more numerous and better equipped. The Aradites, with a sense of the inevitable march of events,[441] not to speak of the robust assaults launched by Mu^{c}āwiya on their city, accepted his assurances for their

---

[437] {Ar. arwād}.

[438] The 'miles' are of shorter length than English or even Roman miles, as can be seen from §§ 164 and 165, below, where reasons are given in the notes for putting our writer's 'mile' at about 300 metres. In reality Arwād lies something like one kilometre off the coast.

[439] Spelt in the Greek way.

[440] {Syr. aqneb} is an error for {Syr. aqreb}.

[441] Lit. 'when they saw the narrowness of the time'.

lives[442] and the choice he offered them of emigrating to Roman territory or of settling wherever they wanted to in Syria. Once the population of that island city had been evacuated, Mu^cawiya ordered its walls to be demolished and its buildings to be set on fire. In this way the Arabs razed it to the ground; and they resolved never to let the city be rebuilt or resettled.

§ 100*.[443] In this year King ^cUthman sent his son Sa^cid to pursue Yazdgird the Persian king. Yazdgird, warned of his coming, left Segestan and went to Marw, the episcopal see of Khurāsān, where he stayed two years as a refugee from Sa^cid. When Sa^cid arrived at Marw, /p. 274/ Yazdgird was afraid that he would be extradited, so he left the city and hid in a mill, where he was discovered by the miller and killed. The miller took his head to the governor[444] of the city, who recognized his master and surrendered Marw to the Arabs. Then Sa^cid took the crown of the Persian kings and sent it to ^cUthmān. Today that crown can be seen in the place of prayer which they call the Ka^cba, for that is where ^cUthmān deposited it. The same year Constans sent a messenger to Mu^cawiya, emir of Syria, in Damascus, suing for peace. A treaty was drawn up between them and Constans sent Gregory, son of Heraclius's brother Theodoric, as a hostage for peace to the Arabs. Gregory died, however, the following year. His body was embalmed and sent to Constantinople and the treaty was annulled.[445]

---

[442] Lit. 'took the word for their lives'.

[443] The *Chronicle of 1234* and Michael omit a notice on the revolt of Pasagnathes, patríkios of Armenia, shared by Theophanes, p. 344 and Agapius, p. 222. [R. H.]

[444] {Pers. marzbān}.

[445] Death of Yazdgird: Agapius, p. 221. Peace: Theophanes, pp. 344-5; Agapius, pp. 221-2. Michael, p. 422:14, 17-20, 26, 11.8a: 'AG 961: [...] After having lain hidden in Segestan for five years, Yazdgird emerged and came to al-Kūfa. [...] A Turk killed him ...'; Michael, p. 418:17-32, 11.7a, adds: 'When Yazdgird, the Persian king, was killed, whether by an Arab or by a Turk, the so-called Sasanid empire and dynasty of the Persians was utterly eradicated. It had lasted 418 years, having begun AG 538 with Ardashīr, son of Pābag {Syr.

§ 101*. AG 966 = year 13 of Constans = AH 37 = year 9 of
^{c}Uthmān:[446] Mu^{c}āwiya, the emir of Syria and of Damascus,
equipped a great fleet to sail to Constantinople and lay siege to it.
These preparations were made on the coast of Tripolis. Abū 'l-A^{c}war
was appointed as admiral of the fleet and they sailed to Phoenicus on
the Lycian coast, where they were met by the great fleet of Constans,
the king of the Greeks,[447] and his brother Theodosius. With the
coming sea-battle on his mind the King that night had a dream. He
dreamt that he was in Thessalonīkē. An interpreter of dreams, when
consulted about this, said, 'O King, if only you had not slept /p. 275/
and had never had this dream. Thessalonīkē signifies that victory
favours your enemies - thes-allō-tēn-nīkēn, literally: set down the
victory to another. In other words, Victory favours your enemies.'

S$^⊃$B$^⊃$Q}, and having ended AG 956 with this last king, Yazdgird, in
the reign of Heraclius, king of the Romans, and of ^{c}Umar b.
al-Khattāb, king of the Arabs. After the Persian king had been killed
and their empire had ceased, the Arabs became masters of all Persia,
which brought them much power. They saw that they were everywhere
victorious in war, because the Lord was helping them. So they came
to Aleppo and Antioch, where they killed many people.' Although the
total regnal years of the Sasanids is correct and the date of year 1 of
Ardashīr is also right, the end-date should be AG 962 or 963; see
Nöldeke, Anhang A. Again, Michael, p. 422:34-36, 423:2-12, 11.8a,
adds: 'At this time (c.AG 953/4) the Arabs destroyed Caesarea in
Palestine. [...] Mu^{c}āwiya surrounded it by sea and by land and kept it
under attack by day and by night, from the beginning of December
until the month of May. Yet they would not take the word for their
lives. Though seventy-two catapults bombarded it continually with
rocks, the wall was so solid that it did not crack. Finally the attackers
made a breach, through which some entered, while others climbed onto
the wall with ladders. For three days the fighting continued, before the
ultimate Arab victory. Of the seven-thousand-strong Roman garrison
some escaped on ships. Mu^{c}āwiya took the treasures and obliged the
population to pay tribute.'
    446 Agapius, p. 223 has AH 34, which is a very simple
palaeographical amendment from 37 in Syriac. This would give year
11 of ^{c}Uthmān but, since ^{c}Umar is given 12 years instead of 10, it
equates to year 9 in Dionysius's reckoning. [R.H.]
    447 {Syr. yawnōyē}, for the first time in this text; the usual word for
the Byzantines is {Syr. rūmōyē}.

The King pooh-poohed this interpretation and gave the order to engage in battle. The two sides persisted stubbornly in their struggle on the sea, but the Greeks were defeated in the end. The King himself might have fallen into enemy hands, had not the son of the bugler[448] leapt onto the royal ship, got the King onto another ship and remained himself in that of the King, surrounded by enemies who took him for the King. He was cornered and killed, though not before he had killed a large number of them. The Arabs pressed their pursuit of the Romans[449] as far as Rhodes. So violent had this sea-battle been that the foam rose up between the ships like dust from dry land, so it is said. Abū 'l-A^{C}war ordered the corpses of the Romans to be hauled up out of the water and counted; and their number was twenty thousand. So the Arabs, who had not only won a historic victory, but had also captured men and property of every kind, set sail for home.[450]

---

[448] {Lat. buccinator}.

[449] Rather than 'Greeks', here and below.

[450] Text No. 10, AG 963; Theophanes, pp. 345-6; Agapius, pp. 223-4; Michael, p. 430:40-431:5, 11.11a: 'Then two dedicated men released the prisoners shut up in Tripolis, where the ships were moored. After killing the Arabs and the emir, they set fire to the whole fleet of ships. They themselves got away in a small boat and escaped to Roman territory.' Michael, p. 430:22-31, 11.10a, adds: 'AG 965: Abū 'l-A^{C}wār and his army sailed to the island of Cos. By the treachery of the bishops (read 'bishop'?) there they took it, wasted and pillaged all its wealth, massacred the population, leading the survivors away as captives, and destroyed its citadel. Then he carried out a raid on Crete and another on Rhodes. The bronze colossus (of Rhodes) was a magnificent work, which was considered one of the great wonders of the world. They made up their minds to break it up to get hold of the Corinthian bronze of which it was made. It had the form of a man standing upright. By lighting a fire around the base they discovered that it was attached to the bedrock by massive iron tendons. Many men were set to haul on long ropes attached to the colossus and suddenly it gave way and fell to the ground. They say that it was 107 foot high. They found three thousand loads of bronze in it and this was bought by a Jew from the city of Emesa.' cf. Theophanes, p. 345; Agapius, p. 222.

§ 102*. We have already related how the Arabs took exception to ^cUthmān from the start, because he did not follow in his predecessors' footsteps. Muḥammad, Abū Bakr and ^cUmar had lived in modesty and self-abasement, as a prophet ought to live. But this man had carriages made for himself and many-coloured banners; drummers, trumpeters and buglers went before him. Worst of all he stood on the topmost step of the minbar.[451] The minbar is a pulpit-like construction with steps. Muḥammad, their prophet, had used it at times of prayer. When Muḥammad had died, his successor Abū Bakr had had the humility to stand and preach, as is their custom at the time of prayer, on the step /p. 276/ below that on which Muḥammad had stood. Likewise, when Abū Bakr had died, his successor ^cUmar b. al-Khaṭṭāb had been humble enough to take another step down, below the place where Abū Bakr had been accustomed to stand, and to stand there and preach as is the custom. But when ^cUmar died and was succeeded by ^cUthmān, ^cUthmān went up and stood on the topmost step, where Muḥammad had been accustomed to stand. This excited the indignation of the Arabs against ^cUthmān and disposed them to kill him.

§ 103. But it was another matter which actually brought about ^cUthmān's assassination. A relative of their prophet, the son of Muḥammad's grandfather Abū Bakr, demanded the governership[452] of Damascus and insisted that ^cUthmān should depose Mu^cāwiya in his favour. Although this man - whose name was also Muḥammad - brought great pressure to bear on him, ^cUthmān withheld his consent. Now Muḥammad b. Abī Bakr had, they say, been egged on to ask for the lordship of Damascus by ^cAlī b. Abī Ṭālib, who had been unsuccessful in his ambition to succeed their prophet Muḥammad. ^cUthmān was so irritated by the insistence of the man that he wrote a letter to Mu^cāwiya, sealed it, and gave it to the said Muḥammad with instructions to go and take over power in Damascus; but what he had written in the letter was: 'As soon as Muḥammad gets to you, kill

---

[451] {Gr. bēma}.

[452] Lit. 'kingship'; here a synonym of 'lordship', as will appear.

him.' Muhammad clasped the letter in his hand, delighted, and went
straight to ᶜAlī b. Abī Ṭālib. Now ᶜAlī realized that ᶜUthmān was
in no position to dismiss Muᶜāwiya because he was a member of his
own tribe. He told Muhammad: 'This letter has not been written to
transfer the governorship to you, but to have you killed.' On opening
the letter they discovered that ᶜAlī's hunch had been correct.

§ 104. At the instigation of ᶜAlī, Muhammad went to the mosque
on Friday, when it was packed with Arabs, holding the letter in his
hand. /p. 277/ The moment ᶜUthmān mounted the minbar to preach the
customary sermon, Muhammad stood up with the letter in his hand and
said in front of the people, 'O Commander of the Faithful and
Deputy[453] of the Prophet of God, what penalty ought a person to
pay who, being an Arab, encompasses the death of an adult male Arab
without that man's having wronged him?' ᶜUthmān replied, 'The
penalty of death.' Then, in front of all the Arabs, Muhammad opened
the letter and said, 'You intended to kill me without my having
wronged you.' At this ᶜUthmān denied having written the letter; but
the scribe was summoned and confessed that it was ᶜUthmān who had
commanded him to write it. There ensued a general riot of the Arabs,
who crowded around the entrance to ᶜUthmān's palace, intent on killing
him. ᶜUthmān sent word to ᶜAlī b. Abī Ṭālib and requested his
protection and ᶜAlī sent his two sons, al-Ḥasan and al-Ḥusayn, to
restrain the Arabs. When they arrived they cleared the entrance to the
palace and settled down to guard it. But the Arabs, in a frenzy of rage,
dismantled the enclosure-wall at another point. And so they forced an
entrance and assassinated ᶜUthmān b. ᶜAffān in Yathrib.[454]

---

[453] {Syr. tahlūpō}, etymologically related to {Ar. khalīfa}, 'Caliph',
of which it is a translation.

[454] Texts No. 9 and No. 10, AG 967; Michael, p. 433:22-434:6,
12-13, 11.12a: 'When ᶜUthmān reverted to his (bad) old habits, the
Arabs assembled and asked him, "Why do you not behave as
Muhammad taught us? We see you piling up treasures by preying on
others and you converse with adulterers, fornicators and criminals."
His reply was, "I am King and I do what I like." For that reason they
were alienated from him and snarled every day that they would destroy

§ 105*. Directly after the murder of ^cUthmān, ^cAlī wrote a letter of royal authority,[455] commanding Muhammad b. Abī Bakr to go to Damascus and relieve Mu^cāwiya of power. When Muhammad reached Damascus, however, and showed the letter to Mu^cāwiya, he rejected it and defied ^cAlī, saying, 'I do not consent that ^cAlī should rule the Arabs, unless he sends me ^cUthmān's murderer to pay the price of ^cUthmān's blood.' Mu^cāwiya was supported in this matter by a wise and learned man, ^cAmr b. al-^cĀs, the governor of Egypt, and by all the Arabs in the west. So Muhammad went back to ^cAlī with the man sent by Mu^cāwiya to secure the extradition of ^cUthmān's murderers. When they reached ^cAlī, who was at al-Kūfa, he mounted the minbar on Friday as usual and addressed all /p. 278/ the Arabs who were gathered in the mosque: 'This man has come to demand in the name of Mu^cāwiya the extradition of ^cUthmān's murderer. So let every one who shares responsibility for the assassination of ^cUthmān now sit down on the ground!' The whole congregation sat down. Again he addressed them: 'Now let every one who shares responsibility for the assassination of ^cUthmān stand up!' The assembly rose to its feet as a single man. Then ^cAlī turned to the envoy: 'You have seen it for yourself. No individual is responsible for ^cUthmān's death; he was killed by all the Arabs in the city. So tell your master to submit with a good grace and not to oppose the rule of law.'[456]

---

him. They reassembled, armed, at his gate, shouting, "Change your vile habits, or else you will die forthwith." He wrote to Mu^cāwiya to tell him about the situation and to ask him to send him a force. But the Arabs assembled again and attacked their king ^cUthmān with violence and lynched him, there in the /p. 434/ city of Yathrib itself. Meanwhile, Mu^cāwiya had sent an army under the leadership of Habīb to help the King. At Busrā they learned of the assassination of the King and they went back and told Mu^cāwiya. [...] These things happened in AG 967 = AH 35.'

455 {Lat. sigilla}.

456 §§ 105-9: text No. 10, AG 967, 968; text No. 12, AG 967. Theophanes, pp. 346-7, Agapius, pp. 225-6 and Dionysius have very different accounts of the first Arab civil war; the latter makes considerable use of Muslim sources. [R.H.]

§ 106. At the return of his envoy Mu^{c}āwiya equipped himself for battle. He mustered a force of 120,000 men. ^{c}Alī, too, made preparations for war and led an army of 90,000 men against Damascus. They met on the Euphrates, not far from Callinicum, at a place called Siffīn,^{457} and did battle. The sum of the dead on both sides was 60,000. ^{c}Alī returned to al-Kūfa, Mu^{c}āwiya to Damascus; and the Arab civil war continued, until it reached the point that in all the west and at Damascus a ceremonial curse against ^{c}Alī was spoken from the minbar at the time of prayer, while in the east and at al-Kūfa they cursed Mu^{c}āwiya. Then the Arabs decided to make peace and to put an end to this division. The warring parties agreed in good faith that the supporters of ^{c}Alī should elect a representative and the supporters of Mu^{c}āwiya likewise; and that all the people should consent without discussion to the choice made by these two men and recognize the man they should designate as king, whether it should be Mu^{c}āwiya or ^{c}Alī. As representative of the party of Mu^{c}āwiya was chosen ^{c}Amr b. al-^{c}Ās; the party of ^{c}Alī elected Abū Mūsā, who was called al-Ash^{c}arī.

§ 107. Now ^{c}Amr b. al-^{c}Ās was a devious man. While they were walking alone together on the road, /p. 279/ he put al-Ash^{c}arī to the test. 'Put your ear near my mouth!' he told him, 'I want to tell you a secret.' The fact that al-Ash^{c}arī obeyed revealed to ^{c}Amr that he was a simpleton. For who was there to overhear the secret, that he should need to put his ear near his mouth? So he said, 'Take my advice, Abū Mūsā. Give me your right hand to seal the engagement of your daughter to my son, then we shall both designate my son to be the king. When you mount the minbar on Friday say to the people: I have stripped ^{c}Alī of the kingdom as I take this ring here off my finger. Then I will go up into the minbar myself and say: I have given the kingdom to such-and-such - my son, that is - as this ring goes on my finger.' Abū Mūsā agreed to this plan and when they reached Damascus, he went up into the minbar and recited the lesson he had

---

^{457} {Syr. sepīn}.

learned from ^CAmr b. al-^CĀs: 'I have stripped ^CAlī of the kingdom.'
Then ^CAmr went up after him and said, 'I have stripped ^CAlī of the
kingdom and I have laid it on the shoulders of Mu^Cāwiya.'

§ 108. This outcome did not help matters in the slightest, but only
increased the general indignation. Once again they made ready for
battle. The killing and the struggle for power did not subside as long
as ^CAlī lived, nor even after his death, as we shall soon relate.

§ 109*. Three men driven by indignation at the state of civil war
formed a plot that each of them would kill one of those on whose
account the war was being fought amongst the Arabs, namely ^CAlī,
Mu^Cāwiya and ^CAmr b. al-^CĀs, who was in Egypt. The one who went
to Egypt was caught and killed, as was the one who went to the camp
of Mu^Cāwiya; but the third, whose name was ^CAbd al-Rahmān b.
Muljam went /p. 280/ to al-Kūfa and hid in the mosque at dawn, when
^CAlī came in to pray. He came up behind him and killed him with a
blow from his sword. As he was leaving the mosque he ran into those
coming in to pray and he looked so scared that they laid hold of him.
Inside they found ^CAlī prostrate on the ground and asked him, 'Who
wounded you?' He answered, '^CAbd al-Rahmān b. Muljam here did it.
If I die, deal him one blow with the sword. If that kills him, so much
the better for him. If he lives, then let him be. For he dealt me a
single blow.' Two days later ^CAlī died and the Arabs executed ^CAbd
al-Rahmān. On ^CAlī's death he was succeeded by his son al-Hasan,
who was poisoned shortly afterwards and was succeeded in turn by
al-Husayn. These two sons of ^CAlī were born of Fātima, the daughter
of Muhammad, the prophet of the Arabs.[458]

§ 110. Still the civil war was not over. Mu^Cāwiya did battle with
al-Husayn in the east and al-Husayn's side lost. Most of the army and
al-Husayn himself were killed at a place called Karbalāᵓ. Al-Husayn
was killed by Shamir, an Arab; but first he was tortured by thirst. The
victors slaughtered most of the tribe and kin of ^CAlī. They took their

---

[458] Text No. 10, AG 973; text No. 12, AG 971; Michael, 11.12a.

wives and children and tormented them beyond the limit of endurance.[459] After this the only survivor in power was Mu^{c}āwiya b. Abī Sufyān from the tribe of the Umayyads, who had a son Yazīd, called after his brother Yazīd who had died - this man has been mentioned before (see pp. 144, 150). He moved the capital and the royal granaries from al-Kūfa to Damascus. He had already led the Arabs as a commander for twenty years. He was an honourable man whose tolerance and humanity seemed unlimited. /p. 281/ Insults against his person were heard by him and ignored. This increased his popularity among the Arabs and so contributed to the division of the Arab armies, with those of Yathrib and Babylonia on the one side and those of Egypt and Damascus on the other, until the death of al-Husayn, as we have shown. And still today there is a heresy[460] among the Arabs.[461]

§ 111. The following story is told to illustrate the boundless tolerance of Mu^{c}āwiya b. Abī Sufyān. A certain Arab hit a small son of Mu^{c}āwiya's and the child died. The man was arrested and brought

----

[459] The killing of al-Husayn by Shamir b. Dhī al-Jawshan and the theme of thirst (Tabarī, II, pp. 312-3) identify this as the battle of Karbalāͻ, which Muslim sources place in 680, although it is here made a part of the first civil war. Theophanes, p. 347 does the same and also conflates this battle with that of Siffīn. [R.H.]

[460] {Gr. haíresis}.

[461] Michael, p. 434:34-36, 11.12a: 'Mu^{c}āwiya transferred their kingdom from Yathrib to Damascus' (Agapius, p. 226). Michael, p. 434:40-435:19, 11.12a, adds: 'At this time the Harūrite sect {Gr. haíresis}, named after the village Harūrāͻ, where they met, revolted against this kingdom of the Hagarènes; indeed, they are still now in revolt against it (Theophanes, pp. 347-8; Agapius, p. 227). AG 980 = year 27 of Constans = year 9 of Mu^{c}āwiya = AH 54 (read 48): Abū 'l-A^{c}war made a census of the Christian labourers (the word can also mean 'soldiers') of all Syria. As a matter of fact, Christian labourers had not earlier paid tax under Arab rule. The seven years of the peace-treaty between the Romans and the Arabs were finished and the Arabs pillaged all Asia, Bithynia, and Pamphylia. There was a serious outbreak of pestilence in Mesopotamia. Once again the Arabs left a trail of pillage and destruction as far as the Black Sea {Gr. póntos} and Galatia.'

to Mu^{c}āwiya, who asked him why he had killed the child. He answered, 'By your life, O King, I hit him just once without intending to kill him. Now that he is dead, it is for you to deal with me according to the abundant mercy of your goodness.' Then Mu^{c}āwiya said to him, 'Go! In the eyes of God you are innocent.'

§ 112*. At the time of the civil war between ^{c}Alī and Mu^{c}āwiya, ^{c}Alī had sent word to all Mesopotamians that they should be his allies against Mu^{c}āwiya. When he had reached Siffin on the Euphrates he had sent word to the people of Harrān and they promised to come and help him against Mu^{c}āwiya. But when Mu^{c}āwiya had arrived and the battle had begun, the Harrānites had fought on his side instead. So when Mu^{c}āwiya had returned to Damascus, ^{c}Alī had gone to Harrān and put most of the citizens to the sword. There had actually been blood flowing out at the gate of the city. For this reason many Harrānites marched with Mu^{c}āwiya and fought in that final battle between Mu^{c}āwiya and the partisans of ^{c}Alī. And still today the Harrānites honour Yazīd, the son of Mu^{c}āwiya, because of his undying enmity towards the party of ^{c}Alī. /p. 282/

§ 113*. Now King Constans had killed his brother, which made him hateful to his soldiers. When he realized this and began to fear that they would kill him, he left Constantinople and set up residence in Rome. It was not long before the senators began to complain: 'It is neither suitable, nor is it right that the government should be at Rome, because Rome is too far from the Arabs.' At this Constans left Rome and went to Syracuse on the island of Sicily. He liked it and so decided to settle there. He commanded the lords who accompanied him to build themselves palaces there and to acquire livestock and agricultural estates. He also sent for his sons, who were at Constantinople, but the Constantinopolitans would not let them go, saying, 'We will not allow our kings to abandon us.'[462]

§ 114. AG 976 = year 23 of Constans = AH 44: There was confusion as to the date of the Feast of the Resurrection. While some Christians celebrated the Feast of Hosannas,[463] others celebrated Easter; and when the former were still celebrating Easter, the latter celebrated New Sunday.[464] In this year there was an eclipse of the sun and the stars came out. In this year both Lord John the patriarch and Lord Simeon the metropolitan of Edessa died within the space of a month. At this time Severus Sabūkht, the bishop of Qēnneshrīn, became known for his wisdom[465] and likewise Matthew of Aleppo. And Mu^{c}āwiya invaded Egypt[466] and destroyed all the Romans there, more than five thousand of them - year 5 of Mu^{c}āwiya.[467]

---

[462] Theophanes, pp. 347-8; Michael, p. 432:11-24, 33-38, 11.11a: 'When the Arabs prepared to march once more against Constantinople, Ptolemy came and promised them annual tribute from the land of the Romans. When he cheated them, the Arabs went up and pillaged Isauria. Ptolemy came out again, gave them the gold and made peace with the Arabs for three years. The emperor sent his (actually Heraclius's) brother's son, Gregory, to Mu^{c}āwiya as a hostage for the gold. But even so the Arabs did not keep their promises; but then, the Romans were not exactly to be trusted, whether by the Arabs or indeed by their fellows. Constans, for example, murdered his brother Theodosius, in order to leave the kingdom to his sons. [...] They (the people of Constantinople) said, "We will not let our kings leave us." So he (Constans) proclaimed his three sons Constantine, Tiberius and Heraclius "autokrátores" and bid them reside at the Royal City.' cf. Theophanes, AM 6142.

[463] Palm Sunday.

[464] The First Sunday after Easter.

[465] Severus was, amongst other things, an astronomer who wrote about eclipses; he had taught at the monastic school of Qēnnēshrē, on the Euphrates, not to be confused with Qēnneshrīn, south of Aleppo, his bishopric.

[466] {Gr. aíguptos}.

[467] Matthew of Aleppo, Patriarch John, Simeon of Edessa: text No. 10, AG 955 ad finem, 961; text No. 12, AG 960. Severus Sabūkht: text No. 4, AG 970; according to texts No. 9 and No. 10, AG 976, it was Patriarch Theodore who died in that year (see Appendix I); cf. Michael, 11.9a. Michael, p. 433, 11.12b, gives the date of the dispute about the date of Easter as: 'AG 976 = AH 44 = year 23 of Constans

§ 115*. In year 26 of Constans one of his generals, called Shabuhr, rebelled against him.[468] He sent an envoy to Mu^cāwiya, the Arab king, a man called Sergius, to convey his promise that he would subject Roman territory to his rule, /p. 283/ if he would send him an army and help him to assassinate Constans. When Constantine, the son of Constans, who was in Constantinople, learned of this, he too sent an envoy to Mu^cāwiya, a eunuch called Andrew, who was the Royal Chamberlain.[469] With him he sent precious gifts and royal presents, requesting that he abstain from taking the part of that rebel and from helping him to usurp the throne. The eunuch Andrew set out on a fast post-horse and reached Damascus, where he found that Sergius, the envoy of Shabuhr, had already been admitted to Mu^cāwiya's presence and had been well received.

King Mu^cāwiya had heard that Andrew was on his way - his name was very well known among the Arabs, since he possessed strength of character, both in military prowess and in rhetorical ability, in spite of being a eunuch - but, out of antipathy for Constans, he had ordered that Sergius should be admitted first, then Andrew the Eunuch.

So it happened that Sergius went in first and sat down next to Mu^cāwiya and that Andrew only then received his own instructions to go in. As soon as Andrew had entered and had taken up position in front of Mu^cāwiya, Sergius leapt to his feet and placed himself in front of him and made obeisance to him. The sight of this made Mu^cāwiya angry with Sergius.

'You idiot!' he said, 'You coward! What is wrong with you? Why did you make obeisance to this man? If the servant frightens you so much that you get up and do obeisance to him, what would you not do

---

= year 5 of Mu^cāwiya.' On the solar eclipse, see Michael, p. 421, 11.8b: 'At this time there was a solar eclipse at the third hour on 9 October (but see Appendix I); the stars appeared and a great terror took hold of all who saw this awful sign.'

[468] Shabuhr, or Sapor, is a Persian name which was borne by some of the Sasanid kings.

[469] {Lat. cubicularius}.

if you saw the one who sent him?'

Sergius answered, 'I did it by force of habit, not because I was afraid of him.'

Then Mu^cāwiya asked Andrew, 'Where have you come from and what do you want?'

He replied, 'Emir, I have been sent to you by my King to ask you to expel, if you will, this man who is sitting next to you from your presence.'

Mu^cāwiya said, 'Your king and the man who sent this envoy and /p. 284/ all the rest of you are our enemies. Whoever will embrace our cause and exert himself in our interest can count on my support. Therefore, if your king gives me more gold, we shall help him to suppress his rebellious baron; but if the one who sent this envoy not only outbids him, but also embraces our cause, we shall make him king.'

To this Andrew replied as follows, 'True, O Emir, both parties are your enemies, both my King and the one who has rebelled against him. But some enemies are better than others, just as some friends are better than others. There can be no comparison between the lord and the slave. The one, being a lord, conducts his affairs in a noble and magnificent manner, while the other, whose life has been one of servile subservience, will do business in a thoroughly servile way. As befits low-born people he will promise more than he can deliver; and such promises are never kept. So if my King offers to enter into a covenant with you on certain conditions, whatever they may be, even if he promises you less than that tyrant, it is in him that you should place confidence, nor should you try to haggle. For if that tyrant should attempt to gain your favour by promising more, you may be quite certain that he is a liar and that he will not keep his word. Is it likely that one who has proved himself so ungrateful in recompensing his lord for all his benefits towards him would keep his promises to you, who are his enemy? However, you must do whatever you think best.'

Mu^cāwiya replied, 'You have spoken well. But now you are dismissed. Go and think about what you have heard me say and come back again tomorrow!'

Once Andrew had gone, Mu^{c}āwiya said to Sergius, 'You, too, be off
to your lodgings and make sure you get here first tomorrow! Be on
your guard and do not make obeisance to the eunuch, as you did
today!'

The next day Sergius was there before Andrew. He was admitted to
Mu^{c}āwiya's presence /p. 285/ and Mu^{c}āwiya told him to sit down.
Then Andrew, too, arrived. He, too, was ordered to be seated.
Sergius broke his habit and did not get up when he came in. Then
Andrew glared at Sergius and spoke angrily in Greek,

'Desperate fellow! Thrice-wretched cur! Why did you not rise from
your seat to show respect when I came in, as befits your status as a
slave? Did you remain seated so as to show off your shamelessness to
Mu^{c}āwiya?'

Sergius's answer was wounding, disrespectful and contemptuous. He
called him effeminate: not a man, nor a woman, nor *oudéteros*, which
means 'either of these'.[470]

Then Andrew said to him, 'If the Lord grants me life, you shall pay
for this outrage! I, personally, shall remove your balls and place them
on your palms.'

Thus these two wrangled in front of Mu^{c}āwiya, until he commanded
them to be silent. Then he spoke to Andrew,

'What do you say? Do you agree to make a covenant on the same
conditions as Sergius and will you give as much as he has promised, or
not?'

Andrew replied, 'What are the conditions, O Emir?'

Mu^{c}āwiya said, 'You may keep the name and the privileges of
kingship, but the revenue and the territory[471] must go to the Arabs.
If you approve, give your word and make a covenant; and if you do not
approve, you may withdraw and all the best to you!'

---

[470] I have translated this sentence literally, since its clumsiness
betrays, I think, a Greek original.

[471] The Syriac has 'the revenue of the lands', but this feminine
singular subject is followed by a masculine plural verb, suggesting my
straightforward emendation.

Andrew answered, 'O Emir, what you require would leave the Arabs with the body and us with the shadow in our hands. What advantage would there be for us in that? Do a deal with Sergius, if you like. We shall take refuge in God, who is more able than you to help the kingdom of the Romans.'

So Andrew left Damascus, riding a royal mule, and made his way to Melitene, using the route which Sergius would take on his way back to the one that sent him. He ordered the guards /p. 286/ of the pass to set up an ambush in the steepest part of the defile and to arrest Sergius when he came through.

Sergius, meanwhile, did a deal with Muᶜāwiya, by which Muᶜāwiya was to send an Arab army to help Shabuhr. Then he went ahead to tell the rebel leader that the army was on its way. When he arrived at the defile and found himself hemmed in by the walls of a certain ravine, the ambush was sprung and Sergius was seized. They bound him and his escorts hand and foot and sent him to the Chamberlain, Andrew. When he was confronted with him, he fell on his face and grovelled in the dirt, begging for forgiveness. But Andrew said to him,

'You are Sergius! The one who was so proud of his balls! The one who swanked in front of Muᶜāwiya! The one who called me effeminate!'

Then he ordered his testicles to be extracted and placed them on his palms, before commanding them to impale him on a piece of wood. Such was the revenge which Andrew took on Sergius.

As for Muᶜāwiya, in accordance with the agreement reached between him and Sergius, he sent the general al-Faḍl with a large number of Arabs to assist the rebel Shabuhr. When this horde reached the tyrant, Shabuhr happened just to have mounted a horse to come out through the gateway of his palace. The horse reared up and he was jammed between the wall and the crest of the gate. His head was crushed and he died, just when the Arab army had reached Melitene.[472]

---

[472] The editor needlessly obelizes the Syriac of these two sentences, perhaps because he was unfamiliar with the word 'ear of wheat' with the meaning of 'crest'.

When al-Fadl wrote to Mu^{c}āwiya about what had happened, Mu^{c}āwiya sent his son Yazīd, who caught up with al-Fadl, then invaded the Roman empire with him, taking captives, plundering and generally having their way. Under the pressure of this aggression the Romans offered them gifts and sued for peace and the Arabs went back to their country.[473]

On November 4 of this year, in the middle of the night, there was a great flood at Edessa. The water undermined the walls of the city and breached them /p. 287/ and the whole city was filled with water. Thousands of people were drowned there.[474]

§ 116*. AG 980 = year 27 of Constans = year 9 of Mu^{c}āwiya: King Constans was killed in Sicilian Syracuse, which he had chosen for his royal residence. Andrew, son of Troilus, went in with him to the bath-house. In the process of washing the King, he so covered his head with soap-suds that he was unable to open his eyes. Then he took a silver bucket, which he had placed in front of the King, and brought it crashing down on his head, fracturing his skull. Hurrying out of the bath-house he was caught by no one. They bore the King away to his royal palace and two days later he expired; whereupon the Romans elected as king a certain patríkios called Mizīzī, an Armenian. When Constantine heard of his father's assassination, he sailed to Sicily in force, seized Mizīzī and executed him and all those responsible for his father's death. After this he returned to Constantinople.[475]

---

[473] Theophanes, pp. 348-51; Agapius, pp. 228-9; Michael, pp. 433-6, 11.12b.

[474] Theophanes, p. 351; Agapius, p. 229; Michael, p. 433, 11.12b: 'The following year there was a flood at Edessa during the night. The water mounted up against the wall and a breach appeared. The city was filled with water and many people were drowned.'

[475] Theophanes, pp. 351-2; Agapius, pp. 230-1; Michael, p. 435:29-36, 11.12a: 'Then the Greeks made a man called Mizīzī their king, an Armenian by origin, who enjoyed the rank of patrician. He was brave, beautiful and chaste; and they made him king against his will.'

§ 117*. AG 981 = AH 49 = year 10 of Mu^{c}āwiya: Constantine became king of the Romans with his two brothers, Tiberius and Heraclius. He commanded the assembled senators to remain good subjects both of himself and of his brothers and warned them against insidiously creating division between them through a desire to ingratiate themselves and to be attached to one of them more than to the others. In the first year of his reign an Arab army invaded Africa and returned with 80,000 captives.[476] /p. 288/

§ 118*. In the fourth year of the reign of Constantine on the night from Monday to Tuesday at the third watch of the night a perfect bow was seen in the heavens, a highly unusual phenomenon; indeed it is unnatural for a bow to appear in the night, when the sun is underneath the earth.[477]

---

[476] Theophanes, p. 352; Agapius, p. 231; Michael, p. 436:12-13, 24-26, 31-42, 437:1-12, 11.13a: 'AG 981 = AH 55 (read AH 49; cf. the false synchronism in § 110, which tallies with this one) = year 10 of Mu^{c}āwiya: [...] They (Tiberius and Heraclius, the brothers of Constantine) went off to Gaul and to Italy and subjected all the peoples (*sic*) of the western region. [...] The following year (AG 982) the Arabs once again raided Lycia and Cilicia; returning to Lycia, they besieged a city on the sea-coast. Then three patríkioi of the Romans marched against them and defeated them. That day about 30,000 Arabs died, while those who escaped by ship ran into heavy storms. A carpenter from Baalbek, by name Callinicus, who had come from Syria to the Roman empire as a refugee, concocted a flaming substance and set fire to the Arab ships. With this fire he destroyed the rest of those which were confidently riding (at anchor) out at sea and everyone on board. Since that time the fire invented by Callinicus, which is called naft {Syr. naptō}, has been constantly in use by the Romans' (Theophanes, p. 354; Agapius, p. 232).

[477] Theophanes, p. 353; Agapius, p. 231; Michael, p. 436:31-32, 11.13b: 'All those who saw it thought that the end (of the world) would be in that year' (*ibid.*). Michael, p. 436:12-25, 33-37, 11.13b, adds: 'At that time there was a violent earthquake which ruined many places. AG 980: A harsh winter; much frost, ice and snow; olives and vines shrivelled throughout Syria and Mesopotamia (*ibid.*). AG 983: Solar eclipse in December, on a Sunday (correct for 7 December; Theophanes, p. 354). AG 988: An awesome comet appeared every morning from 28 August to 26 October, sixty days in all. [...] In this same year (AG 989) the rats became numerous in Syria and Phoenicia

§ 119. In the ninth year of his reign certain Romans launched an invasion of Mount Lebanon from the sea, landing on the coasts of Tyre and Sidon.   They were called the 'Mardaïtes'[478] and they controlled the heights from Galilee to the Black Mountain, sallying out all the time into Arab territory to plunder and destroy.[479]

§ 120. AG 950:[480] On the Sunday of the Resurrection a violent earthquake struck S^{e}rūgh and left it in ruins. The ciborium and the two outer sides of the Great Church at Edessa also collapsed and Mu^{c}āwiya commanded that these parts should be restored.[481] At this time Mu^{c}āwiya sent ^{c}Abd al-Rahmān to Roman territory to waste it and enslave the population and he stayed there for two years.

§ 121*. ^{c}Alī's son al-Husayn had perished in the war against

---

and destroyed the crops, causing a great food-shortage (Agapius, p. 232). The following year there were locusts (Theophanes, p. 354).' Theophanes, p. 353 = Agapius, p. 232: 'there was a plague in Egypt'.

[478] {Syr. marīdōyē}: a name perhaps connected with the Syriac verb MRD, meaning to rebel.

[479] Theophanes, p. 355; Agapius, pp. 232-3; Michael, p. 437:14-17, 19-23, 11.13a: 'They were called Marīdōyē or Līpūrē; the inhabitants of Syria called them the Jarājima {Ar. plural of jurjumānī, a native of al-Jurjūma; Syr. gargūmōyē}. [...] They launched raids constantly, for that is why they had been sent by the Romans. Finally the Arabs overcame them; some they killed, while they gouged out the eyes of the rest.' 'Līpūrē' can be explained by reference to Arab sources as 'brigands'; but cf. § 128, which suggests perhaps that 'deserters' may be meant, from the Greek verb: 'leipein'. Michael, p. 437:23-26, 11.13a, adds: 'At this time John, son of Mizīzī, rose up against Constantine. His rebellion lasted seven months, until he was killed by the army which the King had brought to Sicily.'

[480] Read '990'.

[481] Texts No. 10 and No. 12 (a+b), AG 990; Theophanes, p. 356; Agapius, p. 233; Michael, p. 437:1-8, 11.13b: 'They say that he was encamped (add: near Edessa at the time?) and had a dream announcing the ruin of ^{c}Alī and the confirmation of his own kingship; and that he had it (the church) rebuilt for that reason. In this same year there were tremors everywhere; and so it went on for seven years.'

Mu^cāwiya.[482]   Now King Mu^cāwiya also died and was buried at Damascus, AH 59 = year 11 of Constantine. He had led Syria as a general for twenty-one years and he had ruled as king for a further twenty. He was succeeded at Damascus by his son Yazīd.[483]

§ 122. Two years later King Constantine deposed his brothers. His reason for doing this was his son, an arrogant youth called Justinian. Fondly imagining that the boy would make a good king, Constantine looked for a way to remove his brothers from the throne and so to open the way for his son to succeed him. He began to curry favour with the Romans, /p. 289/ now with flattery and gifts, now with deceit and cunning subterfuge. Most of the Roman aristocracy he won over to his designs, but there was a certain Leo, a valiant and distinguished man, who persisted in crossing his will. His attitude was: 'It is not right to reject now men who came to the throne at the same time as the King. Why, even our denarius[484] has three busts portrayed on it. I will not be a partner to treason.' The King ordered that his tongue be cut out and as the hangman[485] dragged him off he began to shout, 'There is a Trinity that reigns in heaven and a trinity that reigns on earth. I will no more reject the trinity on earth than I will deny the Trinity in heaven.' While he was bellowing these words at the top of his voice the sentence was carried out.[486]

§ 123. After this the King invited the Roman aristocracy to be present while he put the following question to his brothers, 'Tiberius and Heraclius, who do you say that I am? Your brother, or your King? If you say your King, I will call you my brothers. But if you say your brother, I will know that you are my enemies.' They answered him,

---

[482] This sentence is included with the previous paragraph in the *Chronicle of AD 1234*.

[483] Text No. 10, AG 988; text No. 12, AG 991; Theophanes, p. 356; Agapius, p. 233; Michael, 11.12a, 11.15a.

[484] {Lat. denarius}, glossed as {Syr. drēkūnō}.

[485] {Gr. dēmósios}.

[486] Theophanes, p. 360; Agapius, p. 234; Michael, p. 437:35-36, 11.13a: 'Constantine ordered that his (Leo's) tongue be cut out and his hands and feet amputated.'

'We have no objection at all to calling you our eldest brother, but we can never acknowledge that you are our king, because we share the royal power with you.' In saying this they were relying on the support of the senators, but when it transpired that these were now against them, not for them, there was nothing they could do to stop Constantine deposing them.[487]

§ 124*. Year 14 of Constantine = AH 63: Yazīd b. Muᶜāwiya, king of the Arabs, died /p. 290/ after a reign of three years and five months. At this time a man called Mukhtār, a lying impostor and a hypocrite posing as a prophet, usurped power in the land of ᶜAqūlō. Because Yazīd left no son old enough to reign as king there was commotion among the Arabs. Those in the east and in Yathrib elected a certain ᶜAbd Allāh b. al-Zubayr as their king, whereas those in Damascus and Palestine remained loyal to the house of Muᶜāwiya and waited for one of Yazīd's sons to grow up and become king. In Phoenicia and in Syria, however, al-Dahhāk b. Qays was made king; this al-Dahhāk came to Damascus, pretending to be an ally of Ibn al-Zubayr, whereas in fact he wanted to seize power for himself. As for Mukhtār, he would not be subjected either to Ibn al-Zubayr or to those who remained loyal to the house of Muᶜāwiya.[488]

---

[487] Michael, 11.13a.

[488] Michael, p. 444:23-445:22, 11.15b, adds: 'At this time a large comet appeared and stayed for eleven days. At this time there was a harsh winter, with much snow and ice. For six days the Euphrates and even the earth itself was frozen. Everywhere the olives were shrivelled and in some places the vines were, too; even the wine froze in the jars. People were in great distress. Cattle and other (domestic) animals and fowl and even many human beings perished from the cold. Afterwards a great comet appeared again, every evening for 41 days; then others appeared opposite it for seven days, beginning in the month of September, AG 995. And when the year 995 was nearly over (lit.: 'had entered', i.e. harvest-home?), on 22 and the 23 September, the Arabs fought a very violent battle amongst themselves. The fighting went on for many days, with much mutual damage and the loss of tens of thousands of lives on both sides. They say that the dead numbered 400,000. This occurred on the river Khāzir {Syr. HZR} in the region

§ 125*. In the midst of this commotion one of the Quraysh emerged from Yathrib, a man by the name of Marwān b. al-Ḥakam. He and his sons came to Damascus and took up residence in the palace of Yazīd. Having summoned those who had been attached to Yazīd, the leading men of Damascus and the freedmen of Mu^{c}āwiya, he addressed them as follows: 'Gentlemen, listen to me. I am an old man - the oldest of all the Quraysh at the present time. I have come here from Yathrib in order with God's help to unite the two sides. For it is not right that members of the same race should be enemies of one another. All should give their consent to one man, who is chosen by God. So, if you agree, let us choose three men and write their names on three arrows; and let these arrows be placed /p. 291/ in the hands of someone innocent of the plan; and let him shuffle them in his hand and loose one of them into the air between the people; and whichever name is found on that arrow, let us make that man our king.'

§ 126. The adherents of the family of Mu^{c}āwiya were all in favour of this plan and resolved to put it into practice. They went to find Ḥassān b. Mālik, the emir of Jordan, at al-Jābiya, for he was a supporter of the family of Mu^{c}āwiya. They told him what Marwān had suggested and he was in agreement with them. He wrote three names on three arrows: the name of ^{c}Amr b. Sa^{c}īd,[489] the name of ^{c}Abd Allāh b. al-Zubayr and the name of Marwān b. al-Ḥakam himself. Then Ḥassān b. Mālik took the arrows in his hand and shuffled them.

---

of Nineveh. A great (civil) war raged among them. They suffered a great loss of power and brought about their own disgrace, for their pride and their impiety had grown excessive.' Michael, p. 444:17-23, 11.15b, adds: 'At this time Yazīd, the king of the Arabs, collected a large work-force of builders, with the intention of digging a canal to Sahsahna (= Dhunb/Dhanab al-Timsāh, otherwise known as Clysmia/Qulzum, on the Red Sea?), but he failed. He had already had a great deal of work done, when he died without seeing the water fill the canal.'

[489] This is ^{c}Amr b. Sa^{c}īd b. al-^{c}Ās al-Umawī, grandson of his namesake (§ 46 above) and known as al-Ashdaq; he later rebelled against ^{c}Abd al-Malik (cf. § 129 below), claiming that Marwān had promised him the succession. [R.H.]

The one he shot turned out to have the name of Marwān b. al-Hakam written on it.[490] Immediately they gave him the right hand of allegiance and made him king. When al-Dahhāk heard what had been done he came to al-Jābiya with a few men and sneaked up to the camp of Marwān and of Hassān like a spy. He was apprehended and brought before Marwān, where he was made to swear allegiance against his will. But when night came he escaped and returned to his army. At dawn, when his disappearance was noticed, Marwān left al-Jābiya to give chase; in the battle which ensued al-Dahhāk was killed. After that his friends swore allegiance to Marwān. Marwān then entered Damascus; and by marrying Yazīd's widow he legitimized his position as King. But Egypt had not yet submitted to his authority, so he made preparations to invade it.[491]

§ 127*. /p. 292/ But Marwān reigned for less than one year and died in Damascus. He was succeeded by his son, ᶜAbd al-Malik, AG 996. This king sued Constantine, king of the Romans, for a mutual cessation of hostilities. This he did because he had so many wars on his hands at once, not the least of his troubles being the aggression of the 'Mardaïtes'[492] of Mount Lebanon. But just then Constantine, son of Constans, died after a reign of sixteen years[493] and was succeeded by his son Justinian.[494]

---

[490] It is unclear why Marwān's suggestion to give the arrows to someone 'innocent of the plan' was not followed.

[491] §§ 124-6: text No. 10, AG 992-3; text No. 12, AG 994. Agapius, pp. 234-6 and Dionysius (Michael, 11.15a) certainly share a common source for the second Arab civil war; Theophanes, pp. 360-1 very likely does, but is too brief to allow us to be sure. [R. H.]

[492] Here: {Syr. maridatē}.

[493] According to Theophanes, Constantine had seventeen regnal years.

[494] §§ 127-8: text No. 10, AG 993; text No. 12, AG 996; Theophanes, pp. 361, 363; Agapius, p. 237; Michael, p. 445:28-30, 33-34, 11.15a: 'Marwān died after a reign of nine months; once more the kingdom of the Arabs was divided amongst numerous leaders. [...] A certain Ibn Hubayb (?) {Syr. HWBB} seized Rhesaina and reigned there as a rebel governor.'

§ 128*. AG 997: In the first year of Justinian's reign ^{C}Abd al-Malik sent letters desiring peace and demanding that he remove the 'Mardaïtes' from Mount Lebanon and restrain his bandits from attacking Arab territory. In the treaty which they signed it was stipulated that the 'Mardaïtes' should evacuate the Lebanon; that there should be peace for ten years; that ^{C}Abd al-Malik would give to the Romans one thousand denarii, one horse and one slave each day for ten years; and that Cyprus should pay tribute equally to both kingdoms.[495] There were 12,000 'Mardaïtes' in Mount Lebanon, not including runaway levies and slaves.

§ 129*. Once peace had been concluded between the kingdoms, ^{C}Abd al-Malik sent Mu^{C}āwiya's brother Zayd against the impostor Mukhtār; the outcome of the battle, however, was that Zayd was killed. Hearing this, ^{C}Abd al-Malik crossed the Euphrates into Mesopotamia. But when he reached Rhesaina he heard that ^{C}Amr b. Sa^{C}īd b. al-^{C}Āṣ had rebelled against him in Damascus.[496] He returned to Damascus[497] to besiege the city and launched a massive attack on it. ^{C}Amr opened the gates on receiving ^{C}Abd al-Malik's assurance /p. 293/ that he would not be harmed. But at a later stage ^{C}Abd al-Malik did kill ^{C}Amr by a trick.[498]

§ 130. Seeing that Ibn al-Zubayr was gaining support in the east, ^{C}Abd al-Malik appointed two generals, his brother Muhammad and al-Hajjāj b. Yūsuf, both powerful men, capable of shedding blood without the slightest pity. To his brother Muhammad he gave authority over Mesopotamia, Mossul and all Armenia; to al-Hajjāj he entrusted the whole of Persia. The first city to which this Muhammad came was Edessa, where he took up residence after being welcomed without

---

[495] Michael, p. 446:8-10, 11.15a, adds to the conditions stipulated in the peace treaty: 'Armenia was to be for the Romans, with Garzan and Arzanene and the northern part of Media, viz Azerbaijan.'

[496] {Ar. dimashq}.

[497] {Syr. darmsūq}.

[498] Theophanes, p. 363. There is a gap in the MS. of Agapius for almost the whole of the reign of ^{C}Abd al-Malik. [R. H.]

resistance. Before long he had recovered the whole of northern Mesopotamia[499] except for Nisibis, which was held by Burayda (?).[500] Al-Hajjāj b. Yūsuf, meanwhile, went against Yathrib to fight ᶜAbd Allāh b. al-Zubayr; and ᶜAbd al-Malik sent word to his brother Muhammad to muster a force and go to al-Hajjāj's assistance. By their combined forces ᶜAbd Allāh b. al-Zubayr's army was defeated and his general, Ibrāhīm b. al-Ashtar, was killed. ᶜAbd Allāh himself escaped with a few men and sought sanctuary in the Kaᶜba, i.e. the house of worship used by the prophet and his followers in Mecca. Al-Hajjāj pursued them there and penned them up within the building, then used catapults to demolish the enclosure wall, thus enabling his men to rush in, take ᶜAbd Allāh b. al-Zubayr and kill him. They cut off his head and sent it to ᶜAbd al-Malik b. Marwān; then they rebuilt the sanctuary. After this ᶜAbd al-Malik made al-Hajjāj lord of al-Kūfa and of Yathrib, of Mecca and of all Iraq.[501]

§ 131*. Given authority over Persia, al-Hajjāj began to wreak destruction pitilessly. He even murdered /p. 294/ the leading men of the Arabs and looted their houses; and Muhammad b. Marwān did the

---

[499] {Syr. gōzartō = Ar. al-jazīra}, meaning 'the island'; the previous reference to Mesopotamia was to {Syr. bēt nahrīn}.

[500] {Syr. BWDYR} or {Syr. BWRYDᵓ} (Michael). This is probably Yazīd (there is a difference of only two diacritical points in the Arabic, which are frequently omitted anyway in MSS.), *scil.* Yazīd b. Abī Sakhr, known as Abū Qārib and named by Muslim sources and one contemporary Nestorian witness as the leader of the revolt at Nisibis. See G. Rotter, *Die Umayyaden und der zweite Bürgerkrieg (680-92)* (Wiesbaden, 1982), pp. 214-6. [R.H.]

[501] Theophanes, pp. 364-5; Michael, 11.15a, 11.16a; Michael, p. 446:*ult.*-447:17, 11.16b, adds: 'AG 1005 = AH 75: There was a solar eclipse in the month of October, on a Sunday, during the third and fourth hours; it was so dark that the stars came out (this was the eclipse of Sunday, 5 October, AD 693). In the same year there was a shortage of rainfall everywhere. The price of corn went up, to such an extent that three modii of wheat cost one denarius. Seven years previously there had been a cruel famine, during which the grain-prices rocketed throughout Syria, to the point that wheat was sold at one modius for three denarii. Men ate bread made of lentils, peas, barley and other grains.'

same in his province, slaughtering leaders and showing no mercy. He also framed charges against the leaders of the Christians and began killing them, too, and looting their houses. He murdered Mardānshāh, son of Zarnōsh, and his son, who were the administrators[502] of Nisibis, and Simeon, son of Nonnus of Halūghō (?), by impaling them on wooden stakes. The Armenian leaders he herded into a church, which he then set on fire, so that they were burned to death. The administrator of Edessa, also, Anastasius, son of Andrew, he murdered and he appropriated all his possessions. Yet Christians still held office as scribes and leaders and administrators in the Arab territories.[503]

§ 132*. Indeed, it was in the reign of ᶜAbd al-Malik that Athanasius Bar Gūmōyē of the city of Edessa became rich and famous. ᶜAbd al-Malik was informed of his reputation as an intelligent man, well trained in the scribal skills, and he summoned him to Damascus, where he made him the guardian of his younger brother ᶜAbd al-ᶜAzīz, whom he had made, still a child, the emir of Egypt. He commanded that Athanasius should be not only his scribe, but the manager of his affairs and that authority and administrative direction should be his, while ᶜAbd al-ᶜAzīz should have the nominal power. So it came about that the distinguished Athanasius ruled Egypt and assigned taxes[504] throughout the land. His sons were put in charge of the region of Gunada,[505] though he sent his eldest son, Peter, to maintain and manage his possessions in Edessa. It is said that, apart from the generous income and privileges which he enjoyed from the King, his sons also had a publicly acknowledged right /p. 295/ to one denarius every year from each man drawing wages in the army. This

---

502 {Syr. mᵉdabbᵉrōnē}.

503 Michael, 11.16a.

504 {Syr. gᵉzītō = Ar. jizya}.

505 {Syr. ꓳTRꓳ D-GWNDꓳ}. From the context it would appear that they were connected specifically with the army, so the Ar. ajnād, meaning 'soldiers' (cf. Pahlavi: gund, 'army, troops') might lie behind the otherwise unknown 'country' of Gunada.

army was 30,000 strong and the period during which they stayed in Egypt was twenty-one years.[506]

§ 133. Athanasius himself was not only wise but also strictly Orthodox. He had great respect for the hierarchy of the Church and he built new churches and renovated old ones, as well as distributing alms abundantly to the orphans and the widows. He collected gold and silver like pebbles and he had four thousand slaves, all bought out of his own purse, besides grand houses, villages, various estates and gardens worthy of a king. In Edessa he had three hundred shops and nine inns. In the Egyptian city of Fustāt he erected two temples and he renovated the glorious temple of the Mother of God in Edessa and another splendid building, to be a baptistery. For this building he built reinforced canals of water, exactly as Bishop Amazonius had done in the great and ancient church of Edessa. He also revetted the walls of it with marble and adorned it with gold and silver.[507]

---

[506] §§ 132-4: Michael, 11.16b.

[507] Michael, p. 448, 11.16b: 'At Edessa he built also a baptistery in honour of the image {Syr. salmō} of Christ which was sent to King Abgar. [...] The reason for the construction of this building {Syr. baytō} was as follows: The Edessans were short of the sum needed to pay the tribute which they owed (to the Arabs) and they were unable to pay it. Some crafty fellow presented himself to Muhammad, the collector of the tribute, with this advice: "If you (threaten) to take the image, they will sell their sons and their very lives rather than part with it." When Muhammad did this, the Edessenes felt ready to give all that they had and to undergo death, /p. 449/ rather than let that man take the image. Being forced to approach Athanasius, that leading citizen, by necessity, they asked him to pay the 5,000 denarii of the tribute and to take the image into his house until the money was paid back. As for Athanasius, he was delighted to take the image into his house and he gave the gold. Then he brought in a certain skilful painter and asked him to paint a duplicate. When the task was finished, the (new) image resembled the original as closely as seemed possible; for the painter had blackened the colours of the image so as they should appear to be ancient. Some time later, when the Edessenes returned the gold and asked him for the image, he gave them the one that had just been made and kept the ancient one in his house. After a while he revealed to the faithful (?) what he had done and he built that wonderful temple of the baptistery and he perfected it at great

§ 134. When ^CAbd al-^CAzīz died in Egypt, Athanasius set off on the journey home.   The caravan of his household and his sons, his possessions, his slaves and his vast wealth arrived at Damascus and filled with envy the secretary of ^CAbd al-Malik at Damascus, Sergius, son of Mansūr, a Chalcedonian, who said to the king, 'Bar Gūmōyē has clawed in the contents of all the vaults in Egypt.' But ^CAbd al-Malik gave Athanasius a serene reception, only remarking pleasantly to him, 'We deem it unjust that all this wealth should belong to a Christian, so give us a part of it and keep a part for yourself.' So the king took a great deal away from him, but what Athanasius was left with was more than enough.

§ 135*. Let us get back now to the affairs of state and tell about /p. 296/ what happened in the reign of ^CAbd al-Malik. At this time ^CAbd al-Malik ordered that all silver and gold coins and denarii be stamped without images and with Arabic⁵⁰⁸ writing on both sides.   On one face they wrote the name of their prophet, Muhammad, and on the other side they wrote the name of ^CAbd al-Malik. It is the practice of the Arab kings still now, that each new king inscribes his name on the die. ^CAbd al-Malik also ordered the pigs to be killed in the cities of

---

expense beyond all measure in honour of the image, in that he knew that the very image which was sent by the hands of Yuhannōn the courier remained in his possession. Some years later he brought it and placed it in the baptistery. The patriarch Dionysius Tel-Mahrōyō, who wrote this, added: ''I took all these things from the 'Stories' of Daniel, son of Samuel of Tūr ^CAbdīn, my own maternal grandfather. But it seems to me that the image had been in the hands of the Chalcedonians because it had been handed down and had remained with them from the time of the Greek kings until it was taken away from them by Athanasius bar Gūmōyē''.' In this quotation read 'Moses' instead of 'Samuel' (cf. Michael, p. 378, 10.21, scholion). By the 'Greek kings' {Syr. malkē yawnōyē} are meant the emperor Tiberius (578-82) and his successors.

⁵⁰⁸ {Syr. arabōyōtō}.

Syria and throughout Mesopotamia.[509]

§ 136. AG 1002: ^CAbd al-Malik was at last free from conflicts, when Justinian shipped the Cypriots into exile, to prevent them paying tribute to the Arabs according to the treaty; but the ships were lost at sea with all hands, except for a few, whom the King settled in the city of Cyzicus. ^CAbd al-Malik regarded this as a breach of the treaty and, although ten years had not yet passed, he commanded his brother Muhammad, the governor of Mesopotamia, to carry out a raid in Roman territory. The booty and the captives which he brought back from this raid were abundant. At this time a certain patríkios of the Armenians called Sambāt betrayed Armenia[510] into the hands of Muhammad b. Marwān.[511]

§ 137. Also at this time a certain bandit or robber of Ishmaelite race, called Shabīb, invaded the territory of al-Ḥajjāj, committed many crimes and began to do murder on a large scale. He even attempted to assassinate al-Ḥajjāj, who escaped by using his wits. No one seemed to be a match for this outlaw, but in the end al-Ḥajjāj found a way to

---

[509] Text No. 12, AG 1008, 1015; Theophanes, p. 365; Michael, p. 447:17-20, 11.16b: 'At this time the Arab king, ^CAbd al-Malik, decreed that crosses should be taken down and pigs slaughtered.' Michael, p. 447:27-30, 11.16a, adds: 'AG 1009: In this year the emir ^CAtiyya carried out a census of foreigners; many of them he forcibly repatriated (Text No. 12, AG 1009 = 1008 + 1).'

[510] A marginal note in Syriac adds: 'Armenia is used here to denote the region of Akhlat and of Mayperqat, the mountains of Sanason (i.e. Sason or Sasun) and Arzanene {Syr. ⌐RZWN} and all the cities of that region.'

[511] Text No. 10, AG 1002; Theophanes, pp. 365, 366; Michael, p. 446:29-38, 11.15a: 'That is why Muhammad, the emir of northern Mesopotamia {Syr. gzīrtō = Ar. al-jazīra}, invaded Roman territory. The Romans engaged in battle with him near Cappadocian Caesarea, but the Slavs, about seven thousand of them, took the side of the Arabs and went with them back to Syria. The Arabs settled them at Antioch and Cyrrhus, gave them women and distributed to them (the revenue from) the poll-tax {Syr. g^ezītō = Ar. jizya} and army wages {Syr. rūzīqō} (Theophanes, p. 366). AG 1006: The Romans entered the Vale of Antioch; the Arabs mustered a force to meet them, which destroyed most of them, while the rest took flight.'

drown him in the Euphrates.[512] /p. 297/

§ 138*. For ten years the leaders of the Romans had endured the insatiable cruelty of Justinian. Now at last they got themselves together and laid hold of him, cut off his nose and sent him into exile beyond the Pontus. To replace him as king they chose an old man, sluggish in the administration of affairs of state, the patrician Leontius, who had been in Armenia.[513]

§ 139. AG 1007 = year 12 of [c]Abd al-Malik: After a reign of three years Leontius was uncrowned by a man called Apsimar, who came from Cilicia to Constantinople at the head of a great army.[514] Far from doing him bodily harm, he granted him the privilege of living on his own in peace. So Apsimar became king of the Romans.[515]

§ 140. AG 1013: [c]Abd Allāh, the son of [c]Abd al-Malik, carried out a lucrative raid on Roman territory and returned to Cilicia. He rebuilt Mopsuestia and garrisoned it with enough troops to protect it, before returning (to Damascus). The following year the Armenian leaders organized a revolt against the Arabs. Muhammad b. Marwān went up and crushed the Romans who had come to Armenia and he also killed many Armenians. Then Armenia reverted to Arab control.[516]

---

[512] Text No. 12, AG 1016; Theophanes, pp. 366-7.

[513] Text No. 12b, AG 992; Theophanes, p. 368; Michael, 11.16a.

[514] Actually early in AG 1010, late in AD 698.

[515] Theophanes, pp. 370-1; Michael, p. 447:37-448:3, 11.16a: 'This Apsimar was a general and they called him Tiberius. When the Slavs revolted against the Romans, Leontius took no measures to prevent them pillaging and wasting Roman territory; at this point Apsimar marched against them and defeated them. This gave him the power to defy and dethrone Leontius.'

[516] Text No. 12, AG 1015; Theophanes, p. 372; Michael, p. 449:36-450:2, 451:9-20, 11.17a, adds: 'AG 1015 = year 19 of [c]Abd al-Malik: [c]Abd al-Malik sent Maslama to Mopsuestia, which he captured. The same year the Arabs of [c]Aqūlō and of Basra revolted against [c]Abd al-Malik and fought against him. [...] AG 1014: The Arabs rebuilt Mopsuestia, which they had occupied a short time before. They gave it very strong walls and other beautiful buildings and they put a garrison in it and made it their frontier with the Romans. King [c]Abd al-Malik went there himself and there, indeed, he died, or, as

§ 141*. The same year Justinian escaped from his place of exile and made his way to the Khagan, the King of the Khazars. He asked for the hand of his daughter in marriage, then, having made her his wife, he sought asylum among the Bulgars. There he mustered his own army and marched against Constantinople. Apsimar panicked at the news of his approach. He took to the run, abandoning the city. When Justinian arrived he rode into the City without a fight, returning to his kingdom after being /p. 298/ an ex-king for ten years. He sent for Apsimar, who was brought before him in chains, and he ordered his execution. He also executed Leontius, the man who had been king for three years. He began to take revenge on all his enemies. Many of the Romans he destroyed without mercy. He murdered and he impaled until there were no men of stature left in the Roman state.[517]

---

others say, was murdered, in this year.'   Michael, p. 450:1-24, 451:1-25, 11.17b, adds: (Earthquake of AG 1017) 'The fort of Sarīn collapsed and many other settlements. In April of this year there was a frost and the olives and the vines shrivelled up. At this same time there was a violent battle on the Tigris between the eastern and the western Arabs; the eastern Arabs were defeated. AG 1019: On 16 July there was a strange phenomenon.   Meteorites shooting or flying through the air, or as some call them, falling stars, were visible over the whole vault of heaven. All night, dense and rapid, they flew, from the south towards the whole north, something unheard of since the Creation. The holy Doctors have written about these, principally James of Edessa and Moses Bar Kīfō. What will those natural scientists now say who claim that the shooting stars are vapours, i.e. dense air, which catches fire when it rises towards the pyrosphere? Let them be asked now: Where does so much dense air come from? Where had it been hidden? And since they will not have a word to answer, let them admit that the Lord does exactly as He wills.   The event proved that these signs announced the Arabs {Syr. arabōyē}, who at this very time invaded the northern regions, wasting, setting on fire and ruining the countryside and its inhabitants.   At this time an edict of Walīd required that all magicians be put to death. They bound them to beams of wood and threw them into the water. Those who floated were executed, those who sank were saved. Most of them were killed.'
[517] Text No. 12b, AG 992; Theophanes, pp. 372-3, 374-5; Michael, p. 450:19-24, 451:1-9, 11.17a: 'He sent a great army to fetch his wife, all of whom drowned in a storm at sea. When the Khagan heard of this, he sent word to him, "You stupid, unthinking fool! You should

§ 142. At his return, Justinian had found six thousand Arab prisoners of war. All these he released and sent back home, having been urged to do so by Elustriya, son of Araq (?), from Ḥarrān, who was also in Roman territory as a prisoner of war. Him, too, Justinian released and sent back to his country loaded with gifts.[518]

§ 143*. AG 1017 = year 2 of Justinian's second term of power = AH 87: ᶜAbd al-Malik died in the month of February, after a reign of twenty-two years, and was succeeded by his son Walīd. On assuming control this man immediately began to demolish the churches of Damascus. He dismantled the great and splendid temple of St John (the Baptist) and built in its place a mosque for their prayers, which he adorned with many ancillary buildings and decorated with gilded mosaic pictures.[519]

§ 144. AG 1019: Maslama, the son of ᶜAbd al-Malik, the brother of Walīd, launched a raid into Roman territory and laid siege to Tyana. He persevered with the assault for nine months. Then the general Theophylact was sent at the head of a large force to relieve the city. But the Romans were defeated in battle by the Arabs and lost

---

have sent just a few. Why, did you imagine that I would keep her from you? No, by the life of your Imbecility, I will not keep her. Just send and take her.'' When Justinian heard this he was ashamed; but he sent for his wife and for his son Tiberius, whom he made his partner in empire' (Theophanes, p. 375; Agapius, pp. 237-8).

[518] Michael, 11.17a; Michael, p. 448:19-25, 11.16a, adds: 'Tiberius Apsimar sent an army of Romans against the Arabs. They invaded the region of Samosata and killed five thousand Arabs; they came back with captives and booty from the whole region.' According to the *Life of Theodotus of Amida* there was a governor of Samosata called Elustriya of Ḥarrān around this time: see Palmer, *Monk and Mason*, p. 165. Michael, p. 449:12-21, 11.16a, adds: 'AG 1014: The emir Walīd b. ᶜAmr died and was succeeded by Ḥārith b. Kaᶜb. After him came Qurra b. Sharīk; and Maslama, the son of ᶜAbd al-Malik, became emir of the region of Qēnneshrīn.'

[519] This is the 'Umayyad' mosque at present standing in Damascus. Text No. 10, AG 1014; text No. 12, AG 1016; Theophanes, pp. 374, 376; Agapius, p. 238; Michael, 11.17b; Michael, p. 451:21-22, 11.17a: '(Walīd) reigned nine years and five months.'

40,000 men. So the Arabs penetrated the city and led the population into slavery in Syria.[520]

§ 145. In this year Walīd forbade the use of Greek to be continued in the offices of his civil service, i.e. in what the Arabs term the dīwān. From this time on Arabic[521] writing had to be used. Up to this time the registers of the Arab kings /p. 299/ had always been kept in Greek.[522]

§ 146. This Walīd was a learned man. But he raised the taxes and increased the general suffering more than any of his predecessors.

§ 147. AH 89: Walīd sent word to his uncle Muhammad that his term of authority over Mesopotamia was at an end and he appointed his brother Maslama instead. Maslama's first action on coming to Mesopotamia and taking over the governorship of all the Jazīra[523] was to commission a survey of the arable land and a census of vineyards, orchards, livestock and human beings. They hung leaden seals on each person's neck.[524] Maslama also raided Roman territory and sacked the city of Amasya, returning at the head of an endless train of booty and of slaves.[525]

§ 148*. AG 1021: The patríkios Philippicus and some other Romans

---

[520] Text No. 10, AG 1028 (misplaced); text No. 12, AG 1021; Theophanes, p. 377; Agapius, pp. 238-9; Michael, p. 451:23-26, 34-36, 11.17a: 'This Walīd made Marthad (?) b. Sharīk emir of Qēnneshrīn and sent Qurra to Egypt. [...] (Tyana was taken) in the month of March.'

[521] {Syr. araboyō}.

[522] Theophanes, p. 376; Agapius, p. 238; Michael, 11.17b.

[523] {Syr. gzīrtō = Ar. al-jazīra}, meaning 'the island', i.e. northern Mesopotamia.

[524] After entering him in the register, presumably.

[525] Text No. 10, AG 1020, cf. AG 1003; text No. 12, AG 1021, 1022; text No. 12b, AG 1020; Michael, p. 451:40-452:3, 20-24, 11.17a: 'AG 1022: Maslama took TYBRND⁻, Gargarūm and Tūranda {Syr. TWND⁻} and many other (forts) in the Hexapolis on the Roman border. An Arab post was established at Tūranda {Syr. TWND⁻}. [...] al-ᶜAbbās b. Walīd also led an invasion and took Antioch in Pisidia; he returned with many captives.'

initiated a revolt and killed Justinian and his son Tiberius.[526] They
stuck his head on a pike and paraded it through the City. He had
reigned for sixteen years in all, divided into two terms of ten and six
years, respectively. This Philippicus was well educated, having both
impressive learning and rhetorical skill and being thoroughly acquainted
with the traditional academic curriculum in profane studies. He
commanded that all Armenians be expelled from his empire; these
exiles sought asylum with the Arabs, who settled them in Melitene and
on its borders. The following year the Romans deposed Philippicus
and gouged out his eyes.[527]

§ 149*. After the deposition of Philippicus the Romans raised up
Anastasius as their king.[528] In the first year of his reign there was
a violent earthquake in the month of February, which left many
settlements in ruins /p. 300/ in the regions of Antioch, Aleppo and
Qĕnneshrĭn. It was the churches and the temples which suffered the
greatest damage.[529]

---

[526] Actually in November, AD 711.

[527] Text No. 12b, AG 992; Theophanes, pp. 377-83; Agapius, pp.
239-40; Michael, p. 452:7-11, 11.17a: 'At this time (AG 1022, to
which this source dates the revolt of Philippicus) King Walĭd issued
an edict concerning the Christian captives and they were slaughtered
inside the churches in all the cities of Syria.' Michael, p. 452:17-26,
11.17b, adds: '(The Arabs settled the Armenians in Melitene) and in
Armenia IV. The Armenian population of these regions became very
numerous and strong. They became allies of the Arab kingdom and
enemies of the kingdom of the Romans. By such affairs (as the
expulsion of the Armenians to the disadvantage of Byzantium) the
Romans proved themselves to be bad administrators, men with a
contemptible mentality, incapable of reflection, because of their hatred
for all the Orthodox.' N.B. the expelled Armenians were
anti-Chalcedonians.

[528] Text No. 12b, AG 992; Theophanes, p. 383; Agapius, p. 240.

[529] Text No. 12, AG 1024; Theophanes, p. 383; Agapius, p. 240;
Michael, p. 451:37-39, 11.17b: 'AG 1024: There was a very violent
earthquake on February 28.' With 'churches and temples' the author
probably includes all Christian places of worship, both major and
minor; but 'chapels' would not do justice to the range of the second
word {Syr. hayklē}.

§ 150. AG 1026 = year 1[530] of Anastasius = AH 96: The Arab king Walīd died in the month of February and was succeeded at Damascus by his brother Sulaymān.[531]

§ 151*. Year 2 of Anastasius: (Anastasius) sent armies to the West to fight with his enemies, but the armies mutinied against their general. They brought someone called Theodosius and made him their king. As for that general, they killed him. After these mutineers had raised Theodosius as their king, news of the matter reached Anastasius, who fled in terror to Nicaea in Bithynia. But Theodosius sent an army after him to arrest him; he himself went straight to Constantinople, where they received him with rapture and proclaimed him king. Meanwhile, those who had been sent to Nicaea seized Anastasius, shaved his head and sent him to Theodosius, who banished him. This happened after he had reigned for one year and three months. Now* Leo, the general of the Anatolikón,[532] did not consent to the rule of Theodosius and carried on the struggle on Anastasius's behalf.[533]

§ 152. The following year Sulaymān, the king of the Arabs, told

---

[530] Actually year 2.

[531] Text No. 10, AG 1026; Theophanes, p. 384; Agapius, p. 240; Michael, p. 452:38-40, 11.18a, adds: 'Maslama invaded Turkish territory, took many captives and returned.'

[532] The 'Anatolikón', one of the Byzantine military provinces or 'themes' in the area of present-day Asian Turkey, originally extended from Cappadocia to the Mediterranean and the Aegaean Seas, not including the south-western and north-western parts of Asia Minor. It was later subdivided into 'Kappadokía' in the East, 'Thrakēsion', including Pergamum and Ephesus, in the West, 'Seleukeía' (including Cilician Seleucia) in the South, and the central theme 'Anatolikón', including Amorium and Iconium. The general of a theme was also the provincial governor.

[533] Theophanes, pp. 384-6; Agapius, p. 241; Michael, p. 452, 11.17a, adds: 'In this same year (AG 1026) Maslama invaded the country of Galatia and occupied the fortresses which were there; he returned with many captives' (Theophanes, p. 383; Agapius, p. 240).

Maslama[534] to get ready for an expedition into the Roman empire in order to besiege Constantinople.[535] He mustered an army of 200,000 and built 5,000 ships, which he filled with troops and provisions. As leader of these troops he appointed ᶜUmar b. Hubayra, who was to be answerable to Maslama. He collected furthermore 12,000 workmen, 6,000 camels and 6,000 /p. 301/ mules to bear provisions for the animals and the workmen. The camels he loaded . with weaponry and catapults. For this force he prepared supplies to last for many years; for Sulaymān had said, 'I shall not cease from the struggle with Constantinople until either I force my way into it, or I bring about the destruction of the entire dominions of the Arabs.' On his invasion, (Maslama) was joined by about 3,000 unemployed and unoccupied people, who belonged to the class of Arabs without possessions whom they call 'volunteers'.[536] They were also joined by many Arab owners of capital,[537] who had provided mounts for the troops on the basis of hire or sale, in the hopes of being recompensed from the booty to be got out of the Royal City.

§ 153. Maslama ordered Sulaymān b. Muᶜawwid[538] and al-Bakhtarī to proceed by land and ᶜUmar b. Hubayra by sea. After an extended march to the city of Amorium, al-Bakhtarī and Sulaymān encountered there Leo, the general who, as we have told, had held out against Theodosius. This man made a covenant with the Arabs, whom he led to believe that he would help them to capture Constantinople.

---

[534] The name is spelt {Syr. MWSLM}; Michael, who is also drawing on Dionysius, calls him Maslama, which is correct.

[535] §§ 152-63 The Siege of Constantinople: text No. 10, AG 1028; text No. 12, AG 1027-8; Theophanes, pp. 386-99; Agapius, pp. 241-2. Michael's version of these events is on pp. 452-5 of his Chronicle, where this chapter (11.18a) is headed: 'On the second Arab siege of Constantinople'; curiously enough, in view of this description, the first Arab siege, which was ended, after four years of blockades, in AD 678, is not described in the Syriac chronicles.

[536] {Ar. mutatawwiᶜīn}.

[537] Lit. 'of gold'.

[538] Fiey, in his index to this chronicle, writes 'Sulaymān b. Muᶜād'.

Maslama, who was still on the road, travelling behind them, was informed about this in written despatches; he was delighted with Leo's promises and he promised him in return that he would not permit the Arab army to cause any damage in Leo's province.[539] So when the Arab army arrived, Maslama gave orders that no one should do any harm in that region, not even by (the theft of) a loaf of bread. Leo, for his part, gave orders that a travelling market be loaded up for the Arab army; and the Romans bought and sold in good faith without fear. But Leo's whole concern was to appropriate the Roman kingdom for himself.

§ 154. As soon as the Arabs had left Leo's territory, they began to do all sorts of /p. 302/ mischief and to commit all kinds of outrage in Roman territory, burning down churches and houses, looting, shedding the blood of men and taking children captive. Many cities in the region of Asia fell to them that summer and they ruined them and took captives and looted, slaughtering the men and sending the children and the women back as slaves to their own country. That winter the Arabs spent in Asia. And Maslama sent Sulaymān b. Mu^cawwid with 12,000 men to lay siege to the city of Chalcedon, to cut off supplies from that approach to Constantinople and to lay waste and pillage Roman territory in general.

§ 155. When Theodosius received intelligence of the covenant which Leo had made with Maslama, he sent men to round up his relatives and to shut them up in Amorium; and he gave orders to the governor of Amorium to guard them with vigilance. Leo, on hearing that his

---

[539] Michael, p. 453:36-38, 11.18a, has a different promise: 'Maslama promised Leo that once he had conquered the city he would make him king of the Romans.' He continues (p. 453:39-44, 454:1): 'Leo returned to Constantinople and the Arabs passed by various cities, giving them assurances of peace. King Sulaymān himself came with 12,000 men and pitched camp at Chalcedon, to stop provisions getting into Constantinople.' Michael has abbreviated the passage and in so doing has confused the general Sulaymān b. Mu^cawwid with his namesake, the caliph Sulaymān.

relatives had been imprisoned in Amorium, marched in haste with his army until he reached Sulaymān b. Mu^cawwid at Chalcedon; for Maslama and the (main) force of the Arabs were encamped in Asia at the time. He demanded an army from Sulaymān to go and put fear into the inhabitants of Amorium, so that they would give him back his relatives; and Sulaymān gave him an escort of six thousand horse. So Leo returned to Amorium and pitched camp there. When the citizens realized that they were under siege, they were afraid of Leo. But he went up to the wall and spoke with the leaders and the foremost men of the city. When they understood that his intentions were totally opposed to the betrayal of the Romans and that his relationship with Maslama was a pretence, designed to save his territory from destruction, and when they reflected that Theodosius was incapable of managing the empire and that there was no one more suitable to be king than Leo, who was in a position to save the Royal City by this manoeuvre of his, they exchanged with him oaths of fidelity and returned his relatives to him. Then Leo dismissed /p. 303/ his Arab escort, after giving each man twelve denarii.

§ 156*. When Leo had dismissed the Arab cavalry, he set off with his own army towards Constantinople. On the way he pitched camp in a certain ruined city on the sea coast. While they were encamped there, a force sent by king Theodosius caught up with them. Their orders were to do battle with Leo and, when he had been defeated, to crown Theodosius's son, who had been sent with them as general of their force.[540] They had with them the crown and the purple (clothes) of empire, with which to invest his son as king - once they had defeated Leo. But when they reached Leo's camp and the two armies met, the Romans on Leo's side and those who had been sent by the King agreed unanimously to make Leo king. They placed the crown which they had brought with them on his head and invested him with the purple; and they delivered Theodosius's son to him. Then they all marched to the Royal City, where all the citizens welcomed them with

---

[540] Perhaps as Caesar or 'heir-apparent'.

a festive escort. Theodosius was deposed from the throne after a reign of one year and four months and Leo took control over the kingdom AG 1028.[541]

§ 157. When Maslama heard that Leo had become king, he was overjoyed, supposing that he would thereby find an opportunity to fulfil his promise and deliver the city to him. And Leo, from the moment of his elevation to the throne, wrote constantly to Maslama, encouraging him in his vain hopes. At the same time he was restoring and strengthening the city and gathering into it plenty of supplies. He was also having ships prepared for combat with the enemy. And he came to a financial arrangement with the Bulgars, by which they agreed to help the City. In short, he took every possible precaution to ensure the City's impregnability. /p. 304/

§ 158*. Winter passed away and Maslama understood the deceit which Leo had practised upon him. He made ready his army and his ships; and in June of the same year he crossed over to the far side.[542] Leo, for his part, had received intelligence that Maslama was getting ready to cross over and he sent men to scorch the earth in the whole region to the west of the City. Maslama's army crossed to a point about six 'miles' below the City,[543] but Maslama himself with his escort of 4,000 horse landed after the rest at a distance of about ten 'miles' from the camp of those who had preceded him. That night the Bulgarian allies of the Romans fell upon him unsuspecting and slaughtered most of the force which was with him. Maslama escaped by a hair's breadth and reached the safety of the greater encampment.

§ 159. Then the whole army moved up to the west side of the City and pitched camp near the wall, opposite the so-called Golden Gate. They dug a ditch in front of the camp, between it and the City, and another behind it, between it and the Bulgars; to the right and to the

---

[541] Michael, p. 454:25, 11.18a, adds: 'AH 98'.

[542] i.e. to the shore of Europe.

[543] i.e. further down the coast of the Sea of Marmara?

left of the camp was the sea, with a force of about 30,000 Arabs on board the ships. Maslama also instructed the Egyptian crews to stay at sea and to defend his ships from the ships of the Romans. A further force of 20,000 under the command of Sharāhīl b. ʿUbayda was sent out to guard the (landward) approaches of the camp against the Bulgars and the seaward approaches against the Roman ships. On the opposite coast they had to combat the Roman scouts who tried to draw them off and to prevent supplies from reaching the Arabs.

§ 160. One day the Bulgars gathered against Sharāhīl and his army, did battle with them and killed a large number of them, so that the Arabs came to fear the Bulgars more than the Romans. Then their supplies were cut off and all the animals they had /p. 305/ with them perished for want of fodder. Nowhere in all Syria could any further news of them be obtained. For they were surrounded by water and the Roman scouts[544] prevented anyone leaving or entering the camp by sea. Outside (the City) the Arabs and inside, the Romans: both were in this critical state, when winter came upon them with a vengeance. The Arabs, for their part, were all in despair. They dreaded going back without their king's permission; and in any case, the sea was so rough as to prevent them going anywhere. Moreover, they were afraid of the Bulgars to the west of them. Straitened thus on every side with the spectre of their death before their eyes, they abandoned (all hope of) anything whatsoever. As for Maslama, he deceived the Arab army with the expectation that, today or tomorrow, the Romans would surrender the City.[545] He also held out false hopes to them of the donations and supplies which were supposedly about to arrive from the Arab king, Sulaymān. But after many interrogations they ascertained that all this was a pack of lies. From that time onwards they would not

---

[544] A marginal note: 'that is, the spies'.

[545] Dionysius may have known the tradition reported by text No. 10 that Maslama continued during the famine to remind Leo of his promise and did not perceive the trick until later; he himself found this incredible and assumed that the tradition derived from Maslama's attempts to keep the army's morale high.

believe him, even when he told the truth.* And in this dire situation, where both sides were in such extraordinary danger, above all the Arabs, who were suffering cruelly from starvation, of a sudden the sun of salvation shone out upon them. For although the Romans considered the Arabs to be their prisoners, they were actually in even greater danger themselves.[546]

§ 161. The Romans had inflicted such deprivation on the Arabs that they had begun to eat dead animals and corpses and dung. In the Arab camp a modius of wheat had reached the price of ten /p. 306/ denarii and a head of dead livestock was being sold for two or three denarii; and many of them used to walk down to the ships and tear off the pitch from them and chew on it all day long.[547]* While they were thus sorely afflicted, their king, Sulaymān, the son of ꜥAbd al-Malik, died and so did his son, Ayyūb, to whom the Arabs had sworn allegiance with their right hand as his father's successor designate. His death had actually occurred in October[548] at the beginning of this winter and he had been succeeded by ꜥUmar, the son of ꜥAbd al-ꜥAzī z the son of Marwān, a man with a reputation for piety, truthfulness and the avoidance of evil. As soon as he became king, he put all his energies into rescuing the Arab people who were trapped in the Roman empire.

§ 162. Seeing that news of them was unobtainable, he appointed a trustworthy man, gave him a sufficient escort and sent him into the Roman empire; he ordered him not to return without accurate information about Maslama and his army. This man found his way into the Arab camp and learned all about the situation of the army; then Maslama gave him a letter full of lies to take to ꜥUmar, saying, 'The army is in excellent condition and the City is about to fall.' When the man returned to ꜥUmar, he related to him the very opposite of the good

---

[546] cf. Michael, p. 455:18-19, 11.18a: 'Although the Romans were hemmed in, the Arabs were more surely imprisoned.'

[547] Michael, p. 455:21, 11.18a, adds: 'They found soft stones and ate them; and that actually did them good.'

[548] Text No. 12, AG 1028, has 'September'.

news contained in Maslama's letter. Then, indeed, the King shed tears and grieved deeply for the ruin of the Arab army. He waited until winter had passed, then sent another envoy, bearing a harsh letter to Maslama, in which he forbade him to be the cause of ruin to the Arab army. He was to remove his army and leave. To the army he wrote: 'If Maslama refuses to leave, abandon him and come!' When the envoy from King ᶜUmar arrived and gave the letter to Maslama, he used a trick to conceal the command from the army. But the army /p. 307/ came to know what the King had commanded and proclaimed it publicly throughout the camp: 'King ᶜUmar has commanded you to leave and to return to your own regions!' On receiving such good news, they were filled with utter joy, especially when they heard that they had ᶜUmar b. ᶜAbd al-ᶜAzīz for their king.[549]

§ 163. Then Maslama set off home against his will, with the curse of both sides upon him. They embarked on their ships and set sail on the sea and the Romans did battle with them there and burned many of their ships. The survivors were caught at sea by a storm and most of their ships went down. Some were wrecked and thrown up on the barbarian[550] coast. Such was the terrible fate of the Arab expedition after two years in Roman territory. King ᶜUmar, however, sent reinforcements to encourage those who had come away by land, with more than 20,000 mules and some horses; for all the Arabs were unmounted when they left (Constantinople), because all their livestock had perished of starvation. The King sent much gold also for distribution, ten denarii for every man. He also sent instructions

---

[549] cf. Michael, p. 455:25-30, 11.18a: 'When the envoy learned that he (Maslama) had written the opposite of what was in the camp, he sent him word to take his army and leave. But since it was still winter, they were quite unable to leave. When the rigours of winter had passed and Maslama had not told the Arabs about Sulaymān's death, the Romans told them from the wall, "Your king is dead!" And great fear fell upon the Arabs. Then the envoy of the King arrived bearing the command for Maslama to withdraw and for the people, if he refused, to withdraw regardless.'

[550] This is perhaps a mistake for 'Bulgarian'.

throughout his empire that everyone who had a brother or other relative in the army which was under Maslama's command should go out to escort him home, taking provisions for the journey; and many did go out to meet them and did all they could to save them.[551]

§ 164. /p. 142/[552] *On the first foundation and construction of the City of Byzantium*: In olden days the lands of the Romans were ruled by many kings. One king ruled in Italy, another in Macedonia, another in Thrace and other kings elsewhere. At that time the ruler of Asia and of Thrace was King Byzas. He wanted to find a defensible site on which to build his royal city, so he summoned a certain experienced surveyor and sent him on a tour to search for a place which fitted his ideal. The surveyor, having received this command, /p. 143/ proceeded to travel about in many regions. One day, weary and weighed down by his cares, he cast himself down on the ground to rest. He took the measuring rod, the cord and the right-angle which he had with him and he wrapped them in a red cloak to make a pillow; and then he fell asleep. At this moment a hungry eagle was circling on high in search of food. It caught sight of the red cloak and, thinking it was meat, stooped to snatch it. The flurry of its wings set up such violent currents of air that its claws became entangled, both in the cloak and with the cord. As for the man, he was awakened by the scuffle of the eagle's flurrying feathers and sat up, scared. The eagle, too, was frightened of the man and launched itself into the air, carrying the

---

[551] Michael, p. 455:34, 11.18a, ends his account with the words: 'and the City was delivered.'

[552] In the *Chronicle of 1234* this passage forms part of the narrative of the reign of Constantine the Great, where it is inserted between rubrics 23 and 24 on pp. 142-5; but Michael, 11.18b, who has an abbreviated version, tells us (p. 452:33-34) that it comes from the work of Dionysius of Tel-Mahrē, where it followed on the account of the second Arab siege of Constantinople in AD 717-18. If so, Dionysius may have known and rejected the story reported in text No. 10, that Maslama had been given a three-day tour of the antiquities of Constantinople by Leo before ending the siege, while taking from it the inspiration to append this excursus to his account of the siege.

cloak and everything that was in it. The load was too heavy for it to
carry far, so, after flying a short distance, it alighted on the ground in
a certain place, freed its legs from the cloak and then was airborne once
more, leaving it behind. The man observed where the eagle had
alighted and went to fetch his cloak and his tools. In so doing he
traversed and surveyed that place and came to the conclusion that it was
most suitable for human habitation and answered perfectly to the wishes
of the King. For it was both spacious and well defended by nature, in
that it was surrounded by the sea on three sides and very abundant in
springs of fresh and pleasant water. Then he went to the King and told
him what had happened. The King was amazed and understood that
God had had a hand in these events. He went to see the place himself,
then ordered a city to be marked out there with a length of ten 'miles'.
Its breadth was to be the distance from shore to shore. But while they
were still building it, before it was complete, King Byzas died. He was
succeeded by his brother Antius, who completed the construction of this
city. For this reason its name was formed out of these two names:
Byzantium. /p. 144/

§ 165. *On the construction and the extension (of the City) in the
reign of Constantine*: When all of what we call 'Romania'[553] came
under a single ruler and this ruler was the believing Constantine, he
found Byzantium an exceedingly well favoured site, more suitable than
all the other cities in his empire. So he ordered it to be extended to the
west by two 'miles', making the length of it henceforth twelve
'miles';[554] and he built it up and adorned it with all things lovely.
This city is built on seven hills. He built a harbour for ships with one

---

[553] {Syr. RWMNYʾ}; this passage, in combination with the
beginning of the previous paragraph, shows that the Syriac name
'Romania' covers the whole Roman empire from Italy to Asia.

[554] The distance from the Constantinian walls to the tip of the
peninsular is about four kilometres, so that our writer's 'mile' would
seem to be about 333 metres. If the length of a 'foot' is one third of
a metre, this corresponds to 1,000 'feet'. That would mean that {Syr.
mīlē} in this passage and elsewhere in text No. 13 (e.g. at § 99)
translates {Lat. milia pedum} instead of {Lat. milia passuum}.

of these hills on either side. It is guarded by two mighty towers, between which a robust iron chain is fixed. This chain prevents the ships which are in the harbour from sailing away without permission from the governor and hinders enemy vessels from sailing in. On three sides the City is surrounded by the sea, but on the west side there is land, with a great wall at a distance from the City, stretching from shore to shore, which is called *Makrón Teîkhos*, which means 'Long Wall'. Between the wall and the City is contained a great open area. The width of the sea between the City and the land to the east and to the north is four 'miles'[555] (in both directions?) and its depth is unsoundable. When the construction of the City was complete, Constantine enriched it with many mighty buildings to make it a rival for the great city of Rome; and he called it Constantinople, which means 'the City of Constantine'. But he decreed by law that it should be entitled 'the Second Rome'. He also built a great and splendid city named after his mother: Helenopolis, for by that time she, too, wore a crown and was striking her own coins. Likewise, he built splendid temples in Constantinople: the church of Eirēnē and another dedicated to the Apostles. /p. 145/ Obelisks and many sacred objects[556] were also set up in the City, most of which have been preserved until today. When the last touch had been put to everything, he established his throne and his royal residence there and stored all his royal treasures in it. There he appointed his generals and his governors and it was called the 'Royal City', as it is still today.[557]

END OF EXTRACT

---

[555] If a 'mile' is about 300 metres, then this is about right, at least for the distance to the coast of Asia; it is somewhat exaggerated for the mouth of the Golden Horn.

[556] {Gr. ektelésmata}.

[557] Michael, 11.18b; Michael, 11.18c, shows that AD 718 was a watershed in Dionysius's Church History, too.

PART THREE

TWO RELATED APOCALYPTIC TEXTS DATED AD 691/2

14.   AN   EXTRACT   FROM   THE   APOCALYPSE   OF
PSEUDO-METHODIUS

INTRODUCTION

The *Apocalypse* attributed to Bishop Methodius of Olympus (martyred
312) is a product of north Mesopotamia belonging to the second half
of the seventh century; the original language was, without any doubt,
Syriac.[558]   The work shares with the writings of the mystic St
Isaac the Syrian, its almost exact contemporary, the distinction of being
one of the very few Syriac works of the Arab period to have been
translated into Greek.   The several different recensions of the Greek
which survive show how the *Apocalypse* was periodically updated for
the benefit of later readers, in order to accommodate the lapse of time.
From Greek it was soon translated into Latin (the earliest manuscript
belongs to the eighth century) and into Slavonic.   In all these languages
it proved immensely influential, providing the source for the Legend of
the Last Emperor.
    The *Apocalypse* is described in the Syriac title as: 'A discourse
composed by Methodius, bishop and martyr, concerning the succession
of kings and the end of times.'   This 'discourse' takes the form of a
compact world history, divided into seven millennia, running from the
Fall of Adam and Eve to the Second Coming; the writer is, however,
chiefly interested in the biblical period, in the interrelationships
between the different kingdoms and in his own times.   Chapters I-VII,
which take the reader down to the rebuilding of the Temple (538 BC)
make use of a number of interesting non-biblical sources, notably the

---

[558] Some doubts have been expressed about this, but Reinink has
conclusively shown that Syriac was the original language (see especially
his 'Ismael, der Wildesel in der Wüste' [see Bibliography for details];
cf. also Alexander, *The Byzantine Apocalyptic Tradition*, pp. 31-33).

Syriac *Cave of Treasures*,[559] which provided the schema of six millennia, extended by our author to seven. Considerable attention is paid to Noah's fourth son, Yonton,[560] and to Nimrod, and excursuses are made into legendary genealogical links between the various kingdoms.

Chapter VIII introduces the famous theme of how Alexander the Great confined Gog and Magog, along with twenty other nations, all descendents of Japhet, behind the iron gates of the north.[561] At the same time it provides a mythical genealogy which is designed to show how he, along with, the Greek and the Romans (ch. IX), all had Ethiopian blood:

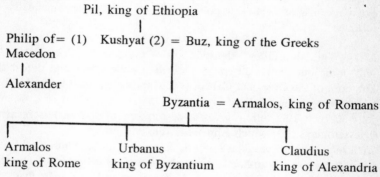

The whole purpose of this remarkable family tree is to provide an eschatological exegesis of *Psalm* 68:31, 'Kush will surrender to God', whereby Kush can be identified, not as the Ethiopian kingdom of the author's own time, but with the Byzantine Empire; theirs will be the

---

[559] English translation by E. A. W. Budge, *The Book of the Cave of Treasures* (London 1927).

[560] Also derived from the *Cave of Treasures*. On Yonton (Ionetos/Moneton in Greek, Ionitus in Latin) see S. Gero, 'The legend of the fourth son of Noah', *Harvard Theological Review*, 73 (1980), pp. 321-30.

[561] For this famous episode see A. R. Anderson, *Alexander's Gate. Gog and Magog and the Enclosed Nations* (Cambridge, Mass., 1932); Alexander, *The Byzantine Apocalyptic Tradition*, pp. 185-92.

only kingdom left on earth when the Son of Perdition appears. What Kush (i.e. the last Byzantine emperor) will surrender to God emerges in ch. XIV: 'The king of the Greeks shall place his crown on the top of the holy Cross [on Golgotha], stretch out his hands towards heaven, and hand over the kingdom to God the Father.[562] And the holy Cross upon which Christ was crucified will be raised up to heaven, together with the royal crown' (XIV:3-4). The author sees himself as living on the eve of the last times: the immediate antecedents to the appearance of the Son of Perdition are the Ishmaelites (i.e. Arabs) whose initial conquests and ultimate defeat are 'foretold' in the chapters translated below. The apocalyptic sequence of events, making extensive use of biblical typology, can be set out schematically as follows:

XI:1-3 The Ishmaelites, 'the wild ass of the desert' (*Genesis* 16:12), will come out of the desert of Yathrib (i.e. Medina) and defeat the kingdom of the Greeks at Gab^Cot (i.e. Gabitha, adapted to the biblical toponym of *Judges* 7:1).

XI:4-XIII:1 The author gives a description of the chastisement (2 Thessalonians 2:3) which Ishmaelite rule will effect.

XIII:2-10 Ishmaelite victory will be completed in the 'tenth week' (i.e. after 70 years; the author is using the apocalyptic 'week' of Daniel). Double affliction will ensue, and the taunt will be made that 'the Christians have no Saviour'.

XIII:11-13 All of a sudden the king of the Greeks will go forth in anger and fall upon the Ishmaelites, slaughtering or enslaving them.

XIII:14-18 There will be peace and the faithful remnant will return.

XIII:19-20 The Gates of the North will be opened and the confined peoples will issue forth to devastate the earth.

XIII:21 After one week they will be destroyed by an angel in the vale of Joppa. The king of the Greeks will then come down and reside in Jerusalem for one and a half weeks, or ten and a half years, after which the Son of Perdition (whose birthplace is specified in XIV:1) will appear.

XIV:2-6a The king of the Greeks will stand on Golgotha and hand over

---

[562] The motif derives from the so-called *Julian Romance*.

his crown and kingdom in fulfilment of *Psalm* 68:31; he will then yield up his soul.

XIV:6b-13 The Son of Perdition will be revealed, in accordance with the prophecy of Jacob (*Genesis* 49:17-18); he will enter Jerusalem and seat himself in the Temple, but at the Second Coming of Christ he will be delivered over to Gehenna.

Date and provenance

Various dates within the seventh century have been proposed. Among recent writers Alexander and Suermann argue for a date after AD 644 but prior to the unsuccessful Arab siege of Constantinople in 674-8.[563] A more precise date of *c*.655 for the Syriac original and *c*.674 for the Greek translation is suggested by Lolos.[564] I have proposed a somewhat later date, *c*.690-91, just before ʿAbd al-Malik's tax reforms, on the assumption that the author was living near the end of the 'ten weeks' of Arab rule; this has been accepted by Reinink and, with a slight modification, by Martinez, who advances it a little to 688/9.[565]

The ecclesiastical community to which the author belonged remains unclear. The surviving manuscripts are all Syrian Orthodox, and both Nau and Alexander held that the author belonged to that community;[566] but it is also a fact that the earliest quotations in Syriac from the work are to be found in East Syrian writers of the ninth and tenth centuries, while chapters XI-XIV are incorporated in abbreviated form by the East Syrian writer Solomon of Bostra into his *Book of the Bee* (thirteenth century). On the other hand, the fact that

---

[563] Alexander, *The Byzantine Apocalyptic Tradition*, 25; Suermann, *Die geschichtstheologische Reaktion*, pp. 160-1.

[564] Lolos, *Die Apokalypse des Pseudo-Methodius*, pp. 20-2.

[565] Brock, 'Syriac views', 19; Reinink, 'Die syrischen Wurzeln', p. 206 note 9; Martinez, *Eastern Christian Apocalyptic*, pp. 30-1.

[566] F. Nau, 'Methodius-Clément-Andronicus', *Journal Asiatique* XI,9 (1917), p. 446; Alexander, *The Byzantine Apocalyptic Tradition*, p. 29 (but, as the editorial footnote 49 points out, he subsequently modified his opinion). Suermann, *Die geschichtstheologische Reaktion*, p. 161, also considers this view to be the most likely.

the work was translated into Greek suggests strongly that the author was a Melkite (Chalcedonian);[567] this would seem to be supported by the pro-Byzantine ideology of the work, something that would be most surprising in a Syrian Orthodox or an East Syrian writer. Another possibility, suggested by Reinink,[568] is that the author deliberately set out to be non-sectarian - and so came to be used by people belonging to each of the three christological traditions.[569]

The *Apocalypse* of Ps.-Methodius survives complete in Syriac in Vatican syr. 58 of AD 1584/6 and it is from this manuscript that the present translation has been made.[570] In order to facilitate comparison with the Greek translation, the chapter and verse-numbers of the edition of the earliest form of this by A. Lolos have been incorporated, together with the folio numbers of Vat. syr. 58. The text of Vat. syr. 58 is sometimes corrupt, but this can often be corrected with the help of the Greek translation and the summarized form of chapters XI-XIV to be found in chapters 53-55 of Solomon of Bostra's *Book of the Bee* (a miscellany of biblical history and legends). Dr Reinink has given further help in correcting corrupt words by comparison with the manuscripts from Mardin.

---

[567] This has recently been argued by Brock, 'Syriac views', pp. 19-20, and (more hesitantly) by Martinez, *Eastern Christian Apocalyptic*, p. 28.

[568] Reinink, 'Der Verfassername "Modios" ', pp. 63-4 (earlier he had suggested that the author came from 'syrisch-nestorianische Kreisen': 'Ismael', p. 344). More recently, in his 'Ps.-Methodius und die Legende vom römischen Endkaiser', he has plausibly seen the work as pro-Byzantine propaganda aimed at winning over the Syrian Orthodox.

[569] The last five articles by Reinink cited in the bibliography postdate this introduction.

[570] In the few places where V's reading is given in brackets, the text translated is based on an obviously correct reading in Mardin Orth. 368 (= M, kindly supplied by Dr Gerrit Reinink, cf. Reinink, 'Neue Erkenntnisse').

Bibliography

(1) Syriac text.
A poor edition of Vatican syr. 58 is provided by H. Suermann, *Die geschichtstheologische Reaktion auf die einfallenden Muslime in der edessenischen Apokalyptik des 7. Jahrhunderts* (Frankfurt a/M, 1985), pp. 34-85. Much more satisfactory is the edition by F. J. Martinez in his unpublished dissertation, *Eastern Christian Apocalyptic in the Early Muslim Period: Pseudo-Methodius and Pseudo-Athanasius* (Catholic University of America, Washington DC, 1985), pp. 58-121. A new edition by G. Reinink, using all the known manuscripts, is forthcoming in CSCO.

(2) Greek and Latin translations.
The earliest form of the Greek translation is edited by A. Lolos, *Die Apokalypse des Ps.-Methodius* (*Beiträge zur klassischen Philologie*, 83; 1976); he has also edited two later forms of the text, *Die dritte und vierte Redaktion des Ps.-Methodius* (*Beiträge zur klassichen Philologie*, 94; 1978). The Latin translation is to be found in E. Sackur, *Sibyllinische Texte und Forschungen. Pseudomethodius, Adso und die tiburtinische Sibylle* (Halle, 1898; reprint Turin, 1963), pp. 60-96. New editions of the Greek and Latin texts have now been prepared by W. J. Aerts and G. A. A. Kortekaas; they will be published together with G. J. Reinink's edition of the Syriac text in CSCO.

(3) Modern translations.
There are complete English translations by P. J. Alexander, *The Byzantine Apocalyptic Tradition* (Berkeley, 1985), pp. 36-51 (not always quite accurate), and by Martinez, *op. cit.*, pp. 122-54 (good; followed by annotation, pp. 155-246). The German translation by Suermann, *op. cit.*, is not very reliable.

(4) Recent studies.
P. J. Alexander, *Religious and Political History and Thought in the Byzantine Empire* (London, 1978) [reprints several of his earlier studies on Ps.-Methodius].
idem, 'The medieval legend of the last Roman emperor and its messianic origin', *Journal of the Warburg and Courtauld Institutes*,

41 (1978), pp. 1-15.

idem, 'The diffusion of medieval apocalypses in the West and the beginnings of Joachimism', in A. Williams, ed., *Prophecy and Millenarianism. Essays in Honour of Marjorie Reeves* (London, 1980), pp. 55-106.

idem, *The Byzantine Apocalyptic Tradition* (Berkeley, 1985).

S. P. Brock, 'Syriac views of emergent Islam' [see the bibliography at the end of the introduction of this book].

F. J. Martinez [see (1)].

idem, 'The apocalyptic genre in syriac: the world of Pseudo-Methodius', in H. J. W. Drijvers, R. Lavenant, C. Molenberg and G. J. Reinink, eds., *IV Symposium Syriacum (Orientalia Christiana Analecta*, 229; 1987), pp. 337-52.

G. J. Reinink, 'Ismael, der Wildesel in der Wüste. Zur Typologie der Apokalypse des Pseudo-Methodius', *Byzantinische Zeitschrift*, 75 (1982), pp. 336-44.

idem, 'Der Verfassername "Modios" der syrischen Schatzhöhle und die Apokalypse des Pseudo-Methodius', *Oriens Christianus*, 67 (1983), pp. 46-64.

idem, 'Die syrischen Wurzeln der mittelalterlichen Legende vom römischen Endkaiser', in M. Gosman and J. van Os, eds., *Non Nova, sed Nove. Mélanges de civilisation médiévale dédiés à W. Noomen* (Groningen, 1984), pp. 195-209.

idem, 'Tyrannen und Muslime. Die Gestaltung einer symbolischen Metapher bei Pseudo-Methodius', in H. L. J. Vanstiphout, K. Jongeling, F. Leemhuis and G. J. Reinink, eds., *Scripta Signa Vocis. Studies about Scripts, Scriptures, Scribes and Languages in the Near East presented to J. H. Hospers* (Groningen, 1986), pp. 163-75.

idem, 'Pseudo-Methodius und die Legende vom römischen Endkaiser', in W. Verbeke, D. Verhelst and A. Welkenhuysen, eds., *The Use and Abuse of Eschatology in the Middle Ages* (Leuven, 1988), pp. 82-110.

idem, 'Der edessenische "Pseudo-Methodius"', *Byzantinische Zeitschrift* 83 (1990), pp. 31-45.

idem, 'Pseudo-Methodius: A Concept of History in Response to the Rise of Islam', in Cameron and Conrad, eds., *The Byzantine and Early Islamic Near East* (see the bibliography at the end of the introduction of this book), pp. 149-88.

idem, 'The Romance of Julian the Apostate as a Source for the Seventh-Century Syriac Apocalypses', in P. Canivet and J.P. Rey-Coquais, eds., *La Syrie de Byzance à l'Islam, VIIe-VIIIe* siècles (Damascus, 1992), pp. 75-86.

idem, 'Neue Erkenntnisse zur syrischen Textgeschichte des "Pseudo-Methodius" ', H. Hokwerda and E. Smits, eds., *Polyphonia Byzantina: Studies in Honour of W. J. Aerts*, forthcoming in the Series Mediaevalia Groningana (Groningen, 1992).

H. Suermann [see (1)].

idem, 'Der byzantinische Endkaiser bei Pseudo-Methodios', *Oriens Christianus* 71 (1987), pp. 140-55.

Selected Variants: V = Vatican Syr. 58; M = Mardin Orth. 368; G
= Greek versions; L = Latin versions

X:6. /f. 127b/ After the kingdom of the Hebrews[571] had been
extirpated, in its place the Children of Ishmael, son of Hagar, waged
war on the Romans. These are the people whom Daniel[572] calls
'the arm[573] of the South'. And he (Ishmael) will be waging war
with it for seven[574] weeks of years, for the end is known,[575]
and there is no extension in-between.

XI:1. In this last millennium, which is the seventh, during which
the kingdom of the Persians will be extirpated, the Children of Ishmael
will come out from the desert of Yathrib[576] and all come and
collect there at Gab^cot Ramta.[577] 2. And there the word of our Lord
will be fulfilled[578] /f. 128a/ which says, 'They resemble the wild
animals of the wilderness and the birds of the sky'; and he will
summon them, (saying) 'Gather and come, for I am going to make a
great sacrifice for you today; eat the flesh of fattened (men) and drink
the blood of warriors'. 3. For in Gab^cot the fattened - the kingdom
of the Greeks[579] - will be devastated. Since they devastated the
kingdom of the Hebrews and of the Persians,[580] they too will be
devastated at Gab^cot by Ishmael, 'the wild ass of the desert',[581]

---

[571] G: 'Persians'.

[572] *Daniel* 11:5.

[573] V: 'seed'.

[574] V: 'ten'; cf. V:9, XIII:2.

[575] M: 'the time of the end has arrived'.

[576] i.e. Medina.

[577] Or 'lofty Gab^cot', cf. *Judges* 7:1, in Syriac: Geb^cat Ramta; an
allusion to Gabitha, the site of the famous battle of AD 636, which
came to be known as the Battle of the River Yarmūk.

[578] cf. *Ezekiel*, in Syriac, 39:17-18.

[579] M: 'the fattened ones of the Greeks'; cf. G and L.

[580] The author may have in mind Heraclius's successful campaigns.

[581] *Genesis* 16:12, in Syriac; on this see Reinink, 'Ismael'. The
second half of this verse is used with reference to the Ishmaelites/Arabs
by John of Phenek (late 7th century) in his *Rīsh Mellē*, Book XV
(English translation by S. P. Brock, 'North Mesopotamia in the late

who will be sent in the fury of wrath against mankind, against wild animals and domestic beasts, against trees and plants. 4. It is a merciless punishment.

And these four heads will be sent before them over[582] the whole earth: Destruction and the Destroyer, Devastation and the Devastator, destroying every town that he comes upon, and Devastation which devastates everything. 5. For he said through Moses,[583] 'It is not because the Lord your God loves you that he is bringing you into the land of the Gentiles for you to inherit it, but because of the wickedness of its inhabitants'. Similarly with these Children of Ishmael: it was not because God loves them that he allowed them /f. 128b/ to enter the kingdom of the Christians, but because of the wickedness and sin which is performed at the hands of the Christians, the like of which has not been performed in any of the former generations. 6. For men have garbed themselves in the lascivious clothes of women who are prostitutes, adorning themselves like unmarried girls, standing openly in the streets of towns, crazed with drunkenness and dissolute behaviour, having no shame, cohabiting with one another. Prostitutes, too, would stand openly in the streets: a man would go in, fornicate, and then leave; then along would come his son and defile himself with the same woman. 7. Brothers, fathers, sons, all together would defile themselves with one and the same woman. For this reason Paul the Apostle said,[584] 'Their males have abandoned nature's use of females, and have been inflamed with lust for one another, one male performing an act of shame with another'. And again, in the case of women, as follows:[585] 'They (fem.) have abandoned nature's use of men, and have made use of something that is unnatural'. 8. For this

---

seventh century: Book XV of John bar Penkāyē's *Rīsh Mellē*, *Jerusalem Studies in Arabic and Islam* 9 (1987), 51-74; reprinted in id., *Studies in Syriac Christianity: History, Literature, Theology* [Collected Studies Series, 357; London, 1992], chapter II; see especially p. 54 notes 19, 58, 73).

[582] Or: 'against'.

[583] cf. *Deuteronomy* 9:5.

[584] *Romans* 1:27.

[585] *Romans* 1:26.

reason God will hand them over[586] to the foul action of the barbarians, and men who are warriors will be tormented with punishment of afflictions, /f. 129a/ while their wives will be defiled by children of defilement.

While I beheld and saw these four heads of punishments, Devastation and the Devastator, Destruction and the Destroyer, they cast lots over the land:[587] 9. The land of the Persians was given to Devastation for him to devastate it, sending its inhabitants to captivity, slaughter and devastation; Syria[588] (was given) to the sword of Devastation, its inhabitants to captivity and to slaughter; 10. Sicily[589] (was given) to Destruction and to the sword, and its inhabitants to captivity and to slaughter; 11. Hellas (was given) to the sword of Devastation, and its inhabitants to captivity and to slaughter; the Roman empire[590] (was given) to Devastation and to the sword, and its inhabitants to flight, plunder and captivity; the Islands of the (Aegaean) Sea (were given) to flight, and their inhabitants to captivity and destruction. 12. Egypt and Syria, and the regions of the Orient, shall be put under the yoke of tribute and taxation - seven times worse than the affliction of those in captivity. 13. The Promised Land will be filled with people from the four winds of heaven - like locusts gathering in a storm; there shall be famine there and affliction and plague. The Devastator[591] shall grow strong and his horn will be raised: he will ride in exaltation and be wrapped in pride until the time of wrath. He will seize the entrances to the North, the roads /f. 129b/ of the East, and the crossings of the Sea. People will be placed under the yoke of servitude to them; domestic and wild animals, birds and the waters of the seas will be subjected to them. 14. Deserted lands, which have been left, like widows, without cultivation, shall belong to

---

[586] cf. *Romans* 1:24 and 26.

[587] For the following, compare the apocalypse in I. E. Rahmānī, ed., *Testamentum Domini nostri Jesu Christi*, Syriac and Latin (Moguntiaem 1899), p. 10.

[588] M: 'Cilicia'; G has 'Isauria', and before this inserts references to Armenia, Cappadocia and Cilicia; see further Martinez, pp. 202-5.

[589] M: 'Syria'.

[590] {Syr. ar^{c}ō d-rūmōyē}.

[591] The author may have Mu^{c}āwiya or ^{c}Abd al-Malik in mind.

them: the tyrant will inscribe (them) as his own. (To him) will belong the fish in the sea, the trees in the forests, plants and their fruits, the dust of the earth, along with its stones and produce, the merchandise of merchants, the agricultural labour of peasants, the inheritance of the wealthy, gifts and ornaments of gold, silver, bronze or iron, clothes and all sorts of garments, splendidly adorned, foods and delicacies - everything that is desirable and luxurious shall belong to him. They will be so elated in their wrath and pride that he will even demand tribute from the dead who lie in the dust. He will take a capitation tax from orphans, from widows, and from holy men. 15. They will have no mercy on the poor, nor will they give judgment to the afflicted; they will treat the old roughly and grieve the spirit of the oppressed. They will not spare the sick, or show mercy to the weak; rather, they will laugh at the wise, /f. 130a/ mock at lawgivers, and jeer at men of understanding. The veil of silence will be spread over all mankind, and all the inhabitants of the earth will live in stupor and in death-pangs. Their wisdom[592] is from them and in them.[593] The insignificant will be accounted as important, the despicable as someone of honour. Their words will cut as though with swords, and no one will be able to alter the argument of their words.

16. The path that their journey fills shall be from sea to sea,[594] from the north to the desert of Yathrib: the path will lead to afflictions, and on it will travel aged men and aged women, rich and poor, all hungry and thirsty, and so tormented by harsh fetters that they will call the dead happy.[595]

17. This is the chastisement of which the Apostle[596] spoke: 'The chastisement must come first, only then will that Man of Sin, the Son of Destruction, be revealed.' This chastisement is not being sent only upon human beings, but also upon everything that is on the face of the

---

[592] V: 'the path of their journey'; cf. the beginning of section 16.
[593] This passage is discussed by Reinink in 'Neue Erkenntnisse'; he translates it: 'Und es wird ihre Weisheit nur von ihnen selbst sein.' This is close to the Greek version.
[594] M, G and Solomon of Bostra add 'and from east to west'.
[595] cf. *Ecclesiastes* 4:2.
[596] 2 *Thessalonians* 2:3, reading 'chastisement' for 'rebellion', {Gr. apostasía}.

entire earth - on men, women, children, animals, cattle, birds. People will be tormented /f. 130b/ by that punishment - men, their wives, sons, daughters and possessions; the old who are weak, the sick and the strong, the poor along with the rich. For God called their forefather Ishmael 'the wild ass of the wilderness',[597] and the gazelles, along with all the animals, both of the wilderness and of the cultivated land, will be oppressed by them. People will be persecuted, wild animals and cattle will die, the forest trees will be cut down, the most beautiful mountain plants will be destroyed, and prosperous cities will be laid waste. Regions will lie desolate[598] without anyone passing through; the land will be defiled by blood and deprived of its produce.

For these barbarian tyrants are not men, but 'children of desolation'; they set their face towards desolation, and they are destroyers: they shall be sent for [or, to] devastation; they are destruction, and they shall issue forth for the destruction of everything. They are defiled, and they love defilement. At the time of their issuing forth from the wilderness they will snatch babies from their mothers' arms,[599] dashing them against stones, as though they were unclean beasts.

18. They will make a sacrifice of those who minister in the sanctuary and they will even sleep with /f. 131a/ their wives and with captive women inside the sanctuary. They will appropriate the sacred vestments as clothing for themselves and their children. They will tether their cattle to the sarcophagi of martyrs and to the graves of holy men. They are insolent murderers, destructive shedders of blood; they are a 'furnace of testing'[600] for all Christians.

XII:1. The blessed Apostle said:[601] 'Not all who belong to Israel are Israel;' nor are all those who are called Christians Christians. For in the days of the prophet Elijah only 7000 of the Israelites were left who worshipped the Lord God, but through them the whole of

---

[597] *Genesis* 16:12.
[598] Read: {Syr. SDYN}.
[599] G and Solomon of Bostra add 'tear open pregnant women and'.
[600] cf. XIII:4.
[601] *Romans* 9:6.

Israel was saved.[602] 2. So too at the time of chastisement by these tyrants a few people out of many will remain as Christians, as our Saviour shows us in the Holy Gospel[603] when he says, 'When the Son of Man shall come, will he find faith on earth?' Even those who are perfect in the countries[604] will be disheartened during those days of chastisement. 3. Many people who were members of the Church will deny the true Faith /f. 131b/ of the Christians, along with the holy Cross and the awesome Mysteries: without being subjected to any compulsion, or lashings or blows, they will deny Christ, putting themselves on a par with the unbelievers. 4. For this reason the Apostle, too, proclaimed concerning them,[605] 5. 'At the latter times people will leave the Faith and go after unclean spirits, and after demonic teaching'; they will be rebels and accusers, haughty, hating anything good, traitors and savages.[606] 6. All who are false and weak in the faith will be tested and recognized during that chastisement: they will separate themselves of their own will from the Christian assembly, for the occasion itself will invite them to go after its defilement.

As for the humble, the gentle, kind, quiet, truthful, noble, wise and elect, such people will not be south out at that time, for they will be rejected and despised. 7. In their place the proud, haughty, and boastful will be sought out, along with deceivers, detractors, accusers, trouble-makers, the licentious and those destitute of any compassion, rapacious men, embezzlers, cruel and ignorant, crass people lacking intelligence and the fear of God, who revile /f. 132a/ their parents, blaspheme against the Holy Mysteries and deny Christ, boorish men who do not possess any of God's wisdom. 8. These people shall be ministers at that time;[607] their lying words will be believed, and people will listen to whatever is said by them. But the truthful, the clergy, the wise and the good will all be despicable in their eyes and

---

[602] cf. *1 Kings* 19:18; *Romans* 11:4.

[603] *Luke* 18:18.

[604] V: 'who perform miracles'.

[605] cf. *1 Timothy* 4:1, in Syriac.

[606] cf. *2 Timothy* 3:2-4.

[607] V omits this word.

treated as dung.

XIII:1.   People will undergo[608] chastisement by the Ishmaelites; they will enter into various afflictions to the point of despairing of their lives. Honour will be taken away from priests, the Divine Office and the Living Sacrifice will come to an end in the Church; priests will be like the people at that time.[609]

2.   In the seventh[610] week, during which their victory will be completed, affliction will increase, a double chastisement affecting people, cattle and wild animals: there will be a great famine,[611] and many will die; their corpses will be thrown, like mud, into the streets, for want of anyone to bury them. On one of those days plagues of wrath will be sent upon humanity, two or three in a single day. 3. A person will sleep in the evening and rise up in the morning to find outside /f. 132b/ his door two or three men who use force as they demand tribute and money.   All accounting of what is given and received will disappear from the earth.   At that time people will sell their bronze, their iron, and their burial[612] clothes.   4.   In that seventh[613] week, when everything else is finished up, they will give their sons and daughters to the unbelievers for money. Shall God, for whatever reason, avert his gaze and refuse to help the faithful to endure these afflictions?   This is in order that the faithful may be tested and separated out from the faithless, the rejected tares from the chosen wheat;[614] for that time is the 'furnace of testing'. 5. God will be patient while his worshippers are persecuted, so that through chastisement they may be recognized as children, just as the Apostle[615] proclaimed to us beforehand, 'If we are without

---

[608] V: 'during the'.

[609] cf. *Hosea* 4:9.

[610] V: 'tenth'.

[611] Compare the description of the famine of AH 67 = AD 686/7 in John of Phenek, *Rīsh Mellē* XV (English tr. by Brock [see note on XI:3], 69).

[612] V omits this word.

[613] V: 'tenth'.

[614] cf. *Matthew* 13:24-30.

[615] *Hebrews* 12:8.

chastisement, then we will become aliens, and not sons'. Our Saviour himself exhorted us[616] saying, 'Blessed are you when people revile and persecute you, saying all sorts of bad things about you falsely for my Name's sake: rejoice then and exult, for your reward is great in heaven. For thus they persecuted the prophets who were before you'. /f. 133a/ And: 'He who endures to the end shall have life'.[617]

6. After these afflictions and punishments from the Children of Ishmael at the end of that week, when people are thrown into the peril of chastisement, and there is no hope that they will be delivered from that harsh servitude, being persecuted and afflicted, oppressed with hunger and thirst, tormented by the harsh punishment, these barbarian tyrants will be enjoying luxurious foods and drink, at ease as they boast over their victory, how they have devastated and destroyed the Persians, Armenians, Cilicians, Isaurians, Cappadocians, Africans,[618] Sicilians, the people of Hellas,[619] and those who live in the land of the Romans and all the Islands of the Sea. They will be dressed as bridegrooms and adorned as brides; they will blaspheme, saying, 'The Christians have no Saviour'.[620]

11. Then, all of a sudden, the pangs of affliction will be awakened, like those of a woman giving birth,[621] and the king of the Greeks shall go out against them in great wrath; he will be awakened against them like 'a man who has shaken off his wine'[622] - someone who had been considered by them as though dead. He will go forth against them from the sea of the Kushites, and will cast desolation and destruction /f. 133b/ on the wilderness of Yathrib, and in the midst of their forefathers' dwelling place. And the sons of the kings of the

---

[616] Matthew 5:11-12.

[617] Matthew 10:22; 24:13.

[618] V omits this.

[619] V: {Syr. ꝺLDNYꝺ}.

[620] G has a long addition here (XIII:7-10) about events to take place 'in the first month of the ninth indiction'.

[621] cf. 1 Thessalonians 5:3.

[622] Psalm 78:65, in Syriac; see especially Reinink, 'Syrische Wurzeln', pp. 199-200; Alexander, The Byzantine Apocalyptic Tradition, p. 167.

Greeks will descend upon them from the countries of the west[623] and finish off with the sword the remnant left over from them in the Promised Land. 12. Fear shall fall upon them from all who are round about them. They, their wives, their children, their leaders, all their encampments, all the land of the wilderness which belonged to their forefathers shall be delivered into the hand of the kings of the Greeks; they shall be given over to the sword and devastation, to captivity and slaughter. 13. The yoke of[624] their servitude shall be seven[625] times more oppressive than their own yoke, and they shall be in harsh affliction, from hunger and from exhaustion; they shall be slaves, together with their wives and children, and they shall serve in slavery those who were (previously) serving them. Their slavery shall be a hundred times more bitter than the one they imposed.

14. Then the land which had been devastated of its inhabitants shall be at peace, and the remnant left over shall return, each to his land and to the inheritance of his forefathers - Cappadocians, Armenians, Cilicians, Isaurians, Africans,[626] Greeks,[627] Sicilians[628] - all the remnant /f. 134a/ left over from captivity; and everyone who was in captive servitude shall return to his region, to his ancestral home. 15. People shall multiply like locusts in the land which had been devastated. While Egypt[629] shall be devastated and Arabia shall be burnt, and the land of Hebron shall be laid waste; but the tongue of the sea shall be at peace. And all the fury of the wrath of the king of the Greeks shall be completed upon those who have denied Christ.[630] There shall be peace in the land, the like of which has never been, for this is the final peace of the end of the world. 16. There shall be joy in all the land and people will live in great peace: churches will be renovated, towns will be rebuilt, priests will be freed

---

[623] V: 'will take the regions of the desert'.
[624] V omits these words.
[625] V: 'a hundred'; cf. G.
[626] V: {Syr. PRYQYꓸ}.
[627] V: {Syr. ꓸLDYꓸ}.
[628] V: {Syr. SYLYQYꓸ}.
[629] V {Gr. aíguptos}.
[630] V omits this word.

from tax. Priests and people will have rest at that time from toil, fatigue and oppression; 17. for this is the peace of which he spoke in his Gospel,[631] 'There shall be great peace, the like of which has never been. People will live in quiet, and eat and drink, rejoicing with joy of heart. Men shall marry wives, and women will be given in marriage to men. They shall build buildings and plant vineyards.'

18. And while they are eating and drinking, rejoicing and exulting, there being no evil person or any thought of evil, no fear or terror /f. 134b/ in their hearts, during that peace, 19. the gates of the north shall be opened and the armies of those people who had been confined there[632] shall come forth. The land will quake before them and people will be terrified and will flee, hiding themselves on mountains and in caves and tombs. They will die of fear and of hunger; there will be no one to bury them, they will be devoured in the presence of their parents as they look on. 20. For these peoples who will issue forth from the north eat human flesh and drink the blood of animals; they eat the vermin of the earth, mice, snakes, scorpions and all unclean reptiles that creep on the earth, the bodies of foul animals, the stillborn offspring of cattle. They will sacrifice children and give them to their mothers, forcing them to eat the bodies of their own children. They eat dead dogs and kittens and every kind of foul thing. They will devastate the earth and no one can withstand them. 21. After one week of affliction they will all gather to the vale of Joppa, for it is there that all these peoples will gather; they and their wives /f. 135a/ and their children. Thither will God send against them one of the commanders of the angels, and he will destroy them in a single moment.

Then the king of the Greeks will come down and reside in Jerusalem for one week and a half of a week, ten and a half years in number.

Then the Son of Perdition shall appear, the False Messiah. XIV:1. He will be conceived and born[633] in Chorazin, brought up[634]

---

[631] cf. *1 Thessalonians* 5:3, *Matthew* 24:21, 38 and *Ezekiel* 28:26.

[632] The confinement of twenty-two nations by Alexander the Great was described in VIII; on this tradition see Alexander, *The Byzantine Apocalyptic Tradition*, pp. 185-92.

[633] V omits these two words.

[634] V: 'born'.

in Bethsaida[635], and he will reign in Capernaum. Chorazin shall boast of him, because he was born there, Bethsaida[636] because he was brought up there, and Capernaum because he reigned there. For this reason our Lord applied 'Woe' to the three of them in his Gospel,[637] saying: 'Woe to you, Chorazin, woe to you, Bethsaida, and you, Capernaum who was raised up to heaven: you shall be brought down to lowest Sheol.'

2. The moment the Son of Perdition appears, the king of the Greeks shall go up and stand on Golgotha and the holy Cross shall be placed on that spot where it had been fixed when it bore Christ. 3. The king of the Greeks shall place his crown on the top of the holy Cross, stretch out his two hands towards heaven, and hand over /f. 135b/ the kingdom to God the Father[638] 4. And the holy Cross upon which Christ was crucified will be raised up to heaven, together with the royal crown.

For the holy Cross, upon which Christ was crucified - for the salvation of all people who believe in him was he crucified - is the sign which will be seen prior to the Advent of our Lord,[639] to the confusion of unbelievers. 5. And the word of the blessed David, when he prophesied concerning the end of times,[640] saying, 'Kush shall hand over to God', will be fulfilled, for a son of Kushyat,[641] daughter of Pil, king of the Kushites, is the person who will 'hand over to God'. 6. And the moment the holy Cross is raised up to heaven, and the king of the Greeks yields up his soul to his Creator, then all rule, sovereignty and power will be rendered void. Then suddenly the

---

[635] V: {Syr. BSYDN}.

[636] V: {Syr. BẎTSYDN}.

[637] Matthew 11:21, 23; Luke 10:13, 15.

[638] cf. 1 Corinthians 15:24. The motif of the crown and the Cross is taken from the so-called Julian Romance (J. G. E. Hoffmann, ed., Iulianus der Abtrünnige: Syrische Erzählungen, Leiden, 1880), pp. 200-1, where Jovian places the crown offered him on the top of the Cross (cf. text No. 13, § 100, in which the caliph ᶜUthmān places the crown of the Persian kings in the Kaᶜba at Mecca).

[639] cf. Matthew 24:30.

[640] Psalm 68:31.

[641] V: 'Kushat'.

Son of Perdition will be revealed. He is from the tribe of Dan, according to the prophecy of Jacob, who prophesied concerning him saying,[642] 'Dan shall be a deadly snake lying by the road' that leads to the Kingdom of Heaven. 7. The words 'he bites the horse' refer to words which have the semblance of justice. The phrase 'he throws his rider /f. 136a/ backwards' refers to the holy ones who turn aside after his error. The 'heel' indicates for us the consummation of the ages and the end of years. 8. In the case of the saints who will be living at that time, who ride on the word of truth and humbly abase themselves with labours of righteousness, he (sc. the Son of Perdition) will 'bite' them by means of the illusory and deceptive signs which he will perform: they will run after the Deceiver when they see lepers being cleansed, the blind having their sight restored, the paralysed walk, and demons depart. When he looks at the sun it will be darkened; when he gives orders to the moon, it will be changed to blood. [He will make] trees produce fruit from their branches, the earth to sprout vegetation, springs of water to dry up. By means of these illusory signs he will deceive the saints themselves.[643] This is why (Scripture) said, 'He will bite the horse on its heel'.

When any harm is inflicted on the body by means of metal, or by means of bites, a scar appears on it as long as that body is alive. Similarly, in the case of every sin which is performed in the soul, /f. 136b/ fire and eternal torment are reserved for it.

'Backwards' indicates the left side.[644] 9. When the blessed Jacob gazed with the eye of the spirit and saw the affliction that would take place at that time, he spoke as follows,[645] 'I have awaited your salvation, Lord'. Again, our Lord said,[646] 'If he is able to do so, Satan will even deceive the elect'. 10. This Son of Perdition

---

[642] *Genesis* 49:17. The author draws here on a widespread tradition that the Antichrist will be from Dan. The double revelation (XIV:2 and 6) of the Son of Perdition, before and after the handing over of the crown, is probably due to the fusion of two different traditions: see Alexander, *The Byzantine Apocalyptic Tradition*, pp. 198ff

[643] cf. *Matthew* 24:24.

[644] cf. *Matthew* 25:41-46.

[645] *Genesis* 49:18.

[646] *Matthew* 24:24.

will enter Jerusalem and take his seat in God's Temple, acting as if he
were God.[647]   11.   Now this Man of Sin will be someone who
will become embodied through the agency of male semen; he will be
born of a married woman from the tribe of Dan.[648]   12.   This
Child of Perdition will deceive everyone, if possible, by means of the
bitterness of his disposition, seeing that he will become the dwelling
place for all the demons, and all their activity will be carried out in
him.   13.   But at the Advent of our Lord from heaven he will be
delivered over to 'the Gehenna of Fire'[649] and to 'outer darkness',
where he will be amidst 'weeping and gnashing of teeth'.[650]

As for us, may our Lord Jesus Christ hold us worthy of his heavenly
Kingdom, along with all who perform his will.   And may we offer up
praise, honour, worship and exaltation, now and always, for eternal
ages.   Amen.

---

[647] *2 Thessalonians* 2:4.

[648] The Greek ending differs from what follows in the Syriac and
introduces Enoch and Elijah, who will come 'to refute the Adversary';
in revenge he will kill them, whereupon the *parousia* (Second Coming
of Christ) will take place. The *Apocalyptic Fragment*, translated below,
likewise introduces Enoch and Elijah, but instead of being killed by the
Son of Perdition they cause him to melt away 'like salt before water';
cf. Alexander, *The Byzantine Apocalytic Tradition*, pp. 212ff.

[649] *Matthew* 5:22.

[650] *Matthew* 8:12.

15. THE EDESSENE APOCALYPTIC FRAGMENT

INTRODUCTION

The following apocalyptic fragment has a number of features in common with Ps.-Methodius, and its first editor, F. Nau, thought that it represented the original form of Ps.-Methodius, written *c.*683. In the light of Vatican syr. 58 (which Nau did not know), however, the fragment must now be seen as a separate work which here and there draws on Ps.-Methodius (there are very few verbal allusions, but most of the basic themes are in common). Nau's date of *c.*683 (followed by Suermann) depends on the assumption that the '694 years' mentioned near the beginning of the fragment, refer to the Christian era, but this is hardly likely, since the Syrians did not begin to use the Christian era until recent times; Martinez has suggested that the Hijra era may be meant, which would give AD 1294-5 (*Eastern Christian Apocalyptic*, pp. 218-9). It is also possible that the author has in mind the 'seven' (or 'ten') 'weeks of years' mentioned in Ps.-Methodius X.6, during which the Ishmaelites would be waging war. Although the starting point of this period is left unclear, it would seem that its end was meant to be coterminous with the end of the 70 years of Ishmaelite domination over the Byzantines/Greeks (XIII.2, 11); this would provide much the same sort of date as that suggested by Nau, though reached by different means. The matter should probably be left open for the present.[651] The specific reference to the inviolability of Edessa and its four monasteries suggests that the work was produced somewhere in the vicinity of Edessa.

Nau edited the text from Paris syr. 350, an East Syrian manuscript

---

[651] Reinink now ('Der Edessenische "Pseudo-Methodius" ') relates the 694 years to the Edessene date for the Epiphany of Christ and so regards it as referring to AD 692. A point in favour of this is that James of Edessa's *Chronicle*, in which he included a translation of Eusebius, had just been finished in AD 691/2 (see the discussion of text No. 5). Following the priest Thomas (see Palmer, 'Une chronique syriaque contemporaine de la conquête arabe'), James corrected Eusebius on the crucial point of the date of Christ's birth, substituting the Edessene date for that given by Eusebius and revising the chronology accordingly. [A. N. P.]

of 1645/6, and Cambridge Add. 2054 of the eighteenth century, also East Syrian, in 'Methodius-Clément-Andronicus', *Journal Asiatique* XI,9 (1917), pp. 415-71.   The text has been re-edited, with introduction, English translation and annotations, by Martinez (pp. 206-46), and, with a German translation, by Suermann (pp. 86-97, 162-74). On this text see now G. Reinink, 'Der Edessenische "Pseudo-Methodius" ', and 'The Romance of Julian' (see the bibliography on Pseudo-Methodius, pp. 227-29 above).   N.B. For reference to Pseudo-Methodius the abbreviation 'PM' is used in the notes to the following translation.

.../f. 98r/ as a result of the oppression and evils (brought about) by the Children of Hagar. The Orient will be laid waste by the sword and by many wars, for nation will stand against nation, and kingdom against kingdom.[652]   Their own sword will fall among them.   Armenia will be laid waste, and part of the territory of the Byzantines will be laid waste, (including) many cities.

When of the said (number of) years a week and a half, that is, ten and a half years,[653] are left to the Children of Hagar, their oppression will increase: they will take everything made of gold, silver, bronze and iron, and their clothes, and all their habitation from the...[654] of the dead, until the living will pass by the dead and exclaim, 'Happy are you who have not remained alive at this time'.[655]   And seven women will seize hold of /f. 98v/ a man and say to him[656] [...], as it is written in the good news of the Gospel:[657] 'A man will flee from his wife and his children, and a wife from her husband' as a result of oppression, distress and famine. The rains will be withheld, spring water will fail, the fruits of the trees and all the bounty of the land will be scarce at that time, as a result of

---

[652] *Matthew* 24:7.

[653] Not in PM.

[654] The text is corrupt; Martinez, by means of a small emendation, obtains: 'Their whole living area will be near the dead' (p. 232).

[655] cf. *Ecclesiastes* 4:2 and PM XI:16.

[656] *Isaiah* 4:1a; there must be a lacuna.

[657] The source of this allusion is unclear.

the unbelief of the Children of Ishmael.

When the said (number of) years, that week and a half, has passed, at the end of 694 years,[658] then the king of the Greeks[659] will come forth, having a sign in the city of Rome [concerning] the nails which were in the hands of our Lord Jesus Christ and in the hands of the thief: they were mixed together and no one knew those of our Lord from the others. Then they cast /f. 99r/ them into the fire all together and forged a bit or bridle, which they suspended in a church.[660] When a horse that has never been ridden and never even been fitted with a bridle puts its head into that bridle of its own accord, then the Romans will know that the kingdom of the Christians has come: they will 'take the kingdom of the whole earth from the Children of Hagar etc.'[661] Subsequently (the king) of the Greeks will hand over the kingdom to God, as is written.[662] Now the bridle is still there today.

Then the king of the Greeks shall go forth from the west, and his son from the south, whereupon the Children of Ishmael will flee. They will reassemble in Babylon, /f. 99v/ but the king of the Greeks will catch up with them in Babylon,[663] and they will flee thence to the town of Mecca, where their kingdom shall come to an end; and the king of the Greeks will rule the entire earth. Bounty shall return to the earth, the fruits of the trees, the rains, and water shall be plentiful, and so will the fish in the seas and rivers. There will be well-being and peace in the whole of creation and among all nations and peoples. Then once again the living will pass by a dead person and say, 'You

---

[658] See the introduction to text No. 14.

[659] {Syr. yawnōyē}.

[660] This derives from the various cycles of texts surrounding the Finding of the Cross (either by queen Protonice, wife of Claudius, or by Helena). There is also an allusion to *Zechariah* 14:20, in Syriac.

[661] The author is evidently referring to a well-known text.

[662] cf. *1 Corinthians* 15:24; perhaps cf. *Psalm* 68:31, an important text for PM.

[663] No reference to Babylon occurs in PM, but in the *Lexicon* of Bar Bahlūl (col. 1011) there is a note saying, 'I found Methodius, who says that the Children of Ishmael were chased as far as Babylon, the city of the giants'.

would have been fortunate if you had been alive today in this kingdom.'

The kingdom of the Greeks will endure for 208 years.[664] Subsequently sin will increase in the world once again, and there will be fornication openly, like beasts, without cover, in the streets and meeting places, /f. 100r/ as formerly; and the earth will be polluted by sin.

Then the gates of Armenia will be opened, and the descendants of Gog and Magog shall issue forth: they were twenty-four tribes, with twenty-four languages.[665] When King Alexander saw these people eating the reptiles of the earth and all sorts of polluted things, including human flesh, eating the dead and every kind of unclean thing, performing magic rites and all kinds of evil deeds, he gathered them together, took them to the interior of these mountains, and confined them there. He then besought God that the mountains should come together, which came to pass, leaving a gateway [only] twenty[666] cubits wide between the mountains. This gateway he closed up with the stones /f. 100v/ called 'magnetic',[667] of a substance which clings to iron, extinguishes fire at contact and resists all enchantment.

At the end of times these gates will be opened,[668] and they will come out and pollute the earth. They will take a son from the womb of his mother, kill him and give him back to his mother to cook; and if she does not eat him, they will kill her. They (will) eat mice and all sorts of unclean reptiles. God's mercy shall be far removed from the inhabitants of the earth; people shall live to see all sorts of evils, famine, drought, cold, frost and widespread oppression, such that people bury themselves in the ground, while they are still alive. Had

---

[664] This figure is not found elsewhere.

[665] PM, who recounts this episode at an earlier point (ch. VIII), lists twenty-two, not twenty-four. In the ensuing narrative our text has a few verbal parallels with PM. For the theme of Alexander and the enclosed nations see the introduction to text No. 14.

[666] PM VIII has 'twelve'.

[667] PM VIII:8 has: 'He anointed (the gate) on the inside with T꜒SQTYS' (with various spellings in the different witnesses); cf. {Gr. asunkitē_i}.

[668] cf. PM XIII:19.

not God shortened /f. 101r/ those days, no flesh would have survived.[669]

Some people say they will reign for two years and eight months[670] from the time they issue forth to the time when they perish. When they go around the whole creation and rule over the whole world, God will have compassion on His servants; He will gather them to that land where the Children of Ishmael perished, that is, to Mecca.[671] Then God will bid the angels to stone them with hailstones, so that not one of them survives: they shall all perish. During their lifetime [fairness in] weights and measures will be obsolete. Their faces are ugly, and everyone who sees them will abhor and fear them. The stature of each one of them is an arm's length.[672]

At that time the Son of Perdition, who is named 'the False Messiah', shall emerge.[673] He will seize the world by fraud and deceit, without (the use of) the sword. His sin will be even greater than Satan's. This is what Jacob Israel said to his children,[674] 'Gather around and I will show you what shall happen to you at the end of days.' He was hinting to them at the time; and what our Lord hinted will be fulfilled, (namely) that Satan would be united with this False Christ. He will perform signs,[675] open ones but useless - just as the Divinity /f. 102r/ was united with the Humanity and performed signs and wonders. He will utter false and distant rumours, he will raise the dead through falsehood and magic; (likewise he will heal) the paralysed and the blind.

His birth will take place in (the region of) Tyre and Sidon, but he

---

[669] cf. *Matthew* 24:22.

[670] PM XIII:21: 'a week'.

[671] PM XIII:21: 'the Vale of Joppa'.

[672] i.e. they are Pygmies (who almost certainly feature in the list of twenty-two nations given in PM VIII).

[673] PM XIII:21, at the end.

[674] *Genesis* 49:1.

[675] cf. *Matthew* 24:24.

will live in Capernaum.[676] For this reason our Lord (said),[677] 'Woe unto you, Chorazin, woe to you Bethsaida, and you, Capernaum: how long will you be exalted?[678] You shall be brought down to Sheol.' He will gain control of the whole world without a fight. He will say that he is the Christ. He will move from one place to another, his band with him /f. 102v/ - many thousands of demons will be with him, tens of thousands, (demons) without number. He will put an end to (liturgical) offerings and altars. The first to follow him out into error are crowds of Jews, who will say, 'He is the Christ.' Brides will abandon their husbands and go after him. He will reign over the whole earth; however he will not enter the city of Edessa, for God has blessed and protected her.[679] Nor will he enter these four monasteries, which will endure as the first ones in the world.

Finally he will enter Jerusalem and the Sanctuary, as the Gospel says,[680] 'When /f. 103r/ you see an abomination in the Holy Place.' This refers to wickedness, sin and fornication, for the False Christ is the abomination and when he enters Jerusalem, Enoch and Elijah[681] shall come out of the Land of the Living; they will take their stand, fighting and cursing him. When he sees them, he will melt away like salt in contact with water. He will be judged first of all, before humanity, along with the demons who had entered him.

Then the king of the Greeks will come to Jerusalem, climb

---

[676] cf. PM XIV:1. Tyre, instead of Chorazin, will be a further consequence of the corruption of Bethsaida into Sidon (see note 635 to PM XIV:1).

[677] *Matthew* 11:21-3; *Luke* 10:13-15; PM XIV:1.

[678] The text of Matthew has: 'Do you believe you will be raised up to heaven?'

[679] Nothing corresponding to this is to be found in PM; the reference to the protection of Edessa is based on the promise of Christ to King Abgar of Edessa in the legendary *Teaching of Addai* and strongly suggests that the present text is of Edessene provenance.

[680] cf. *Matthew* 24:15.

[681] Neither Enoch nor Elijah features in PM, but their role at the end of time is well known from other sources; cf. Alexander, *The Byzantine Apocalyptic Tradition*, pp. 211ff and the note on PM XIV:11.

Golgotha,[682] where our Saviour was crucified, and in his hand will be the Cross of our Lord. /f. 103v/ Now this king of the Greeks shall be descended from Kushyat, daughter of Kushyat (*sic*), of the kings of Kush;[683] they are (also) called Nub(ians). As he goes up with the Cross in his hands, the crown which descended from heaven upon the head of King Jovian of old will pass over the top of our Lord's Cross and he will raise up the Cross and the crown towards heaven.[684] And Gabriel the archangel will descend and, taking the Cross and the crown, will raise them up to heaven.[685] Then the king will die, along with every human being on earth and all wild animals and cattle: nothing will remain /f. 104r/ alive.

As for the light which God created for the Children of Adam, the sinner, that light was created for them (alone): God, whose honour be revered, has no need of light, or of anything else. The stars will fall like leaves, and the earth shall revert to its original chaos and confusion.[686]

Once all created things have come to an end, all of a sudden, as in a twinkling of an eye, a horn and a trumpet shall give out a sound: then good and bad will be gathered together, for there is a single resurrection for human beings and for everyone. Pangs shall smite the earth, like (those of) a woman who is on the very point of giving birth.[687] Adam shall come forth, and all his children. No human being shall remain behind who will not rise at that moment. Then light will shine out from the east, more intense than the light of the sun and our Lord Jesus Christ shall come, like lightning[688] and fulfil everything that the prophet David has spoken:[689] 'A mighty sound

---

[682] cf. PM XIV:2 (where this occurs when the Son of Perdition first appears, rather than after his defeat).

[683] cf. PM XIV:5.

[684] cf. PM XIV:4. The reference to Jovian (absent from PM) points to the source of this legendary episode, the Syriac *Julian Romance* (see the note on PM XIV:3).

[685] Not in PM.

[686] *Genesis* 1:2.

[687] cf. *Isaiah* 13:8; *1 Thessalonians* 5:3; PM XIII:11.

[688] cf. *Matthew* 24:27.

[689] cf. *Psalm* 68:33, in Syriac.

shall issue from the east and be heard in heaven.'

The light shall distinguish[690] between the good and the bad, for they (i.e. the good) will see light the like of which never existed before for them to see. The resurrection is the same /f. 105r/ for all, but the reward will not be the same. There shall be no greater torment for sinners than when they do not see that light. Then the moment of reckoning and of Judgment shall come. Judgment is the separation of the sinners from the wicked.[691] Languages and dialects will cease. The good and the wicked alike will go up to the judgment. The good will ascend to heaven, while the bad will remain on earth - this is the Gehenna of the wicked. Thus Lord Ephraem the teacher said,[692] 'The fire inside a person /f. 105v/ comes from himself and acts like a hot fever: Gehenna is within them.' Thus the good ascend to heaven and to the kingdom; the reward will not be the same for all, but everyone will be rewarded at that time in accordance with what he has done.

---

[690] The MS., probably corrupt, has 'come out'.

[691] Perhaps what is meant is the separation of mere sinners, who can be forgiven, from the truly wicked, who cannot.

[692] Unidentified, but compare Ephraem's *Letter to Publius*, 22 (*Le Muséon* 89 (1976), 292), 'Maybe the Gehenna of the wicked consists in what they see ... their mind acts as the flame'.

EPILOGUE

'... everything the poor can produce vanishes like smoke. There is no saviour and no king whose door is open. Worse still, God has turned His Face away. When we call upon Him, He does not listen. We have angered Him by our evil deeds, [...] and because of such practices, God has delivered the Christians into the hands of the enemy and they are ruled by those who hate them. They oppress us in order to extinguish that nobility which used to be displayed in the Christian way of life. [...] But which of our people repents in the slightest? Who has a conscience or a rule of life? They all shoot out their lips, wag their heads and scorn the law and the lawgiver alike. This people would have their just deserts if what was said to Jeremiah was applied to them: "Do not pray for this people, because I will not listen to you." [...] Therefore let us say, with Paul, "the time has been cut short" (*1 Corinthians* 7:29) and the dreaded sword approaches. Many are the signs of it, one being that rebellion about which the Apostle spoke, saying that when it comes the Son of Perdition will be revealed (*2 Thessalonians* 2:3ff).'[693]

This extract from the epilogue of Dionysius's chronicle, the lost work which lies behind text No. 13, documents the assertion that his purpose in writing history was essentially a moral one. This is not incompatible with the suggestion in his preface, that history is entertaining; but entertainment, for this historian, is a means, rather than an end. He appears to regard history as a study which should lead the attentive reader to repentance. Perhaps his chief purpose is to shame the Syrian Orthodox people into improving their behaviour and renewing their faith. Dionysius sometimes refers to the Byzantines as 'the Gentiles', implying that he sees his own people as analogous to the Jews of the Old Testament.[694] As the martyrs of the early Church converted by their example the rulers of the Roman empire, which had persecuted

---

[693] On the events of Syrian Orthodox church history to which the word 'rebellion' alludes, see Palmer, *Monk and Mason*, chapter 5, towards the end; chapter 6 is also relevant.

[694] See Michael, p. 452, 11:18c, last word, and compare Michael's own usage of the term 'Gentiles' in a similar context on p. 545, line 2.

them, and so introduced the victory of the Cross to the field of war, so the Jacobites should be such a shining light in the darkness that Byzantium sees the error of its ways, renounces Chalcedon and regains that Grace which alone can lead to justice in a united earthly kingdom. In this way Dionysius shows that there is one fault, the correction of which lies within the power of his readers, a fault which is still preventing God's plan for the history of the world from being completed, namely the sinfulness of the Jacobite community itself. It must be admitted, however, that we have no direct evidence that Dionysius had not completely given up all hope that Byzantium would repent of its 'heresy'.

However that may be, Dionysius's reference to the dreaded end approaching, which he goes on to contrast with his own most welcome death, conveys the urgency of repentance. In the inscriptions at Ehnesh (text No. 11), whose author was not far removed from Dionysius in space and time, the march of history seems to be accelerated. The sins of the author's community are the cause of the evils which have occurred shortly before the inscription was written. There is a strong suggestion that the author lives in 'the last days'. But we should be wary of putting apocalyptic and chronography on the same level and interpreting them with reference to one another, even when chronography is written with a certain conception of the future and although the rhetoric of apocalyptic requires that it be related to historical reality.

The historian reading the texts collected in this book will be aware that they are, in the first instance, documents of the mental world of certain Christian communities in the early days of the Muslim empire. That is one aspect of their interest for historians today. At the same time, history is not just rhetoric, it uses records. One of the aims of this book is to show that scattered and incomplete records were made by Syrians in the seventh century, some of which were collected together by other Syrians in the eighth century. The culmination of this process was a magisterial redaction, supplementing the Syriac sources from Greek and Arabic sources, and integrating them in a nearly continuous narrative of the period. This was the early ninth-century chronicle of Dionysius.

The Syriac records provide a control for the largely oral tradition of the Muslim Arabs concerning the first century of their era, and they supplement the meagre records of the Byzantine chronicles covering the period after Heraclius. There was some exchange and contamination between these three traditions, which makes it, at the present, difficult to be sure when they are giving independent information on the same events. One should remember that the Syrian clerics who wrote these chronicles composed them with other purposes in mind than that of merely recording events; this led them to distort the historical record at times for rhetorical, symbolic or partisan purposes.

Some problems concerning the dates of rulers and of patriarchs

Roman regnal years

Dionysius made Heraclius's reign begin one year too late. This mistake may have been caused by a confusion between the Roman Indiction, which began on 1 September, and the Seleucid year, which begins on 1 October. He dated Heraclius's accession to 1 September, AG 922, instead of 1 September, AG 921. Therefore, all Dionysius's regnal years for Heraclius must be corrected by adding one, when they are synchronized with the Seleucid era. This does not, however, apply, to those of Heraclius's regnal years which are numbered independently of the Seleucid era. At § 32, for example, Chosroēs gives the order for the Edessenes to be deported 'in year 18 of Heraclius' (AD 627/8). Chosroēs died on February 9, AD 628, whereas year 19 of Heraclius began on September 1 of that year. Again, at § 38, Shīrōē's accession (actually February 25, AD 628) is dated to year 19 of Heraclius (beginning in September of 628) and year 7 of Muhammad (beginning in May, 628). Indeed, it is only the presence of a Seleucid date which can have compelled Dionysius to alter the regnal years in order to conform with the false synchronism in § 23. I am grateful to Walter Kaegi and Michael Whitby for preventing me from following Dionysius in his error, and especially to Robert Hoyland for suggesting the solution of this problem.

Since the false synchronism of Heraclius's regnal year with the Seleucid era is found in both witnesses to Dionysius's text, the *Chronicle of AD 1234* and Michael, it probably goes back to Dionysius himself. At § 33, it is true, we read, in the *Chronicle of AD 1234* and in Michael, two synchronisms for the siege of Constantinople, which is dated by *Chr. Pasch.* to 626:

a) 'AG 936, Heraclius 14, Chosroēs 35, Muhammad 3'
b) 'AG 936, Heraclius 15, Chosroēs 35, Muhammad 4'.

It is unlikely that the Seleucid date and the year of Chosroēs have been corrupted, so Dionysius intended to date the siege, albeit wrongly, between October 1, AD 624 and September 30, AD 625. All but the last month of this year falls in Heraclius 15, which Dionysius, consistent in his error, numbered as 'Heraclius 14'. Muhammad's year 3 began on June 24, 624, his year 4 on 13 June 625, ending 1 June, 626. If Dionysius's text originally synchronized AG 936 with Muhammad 3 (which is the same as AH 3) and with Heraclius 14, a comparison with § 38 (Muhammad 7 = Heraclius 19) may have suggested to a scribe the emendation 'Muhammad 3 = Heraclius 15'. But then a comparison with § 25 (Heraclius 12 = Muhammad 1) might have suggested to another scribe the emendation 'Heraclius 15 = Muhammad 4'. If, on the other hand, Dionysius's text originally synchronized AG 936 with Muhammad 4 and with Heraclius 14, a comparison with § 25 (Heraclius 12 = Muhammad 1) may have suggested the emendation 'Heraclius 14 = Muhammad 3', which is what we find in the *Chronicle of AD 1234*. Independently, a comparison of the original text with § 38 (Muhammad 7 = Heraclius 19) might have suggested the emendation 'Muhammad 4 = Heraclius 15', which is what we find in Michael. The latter explanation of the two variants is preferable, because it does not posit an intermediate stage of intelligent corruption. Therefore the original text should be reconstructed as 'AG 936, Heraclius 14, Chosroēs 35, Muhammad 4'.

Dionysius was correctly informed, both as to the year of Heraclius's death and the length of his reign; but he failed to draw the consequences by correcting his tally of the regnal years and righting his error at § 23 (see my note on § 85).

Persian regnal years

For Dionysius, the Persian regnal year ended shortly after 15 September. This can be inferred from Michael's supplement to text No. 13, § 32. The solar eclipse reported there actually occurred in China on 15 October, AD 627; but it was reported by text No. 2, a source known to Dionysius, as having occurred on 15 September, AD 627. This latter date is pinpointed by Dionysius's synchronism (after the alteration of Heraclius's regnal year, on which see above) to AG 938 (starting October 626), Heraclius 18 (starting September 627), Muhammad 6 (starting May 627) and Chosroēs 37. The constancy with which the Persian regnal years otherwise march with the Roman in this chronicle shows that the last number is an indication that 15 September was shortly before the end of Dionysius's Persian year. Probably Dionysius made the regnal years of the shahs begin at the Seleucid New Year, on 1 October.

Arab regnal years

The regnal years of the caliphs are problematic for our authors. The Syriac sources, besides suppressing the caliphate of ^CAlī and omitting to notice the short-lived Mu^Cāwiya II, are in considerable confusion as to the lengths of the several caliphs' reigns. This confusion is probably due in part to their failure to notice that lunar years were a few days shorter than solar years. Even Dionysius of Tel-Mahrē, who occasionally used the lunar years, apparently had only a rough-and-ready calculus for converting them into solar years, for his calculations do not always quite coincide with those of Wüstenfeld and Mahler. At least Dionysius (unlike Michael after him) rejected the seven-year reign accorded to Muhammad by James of Edessa, which had been, thanks to James's authority, a serious aggravating factor in Syriac calculations. The important source which Dionysius shares with Theophanes and Agapius, on which see the introduction to text No. 13, gave twelve years to ^CUmar b. al-Khattāb; this accounts for the equation of AD 654/5 with ^CUthmān's year 9, instead of his year 11 (§ 101), and perhaps also for the omission of the length of his reign from the narrative of his death, which Dionysius dated securely to 655/6 (see the note) and the failure to specify how long the subsequent civil war continued. Dionysius's tally of the Arab regnal years is accurate again from Mu^Cāwiya onwards.

Syrian Orthodox Patriarchs

The regnal years of the Syrian Orthodox (Jacobite) patriarchs are given according to the table in Hage, *Die syrisch-jakobitische Kirche*, supplemented and corrected from Dionysius of Tel-Mahrē's Church History (as represented in the *Chronicle of AD 1234*, II, p. 257: Peter of Callinicum raised to the patriarchate in AG 894) and from the chronicle of the priest Thomas (text No. 2). Hage himself, using

Thomas, names 6 November as the date of Athanasius I's consecration; but he follows Michael in giving the year as AD 594 (Michael, p. 378, 10.23c). Assuming the month-date is correct (Brooks marks the number '6' in '6 November' as doubtful, but Brock, who has re-examined the manuscript, finds it 'absolutely clear'), it might show that he was consecrated in AD 589, 595, 600 or 606, if patriarchal consecrations, like episcopal ordinations, took place by canonical prescription on a Sunday (*Vitae virorum apud monophysitas celeberrimorum*, ed. E. W. Brooks, CSCO 7, 1907, p. 53). But text No. 2 gives AD 603 as the year. The authority of this chronicle is considerable as it was written within forty years of this date and could draw on good sources at Edessa and at Qēnneshrē; besides, it enjoys the support of James of Edessa (see the discussion of text No. 5 and of text No. 10). For this reason I depart from Michael's date for the accession of Athanasius, giving him 29 years in office instead of the phenomenal 37. Perhaps he was indeed consecrated on a Wednesday.

Michael's earlier date is presumably due to the anxiety he or his source felt about the apostolic succession in the Syrian Orthodox Church; if there was a vacancy of nine years before Athanasius's reign, that did not look good on the Church's pedigree. But such a vacancy, far from being improbable, helps to explain the renewed persecution of the Jacobites by the Chalcedonians in 598/9 and their expulsion from many churches (see for example text No. 2, AG 910, and text No. 13, § 21); it also suggests a connection between the death of Maurice in AD 602, the stoning of the Chalcedonian bishop of Edessa in 603 and the restoration of the Jacobite patriarchate at the end the same year, three events juxtaposed (intentionally, as I think) by James of Edessa.

It is to be noted that the *Chronicle of AD 1234* gives rather wild dates for the deaths of at least two patriarchs, making one of them coincide with a total eclipse of the sun, while the other coincides with a series of natural catastrophes. It is not impossible that Dionysius of Tel-Mahrē, from whom this chronicle is derived, gave correct dates for the patriarchs in his History of the Church, but used this device with intentional flagrancy in his Secular History to accentuate certain events. In the Secular History he only refers incidentally to patriarchs and bishops. Compare the liberties taken by Syriac chroniclers with the records of solar eclipses, presumably on the understanding that the facts could be found elsewhere (see Appendix II). The loose expression 'at this time' enabled Dionysius to bring the patriarch Peter's death (591) into close proximity with portents which occurred later, in 598 and 601 (see p. 119, above, with the notes). But there is nothing vague about the expression 'in this year', which links the deaths of the patriarch John and the metropolitan Simeon of Edessa (probably 648, though dated 649/50 by text No. 10) with events in the years 664ff, including a total eclipse of the sun which actually occurred in 667. The fact that the patriarch Theodore may have died in 667 (though texts No. 10 and No. 12 date his death to 664/5) suggests a confusion between this prelate and the patriarch John; and the fact that the expression 'in this year' is used twice in two lines (p. 188, above), without even a conjunction before the second occurrence, suggests that someone may have spliced the anachronism, lifted from text No. 10, AG 961, or a related source, into place, where Dionysius, perhaps, originally had a correct synchronism with Theodore's death. After all, Dionysius had access, as did Michael after him, to the archives of the patriarchate; and there is no apparent motive, as there was in the case of the patriarch Athanasius, for distorting the facts at this point.

APPENDIX II

Solar eclipses in Syria during the seventh century

The chief publications are the following:

Hofrath Prof. Th. Ritter von Oppolzer, *Canon der Finsternisse* (Denkschriften der kaiserlichen Akademie der Wissenschaften: mathematisch-wissenschaftliche Classe, 52; Vienna, 1887);

F. K. Ginzel, 'Astronomische Untersuchungen über Finsternisse', *Sitzungsberichte der kaiserlichen Akademie der Wissenschaften, II. Abtheilung*, 88 (1883), pp. (629-755) = 1-127;

H. Mucke and J. Meeus, *Canon of Solar Eclipses -2003 to +2526* (Vienna, 1983);

D. J. Schove, in collaboration with A. Fletcher, *Chronology of Eclipses and Comets AD 1-1000* (Woodbridge, 1984).

Listed below are the eclipses which might have been visible in the course of the seventh century in Syria. Those printed in italics occurred more or less directly overhead, i.e. the centre of the cone of the moon's shadow traversed some part of Syria. T, A and P stand for TOTAL, ANNULAR and PARTIAL. To the right of these objectively calculated eclipses are listed the eclipses recorded in the Syriac chronicles here translated. The texts are referred to by their number, followed after a colon by the AG date, or, in the case of text No. 13, after a comma by the paragraph-number. There is another kind of list in Schove and Fletcher, which takes as its point of departure the dates given in the chronicles. According to these authors, eclipses were signalled in Syria and Mesopotamia in 601, 604, 617, 618, 632, 644, 671 and 693. They also give a check-list of comets, with seventh-century comets between pages 292 and 294.

Table of solar eclipses

601 March 10	T 10:912; 12a:912; 12b:912; 13, §10, note
604 December 26	A
606 June 11	*A*
613 July 2314	T 13, §24, note: 'In year 1 of Heraclius'
616 May 21	*T*
620 September 2	T 5:2L (referred to 604 by Schove and Fletcher, p. 113)
- - -	2:938 (there was an eclipse in China, 627 October 15)
634 June 1	*A*
638 March 21	A
639 September 3	T 13, §60, note
646 April 21	*T* 13, §114? (Patriarch John died 648)
655 April 12	T
660 July 13	A
661 July 2	A
667 August 25	*T* 13, §114? (Patriarch Theodore died 667)
671 7 December	A 13, §118, note
672 November 25	P
678 July 24	A
679 July 13	A
686 February	TA
688 July 3	A
692 April 22	A
693 October 5	*T* 13, §130, note (cf. Schove and Fletcher, pp. 137-42)
696 February 19	*T*
698 December 8	*A*
700 May 23	*T*
702 September 26	T
707 July 4	T

Note that each individual chronicle apart from 13 has only one eclipse (unless the original text of Dionysius had that recorded by Michael, 10.23b, as well) and that 13 is a compilation from a number of different chronicles.   Having said that, 5 is only preserved in a fragment and may have contained more eclipses, which should be among those preserved in Michael, if Michael is being accurate when he says that he incorporated all 5's material.   But even from the preserved portion of 5 it appears that James of Edessa was selective in recording eclipses and there is a *prima facie* case for the claim that he used them to underline certain events in history, just as the other chroniclers did.   There was a body of astronomical literature (cf. p. 188n, above) and this must have assured that the observation of eclipses remained scientific, even while they were being put to imaginative uses by the chroniclers, who presumably took liberties on the understanding that the sober facts could be found elsewhere.   The chronicles record some eclipses with accuracy, some approximately and some quite wrongly.   Where the date is vague ('at this time') one suspects that the synchronization of the eclipse with the event it symbolized was artificial.   2 is the only chronicler who seems to have reported an eclipse which was observed in another part of the world.

It seems fair to say that the Syrian chroniclers here surveyed were not interested in eclipses for their own sake, but only if they made an effective combination with events on the human stage.   For example, 2 imports an eclipse from China to mark the death of Chosroēs II, whereas 5 juxtaposes the first appearance of Muhammad with a solar eclipse.   10 appears to evoke the eclipse which accompanied Christ's Passion; he makes the eclipse of AD 601 last for three hours, like that which coincided with the Crucifixion of Jesus, before 'the darkness was drawn back and day reappeared as usual' (*Mark* 15:33; *Matthew* 27:45; *Luke* 24:45).   The word 'drawn back' is properly used of a curtain; involuntarily one thinks of the 'veil of the temple' which 'was rent in the midst' during the eclipse in the Gospels (*Mark* 15:38; *Matthew* 27:51; *Luke* 24:45), two events combined in a single verse by Luke. Yet 'was drawn back' is different from 'was rent' and makes one think of the stone which was 'rolled back' from the tomb at Jesus's resurrection, especially since the verbs in Syriac ({Syr. etgallag} and {Syr. et^{c}aggal}) are phonetically similar. The purpose of this writer is literary, not merely informative.

13, on the other hand, depicts the persecution by Domitian of Melitene (§ 9) as the temporary 'eclipse' of oriental monasticism in a dark, blood-filled ditch outside the Sun-Gate of Edessa. By doing so the author associates himself with 12a, which suggests, by juxtaposition, that the eclipse of AD 601 was a sign of God's anger on account of these persecutions. The plague, the earthquake and the death of a patriarch form together with the eclipse a portentous drum-roll. The eclipse itself is omitted from the *Chronicle of AD 1234*, but we find it in the parallel passage in the *Chronicle* of Michael, so it was probably in Dionysius of Tel-Mahrē's original text. Here again an allusion to Good Friday is made by making the eclipse last 'from the third hour until the sixth'; and 'everyone said that the sun had been darkened because of the murder of those monks who served Christ' (Michael, p. 387, 10.23b.) 13 also borrowed from 2 the eclipse of AD 627, but linked it with the deportation of some of the citizens of Edessa. See text No. 13, § 32: 'In this year the sun was darkened and lost the light of half its orb. It remained so from October until June, so that people began to say that the full orb of the sun would never be restored.' These seven months of semi-darkness correspond to the exile of a part of the Edessene population. By connecting the end of the eclipse implicitly with the return of the survivors after Chosroēs's death in February, AD 628, 13 retains a link with 2.

Solar eclipses thus play a particular role in the chronicles. They are also to be found in apocalyptic texts such as 11 and 14: 'When he looks at the sun it will be darkened; when he gives orders to the moon, it will be changed to blood' (XIV.8).

APPENDIX III
Maps

The outlines of maps I, II, III and IV were traced from *Muir's Historical Atlas: Ancient and Classical*, 6th ed. (London, 1963), the outline of map V from *Türkei und Naher Osten 1 : 800,000* (Reise- und Verkehrsverlag, ISBN 3.575.11199.6). Both of these sources were used, together with the following:

Atlas zur Kirchengeschichte (Freiburg im Breisgau, 1987);
W. Brice, *An Historical Atlas of Islam* (Leiden, 1981) - good for visualizing the relief, but thin on Syria;
T. Cornell and J. Matthews, *Atlas of the Roman World* (Oxford, 1982);
R. Dussaud, *Topographie historique de la Syrie antique et médiévale* (Paris, 1927);
Institut géographique national, *Bassin méditerranéen, échelle 1 : 2 500 000* (Paris, 1981);
Palästina: Historisch-archäologische Karte, 1 : 300 000 (Göttingen, 1979);
R. Roolvink, ed., *Historical Atlas of the Muslim Peoples* (Amsterdam, no date (*c*.1958));
W. Smith, *Dictionary of Greek and Roman Geography*, 2 vols. (London, 1856 and 1857);
The Times Atlas of the World, Comprehensive Edition, 5th ed. (London, 1975);
Turkey: motoring map 1 : 1,600,000 (Geographia, ISBN 0 092121705);
M. Whitby, *The Emperor Maurice and His Historian* (Oxford, 1988);
Yāqūt, *Mu'jam al-buldān* (topographical encyclopedia, in Arabic, made accessible to me by Geert Jan van Gelder), ed. F. Wüstenfeld, 6 vols. (Leipzig, 1866-73).

N.B. A question-mark after a name indicates that an element of guess-work was involved in locating it. On Map V, the horizontally printed names are those of settlements, those on a rising diagonal refer

to rivers, lakes and seas, those on a descending diagonal refer to
regions, mountains and districts (e.g. Siffin, which would appear
(*pace* Roolvink, ed.) to have been a district rather than a settlement; cf.
text No. 13, § 106: {Syr. dukk^{e}tō d^{e}metqaryō S$^{\supset}$PYN} and *Türkei*,
cited above, just above the symbol SYR: {Ar. 'Ard Safayn}).

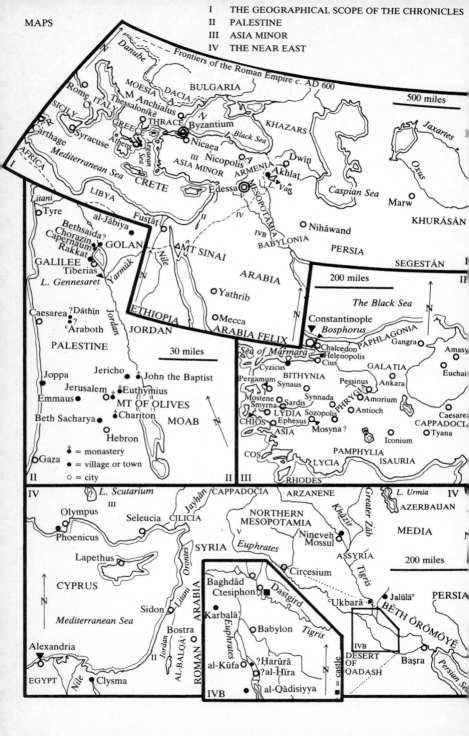

MAPS

I THE GEOGRAPHICAL SCOPE OF THE CHRONICLES
II PALESTINE
III ASIA MINOR
IV THE NEAR EAST

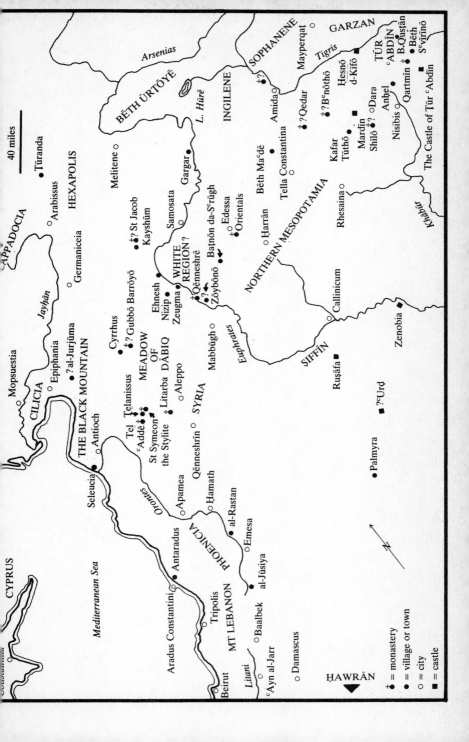

N.B. Names followed by initials are those of scholars. Emperors, Caliphs, Shahs, Popes, Jacobite Patriarchs and Patriarchs of Constantinople are listed with their dates of office. Persons active in the period 582-718 are listed with the date of their death or with a *floruit* normally taken from this book. Other entries are more or less approximately dated. All dates are AD except where marked as BC. 'Arab', 'Byzantine' and 'Roman' are too frequent to be usefully indexed; the same applies to 'Persian', which, however, is indexed from p. 179 onwards (after the end of the Persian empire). A Roman numeral within brackets beside an entry in the index refers to the map or maps on which that place-name can be found. The Arabic defining prefix 'al-' is written, but disregarded for the purpose of alphabetical ordering. Where there are many entries for one name (a good example is 'John'), these have been ordered according to the first substantive following the name.

Aaron, brother of Moses 131n

Aaron, 'the Persian exegete' (*fl.* 665) 59

^{C}Abbāsid xxvii, 97

al-^{C}Abbās b. ^{C}Abd al-Muttalib (*fl.* 635) 144, 161

al-^{C}Abbās, the same, confused with ^{C}Alī 59, 66

al-^{C}Abbās b. al-Walīd, Arab general (*fl.* 711, 718) 64, 209n

^{C}Abd al-Malik b. Marwān, Caliph (685-705) xxiv, 43-45, 48, 50, 51, 60, 66, 78, 109, 198n, 199-202, 204-206, 208, 225, 232n

^{C}Abd al-Muttalib, grandfather of Muhammad 144

^{C}Abd al-Rahmān b. Khālid (*fl.* 664) 33-35, 77, 195

^{C}Abd al-Rahmān b. Muljam (d. 658/660) 185

^{C}Abd al-^{C}Azīz, brother of Caliph ^{C}Abd al-Malik xxii, 202, 204

^{C}Abd Allāh b. ^{C}Abd al-Malik (*fl.* 702, 704) 78, 206

^{C}Abd Allāh b. ^{C}Abd al-Muttalib, father of Muhammad 144

^{C}Abd Allāh al-Ma$^\supset$mūn, Caliph (813-833) 83

^{C}Abd Allāh b. al-Zubayr (*fl.* 682/3) 197, 198, 200, 201

Abgar, king of Edessa (1st cent.) 203n, 248n

Abouna, A. 103

Abraham, father of Ishmael 8, 144

Abramowski, R. 41, 86, 87, 98n, 102

Abū 'l-Anwar, in error for Abū 'l-A^{C}war 176n

Abū 'l-A^{C}war, Arab general (fl. 654) 176+n, 179, 180+n, 186n

Abū Badr, Arab governor of Edessa (fl. 640) 77, 163

Abū Bakr b. Abī Quhāfa, Caliph (632-634) 38, 43, 49, 51, 52, 57, 66, 76, 107, 144-146, 150, 168n, 169, 181

Abū Bakr, grandfather of Muhammad 181

Abū 'l-Faraj = Barhebraeus, q.v.

Abū Ju^{C}ayd(id) of Jerusalem (fl. 636) 161+n

Abū Jafnā = Nu^{C}mān b. al-Mundhir, q.v.

Abū Mūsā al-Ash^{C}arī 184

Abū Qārib = Yazīd b. Abī Sakhr 201n

Abū Sufyān, Arab general (fl. 636) 157

Abū ^{C}Ubayda = ^{C}Umar b. ^{C}Abd Allāh b. al-Jarrāh, q.v.

Acacius, Patriarch of Antioch (fl. 456) 13, 14

Acacius, Patriarch of Constantinople (471-489) 14

Acindynus, governor of Harrān (d. c.589) 114

Adam, the first man 8, 51, 91, 131, 222, 249

Adavīn = Dwīn, q.v.

Adarmahān, Persian general (6th cent.) 16

Adbeel, son of Ishmael 144

Aegaean Sea, The, 'the Islands of the Sea' (I) 211n, 232, 237

Aerts, W.J. 227

Africa (I), African xi, xiv, 126, 167, 194, 237, 238

Africanus, Sextus Julius (fl. 200) 91, 95n

Agapius of Manbīj, historian (d. c. 950) lxiv, 32n, 96, 97, 111-221nn passim, 257

Agathias, historian (6th cent.) xviiin

Ahīshmō, Nestorian bishop of Edessa (fl. 609) 126n

^{C}Ā$^⊃$isha, favourite wife of the prophet Muhammad 144

al-Ajnādayn (II) 19n, 149, 156n

Akhlat (I) 205n

Aleppo (V) = Beroea 26, 82n, 84, 104, 107, 125n, 160n, 179n, 188n, 210

Alexander the Great (4th cent. BC) xxxiv, 6, 13, 43, 45, 51, 173, 223, 239n, 246+n

Alexander, P.J. xxvin, 222-224, 227, 237, 239n, 241n, 242n

Alexandria by Egypt (IV) xxiiin, 17, 38, 39, 93, 94, 126n, 128+n, 146, 159, 160, 173-175

^CAlī b. Abī Tālib (cf. al-^CAbbās) (d. 658/660 ?) 29, 30+n, 31n, 44, 59n, 66, 77, 108, 161, 181-185, 187, 195+n, 257

Amasya (III) 209

Amazonius, bishop of Edessa (fl. 550) 203

Amida (V) = Diyarbakir 21, 38, 53, 57, 58, 68, 70, 77, 87, 122n, 163, 165n

^CĀmir, ^Cal-M.^CA. A. xivn

Amorium (III) 34, 35, 87, 168n, 211-214

Amos (?), a church at Antioch? 16

^CAmr b. al-^CĀs, Arab general (fl. 656) 144n, 158, 160n, 183-185

^CAmr b. Sa^Cd = ? ^CUmayr b. Sa^Cd, q.v.

^CAmr b. Sa^Cīd b. al-^CĀs, grandfather of following (fl. 635) 144

^CAmr b. Sa^Cīd b. al-^CĀs al-Ashdaq al-Umawī (fl. 685) 198+n, 200

Anastasius I, Emperor (491-518) 11, 13, 21, 26, 111

Anastasius II, Emperor = Artemius (713-715) 62, 65, 81, 110, 210, 211

Anastasius, Byzantine general (fl. 590) 116

Anastasius, Patriarch of Antioch (fl. 571, 590) 27, 117, 125n

Anastasius the Sinaite (7th cent.) xixn

Anastasius, son of Andrew of Edessa (d. c.693) 202

Anatolikón Theme (III) 211

Anchialus (I) 112n

Ancyra = Ankara, q.v.

Anderson, A.R. 223n

Andrew, the Edessene (fl. 690) 202

Andrew the Eunuch, cubicularius (fl. 667) 189-192

Andrew, son of Troilus (fl. 668) 193

Andronicus, chronographer 91

Andronicus, Patriarch of the Copts (fl. 628) 39

Anhel (V) 100

Ankara (III) = Ancyra 133+n
Ankara, Synod (allegedly 116) 21
Annianus of Alexandria, chronographer (*fl.* 412) xxiv, 91
Antakya = Antioch on the Orontes, q.v.
Antaradus (V) = Ṭarṭūs 177
Antes 112n
Anthimus, Patriarch of Constantinople (536) 13
Antichrist, 'Son of Perdition', 'Deceiver', the 74, 233, 239-242, 247-249, 251
Antigon (?), fortress 80
Antioch on the Orontes (V) = Antakya xiv, 6-8, 11, 14-16, 19, 21, 46, 78, 93, 94, 107, 113, 114, 120, 125n, 127, 141, 146, 149n, 152n, 156, 158, 163, 179n, 205n, 210
Antioch in Pisidia (III) 209n
Antioch, Synod (allegedly 220) 21
Antius, king, brother of Byzas 220
Anzitene = Bēth Ūrtōyē, q.v.
Apamea (V) 16, 25, 127
Aphrahaṭ, Syriac author (4th cent.) 11
Apostles, church at Constantinople 221
Apostles, church at Ctesiphon 118n
Apsimar = Tiberius II, Emperor, q.v.
Aqīd, son of Ishmael 144
^cAqūlō = al-Kūfa, q.v.
Arabia (I) 39, 128n
Arabia Felix (I) 129
Arabia, Roman (IV) 150
Arabissus Tripotamus (V) 13, 18, 111, 112n
Arab = 'Christian Arab' (q.v.) 55, 57, 58, 71, 78, 113
^cAraba 19n
^cAraboth (II) 19n
Aradus Constantini (V) = Arwād 58, 68, 108, 173n, 177+n
Aramaean, 'son of Aram' 60
Araq, of Ḥarrān 208
Ardashīr I, Shah, son of Pābag (227-243) 178f.n

Ardashīr III, Shah (628-630) 18, 38, 142+n
Ardigān, Byzantine general 156+n
Arius, heresiarch (d. c.336) 28
Arian(ism) 17, 18, 20, 89n
Armalos, 'king of the Romans' 223
Armalos, 'king of Rome' 223
Armenia (I), see also Inner Armenia 20, 21, 125n, 137, 138, 153n, 156, 158, 167n, 200+n, 205+n, 206, 232n, 244, 246
Armenia I 114n
Armenia III 112n
Armenia IV 165n, 210n
Armenian 57, 70, 86, 109, 137, 156, 159, 164n, 165, 168n, 193+n, 202, 205, 206, 210+n, 237, 238
Armenian division of the Byzantine army 16
Arsenias, river 62
'al-Artabūn', 'Aretion', 'Tribunus'? 156n
Arwād = Aradus Constantini, q.v.
Arzanene (IV) 200n, 205n
Arzūn = Arzanene, q.v.
Ashbrook-Harvey, S. xxiiin
Asia, continent xi, 137, 221n
Asia Minor (I, III) xviiin, 29, 39, 68, 211n
Asia, province in Asia Minor (III) 62, 80, 84, 186n, 213, 214, 219, 220n
Assyria (I) 126n, 137, 138
Athanasius, bishop of Arabissus (fl. 630) 143n
Athanasius Bar Gūmōyē, noble of Edessa (fl. 690) xxii, lviii, 93, 100, 109, 202-204
Athanasius I, Patriarch of the Jacobites (603-31) 16, 25, 38, 42, 55, 67, 76, 142+n, 143, 258, 259
Athanasius II, Patriarch of the Jacobites (684-7) 60, 67, 82
al-Athārib = Litarba, q.v.
Athens xvi
cAtiyya, Arab governor (fl. 698) 78, 205n
Atlas zur Kirchengeschichte 264

Attic language 87

Augusta, consort of the Emperor Maurice 111, 112n

Aurelian, Emperor (270-275) 20

Avar xivn, xix, 112n

^{C}Ayn Gērō = ^{C}Ayn al-Jarr, q.v.

^{C}Ayn al-Jarr (V) 79

Ayyūb b. Sulaymān b. ^{C}Abd al-^{C}Azīz (d. 717) 217

Āzarmēdukht, daughter of Chosroēs II, Queen of Persia 39, 143

al-Azdī, historian 19n, 145n, 156n

Azerbaijan (IV) 137, 200n

Baalbek (V) = Heliopolis 149, 155, 194n

Baanēs, Byzantine general (d. 634) 107, 149

Babylon (IV B) 245+n

Babylonia (IV) 186

Babylōnē = Fustāt, q.v.

Badrān, ^{C}A.al-Q. 156n

Baghdād, founded AD 752 (IV B) 165n

al-Bakhtarī, Arab general (fl. 717) 212

al-Balādhurī, historian 19n, 169n

al-Balqāɔ (IV) 150, 155

Banū Tanūkh, Christian Arab tribe 71, 171+n

Bar Bahlūl, Syriac lexicographer (10th cent.) 245n

Bardaysōn, philosopher of Edessa (fl. 200) 20

Barhebraeus, Gregory Abū 'l-Faraj (d. 1286) 85f, 126n

Barnish, S. xviiin

Barsawm, I.E. 7, 10, 75, 83, 103

Bashear, S. xxivn

Basil, bishop of Emesa (fl. 630) 142n

Basil, bishop of Kafar Tūthō (fl. 605) 122n

Basra (IV) xxii, 206n

Baššār b. Burd (715-785) xxii

Batnōn da-S^{e}rūgh (V) 57, 59, 60, 68, 77, 78, 81, 171, 195

Baumstark, K.A. 7, 73n

Beacham, R.C. xvin

Beeston, A.F.L. xxii

Benjamin, Patriarch of the Copts (*fl.* 628) 39, 107, 158-160

Beroea = Aleppo, q.v.

Bēth Hālē (IV) xxin

Bēth Ma^{c}dē (V) 87, 164

Bēth Ōrōmōyē (IV) 138

Bēth Qustān (V) 76

Beth Sacharya (II) 4

Bethsaida (II) 240, 248+n

Bēth S^{e}virīnō (V) 75

Bēth Shemesh, Gate, the 'Sun-Gate' of Edessa 118

Bēth Ūrtōyē in Armenia IV (V) = Anzitene 165n

B^{e}nōthō, monastery (V) 6, 19, 150+n

Bidez, J. 113n

Bithynia (III) 39, 186n, 211

Black Mountain, The (V) = Mons Amanus 62, 195

Black Sea, The (I, III) = Pontus 39, 112n, 128n, 186n, 206

Blastīn ? = Euchaita, q.v.

Boor, C. de lxv

Bōrān, daughter of Chosroēs II, Queen of Persia (631) 39, 143

Bosphorus (III) 63

Bostra (IV) = Busrā 150, 156n, 183n

Boukellarion division of the Byzantine army 116

Brice, W. 264

Britain xiv

Brock, S.P. xxin, xxviin, 1, 2n, 3n, 27n, 30n, 45, 152n, 171n, 225n, 226n, 228, 230n, 258

Brooks, E.W. xxvn, lxiv, 1, 2n, 5-7, 20n, 41, 75, 83, 95n, 100, 258

Brown, P.R.L. xixn, xxn

'Buccinator', 'Buqantar', Byzantine general 156+n

Bucellarion = Boukellarion, q.v.

Budge, E.A.W. 223n

al-Bukhārī, historian 156n

Bulgar (I) 80, 84, 112n, 120n, 207, 215, 216, 218n

Bulgaria 80

'Burayda' = Yazīd, q.v.

Busr b. Abī Artat (*fl.* 663) 32n

Busse, H. 161n

Butler, A. 156n

Buz, 'king of the Greeks' 223

Busrā = Bostra, q.v.

Byzantia, 'daughter of Buz, king of the Greeks' 223

Byzantium xiii, xviii, xxiii, xxxi, 6n, 11, 50, 65, 73, 110, 141, 210n, 219, 220, 223, 252

Byzas, 'king of Asia and of Thrace' 219, 220

Caesarea in Cappadocia (III) 69, 77, 127, 168n, 205n

Caesarea in Palestine (II) 19n, 57, 68, 69, 108, 146, 147, 165, 179n

Cain, son of Adam and Eve 31

Callinicum (V) = Raqqa 17, 184

Callinicus of Baalbek, inventor of 'Greek Fire' (*fl.* 671) 194n

Cambridge, Cambridgeshire 244

Cameron, Alan xvin

Cameron, Averil xivn, xvn, xviin, xxn, 228

Canard, M. 32n

Canivet, P. 229

Capernaum (II) 240, 248

Cappadocia (V), Cappadocian 20, 62, 125, 168n, 211n, 232n, 237, 238

Carthage (I) xiv

Caspian region, the (I) 137

Castle of Tūr ᶜAbdīn (V) 38

Cecrops, king of Athens 9

Cetura, father of Midian 130n

Chabot, J.-B. xxviin, xxxii, lxiv, 53, 54, 61n, 71, 72, 85n, 92n, 93n, 98n, 102, 103, 130n

Chalcedon (III) 119, 125n, 128n, 213+n, 214

Chalcedon, Council (451), Chalcedonian etc. xii, xiii, xxiii, xxx, 10-13, 22, 25-29, 38, 48, 66, 69, 86, 89n, 92-97, 101, 106, 113, 114n, 118n, 120, 122, 125, 126n, 128, 140, 141, 143n, 148, 153n, 159, 160, 204+n, 226, 252, 258

Chalcis = Qēnneshrīn, q.v.

Charrae = Harrān, q.v.

China 24, 98, 256, 261, 262

Chorazin (II) 239, 240, 248+n

Chosroēs I, Shah, Anōshirvān (531-579) 14, 16

Chosroēs II, Shah, Parwēz (590, 591-628) 17, 18, 24, 36, 39, 88, 105, 106, 115-117, 119-129, 133-138, 143+n, 151+n, 255, 256, 262, 263

Chosroēs III, Shah (631) 39

Christ ('the Messiah,' Jesus, 'our Lord' etc.) xi, xii, xvii, xx, 9+n, 10, 15, 21, 22, 25, 31, 47, 48, 71, 73, 74, 94, 119n, 131+n, 132n, 170, 203n, 224, 225, 235, 238, 240, 242, 243n, 245, 248, 249, 262

Christian, used to mean 'Jacobite' 115

Christian Arab 78, 145, 146, 158, 166, 169n, 171n

Cilicia (III), Cilician 206, 232n, 237, 238

Circesium (IV) 17

Cius (III) 35

Claudius, 'king of Alexandria' 223

Claudius, Emperor (41-54) 245n

Clysma (IV) = Qulzum, Dhunb/Dhanab al-Timsāh 198n

Collins, J. xxvi

Conon, leader of a sect of anti-Chalcedonians (fl. 619) 17

Conrad, L.I. xxivn, 97+n, 98, 173n, 176n, 228

Constans II, Emperor (641-668) 30, 31, 33, 58, 65, 97, 108, 109, 167, 178, 179, 186-189, 193, 199

Constantina on Cyprus (V) = Salamis 174, 176

Constantina = Tella, q.v.

Constantine I, Emperor (307-337) xi, xii, xvii, 8-10, 20, 21, 86, 90, 91, 110, 219-221

Constantine III, Emperor (641) 39, 58, 65, 128n, 166, 167

Constantine IV, Emperor (668-685) 31, 33, 60, 61, 65, 89, 109, 188n, 193-197, 199

Constantine V, Emperor (741-775) 95n

Constantine, successor to Anastasius = Theodosius III, q.v.

'Constantine', successor to Constantine III = Constans II, q.v.

Constantinople (III), 'the (Royal) City' xi, xii, xiv, xvin, xviii-xx, xxiv, xxv, xxvii, 13, 15, 21, 25-27, 32n, 51, 62-64, 68, 86, 88, 90, 93-95, 101, 103, 106, 108, 110-113, 118, 119, 125, 127, 135-138, 158, 160, 164n, 178, 179, 187-189, 193, 206, 207, 210-221, 225, 255

Constantinople, Council (381) 22

Constantinople, Council, 'the Sixth Council' (680/1) xx, 25, 26, 29, 88, 89

Cook, M. 169n

Copt xxiii, 94, 101

Cornell, T. 264

Cos (III) 180n

Cosmas, bishop of Cilician Epiphania (fl. 630) 142n

Cosmas Indicopleustes (6th cent.) xvn

Cosmas, son of Araby 140

Crete (I) 18, 180n

Crispus, in error for Priscus, q.v.

Crone, P. xxiin, xxivn, 169n

Crusades xiii

Ctesiphon (IV B) 117, 138, 153, 154

Cubicularius, in lieu of a name 149n

Cush, Cushite, equivalent to Ethiopia, Ethiopian, q.v.

Cutler, A. xvn

Cyprus (IV) 58, 68, 108, 173, 174, 176, 200, 205

Cyriac (the former), bishop of Amida (d. c.608) 55, 126

Cyriac (the latter), bishop of Amida (d. 623) 56

Cyriac, bishop of Edessa (649-665) 58, 59n

Cyriac, Patriarch of the Jacobites (793-817) 99n

Cyril, Patriarch of Alexandria (412-444) 143n

Cyrrhus (V) 205n

Cyrus, Chalcedonian bishop of Edessa (628-639) 153n

Cyrus, governor of Edessa (fl. 625) 99, 133, 134n

Cyrus, Patriarch of Alexandria (fl. 625) 38, 39, 158-160

Cyrus of Batnae, priest, church historian (fl. 582) 85n, 92

Cyzicus (III) 205

Dābiq, the Meadow of (V) 80, 84

Dacia (I) 112n

Dagron, G. xvin, xixn, xxviin

al-Dahhāk b. Qays, Arab pretender (d. 684) 197, 199

Damascus (V) 2-4, 17, 30, 32, 76, 107, 128, 145, 149-151, 154-157, 160, 165+n, 169, 170n, 177-179, 181, 183, 184, 186+n, 187, 189, 192, 196-200, 202, 204, 206, 208, 211

Damianites, sect of anti-Chalcedonians in Egypt (c. 618) 17

Dan, the Tribe of 241-242

Daniel, bishop of Edessa (665-84) 172n

Daniel, bishop of Harrān (fl. 630) 142n

Daniel, prophet of Israel xxvi, 230

Daniel, son of Moses, historian (fl. 750) 92, 93, 100, 103, 204n

Daniel ^cUzzōyō, bishop of Tella etc. (614-633) 76

Danube, river (I) 20

Dara (V) 16, 17, 21, 24, 38, 57, 68, 76, 77, 117+n, 122, 163

Dastgird (IV B) = Sōqartō 134, 138

Dāthin (II) 19n

David the Armenian, Byzantine general (d. c.643) 86, 87, 107, 108, 164+n, 165+n

David, bishop of Harrān (8th cent.) 83

David, king of Israel, prophet 167, 240, 249

Dawūd, son of the Caliph Sulaymān (fl. 717) 80

de Boor, C. lxv

de Goeje, M.J. xivn, 4n, 19n, 149n, 155n, 156n

de Halleux, A. 27+n

Déroche, V. xivn, xvn, xixn, 55n

Dhū 'l-Kalā^c 145n

Diakonov, A.P. 85n

Dickens, Charles xxi

Dīnār b. Dīnār, Arab general (fl. 695) 78

Dindorf, L. lxiv

Diocletian, Emperor (284-305) 20, 95

Dionysius of Tel-Maḥrē, historian, Patriarch of the Jacobites (817-845) xxv, xxvi, xxviiin, xxix, xxxii, xxxiii, lviii, 9-11, 19n, 27n, 35, 36, 69, 85-105 *passim*, 135n, 141n, 144n, 155n, 156n, 166f.n, 168n, 169n, 171n, 173n, 179n, 183n, 204n, 216n, 219n, 221n, 251, 252, 255-259, 262, 263

Dioscorus, Patriarch of Alexandria (444-451) 22

Diyarbakir = Amida (q.v.) xxin, 53

Domitian, bishop of Melitene (578-602) 17, 111, 117, 125, 126n, 263

Donner, F.M. xxin, 4n, 145n

Dothan 19n

Drijvers, H.J.W. xxin, xxviin, 228

'al-Drungār', i.e. Drungarius 156n

Ducellier, A. xxivn

Dumah, son of Ishmael 144

Dussaud, R. 264

Dwin (I) 57, 68, 70

Edessa (V) = Ūrhōy, Urfa, Edessene xiii, xxv, xxix, 9, 11, 17, 21, 38-40, 55, 57, 59n, 60, 67, 68, 70, 76, 77, 88, 93, 99, 100, 103, 104, 106, 115, 116, 118, 120-126, 133, 134+n, 136n, 139-141, 147n, 149, 153n, 163, 165, 193+n, 195+n, 200, 202, 203+n, 243, 248+n, 255, 258, 263

'Edessenes' meaning 'Chalcedonians of Edessa' 203f.n

Egypt (IV), Egyptian, see also 'Copt' xiv, xxii, 23, 24, 38, 39, 94, 100, 107, 126n, 128, 137, 142, 146, 158-160, 173-175, 183, 185, 186, 188, 195n, 199, 202-204, 209n, 216, 232, 238

Ehnesh (V) 23, 71, 72, 73n, 252

Eirēnē, churches dedicated to = Hagia Eirēnē, q.v.

Elijah, biographer of John of Tella (*fl.* 537) 91, 92n

Elijah, chronographer, of Nisibis (11th cent.) 41

Elijah, Patriarch of the Jacobites (709-724) 45, 67

Elijah, priest (*fl.* 636) 2

Elijah, prophet 234, 242n, 248+n

Elustriya, governor of Samosata (*fl.* 705) 208+n

Emesa (V) = al-Ḥims 2-4, 17, 33, 107, 127, 143n, 148, 149, 151, 155, 156, 169n, 170n, 180n

Emmaus (II) 162

England xxi

Ennaton of Alexandria, near Alexandria 126n

Enoch 242n, 248+n

Ephesus (III) 211n

Ephesus, Council, I (431) 22

Ephesus, Council, II (449) 22

Ephraem, Syriac hymnographer (d. 373) 16, 21, 172+n, 250+n

Epiphania in Cilicia (V), see Cosmas, bishop of Epiphania

Epiphanius, bishop of Salamis (367-403) 175

Ethiopia (I), Ethiopian 128n, 223, 224, 237, 240, 249

Euchaita (III) 108, 166

Eudocia, daughter of the Emperor Heraclius 137

Eugenius, leader of a sect of anti-Chalcedonians (*fl.* 619) 17

Euphrates, river (IV, IV B and V) xi, xiii, xxxi, 6n, 11, 13, 16-18, 21, 23, 56, 71, 122n, 125+n, 126n, 129, 140-142, 147, 151, 160n, 163, 171, 184, 187, 188n, 197n, 200, 206

Europe (I) xi, 137, 215n

Eusebius, bishop of Caesarea, Palestine (d. 339) xxv, xxix, xxx, 9-11, 42, 69, 70, 91, 93, 243n

Euthymius, monastery of Abba (II) 31

Eutyches, archimandrite (*fl.* 448) 22

Evagrius, ecclesiastical historian (d. *c.*600) 113n

Eve, the first woman 222

Evetts, B. xxiiin

Ewald, P. xvin

al-Fadl, Arab general (*fl.* 667) 192, 193

Fāṭima, daughter of the Prophet Muhammad 161, 185

Fehim, Paul and Peter, father and son, of Gargar 103

Fiey, J.M. 99n, 103, 212n

Flavian, Patriarch of Constantinople (447-449) 22

Fletcher, A. 260, 261

Flusin, B. xixn

France xxi, 75, 103

Frankia xiv

Frendo, J.D.C. xviiin

Fustāt (I) = Babylōnē 159, 203

Gabitha = al-Jābiya, q.v.

Gabriel, the archangel 249

Gabriel, bishop of Dara etc. (634-648) 76, 77

Gab^{C}ot Ramta 224, 230

Galatia (III) 125+n, 133, 136, 186n, 211n

Galilee (II) 2, 4, 128n, 195

Gangra, Council (340/341) 21

Gargar (V) 103

Gargarūm = al-Jurjūma, q.v.

Garzan (V) 200n

Gaul xiv, 194n

Gaza (II) 18, 19+n

Gehenna 225, 242, 250

Gelder, Geert Jan van 264

Gennadius I, Patriarch of Constantinople (458-71) 13

George, bishop of the Christian Arabs (*fl.* 688) 78

George, bishop of S^{e}rūgh etc. (*fl.* 697) 78

George, church of Saint, at Aleppo 104

George of Raggath, historian = (?) George Syncellus, q.v.

George, Patriarch of the Jacobites (758/9-790) 99n

George, prefect (húparkhos) (*fl.* 617) 55, 68

George, stylite of Tar^{C}ēl (d. 700) 78

George Syncellus, chronographer (d. after 810) 91, 95, 98

Germaniceia (V) = Mar^{C}ash 66, 71, 74

Germanus, Byzantine general (*fl.* 588) 112n, 113

Gero, S. 223n

Gethsemane, the Garden of 31

Gibb, H.A.R. xxivn

Gīhōn, = Jayhān, river, q.v.

Gil, M. 19n

Ginzel, F.K. 260

God, as agent in history xii, xxi, xxviii, 9, 15, 18, 20, 24, 31, 35,
    46, 47, 73, 86, 110, 126n, 141, 148, 152f.n, 153, 158, 163, 165,

170, 175, 179n, 220, 231, 232, 246, 247

Goeje, M.J. de, see 'de Goeje'

Gog and Magog 223, 246

Golan Heights (II) 4

Golden Gate of Constantinople 215

Golden Horn, The 221n

Golgotha 31, 48, 153n, 224, 240, 249

Gosman, M. 228

Greece (I) xi, xiv

Greek (see also 'Attic') xi, xiv, xvi, xxiv, xxxiv, 9, 11, 13n, 32, 35+n, 43, 45, 48, 80, 91, 93, 95-98, 101, 120n, 126n, 179, 180, 191, 193n, 195n, 204n, 209, 222-250 *passim*, 252

Gregorius, incumbent Jacobite bishop of Aleppo 82n, 104

Gregory = Barhebraeus, q.v.

Gregory, patrician posted in Africa (*fl.* 610) 126

Gregory, patríkios of Africa (*fl.* 644) 167

Gregory I, Pope (590-604) xvin

Gregory, son of Heraclius's brother Theodoric 178, 188n

Griffith, S. 49n

Gubbō Barrōyō, monastery of, 'in the desert' 45, 79

Gümüşgün = Ehnesh, q.v.

Guidi, I. lxiv

Gūmōyō, rich family of Edessa 99

Gunada, region of Egypt? 202

Gūryō, Syriac historian of 6th-7th cent. 85n

Ḥabīb, bishop of Edessa (*fl.* 710) 76

Ḥabīb, general of the Arabs (*fl.* 653) 58, 68, 167n, 183n

Ḥabīb b. Maslama, governor of Emesa (*fl.* 634) 155, 156, 160

Ḥadar, son of Ishmael 144

Hadrian, Emperor (117-138) 21

Hagar, Hagarenes, Sons/Children of Hagar 10, 49, 51, 60, 107, 130n, 144, 168n, 173, 186n, 230, 244, 245

Hage, W. xlvii, 67, 257

Hagia Eirēnē, church at Arabissus Tripotamus 13, 18

Hagia Eirēnē, church at Constantinople 221

al-Ḥajjāj b. Yūsuf, Arab governor (*fl.* 690)   109, 200, 201

Haldon, J.F.   xvn, xviiin, xxn

Halleux, A. de   lxiv, 27+n

Hamath (V), Epiphania in Phoenicia   165n

Ḥārith b. Kaʿb, Arab governor (*fl.* 703)   208n

Ḥarrān (V) = Charrae   17, 77, 78, 83, 105, 109, 114, 141, 163, 165n, 187, 208+n

Hartmann, L.M.   xvin

Ḥarūrāᵓ (IV B), Harūrite   186n

al-Ḥasan, son of ʿAlī b. Abī Ṭālib (d. *c.*661)   31n, 182, 185

Ḥassān b. Mālik, emir of Jordan (*fl.* 685)   198, 199

Ḥawrān (V)   155

Hawting, G.R.   xvn

Ḥayy al-Suryān, quarter in Aleppo   104

Ḥebron   238

Hebrews, the kingdom of the   230

Helena Augusta, mother of Constantine I   245n

Helenopolis, named after Helena Augusta   221

Hellas = Greece (q.v.)   232, 237

Hendy, M.   xvn

Heraclonas, Emperor (641)   137, 167

Heraclius, Emperor (610-641)   xviin, xx, xxix, xxx, xxxiii, lviii, 5-7, 10-13, 18, 23-28, 37-40, 50-52, 56-58, 65, 68, 81, 84, 85n, 99, 106-108, 120n, 127-129, 134-149, 156+n, 158, 161-163, 166n, 167+n, 178, 179n, 188n, 230n, 253, 255, 256, 261

Heraclius, father of the Emperor Heraclius   126

Heraclius, son and co-successor of Constans II (668-681)   188n, 194+n, 196

Herodotus (5th cent. BC)   xi

Herrin, Judith   xvn

Ḥesnō d-Kīfō (V)   122n

Hespel, R.   54

Hexapolis (V)   209n

Hieropolis = Mabbūgh, q.v.

al-Ḥimṣ = Emesa, q.v.

al-Ḥira (IV B) 30, 151
Ḥirtian 151, 152
Hishām, Caliph (724-743) 50
Hoffmann, J.G.E. 240n
Hokwerda, H. 229
Honorius, governor of Harrān = Iyarius, q.v.
Hormizd, rival of Yazdgird (d. 632 or 633) 39, 143, 151n
Hormizd IV, Shah (579-590) 112n, 115
Hoyland, R. xxivn, xxvin, lviii, 2n, 96n, 98n, 101n, 145n, 255
Hudhayfa (d. 658) 29
Huns xix, 14n
al-Ḥusayn b. ᶜAlī b. Abī Ṭālib (d. 680) 182, 185, 186, 195
Ibn ᶜAsākir, historian 144n, 145n, 156n
Ibn Hishām, historian xxviin
Ibn Ḥubayb (?), usurper at Rhesaina (fl. 685) 199n
Ibn Khālid = ᶜAbd al-Rahmān b. Khālid, q.v.
Ibn Qanāṭir, Ibn Qāṭūr, Ibn Nāṭūr 156n
Ibn Saᶜd, historian 144n
Ibn Saᶜīd = ᶜAmr b. Saᶜīd b. al-ᶜĀs, q.v.
Ibn al-Zubayr = ᶜAbd Allāh b. al-Zubayr, q.v.
Ibrāhim b. al-Ashtar (fl. 686) 201
Ibrāhim, Arab pretender (9th cent.) 83
Iconium (III) = Konya 211n
Ignatius, bishop of Antioch (martyred 108) 20
Ignatius, bishop of Melitene, historian (d. 1094) 103
Indian 14, 77
Inner Armenia 62
Iraq 201
Isaac the Syrian, Saint, mystic (late 7th cent.) 222
Isaiah, bishop of Edessa (fl. 630) 39, 99, 125, 140+n, 142n, 153n
Isauria (III), Isaurian 188n, 237, 238
Ishmaelite, Sons of Ishmael, Ishmael himself 45, 130n, 141, 144, 205,
    224, 230, 231, 234, 236, 237, 243, 245+n, 247
Israel xii, xixn
Istanbul = Constantinople 103, 234

Italy (I) xiv, 194n, 219, 220n

Īwannis, bishop of Dara (fl. 842) 90, 91

Īwannis Rusafōyō, noble of Edessa (fl. 590) 87, 98, 99n, 106, 122-124, 135

ᶜIyād b. Ghanm, Arab general (fl. 639) 57, 77, 162, 163+n, 165+n

Iyarius, governor of Harrān (d. c.589) 114

al-Jābiya (II) = Gabitha 1, 3, 4, 57, 68, 150, 198, 199, 224, 230n

Jacob, bishop of Edessa, 'Baradaeus' (d. 578) xiii, 16

Jacob, bishop of Edessa, 'Philoponus', chronographer = James, q.v.

Jacob, bishop of Sᵉrūgh, 'the Teacher' (d. 521) 15

Jacob of Cyrrhus, monastery of (V) 78

Jacob, founder of the monastery of Bᵉnōthō 150n

Jacob = Israel, father of Hebrew Patriarchs 8, 83, 225, 241, 247

Jacob the Jew (fl. 617) 55

Jacob, monastery of Saint, at Kayshūm (V) 172n

Jacobite, 'Severan', '(Syrian) Orthodox' xiii, xxiii, xxvi, xxx, 10-12, 25, 26, 28-31, 35, 66n, 74, 77n, 78, 79, 82, 84-86, 92, 94, 102, 104, 105, 113, 118, 125, 126n, 140, 141, 143n, 148, 153n, 158, 159, 210n, 225, 226, 251+n, 252, 257-259

Jalūlāᵓ (IV) 154

James, bishop of Edessa, chronographer (d. 708) = Jacob of Edessa xxiin, xxv, xxx, lxiv, 36, 40-44, 49, 59n, 61, 70, 79, 82, 92, 93, 102, 207n, 243n, 257, 258

Japhet, son of Noah 223

Jayhān, river (V), also written Jayhūn = Gīhōn) 71, 74

al-Jazīra = northern Mesopotamia, q.v.

Jeffery, A. xxin

Jeremiah, the prophet 133

Jericho (II) 31

Jerusalem (II) xixn, xxiv, 4, 9, 17, 19, 31+n, 47, 48, 55, 68, 106, 107, 128, 141, 142, 155, 156n, 160-162, 167+n, 224, 225, 239, 242, 248

Jetur, son of Ishmael 144

Jew, Jewish xi, xiv, xv, xix, 19, 26, 40, 47, 48, 55, 68, 79, 125n, 128, 130n, 132n, 139, 147n, 161, 167+n, 169, 170, 180n, 248, 251

Job, Righteous 173n

John of Phenek, author (*fl.* 686) 230n, 236n

John the Baptist, church, at Damascus 170, 208

John the Baptist, church, at Amida 58

John the Baptist, monastery (II) 31

John, bishop of the Christian Arabs (d. 650) 55, 57, 58

John, bishop of Cyrrhus (*fl.* 630) 142n

John, bishop of Ephesus, historian (d. 586) 69, 70, 91+n, 102, 112n, 127n

John, bishop of Tella, son of Crassus (d. 538) 15, 92n

John the Evangelist 20

John, Byzantine general (*fl.* 590) 116, 121

John, Byzantine governor of Mesopotamia (*fl.* 640) 162, 163

John of Antioch, historian = Malalas, q.v.

John of Antioch, historian, not Malalas 91n

John of Asia, historian = John, bishop of Ephesus, q.v.

John the Lydian (6th cent.) xv, xvi

John, Patriarch of Alexandria (*fl.* 571) 27

John III, Patriarch of Constantinople (565-577) 27, 28

John I, Patriarch of the Jacobites (632-648) 16, 39, 45, 57, 67, 77, 108, 170, 171, 188, 259, 261

John III, Patriarch of the Jacobites (846-873) 83

John, Patriarch of Jerusalem (*fl.* 571) 27

John III, Pope (561-574) 28

John, stylite of Litarba, chronographer (*fl.* 724) xxv, 36, 49, 53, 92, 102

John, son of Aphtonia, founder of Qēnneshrē (5th cent.) 172+n

John, son of Mizīzī, rebel (*c.* 677) 195n

John, son of Samuel, historian (7th or 8th cent.) 92, 100

John, son of Sargūn, of Damascus (*fl.* 634) 155

Jonah, bishop of Edessa (*fl.* 610) 126n

Jonah, rabbi (*fl.* 617) 55

Jones, A.H.M. xvin

Jongeling, K. 228

Joppa (II) 224, 239, 247n

Jordan, province (II) xviin, xviiin, 19n, 128n, 155, 176n, 198

Joseph, a Jew of Edessa (*fl.* 629) 139

Josephus, Jewish historian (1st cent.) 20, 91

Joshua, stylite, of Zuqnīn (8th or 9th cent.) 53

Jovian, Emperor (363-364) 240n, 249+n

Julian II, Emperor, 'the Apostate' (360-363) 21

Julian the Ancient, hermit (d. 367) 16

Julian I, Patriarch of the Jacobites (592-593) 16, 67, 76, 119

Julian II, Patriarch of the Jacobites (688-708) 61, 67, 78, 79, 82, 86, 87

Julian, shrine of the martyr, at Antioch 16

al-Jurjūma (V) = Gargarūm 195n

al-Jūsiya (V) 148, 149n

Justin I, Emperor (518-527) 112

Justin II, Emperor (565-578) xvin, xviin, 13, 27, 28, 54, 66, 112

Justinian I, Emperor (527-565) xii, xv, xvi, 13, 21, 27, 54, 66, 85n, 100, 112

Justinian II, Emperor (685-695; 705-711) xxvii, 61, 65, 78, 81, 109, 196, 199, 200, 205-208, 210

Ka^{c}ba, at Mecca 133n, 178, 201, 240n

Kaegi, W.E. xxin, 255

Kafar Tūthō (V) 122n

Karbalā$^⊃$ (IV B) 185, 186n

Kardīgān, Persian general (d. 630) 135+n, 136, 142

Kawad I, Shah (488-496, 498/9-531) 14

Kayser, C. xxiin

Kayshūm (V) 172n

Kazhdan, A. xvn

Kennedy, H. xviiin, xxiiin

Keydell, R. xviiin

'Khagan', unnamed king of the Khazars (*fl.* 628) 137

'Khagan', another king of the Khazars (*fl.* 705) 207+n

Khālid b. Sa^{c}īd b. al-^{c}Ās, Arab general (*fl.* 635) 144n

Khālid b. al-Walīd, Arab general (*fl.* 635) 149, 154, 155, 160

Khazar (I) 112n, 137, 207

Khāzir, river (IV) 197n

Khoury, A.-T. xxivn

Khoury, R. G. 59n

Khurāsān (I) 178

KLYH ͗, river 150n

Koran = Qur ͗ān, q.v.

Kortekaas, G.A.A. 227

Krikor the Armenian, Byzantine general (fl. 636) 156

al-Kūfa (IV B) = ᶜAqūlō 30n, 151, 165n, 171+n, 178n, 183-186, 197, 201

Kush, Kushite, equivalent to Ethiopia, Ethiopian, q.v.

Kushyat, daughter of Pil (q.v.) 223, 240, 249

Kynēgion, place of execution at Edessa 121

Lammens, H. 51n

Land, J.P.N. 5, 7, 19n

Langobard 112n

Lapethus (IV) 176, 177

Latin xvi+n, 12, 35, 222, 233n, 227

Lavenant, R. 228

Lebanon (IV), Mount 27, 62, 109, 195, 199, 200

Leemhuis, F. 228

Lees, W. Nassau xivn

Leo I, Emperor (457-474) 13

Leo III, Emperor (717-741) xxin, xxv, 62-66, 80-84, 110, 211-215, 216n, 219n

Leo, opponent of Constantine IV (punished 681) 196+n

Leo I, Pope, author of the 'Tome' (440-461) 140, 143n

Leontius, Emperor (695-698) 61, 65, 78, 81, 109, 206+n, 207

Libya (I) 39, 128n

Lidzbarski, M. xxviin

Lilie, R.-J. xviiin

Litarba (V), see John, the Stylite of Litarba

Lolos, A. 225-227

Longinus, martyr 15

Lycia (III) 179, 194n

Lydia (III) 79n

Ma^{c}add, Arab tribe 152+n

Mabbūgh (V) = Hieropolis, Manbij 116, 125n, 126n, 140, 142+n, 143n, 165n

Macedonia 219

Macedonius, bishop of Constantinople (342-346; 351-360) 22

MacCormack, S.C. xvn

Madelung, W. xxviin

al-Mahdī, Caliph (775-785) 71, 73, 74, 97

Majdal ^{c}Anjar = ^{c}Ayn al-Jarr, q.v.

Makrón Teîkhos, the Long Wall of Constantinople 221

Malalas, John, historian (6th cent.) 91

al-Ma^{ɔ}mūn, Caliph = ^{c}Abd Allāh al-Ma^{ɔ}mūn, q.v.

Manbij = Mabbūgh, q.v.

Mango, C. xviin, xxn, xxivn, xxvin, xxxiv, lxv, 95n, 111n

Mani, heresiarch (3rd cent.) 20, 72

Manuel, governor of Egypt (*c.* 635) 159-160

Mar^{c}ash = Germaniceia, q.v.

Marcian, Emperor (450-457) 13, 22

Marcion, heresiarch (2nd cent.) 20

'Mardaïte' 109, 195+n, 199+n, 200

Mardānshāh, son of Zarnōsh, of Nisibis (d. *c.* 693) 202

Mardīn (V) 6, 17, 19, 70, 76, 122+n, 150+n, 163, 226, 230

Maria, daughter of Maurice, wife of Chosroēs II 117

Marinus, nobleman of Edessa (*fl.* 590) 120, 121, 122, 123

Marmara, Sea of (III) 215n

Maron, holy man (*c.* 400) 25, 26, 30n

Maronite, monk of the House of Maron xxx, 25-27, 29, 30+n, 35, 81, 143n

Marthad b. Sharīk, emir of Qēnneshrīn (*fl.* 706) 209n

Martin, Pope (I) (649-655) xx

Martina, niece and second wife of Heraclius 137, 167

Martinez, F.J. 225-228, 232n, 243, 244+n

Martyropolis = Mayperqat, q.v.

Marw (I) 178

Marwān b. al-Ḥakam, Caliph (684-685) 50, 51, 60, 66, 78, 109, 198+n, 199+n

Mary, church of the Theotókos, in Ctesiphon 117

Mary, church of the Theotókos, in Zeugma 114n

Mary, mother of Jesus, Theotókos, 'the Godbearer' xx, 31, 131n

Maryūt, in Egypt xxiiin

Maslama b. ᶜAbd al-Malik, Arab general (fl. 718) 62-65, 68, 79, 110, 206n, 208+n, 209+n, 211-219

Massa, son of Ishmael 144

al-Masᶜūdī, historian xxviiin

Massīsa = Mopsuestia, q.v.

Matthew, bishop of Aleppo (fl. 644, 665) 57, 188

Matthews, J. 264

Maurice, Emperor (582-602) 13, 17, 28, 36, 38, 51, 54, 65, 85n, 88, 90, 102, 105, 106, 111-122, 125, 126n, 128n, 258

al-Mawsil = Mossul, q.v.

Maximus Confessor (d. 662) xx, 26, 81, 89

Mayperqat (V) = Martyropolis 105, 113, 114, 205n

Mayyāfāriqīn = Mayperqat, q.v.

Meadow of Dābiq = Dābiq, q.v.

Mecca (I) 201, 240n, 245, 247

Media (IV) 137, 154, 171, 200n

Medina (I) = Yathrib, q.v.

Mediterranean Sea (I, IV) xi, xvi, 69, 211n

Medyanōyē 130n

Meeus, J. 260

Melkite (see also 'Chalcedonian') xxx, 10, 25-28

Melitene (V) 62, 111, 118+n, 192, 210+n

Menas, Patriarch of Constantinople (536-552) 13

Mesopotamia (V) 6n, 12, 57, 68, 69, 77, 106, 107, 115, 118, 122, 126n, 139-141, 153n, 158, 162-165, 186n, 194n, 200, 201n, 205, 209, 260

Mesopotamia, northern (IV) = al-Jazīra xxv, xxix, 57-59, 79, 83, 106, 147, 169n, 201+n, 205n, 209, 222

Methodius, bishop of Olympus (martyred c.312) 222

Meyendorff, J. xxin

Mibsam, son of Ishmael 144

Michael I, Patriarch of the Jacobites, historian (1166-1199) xxvn, xxxi, xxxii, lxv, 27n, 40-42, 79n, 82n, 85+n, 87-90, 92, 93, 95, 96, 99n, 101-103, 111-221nn *passim*, 255-259, 262, 263

Midian, son of Cetura 130n

Migne, J.-P. lxv

Mingana, A. xxviin

Mishma^c, son of 'shmael 144

Mizīzī, Byzantine pretender (d. 669) 109, 193+n

Moab (II) 145, 146

Modestus, Patriarch of Jerusalem (*fl.* 630) 153n

Moesia (I), Upper and Lower 112n

Molenberg, C. 228

Mons Amanus = Black Mountain, q.v.

Montanus, heresiarch (2nd cent.) 20

Mopsuestia (V) = Massīsa 78, 206+n

Moses bar Kīfō, Syriac author (9th cent.) 207n

Moses, the lawgiver 9, 131+n, 132, 133n, 231

Moses of Tūr ^cAbdīn, historian (*fl.* 700) 92+n, 100, 204n

Mossul (IV) 200

Mostene (III) 79n

Mosyna (III) 79n

Mother of God = Mary, q.v.

Mount of Olives (II) 167

Mu^cādh b. Jabal, Arab general (*fl.* 639) 162

Mu^cāwiya I b. Abī Sufyān, Caliph (661-680) 29-33, 35, 43, 48, 49, 51, 58, 59, 66, 77, 78, 82, 108, 109, 163, 165, 166, 167n, 168n, 173-179, 181-196, 198, 200, 232n, 257

Mu^cāwiya II b. Yazīd, Caliph (683-684) 257

Mucke, H. 260

Muhammad b. Abī Bakr, rival of Mu^cāwiya (*fl.* 656) 181-183

Muhammad b. Marwān, Arab governor (*fl.* 690) 79, 109, 200, 201, 205, 206, 209

Muhammad, the prophet of Islam (d. 632) xxviii, xxx, 2, 19, 32, 36, 37, 39, 41-44, 49, 50, 51, 52, 56, 57, 59n, 66, 74, 76, 89, 96, 106-108, 129-132, 135, 138, 142-144, 161, 168n, 169, 181, 182+n, 185, 204, 255, 256, 262

Muhammad, tax-collector 203n

Muir's Historical Atlas: Ancient and Classical 264

Mukhtār, usurper in ^CAqūlō region (*fl.* 683) 197, 200

al-Munajjid, S. al-D. xivn

al-Mundhir III b. Nu^Cmān, king of Hīra (505-554) 14

al-Mundhir, Ghassānid (victor at ^CAyn Ubāgh 570) 15, 119

Murphy, F.X. xxin

Muslim, another name for Maslama, q.v.

al-Mu^Ctaṣim, Caliph = Abū Ishāq al-Mu^Ctaṣim, q.v.

Naphish, son of Ishmael 144

Narsai, Syriac poet (d. 503) 7

Narseh, rebel Byzantine general (*fl.* 603) 38, 55, 68, 76, 81, 106, 120, 121

Nau, F. 45, 53, 81, 171n, 225, 243

Néa Rhōmē, 'the Second Rome' 221

Nebayoth, firstborn son of Ishmael 144

Nestorian = East Syrian 26, 41, 79, 126n, 201n, 225, 226, 243, 244

Nestorius, Patriarch of Constantinople (428-431) 15, 22, 28, 143n

Nero, Emperor (54-68) 19

Nicaea in Bithynia (I) 211

Nicaea, Council (325) 22

Nicephorus I, Emperor (802-811) 95+n

Nicetas, son of Gregory, rival of Heraclius 127

Nicopolis in Pontus (I) 114n

Nihāwand (I) 154

Nikephoros, Patriarch of Constantinople, historian (806-815) 111n, 120n, 127n, 149n

Nile, river (I) 100

Nimrod 223

Nineveh (IV) 198n

Ninus, king of Assyria 9

Nisibis (V) 16, 79, 82, 113, 114, 201+n, 202

Nizip (V) 71

Noah 223

Nōlar, noble family at Edessa 140

Nöldeke, T. lxv, 1-4, 32n, 179n

Nonnus of Halūghō (d. c. 693) 202

Nuᶜaym b. Hammād, author xxviiin

Nubian 249

Nuᶜmān b. al-Mundhir Abū Jafnā, king of al-Hīra (583-c.602) 113, 115

Olympus in Lycia (IV) 222

Oqba = ᶜUkbarā, q.v.

Oppolzer, Hofrath Prof. T. Ritter von, astronomer 260

Orientals, monastery of the, at Edessa (V) 118

Orontes, river (V) 25

Os, J. van 228

Ostrogorsky, G. xvn, xxxiv, lxv,

Ovadiah, A. xviin

Pahlavi 202n

Palästina, Historisch-archäologische Karte 264

Palestine (II, IV), Palestinian, 'Promised Land' xiv, xvii, xxix, 4, 19, 30, 39, 55-57, 68, 69, 95, 107, 125n, 129, 130, 135n, 137, 142, 146, 155, 161, 162, 179n, 197, 232, 238

Palmer, A. N. 2n, 23, 53, 70n, 71n, 73n, 82n, 97n, 98n, 100n, 101n, 243n, 251n

Palmyra (V) 142n, 155

Pamphylia (III) 186n

Panodorus, chronographer (*fl.* 400) xxiv

Paphlagonia (III) 34, 125n

Paradise 132+n

Paris 243

Parmentier, L. 113n

Parwēz = Chosroēs II, q.v.

Pasagnathes, rebel patríkios of Armenia 178n

Paul, 'the Apostle' 19, 48, 172+n, 231, 233-236, 251

Paul, bishop of Edessa (*fl*. 605) 38

Paul, father of the Emperor Maurice 111

Paul Fehim of Gargar, bishop of Edessa (1883-1887) 103

Paul of Samosata, bishop of Antioch (*c*.260-268) 20

Pergamum (III) 35, 80, 211n

Pērōz, Shah (631 or 632) 39

Persia (I, IV and V), Persian i-178 *passim*, 200, 201, 230, 232, 237, 240n, 256, 257

Persian Sea, The 129

Pessinus (III) 35

Peter, the Apostle = Simon Cephas, q.v.

Peter, brother of the Emperor Maurice 111, 118, 119

Peter Fehim, owner of manuscript (*fl*. 1899) 103

Peter, Patriarch of Alexandria (martyred 300) 20

Peter, Patriarch of the Jacobites (584-591) 16, 54, 67, 76, 119, 257, 259

Peter, firstborn son of Athanasius Bar Gūmōyē 202

Philip of Macedon (4th cent. BC) 223

Philippicus, brother-in-law of Emperor Maurice 106, 113, 114, 120+n

Philippicus, Emperor (711-713) 62, 65, 81, 109, 209, 210

Philoxenus, bishop of Mabbūgh (d. 523) 28, 126n

Phlabianos = Flavian, q.v.

Phocas, Emperor (602-610) 13, 28, 36, 38, 42, 51, 52, 55, 56, 65, 68, 81, 106, 120-122, 125-128

Phoenicia (V) 33, 39-41, 69, 107, 125n, 127, 140, 153n, 194f.n, 197

Phoenicus in Lycia (III) 179

Phrabitas, Patriarch of Constantinople (489-490) 13

Phrygia (III) 20, 79

Piccirillo, M. xviin

Pil, 'king of Ethiopia' 223, 240

Pisidia (III) 15, 209n

Pognon, H. 71, 72

Polybius, historian (2nd cent. BC) 91n, 93

Pontus = Black Sea, q.v.

Priscus, Byzantine general (*fl*. 588) 105, 112, 113n

Priscus, son-in-law of Emperor Phocas 120n
Procopius of Caesarea, historian (6th cent.) xviin
Procopius, Byzantine general (fl. 644) 57, 58, 68
Protonice, Queen, consort of Emperor Claudius 245n
Pseudo-Dionysius of Tel-Mahrē = the Zuqnīn chronicler, q.v.
Pseudo-Methodius, Syriac author (fl. 691?) 48, 145n, 222-250 passim
Pseudo-Wāqidī, historian 19n, 156n
Pseudo-Zacharias, Syriac historian (6th cent.) 91+n, 92n
Ptolemy, Byzantine governor (fl. 639) 163, 188n
Pugurian 112n
Pygmy 247n
Qābūs, king of al-Hīra (fl. 570) 15
Qadash = al-Qādisiyya, q.v.
Qadash, Desert of (IV) 151
al-Qādisiyya (IV B), Qadash 151, 153
Qartmīn, monastery (V) xxv, 75-79, 82, 83, 84
Qedar, monastery (V) 6, 19, 150n
Qedar, son of Ishmael 144
Qedemah, son of Ishmael 144
Qēnneshrē, monastery of (V) xxv, 11, 18, 23, 87, 108, 126n, 160n,
     172+n, 188n, 258
Qēnneshrīn (V) = Chalcis 125n, 160, 163, 188, 208n, 210
Qinnasrīn = Qēnneshrīn, q.v.
Quraysh, tribe of Muhammad 77, 129, 161, 168, 169+n, 198
Qurʾān, the holy book of Islam 132, 169+n
Qurra b. Sharīk (8th cent.) 208n, 209n
Qustīn = Bēth Qustān, q.v.
Rabbūlō, bishop of Edessa (d. 435) 16
Raggath, see Rakkat
Rahmānī, I.E. 103, 232n
Rakkat (II) = (?) Raggath 95n
Ramadān 132
Raqqa = Callinicum, q.v.
Raʾs al-ʿAyn = Rhesaina, q.v.
al-Rastan (V) 155

Red Sea, The (I) 129

Rehoboam, son of Solomon 119

Reinink, G. xxivn, xxviin, 45, 222n, 225-228, 230n, 233n, 237n, 243n, 244

Rey-Coquais, J.-P. 229

Rhesaina (V) = Rīsh ^{c}Aynō, Ra$^\supset$s al-^{c}Ayn 6, 11, 17, 38, 77, 81, 98, 117n, 150+n, 163, 199n, 200

Rhodes (III) 18, 133n, 180+n

Riad, Eva 90

Rīsh ^{c}Aynō = Rhesaina, q.v.

Rishīr, monastery named after abbot called 150n

'Roman state', 'the' 164, 165

'Romania', i.e. the Roman empire 112n, 220

Rome (I) xi, xiv, xvi, xxi, 20, 86, 93, 109, 187, 221, 245

Rōmēzān, Persian general = Shahrvarāz, q.v.

Roolvink, R. 264, 265

Rotter, G. 201n

Royal City, the = Constantinople, q.v.

Rōzvēhān, Persian general (d. 628) 137, 138

Rusafōyō, a noble family at Edessa 35, 87-89, 140

Ruṣāfa (V) 115, 142n

Russel, D.S. xxvin

Rydèn, L. xxn

Sabūkht = Severus Sabūkht, q.v.

Sacellarius = Theodore, Byzantine general, q.v.

Sackur, E. 227

Sa^{c}d b. Abī Waqqāṣ, Arab general (fl. 634) 150, 151

Sahmī 144n

Saḥsahna = Clysma, q.v.

Said, S. xviin

Sa^{c}īd b. Kulthūm (fl. 636) = ? Sa^{c}īd b. Zayd 157

Sa^{c}īd b. ^{c}Uthmān, son of the Caliph ^{c}Uthmān 178

Sa^{c}īd b. Zayd, governor of Damascus (fl. 635) 160

Sakellarios, probably in error for Spatharios, q.v.

Sal^c, Mount xxiii

Salamis = Constantina in Cyprus, q.v.

Samaritan 19, 146, 147

Sambāt, Armenian patríkios (fl. 690) 205

Samosata (V) 143n, 172n, 208n

Samuel, bishop of Amida (fl. 610) 126

Samuel, in error for Moses of Ṭūr ᶜAbdīn, q.v.

Sanason or Sasun, mountain west of Lake Van (I) 205n

Sapor, form of the name Shabuhr (q.v.) 189n

Saracen 3n, 33, 47, 130n

Sarah, wife of Abraham 130n

Sardis (I) 80

Sarīn 207n

Sasanid 178f.n, 189n

Satan 134n, 247

Schauer, D. xvin

Schick, R. xxiiin

Schove, D.J. 260, 261

Scotia xiv

Scutarium (?), lake (III) 33

Sear, D.R. xlvi, lxv

Segestān (I) 154, 178+n

Seleucia in Cilicia (IV) 211n

Seleucia, port of Antioch (V) 16, 46

Sergius and Bacchus, martyrs 20

Sergius, bishop of ᶜUrd (fl. 630) 142n

Sergius, church of Saint, at Ctesiphon 117

Sergius, church of Saint, at Ehnesh 23, 71

Sergius, envoy of the rebel Shabuhr (fl. 667) 189-192

Sergius I, Patriarch of Constantinople (610-638) xx

Sergius, patríkios of Caesarea (fl. 632) 19n, 146, 147

Sergius, son of Īwannis Rusafōyō of Edessa, writer (fl. 627) 35, 98-100, 124, 134n, 135+n

Sergius, son of Mansūr (8th cent.) 26, 204

Sᵉrūgh = Batnōn da-Sᵉrūgh, q.v.

Severan = Jacobite, q.v.

Severus, Chalcedonian bishop of Edessa (d. 603) 38, 42, 55, 68, 76, 106, 120

Severus, bishop of Qenneshrin, Sabūkht (fl. 630) 30, 142f.n, 188+n

Severus, bishop of Samosata (fl. 630) 143n, 172n

Severus, Emperor (222-235) 21

Severus, Patriarch of Antioch (d. 538) 13, 15, 26-28, 118+n, 148

Severus, Patriarch of the Jacobites (668-683) 59, 60, 67, 68, 78

Severus, scribe (9th cent.) 83

Shabīb the Harūrite, bandit (d. 705) 79, 205

Shabuhr, Byzantine general and rebel (d. 667) 189+n, 192

Shabuhr I, Shah (241-272) 20

Shahid, I. xviin

Shāhīn, Persian general (fl. 616) 128n

Shahrvarāz, Shah (630) = Rōmēzān 6, 12, 13, 17, 18, 39, 40, 107, 117, 121, 122, 125, 128, 133+n, 135-139, 142, 143+n, 149, 151

Shamir b. Dhī al-Jawshan (fl. 680) 185, 186n

Sharāhīl b. ʿUbayda, Arab general (fl. 717) 80, 84, 216

Sheol 240, 248

Sherwood, P. xxin

Shīlō, monastery of (V) 61, 68, 70, 78

Shiloh, tower of 47

Shimr = Shamir, q.v.

Shīrōē, Shah (628) 18, 37, 39, 76, 106, 138, 139, 142+n, 255

Shurahbīl b. Hasana, Arab general (fl. 633) 144

Sicily (I), Sicilian 187, 193, 195n, 232, 237, 238

Sidon (IV) 195, 247, 248n

Siffīn (V) 43, 59, 68, 71, 74, 184, 186n, 187, 265

Sīkūn, chief of the giants 9

Simeon, bishop of Edessa (d. c.650) 57, 58, 77, 188, 259

Simeon, bishop of Harrān (c.617) 55

Simeon, bishop of Harrān (700-734) 78, 79, 82

Simeon, son of Nonnus of Halūghō (d. c.693) 202

Simon, bishop of Jerusalem (martyred 104) 20

Simon Cephas, the Apostle (martyred 64) 6, 19, 172+n

Simon, doorkeeper of Qedar (killed by Arabs 636) 6, 19

Sinai, Mount (I) 27, 28

Sittas, Byzantine general (*fl.* 588) 113, 114

Slav 18, 112n, 205n, 206n

Smith, W. 264

Smits, E. 229

Smyrna (III) 35

Socrates, church historian (5th cent.) 69, 70, 91

Solomon of Bostra, Syriac author 225, 226, 233n

Solomon, the Temple of, in Jerusalem 48, 162, 167n

Son of YRDN ?, Byzantine general (d. 634) 19+n

Son of Hagar = Ishmaelite, q.v.

Sophanene, incorporated in Arzanene AD 591 (V) 112n

Sophronius, Patriarch of Jerusalem (*fl.* 635) 48, 161, 162

Sōqarthō = Dastgird, q.v.

Southern Sea, The 129

Sozomen, church historian (5th cent.) 91

Sozopolis (III) 15

Spain xiv

Spatharios, 'name' of monks' executor (*fl.* 599) 118n

Stephen, bishop of Ḥarrān (*fl. c.*600) 114

Stephen, Byzantine general (*fl.* 636) 156n

Stephen, the first Christian martyr 19

Stratos, A. xvn

Suermann, H. xxviin, 225+n, 227, 229, 243, 244

Sulaymān b. ᶜAbd al-Malik, Caliph (715-717) 47, 50, 52, 61, 63, 66, 80, 110, 211, 212, 213n, 216, 217, 218n

Symeon the Stylite 16

Symeon, the Stylite, monastery of, at Telanissus (V) 152n

Synaus (III) 34+n

Synnada (III) 34+n

Syracuse (I) 187, 193

Syria (IV, V) xii-xiv, xxiii, xxx, xxxiv, 6, 15, 18-20, 23-26, 29, 39, 41, 45, 50, 51, 63, 65, 68, 76-78, 80, 92, 94, 98, 100, 106, 107, 119, 120, 122n, 125-128, 137, 138, 140+n, 144, 145, 153n, 156,

158, 162-165, 175, 177-179, 186n, 194n, 196, 197, 201n, 205+n, 209, 210n, 216, 232, 260

Syriac, the language and the literature xxiv, xxviii, xxxiv, 1, 9, 11, 14, 59n, 65, 93, 94n, 98-101, 115n, 154n, 169n, 171+n, 192n, 195n, 197n, 220n, 222+n, 235n, 237n, 242n, 245n, 249n, 252

Syrian, ethnic and cultural character xxx, xxxi, 8, 11, 23, 25, 43, 50, 62, 84, 87, 243, 252, 253, 262

'Syrian', used by the Syriac chroniclers 60, 62, 80, 85n, 164, 167n

Syrian Orthodox = Jacobite, q.v.

al-Tabari, historian (9th cent.) xxin, xxviin, 19n, 30n, 31n, 32n, 64n, 144n, 145n, 169n, 176n, 186n

Tanukhids = Banū Tanūkh, q.v.

Tar^{C}ēl = Tel ^{C}Addē, q.v.

Tartūs = Antaradus, q.v.

Ṭayyōyē 10, 39, 129, 130n

Ṭayyōyē applied to Christian Arabs 145

Tel ^{C}Addē (V) = Tar^{C}ēl 78, 82+n, 126n

Tella Constantina (V) = Viranshehir 38, 76, 77, 139, 163

Tel-Mahrōyō, noble family at Edessa 99, 100, 140

Tema, son of Ishmael 144

Theodora, consort of the Emperor Justinian I 13, 21

Theodore, bishop of Edessa, historian (9th cent.) 92, 94n

Theodore, Jacobite bishop (fl. 659) 30

Theodore, Byzantine general (fl. 644) 57, 68

Theodore, Patriarch of Alexandria (fl. 680) xxiiin

Theodore, Patriarch of the Jacobites (649-667) 58, 59, 67, 68, 77, 188n, 259, 261

Theodore, patríkios of Edessa, 'Sacellarius' 3+n, 4, 149+n

Theodore, Saint, unidentified 172

Theodoret, church historian (5th cent.) 91

Theodoric, brother of the Emperor Heraclius 106, 107, 138, 139, 140, 147-149, 178

Theodosius, Chalcedonian bishop of Edessa (fl. 605) 38

Theodosius, brother of the Emperor Constans II 31, 179, 188n

Theodosius I, Emperor (379-395) 13, 22

Theodosius II, Emperor (402-450) 13, 15, 22

Theodosius III, Emperor, Constantine (715-717) 62, 65, 81, 110, 211-215

Theodosius, Patriarch of Alexandria (d. 565) 13, 15

Theodosius, son of the Emperor Maurice 55, 65, 112n, 116n

Theodotus, bishop of Amida (d. 698, not later) 61, 67n

Theopaschites 26

Theophanes Confessor, historian (d. 818) xixn, 3n, 19n, 30n, 32n, 64n, 95-98, 101n, 111-221nn *passim*, 257

Theophilus of Edessa, historian (8th cent.) 92, 96-98, 101

Theophylact, Byzantine general (*fl.* 708) 208

Theotókos, church of the, at Ctesiphon 117

Theotókos, church of the, at Edessa 203

Theotókos, church of the, at Zeugma 114n

Theotókos, 'the Godbearer', title of Mary, mother of Jesus, q.v.

Thessaloníkē (I) 179

Thomas, the Apostle 172+n

Thomas, bishop, ambassador to Arwād (*fl.* 650) 177

Thomas, bishop of Amida (d. *c.*690, not 713) 56, 58, 61

Thomas, bishop of Mabbūgh, Harqlōyō (*fl.* 630) 126n, 142n

Thomas, bishop of Palmyra (*fl.* 630) 142n

Thomas Bardōyō of Edessa (d. 605) 121

Thomas, priest, chronicler (*fl.* 636) xxv, xxix, 6, 7, 10-12, 19, 23, 28, 35, 42, 49, 67, 98, 243n, 257

Thomas, Sanctuary of Saint, at Emesa 17

Thomas, stylite, of Tella (d. 710) 78

Thrace (I) xiv, 32, 80, 84, 112n, 120n, 135n, 219

Thracian division of Byzantine army 116

Tiberius II, Emperor (578-582) 13, 28, 51, 54, 66, 111, 112, 120n, 204n

Tiberius III, Emperor, Apsimar (698-705) 61, 65, 81, 206+n, 207, 208n

Tiberius, son and co-successor of Constans II 188n, 194+n, 196

Tiberius, son of the Emperor Justinian II xxvii, 208n, 210

Tigris, river (IV B, V) xi, 53, 153, 207n

Times, Atlas of the World, The 264

Tisserant, E. 53

Titus, Emperor (79-81) 20

Titus, Syrian leader under David the Armenian 87, 164, 165+n

Tome of Leo, see Leo I, Pope

Trajan, Emperor (97-117) 20

Tripolis (V) 58, 68, 156n, 179, 180n

Tu^Cāyē, Arab tribe 171n

Türkei und naher Osten 264

Tukhāristān xxii

Ṭūr ^CAbdīn (V) 38, 75, 76, 83, 92, 100, 122n

Ṭūranda (V) 79, 209n

Ṭurk 85n, 178n

Turkey and *Turkey: motoring map* 104, 211n, 264, 265

Turkish xiv, 8, 211n

Turtledove, H. lxv

Twair, Q. 59n

Tyana (III) 64+n, 208, 209n

Tyre (II) 195, 247, 248n

^CUbayd, A. 156n

^CUbayda, Arab general = (?) Sharāḥīl b. ^CUbayda, q.v.

^CUkbarā (IV) 112n

^CUmar b. ^CAbd Allāh b. al-Jarrāḥ Abū ^CUbayda (d. 639) 144, 150, 155-157, 160-162

^CUmar II b. ^CAbd al-^CAzīz, Caliph (717-720) xxin, 50, 52, 64, 66, 80, 84, 99n, 110, 217, 218

^CUmar b. Hubayra, Arab general (*fl.* 717) 212

^CUmar I b. al-Khaṭṭāb, Caliph (634-644) xxvi, 43, 44, 48, 49, 51, 52, 57, 58, 66, 76, 77, 107, 108, 150+n, 151, 155, 156, 160-163, 166-169, 179n, 181, 257

^CUmayr b. Sa^Cd, governor of Damascus (*fl.* 686) 108, 169+n, 170+n, 171

Umayyad xxi, xxii, 169+n, 186

Urbanus, 'king of Byzantium' 223

^CUrḍ (V) 142n

Urfa = Edessa, q.v.

Ūrhōy = Edessa, q.v.

^cUrwa b. al-Zubayr (7th cent.) xxiii

^cUthmān b. ^cAffān, Caliph (644-656) xxvi, 43, 49, 51, 58, 67, 77, 108, 168, 169+n, 178, 179+n, 181-183, 240n, 257

Vahrām VI, Shah (590-591) 115, 117

Vahrām, Persian general (*fl.* 612) 127

Valens, Emperor (367-378) xii, 11

Valentine, Byzantine general (d. *c.*644) 57, 68, 164, 167

Valentinus, heresiarch (2nd cent.) 20

Van, lake (I) 70

van Os, J. 228

Vanstiphout, H.L.J. 228

Vasiliev, A.A. lxiv

Vatican 53, 226, 230, 243

Veh, O. xviin

Verbeke, W. 228

Verhelst, D. 228

Vespasian, Emperor (69-79) 20

Viranshehir = Tella, q.v.

Vööbus, A. xxiin

Vries, B. de xixn

Walīd b. ^cAbd al-Malik, Caliph (705-715) 43-45, 47, 50, 51, 60, 61, 64n, 66, 78, 80, 109, 207-211

Walīd b. ^cAmr, Arab governor (d. 703) 208n

Wārdan, Byzantine general (*fl.* 636) 19n

Watson, A.M. xxiin

Welkenhuysen, A. 228

Whitby, L. M. or M. xivn, xxivn, lxiv, 112n, 255, 264

White Region, The (V) 78

Whittow, M. xviiin

Wigram, W.A. xxiiin

Williams, A. 228

Winkelmann, F. xvn, xxn

Witakowski, W. 7, 53, 61n, 69, 100n

Wuensch, R. xvin

Wüstenfeld, F. xxviin, xxxv, 257, 264

Yākūt, geographer 148n, 264

Yarmūk, river (II) 4, 76, 107, 149n, 157+n, 161n, 230n

Yathrib (I) = Medina 50, 51n, 129, 130, 161, 162, 182, 186+n, 197, 198, 201, 224, 230, 233, 237

Yazdgird III, Shah (632-651) 108, 143, 150n, 151+n, 154, 178+n, 179n

Yazīd b. Abī Sakhr, Abū Qārib (fl. 635) 201n

Yazīd b. Abī Sufyān, brother of Caliph Mu^{c}āwiya 144, 150, 186

Yazīd I b. Mu^{c}āwiya, Caliph (680-683) xxiiin, 32+n, 43, 44, 50, 51, 59, 60, 66, 78, 82, 109, 160, 186, 187, 193, 196-199

Yazīd II b. ^{c}Abd al-Malik, Caliph (720-724) 50, 52

Yazīd 'III', Arab pretender (8th cent.) xxin, 83

Yemen, Yemenite 145+n

Yonton, fourth son of Noah 223+n

Yūhannōn, the courier of King Abgar (q.v.) 204n

Zāb, the greater river of that name (IV) 138

Zarnōsh 202

Zayd, brother of Caliph Mu^{c}āwiya 200

Zechariah, Patriarch of Jerusalem (fl. 614) 128

Zechariah = Pseudo-Zacharias, q.v.

Zeno, Emperor (474-491) 11, 13

Zenobia (V) 17

Zeugma (V) 114n

Z^{ec}ūrō, church of, at Amida 58

Zōybōnō, village on the Euphrates 171

Zosimus, in error, for Sozomen 91

Zuqnīn chronicler, the 11, 53, 65, 69

Zuqnīn, monastery (V) 53, 58, 70

Zuraq, Persian general (fl. 529) 21

TRANSLATED TEXTS FOR HISTORIANS
Published Titles

Gregory of Tours: Life of the Fathers
Translated with an introduction by EDWARD JAMES
Volume 1: 176pp., 2nd edition 1991, ISBN 0 85323 327 6

The Emperor Julian: Panegyric and Polemic
Claudius Mamertinus, John Chrysostom, Ephrem the Syrian
edited by SAMUEL N. C. LIEU
Volume 2: 153pp., 2nd edition 1989, ISBN 0 85323 376 4

Pacatus: Panegyric to the Emperor Theodosius
Translated with an introduction by C. E. V. NIXON
Volume 3: 122pp., 1987, ISBN 0 85323 076 5

Gregory of Tours: Glory of the Martyrs
Translated with an introduction by RAYMOND VAN DAM
Volume 4: 150pp., 1988, ISBN 0 85323 236 9

Gregory of Tours: Glory of the Confessors
Translated with an introduction by RAYMOND VAN DAM
Volume 5: 127pp., 1988, ISBN 0 85323 226 1

The Book of Pontiffs (*Liber Pontificalis to AD 715*)
Translated with an introduction by RAYMOND DAVIS
Volume 6: 175pp., 1989, ISBN 0 85323 216 4

Chronicon Paschale 284-628 AD
Translated with notes and introduction by
MICHAEL WHITBY AND MARY WHITBY
Volume 7: 280pp., 1989, ISBN 0 85323 096 X

Iamblichus: On the Pythagorean Life
Translated with notes and introduction by GILLIAN CLARK
Volume 8: 144pp., 1989, ISBN 0 85323 326 8

Conquerors and Chroniclers of Early-Medieval Spain
Translated with notes and introduction by KENNETH BAXTER WOLF
Volume 9: 176pp., 1991, ISBN 0 85323 047 1

Victor of Vita: History of the Vandal Persecution
Translated with notes and introduction by JOHN MOORHEAD
Volume 10: 112pp., 1992, ISBN 0 85323 127 3

The Goths in the Fourth Century
by PETER HEATHER AND JOHN MATTHEWS
Volume 11: 224pp., 1991, ISBN 0 85323 426 4

Cassiodorus: *Variae*
Translated with notes and introduction by S.J.B. BARNISH
Volume 12: 260pp., 1992, ISBN 0 85323 436 1

The Lives of the Eighth-Century Popes (*Liber Pontificalis*)
Translated with an introduction and commentary by RAYMOND DAVIS
Volume 13: 288pp., 1992, ISBN 0 85323 018 8

Eutropius: Breviarium
Translated with an introduction and commentary by H. W. BIRD
Volume 14: 248pp., 1993, ISBN 0 85323 208 3

The Seventh Century in the West-Syrian Chronicles
introduced, translated and annotated by ANDREW PALMER
including two seventh-century Syriac apocalyptic texts
introduced, translated and annotated by SEBASTIAN BROCK
with added annotation and an historical introduction by ROBERT HOYLAND
Volume 15: 368pp., 1993., ISBN 0 85323 238 5

Vegetius: Epitome of Military Science
Translated with notes and introduction by N. P. MILNER
Volume 16: 182pp., 1993, ISBN 0 85323 228 8

For full details of Translated Texts for Historians, including prices and ordering information, please write to the following:

All countries, except the USA and Canada: Liverpool University Press, PO Box 147, Liverpool, L69 3BX, UK (tel 051-794 2235, fax 051-708 6502).

USA and Canada: University of Pennsylvania Press, Blockley Hall, 418 Service Drive, Philadelphia, PA 19104-6097, USA (tel (215) 898-6264, fax (215) 898-0404).